Keepers of the Record

The History of the
Hudson's Bay Company Archives

DEIDRE SIMMONS

McGill-Queen's University Press
Montreal & Kingston · London · Ithaca

© McGill-Queen's University Press 2007
ISBN 978-0-7735-3291-5 (cloth)
ISBN 978-0-7735-3620-3 (paper)

Legal deposit fourth quarter 2007
Bibliothèque nationale du Québec

Printed in Canada on acid-free paper that is 100% ancient forest free
(100% post-consumer recycled), processed chlorine free
First paperback edition 2009

This book has been published with the help of a grant from the
Hudson's Bay Company History Foundation.

McGill-Queen's University Press acknowledges the support of the Canada
Council for the Arts for our publishing program. We also acknowledge the
financial support of the Government of Canada through the Book Publishing
Industry Development Program (BPIDP) for our publishing activities.

Unless otherwise noted, all photographs have been provided by the
Hudson's Bay Company Archives.

The Hudson's Bay Company charter is a trademark of and reproduced
with the permission of Hudson's Bay Company. Image courtesy of Hudson's
Bay Company Archives, Archives of Manitoba.

Library and Archives Canada Cataloguing in Publication

Simmons, Deidre, 1944–
    Keepers of the record: the history of the Hudson's Bay Company
    Archives / Deidre Simmons.

    Includes bibliographical references and index.
    ISBN 978-0-7735-3291-5 (bnd)
    ISBN 978-0-7735-3620-3 (pbk.)

    1. Hudson's Bay Company – Archives – History. 2. Hudson's Bay
    Company – Records and correspondence – History. 3. Canada –
    History – Archival resources. 4. Hudson's Bay Company Archives –
    History. I. Title.

FC3207.S59 2007   026'.971   C2007-903679-1

This book was typeset by Interscript in 10/13 Sabon.

To my parents

Victor James Simmons (1913–1995)
Elizabeth Simmons (1915–2006)

Contents

Foreword

In 1975 the Hudson's Bay Company Archives opened for public research in Manitoba following transfer of the records from Beaver House in London. Some staff members working here today still recall the unusual way in which the documents were loaded onto the shelves in those early years. They were loaded from the bottom up, rather than the top down, in order to prevent the shelves from tipping over under the weight of the volumes. It was amazing how we got used to this arrangement and found it more difficult to adjust to the other way around – that is, scanning the shelves from the top down to locate a record – once the records were relocated to another vault area and this small glitch in an otherwise flawless transfer of the records from London was corrected.

The time since the records were transferred from London has seen a growth in public interest in use of the material for research. Their accessibility in Canada, along with the development of new avenues to disperse information – the Internet and other electronic tools – has contributed to this growth, which has also increased awareness of the resources. Every year the Hudson's Bay Company Archives hosts thousands of inquiries about the records through on-site visits, remote requests, and microfilm interlibrary loan. HBCA resources contribute to numerous websites, CD-ROMs, exhibit projects, and television documentaries. The archives receives several dozen publications every year in which the author has used the HBCA as a major research component of the book or for illustration. The majority of researchers are genealogists and others doing private research. The traditional academic users from history, geography, anthropology, archaeology, and Canadian Studies fields have been joined in recent years by Native land-claims

researchers and those studying forestry, earth sciences, physical education, sociology, accounting, polar studies, art history, law, English, Native Studies, retail history, and business history.

The Hudson's Bay Company's commitment to protecting its records
and the social responsibility it has demonstrated in making this world-
class resource available for research to North Americans and researchers around the world is unprecedented. Twenty years after placing
them on deposit in the Archives of Manitoba, HBC formally donated
the records to the province of Manitoba in 1994 and used the tax pro-
ceeds to set up a foundation (the Hudson's Bay Company History
Foundation) to provide ongoing support for this amazing gift. Improvements to specialized storage facilities appropriate for each medium of records (textual, cartographic, still images, and film-based
records) and increased staff resources have resulted from this financial
support, ensuring the protection and accessibility of the records over
time. Additionally, the Hudson's Bay Company Archives, Archives
Manitoba, continues to be the corporate archives for the HBC's modern
archival records, ensuring the continuity of this magnificent collection
as the Company's history continues to unfold.

The HBCA continues to build on the legacy established by our earlier
colleagues in London and in Winnipeg. As the steward of the HBC
record-keeping legacy, the HBCA uses technological advances and current best practices in the archival profession to improve access to and
intellectual control of the records.

In 2001 the Archives of Manitoba purchased and customized a descriptive database from Minisis, Inc., which is compliant with the Canadian Rules for Archival Description (RAD). At that time, the
Hudson's Bay Company Archives decided to arrange and describe the
records of the HBC using the series system, building on the Australian
series system and the Canadian series approach developed at the Archives of Ontario. This database has given the HBCA the means to dem-
onstrate more fully how records were created, by whom, in what
context, and for what reason. It enables us to show the complexity of
administrative history, organizational relationships, and records creation within the context of one company. Understanding hierarchical
relationships helps archivists and researchers alike to see the interde-
pendency of record creators and to find the records relevant to a particular administrative body to support their particular field of study.

Ian E. Wilson, now Librarian and Archivist of Canada and an ap-
praiser for the textual records of the Hudson's Bay Company Archives in

1993, stated in his appraisal report, "As an integrated record keeping system, maintained for more than 300 years, this is more than so many journals account books, ledgers and letters. It has all the intellectual integrity of the manuscript of a great novel, a famous painting or a multi-volume encyclopedia. All are worth more than their separate elements. The HBC Archives is a similar coherent work, created by many hands over the generations but the outcome of one continuous records system." The Hudson's Bay Company Archives, 1670 to 1920, is listed on the United Nations Educational, Scientific and Cultural Organization's Memory of the World Register, testimony to its significance on a global scale.

Keepers of the Record is the first-ever comprehensive look at the development of the Hudson's Bay Company's Archives, the result of a continuous record-keeping system of the Hudson's Bay Company over more than three hundred years of its history. It describes the many hands that created and cared for the records over numerous generations. The author has pulled together information that is scattered throughout many different record series within the HBCA into a cohesive body of information. This account promotes a better understanding of the archives as a whole and contributes to the knowledge legacy that embodies the contributions of keepers of the records over time.

Maureen Dolyniuk
Manager, Hudson's Bay Company Archives

Acknowledgments

Any acknowledgment of assistance with the writing of this book will be inadequate, considering the encouragement and support I have been the recipient of over many years.

My family – Murray Watkin, Erin Flaim, Lindsay Tedds, and Lynne and Vicki Simmons – have always been thrilled with every minor development in the research, writing, and publication process. My many friends and colleagues have continued to be interested, especially fellow WAGS – Debra Barr, Margaret Hutchison, and Susan Hart – who have been appropriately thrilled, dismayed, encouraging, and accepting.

This book owes its very existence to keepers of the Hudson's Bay Company Archives – Shirlee Anne Smith, who answered my letter, which got the process started; Judith Hudson Beattie, who welcomed, employed, assisted, and encouraged me; and Maureen Dolyniuk, who took up the torch and made things happen. All Archives of Manitoba/HBCA staff members have gone out of their way to be helpful. Thank you to Provincial Archivist Gordon Dodds (retired) for asking me what he could do to help and to Debra Moore, head of acquisition and special media, who prepared all of the photographs in digital format, with the assistance of Steve Halek of The Lab Works in Winnipeg. But more than anyone, Anne Morton, retired head of public programming, has been a friend, colleague, confidante, researcher, editor, and patient adviser of British history and the use of the English language. A special thank-you to the Hudson's Bay Company History Foundation for providing me with a research grant in 1998, to the HBCA for suppling all of the photographs, and to the HBC for permission to reference active records.

Beyond the present, I am indebted to past HBC archivists, Richard Henry Leveson Gower, Alice Johnson, and especially Joan Craig, who

with Gwen Kemp walked with me through the streets of London explaining HBC ghosts. David and Philippa Innes told me about Richard
and the Leveson Gower family over tea at Titsey Place in Surrey, and
Jim and Ann Cooper shared stories over lunch about Governor Patrick
Ashley Cooper and the storage of the HBC records at Hexton Manor
during the Second World War. Also from the past are William Schooling, who was as obsessed as I have been; Hilary Jenkinson, who provided guidance to Richard Leveson Gower; and Douglas Brymner and
Arthur Doughty, who knew there had to be more. Thanks also to authors Alexander Begg, George Bryce, Agnes Laut, Frederick Merk,
Grace Lee Nute, A.S. Morton, and Beckles Willson, who pushed their
way in; E.E. Rich, Douglas MacKay, and, more recently, Peter C.
Newman, who wrote the history they knew was worth writing. I
needed their stories to fill in the background to mine.

I thank all the academic researchers and writers who have provided
stories from the HBCA about all aspects of the Company and the people
involved in it – Stuart and Mary Houston and Tim Ball for asking me to
write an appendix to their book, *Eighteenth-Century Naturalists of
Hudson Bay*, which led me to McGill-Queen's University Press; the late
William Ewart for his commitment to moving the HBCA to Canada;
Glyndwr Williams for meeting with me at the University of London to
reminisce about the HBC archives, the Hudson's Bay Record Society, Alice Johnson, and Beaver House; Germaine Warkentin for helping me understand Pierre-Esprit Radisson; Ian Wilson for sharing Arthur Doughty;
the late Hugh Taylor for explaining old English script; and Richard
Ruggles for writing the definitive work on the HBCA map collection.

My special thanks to Tom Nesmith for working through the concept,
continually asking me questions, and introducing me to JoAnne Yates's
Control through Communication, which provided a model.

Readers of early versions of the manuscript or parts of it were Murray
Watkin, Debra Barr, Margaret Hutchison, Al Scott, the late John Bovey,
Anne Morton, Judith Beattie, Maureen Dolyniuk, and two anonymous
readers for the University of Manitoba Press. Most recently, the comments from two anonymous readers for McGill-Queen's were most helpful in clarifying the content of this final version. Articles based on the
same notes, which helped develop my thoughts, have been published previously in *The Beaver*, *Épilogue*, *Archivaria*, and the conference papers
of the Rupert's Land Colloquium and I-CHORA.

Finally, I thank all my family, friends, and colleagues not mentioned here
for being a part of my life, which ultimately makes them part of this book.

Albany packet box (artifact no. 130) and display of archival documents

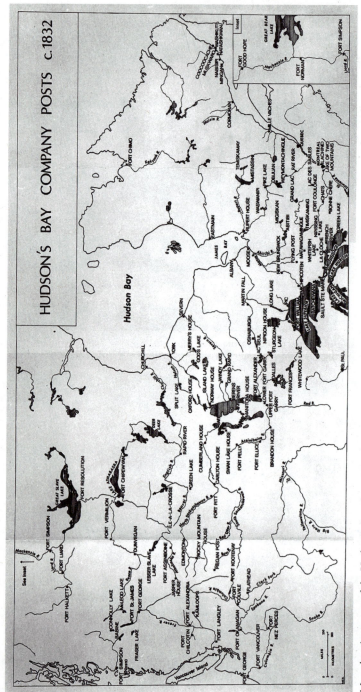

Map showing posts of the Hudson's Bay Company about 1832; reprinted from *Hudson Bay Miscellany, 1670–1870*, ed. Glyndwr Williams (N8134)

KEEPERS OF THE RECORD

Introduction

The Hudson's Bay Company Archives contains the business records of the Hudson's Bay Company, collected, preserved, and protected for more than three centuries as evidence of the Company's legal and professional obligations to its shareholders, to its employees, to the monarchy of Great Britain and Canada, and to the government of Canada. It holds rare and unique evidence and information about business, scientific, historical, political, and archival significance. Over three thousand linear metres of records, including the original vellum and leather-bound minute books, are now maintained in air-conditioned and humidity-controlled space at the Archives of Manitoba in Winnipeg.

This history of the Hudson's Bay Company Archives is an account of how the Company kept its records. It is also a history of the people who were responsible for making and keeping those records. For over 250 years the keeper of the records was the secretary of the Company. In 1931 an archivist was appointed to arrange and describe the historical records. The secretary remained, and remains today, ultimately responsible for the management of the Company's active records and for maintaining the relationship between the HBC and the HBCA. The archivists at the HBCA are responsible for the keeping of the Company's historical records. Although much of the material in the archives has been researched and information from it presented in numerous publications, no history of the keeping of those records and the eventual establishment of an archives has been written.

Throughout the first 200 years of its operations, the Hudson's Bay Company was predominately interested in, and was a prominent element of, the fur trade in North America. The search for new fur supplies and the resultant exploration and mapping led to the gradual expansion of the Company in all directions from the shores of Hudson Bay. Overcoming the problems of making and keeping records in isolated obscurity throughout much of North America and then accumulating those records in London was no small feat. For most of that time, there were no computers, no photocopiers, no fax machines, no telephones. There was, if luck was with the Company, a once-a-year voyage from England to Hudson Bay, which picked up the yearly journals and left behind new ones to be filled in by the post manager or clerk. Occasionally, two years would pass without contact between the Company in London and the posts in North America. The survival rate of business documents in Britain prior to 1800 was quite low.[1] That increasingly changed throughout the nineteenth and twentieth centuries, but the Hudson's Bay Company was already 130 years old in 1800, and its first inventory of records had been completed in 1796. Board minute books, letterbooks, bookkeeping journals and ledgers, registers of members, and staff records were augmented by archival records collected during, but outside, the activity of business such as maps, ships' logs, photographs, post journals, and diaries. There is a large library, including a collection of rare books, in the archives, approximately eight thousand maps and atlases, almost five thousand architectural drawings, approximately 130,000 photographs, and an impressive documentary art collection, as well as sound and moving images.

Sir Hilary Jenkinson, the British archival authority, has explained that archives are not brought together or kept for historical reasons. They are a natural product of an administration which is eventually used by historians for purposes quite different from the original intent.[2] Following Jenkinson's theory, the archival value of these records is enhanced by two major principles: provenance and original order. The fact that the Hudson's Bay Company has been in business since 1670 and has been keeping records over that whole period adds even more to their importance. The interpretation of records is reliant on the reasons for making the records in the first place and, secondly, on the interrelationships between the records and the whole of the collection. The importance of the information in a particular record is increased by the importance the owner put on keeping it. In the case of the Hudson's Bay Company Archives, the provenance has never been lost. Of course, not all the records of the earliest years of the Company have survived. Many unfortunately were lost or destroyed, and a few have strayed into other archives. The conditions, not only of making the records but of keeping them in London and in Rupert's Land in the early years, were not easy to control. Storage of the records that made their way back to London was initially quite haphazard, but many moves and inconsistent storage conditions seem to have had little effect on the preservation of the records in the archives today.

From time to time, a governor and Committee of seven directors in London laid down rules for keeping account books and journals. As early as 1683, the governor and Committee directed the factors of the posts on Hudson Bay to keep daily journals, which were sent to London yearly with the fur cargoes. As well, ships' logs were kept and returned to London by the captains of vessels sailing into Hudson Bay for the Company. The first arrangement of the records and resulting inventory in 1796 listed the records alphabetically, forming the foundation of the Hudson's Bay Company Archives and indicating an emphasis on order and accessibility.

During the first decade of the Company's history, the Committee met in London at various establishments, including the Tower, the Mint, Prince Rupert's house, and Garraway's Coffee House. The records of the "Company of Adventurers" moved with the Committee in a locked, iron-bound chest. The first permanent lease of premises was taken on Fenchurch Street in 1696; there the Company stayed until the move to the second Hudson's Bay House in 1794, almost one hundred years later. Its next move was in 1865. This stability probably aided the keeping of the archives, and credit must be given to the Company for voluntarily maintaining custody and providing some preservation for the records it had kept from the date of its founding. Without any specific management program, the records were kept together and stored in a way that made it possible to complete an inventory and index without any further comment in the minutes about their condition or lack of arrangement. The Company's reasons for keeping its records were related to legal and business concerns rather than a strong commitment to preservation for historical purposes. Legal actions by former employees regarding wages (one of them being Pierre-Esprit Radisson), wars and treaties with France, individual philosophies of various British monarchs, definition of the jurisdiction of the rival North West Company, and fluctuating stock-market returns indicate the range of concerns affecting the Company legally and fiscally. But the fact remains, the Company has kept a continuous record of its day-to-day business in both London and North America since 1670. Throughout most of its first 200 years, accusations were made at various times regarding the Company's use of land, its treatment of the Native people, and its commitment to settlement and exploration. Its charter always proved to be the primary document in any legal discussion of the Company's activities.

The history of the Hudson's Bay Company Archives reflects British archival traditions over the same period of time. Records management and archival science as independent subjects were really only recognized in the twentieth century. How is it, then, that huge accumulations of public, private, and ecclesiastical records of even greater antiquity, not to mention the Hudson's Bay Company Archives, have survived in Britain? The Public Record Office Act in 1838 focused on the public record, leaving considerable numbers of valuable religious, secular, and business records in private hands, at the mercy of time and the environment. Other records survived simply because no one bothered to destroy them. Jenkinson has noted that "as for the older documents accumulated by Companies in their own keeping, preservation has been ... a matter of chance while the Companies survived."[3] The survival of the Hudson's Bay Company meant the survival of its records.

The establishment of an official archives for the Company was, in fact, a gradual process, but the 1920s finally provided a suitable environment for the Company to make a formal commitment to the historical records that had been more or less ignored for 250 years. In considering this period in the history of the archives, it becomes obvious that three main factors influenced the Company's action at this time. First, repeated lobbying from outside researchers, predominately from North America,[4] pressured the Company for access to at least published copies of early records from the Company's archives. Secondly, the growth in the volume of paper records produced by a modern business as extensive as the Hudson's Bay Company in managing interests as diverse as land sales, settlement, retail stores, and fur trade required planned and organized arrangements. Thirdly, Confederation and the interest of the Canadian government in the records made the Company increasingly aware that it had a responsibility to share the archival material it had accumulated over its years of operation both in England and in Rupert's Land. Historically, it had to be accountable for its activities in the fur trade and for its role in the early development of Canada.

The organizers of the celebrations for the 250th anniversary of the Company's founding officially acknowledged the old records as significant historical documents and set the stage for the organization of an official archives. A journalist, Sir William Schooling, was hired to write a history of the Company. In fact, the book, *The Governor and Company of Adventurers of England Trading into Hudson's Bay: during Two Hundred and Fifty Years, 1670–1920*, contained only a brief historical outline. But before the end of 1920, Schooling had convinced the Company to let him write a multi-volume history from the wealth of material in its archives. During the six years of Schooling's efforts, he had a secretary and as many as four assistants, provided by the Company, who indexed and extracted many of the records in a format that has provided later staff of the archives quick and efficient access to volumes of information. And Schooling strongly encouraged the establishment of a formal archives and publication program. Unfortunately, his overly ambitious attempt to publish a history was unsuccessful, but it is a key to discovery of the Company's archives and the opening of that treasure chest.

Richard Leveson Gower became the first Company archivist in 1931.[5] Within a year, in preparation for the opening of the records to scholars, Hilary Jenkinson was one of two consultants invited to inspect the archives.[6] The theories of selection, arrangement, and description of archival material set out in Jenkinson's *A Manual of Archive Administration* were the basis for the classification scheme set up for the archives dating from prior to 1870. The arrangements and resulting finding aids made at that time are the same ones used today, with many of the research tools available electronically and more work being done to describe the records according to Canadian standards of RAD (Rules of Archival Description).

The Hudson's Bay Company fully appreciated the importance of its archives both for historical research and for favourable publicity. It was prepared to encourage interest from outside the Company, but the location of the archives in London presented access problems for researchers, who were, for the most part, in North America. The Company acknowledged this problem by establishing the Hudson's Bay Record Society in 1938 to publish key records in the archives. An agreement for joint publication was reached with the Champlain Society, and E.E. Rich, an historian teaching at Cambridge University, was hired as the first editor. The staff of the Archives Department researched and wrote all the notes to accompany the published text. The

A corner of the archives room, London, 1930s (1987-363-A-19-3)

records society publication program, however, pointed to still unresolved problems relating to access to the Company archives. One of the
remaining restrictions on access, the Company's right to deny publication of information obtained from its records, continued to create
problems for researchers in the late 1930s.

The Company did not want to jeopardize whatever publicity and
profit its own publications would bring to it by allowing researchers to
prepare competitive publications. Its intention was to make the archival material available to students of history and others, but it wanted
to maintain control over what was published. It was difficult to keep
ahead of the North American enthusiasm for access to and publication
of the historical record. Examples of that enthusiasm, almost mythical
at times, have become part of the history of the archives.

Although it would seem that access to the archives was opening up
with the establishment of an Archives Department in 1931, restrictions
continued to be in force. With the establishment of a solid publishing
program, though, it soon became evident that the researchers' interest in
access to the archives and permission to publish information found
therein was not a danger to the Company's own plans. Twelve volumes

of Hudson's Bay Record Society publications were produced jointly with the Champlain Society, and twenty-one more were published between 1950 and 1983 by the Hudson's Bay Record Society alone. As well, hundreds of books and articles by scholars and independent researchers have been written using the historical material in the archives.

The Second World War interrupted the progress of the Archives Department soon after it was established. Both the staff and the records were disrupted. A proposal to microfilm a large number of the most valuable records to save them from war damage was considered and rejected. Instead, the older and more valuable records not required for immediate purposes of classification or publication were moved to the estate of the Company's governor outside London. Research requests declined considerably, but the reduced staff continued to answer inquiries and assist with the Hudson's Bay Record Society publications until the archives were returned to London in 1945.

In the late 1940s the staff, consisting of the archivist and four assistants, continued with the classification and conservation of the records. The Hudson's Bay Record Society published annually, and the number of researchers visiting Hudson's Bay House and, later, Beaver House in London grew. In 1950 the Company was approached by W. Kaye Lamb, Canada's new Dominion archivist, who proposed microfilming the records from 1670 to 1870 as a conservation measure but also as a means of making the contents more accessible to scholars in Canada.[7] The Company supported the microfilming project, and the mere fact that the records would be more readily available in North America on microfilm indicates that it was prepared to entertain and approve more requests for publication of information about its past. Access by academic historians to the pre-1870 archival records and the right to publish information from them was routinely granted. The Company's positive experience with this arrangement soon overcame its remaining doubts about the wisdom of permitting researchers to publish information from its early records.

All varieties of material in the Hudson's Bay Company Archives have been researched and presented in numerous articles and books. Several histories have been written about the Company, most notably E.E. Rich's two-volume work, published by the Hudson's Bay Record Society in 1958 and 1959, and Peter C. Newman's three-volume popular history, published by Penquin Books between 1985 and 1991. Readers are referred to those histories and others for an understanding of the role the Company played in the history of Canada. No full-length official history of the Company has been written, and no previous study has been made of the history of the archival preservation of this large and unique national treasure. This archival history discusses the significance of the Company's administration of its records and its efforts to make them available through public access and publication. Key to the information contained herein are the administrative records of the Archives Department itself, dating from about 1920 to the present.

The book considers the records of the Hudson's Bay Company in the context of the history of the Company, of the history of Britain and of Canada, of business history, and of the history of British and Canadian archival traditions. Other historians search the volumes of primary source material for the minutiae that add so much to our understanding of over three centuries of business, scientific, and social history. As an archivist, I see the history of business record-keeping practices both as evidence of material and format and as anecdotal evidence of the process of keeping records. And beyond their archival and evidential value as records, their artifactual value is also considered. Photographs included in this book provide a visual documentation of their physical character and quality of workmanship through which the reader can imagine the texture and slightly musty smell of soft leather and crisp vellum, the physical weight of rag paper, and maybe even the ghostly presence of the people who laboured over the meticulous script, writing by candlelight in unheated (or overheated, depending on the season) dwellings in the wilderness of Hudson Bay or in the centre of London.

The history of the first 300 years of the Hudson's Bay Company archives also reflects British archival traditions. Britain has unrivalled collections of archives and records dating back many centuries. It is with amazement that we consider the huge accumulations of public, private, and ecclesiastical records of great antiquity, not to mention business archives, that have survived. Similar stories can be found among these archives, but credit must be given to the HBC for voluntarily maintaining custody and providing preservation for the records it has kept from the date of its founding. Admittedly, the tight hold kept on Company records was initially related to legal and business concerns rather than a strong commitment to preservation for historical purposes. But the fact remains that the Company has kept an almost continuous record of its day-to-day business in both London and

North America from 1670. It fully recognized the value of its history in 1920, on the occasion of its 250th anniversary, and the subsequent establishment of the archives and the appointment of an archivist in 1931 is a turning point in this history. The development of the Archives Department, the arrangement and description of the records, and the individual stories of the characters involved is an aspect of the Company's history never before told.

The story of the keepers of the record is interwoven with accounts of significant archival documents representing a small sample of the intriguing and remarkable material in the archives. This is the study of one major company's experience with the keeping of its records. The great significance of the resulting archives to the study of Canadian history is obvious. Over the years, the Company gradually eased control of access to its records, made them more readily accessible on microfilm, and increasingly allowed researchers to publish information found in the records. The 1960s marked the beginnings of another major change for the Company and for the archives. With the centennials of the dominion of Canada in 1967 and the province of Manitoba in 1970, as well as the tercentenary of the Hudson's Bay Company, Canadian historians approached the Company to transfer the archives to a location in Canada. The extent of material relating to the early history of Canada was impressive, and recommendations were made from the government of Manitoba and from the federal government in Ottawa. By the early 1970s, the Company was willing to turn over physical custody of the archives to the government of Manitoba under the most generous terms of access and publication it had ever formally adopted. In 1994 the Hudson's Bay Company completed the process when it announced the donation of its corporate archives and museum collection to the Provincial Archives of Manitoba.

It is in the end an archival success story. Few Canadian companies or businesses have an archives.[8] Many have not responded successfully to the problem of preservation of and access to their corporate archival records. Public archives no longer have the resources to accept large deposits of private business archives. If Canadian business archives are to be preserved, more businesses will have to do so themselves. The Hudson's Bay Company offers an example of how one company has managed to keep its records for over three centuries. The Canadian government provides tax benefits to encourage businesses to participate successfully in the economy of the country and the employment of its citizens. The tax benefit the Company received for its archives and museum collection has been used to establish two foundations – the Hudson's Bay Company History Foundation and the Hudson's Bay Company Foundation. The Hudson's Bay Company History Foundation will ensure the future care, management, and interpretation of these gifts as well as supporting Canada's National History Society, which publishes *The Beaver* magazine, provides support to historical associations, and has established an awards program. The Hudson's Bay Company Foundation supports community-oriented programs related to health, women, and youth.

I

if it can bee Soe Soone done

The First Fifty Years
of Record-Keeping, 1670–1720

If we are to appreciate fully the Hudson's Bay Company's success in keeping its records, we must judge the Company and its records in relation to the time period in which they were created. That requires an understanding of the people involved and their interconnections with the monarchy, government, business, society, and each other. How did the Company get started? What did England look like in the mid-seventeenth century? What is the historical setting for this business and these records?

Charles II was restored to the British throne in 1660 after a decade of the Puritanism of Cromwell's regime. The Restoration, together with the enthusiasm of a broad-minded monarch, provided a firm foundation for a renaissance in science, the arts, and business. The year 1660 also saw the first formal meetings of what would become the Royal Society. Two years later Charles granted a royal charter to incorporate the "Royal Society of London for Improving Natural Knowledge."[1] What this organization has to do with the HBC will become obvious as we progress. The Royal Society was a group of remarkable men, scientists and amateurs, many of them royalists and most of them educated at Oxford or Cambridge, who met regularly at Gresham College in London in pursuit of those scientific activities that had been developing in the Western world over the previous century – medicine, mathematics, exploration – all of which had been stimulated even further by the invention of printing by Gutenberg around 1450 and its introduction to England about twenty-five years later.

Charles II shared the friendship of several of these men, with their interests in physics, mathematics, astronomy, and particularly navigation. As benefactor and patron, he encouraged, supported, and marginally participated in the intellectual and experimental endeavours of the society. A few founding members of the Royal Society, such as Sir Paul Neile and Sir Christopher Wren, were early shareholders in the HBC. Other early members, such as Anthony Ashley Cooper, Earl of Shaftesbury, also found their way into the history of the fledgling company.

If we concentrate on the decades immediately before and after the incorporation of the HBC in 1670, it is hard to imagine an environment less conducive to record-keeping. Although various monarchs, including Charles II, instituted inquiries or issued commissions to search out and recover records belonging to the Crown, a State Paper Office was not set up in London until 1703 and the Public Records Office Act was not passed until 1838.[2] Records of the state, churches, businesses, and citizens were at the mercy of the elements, even if they were provided with an interior storage space. The Great Plague swept through London in 1665, lingering in England for over a year and killing thousands. The disruption to living arrangements and personal possessions can be surmised from the reports that come to us from that era. We can imagine that the reports from the keeper of records in the Tower of London, which mention preserving records from fire, war, water, mould, insects, and general filth, are not exaggerated. If pestilence and plague were not enough, the Great Fire of London in 1666 destroyed untold treasures and added to the confusion of any order that might have been put on what have been described by the same keeper as "rare ancient precious pearls and golden records."[3] With these conditions in mind, we can visualize the shareholders and Committee of the HBC making their way through the streets of London to meet regularly in the Tower, at Whitehall, Prince Rupert's home, or in a Cornhill coffeehouse.

The Restoration brought with it an energy that had far-reaching influences on commerce and trade as well as on science and the arts. A spirit of innovation resulted from the return of stability to the country. Not only did the court re-establish an opulent lifestyle after the years of Cromwell's control, but soon the City of London had to resurrect itself after the miseries of plague and the desolation of fire. The young, bright, and energetic king, thirty years old in 1660, stimulated new attitudes toward commerce and technologies such as shipbuilding and navigation which encouraged expansion of trade and exploration. One way of financing these enterprises was through the joint-stock company. And with the renewed emphasis of Charles II on royal charters, the result was incorporation of several overseas trading monopolies.

The term "joint-stock company" refers to the association of partners in a venture, not necessarily as equal partners, contributing capital to a common pool and sharing in the profits or losses, but trading as individuals. The earliest versions of such enterprise included the powerful group of wool traders known as the Merchants of Staple (c. 1277) and the Merchant Adventurers of England, who received their first charter at the end of the thirteenth century and were further encouraged with royal charters by Edward III and Henry VII. The Merchant Adventurers were active until 1807. Overseas traders, organized in this manner, might receive royal acknowledgment, which allowed a guild-like system of control and self-government in foreign territories. This interconnection between business and government provided the structure for administrative record-keeping beyond the immediate requirements of trading companies. Records were kept as a reporting mechanism to the monarch and Parliament. Chartered companies were private enterprises, but their charters provided them with public support in the event of foreign competition or hostility. A monopoly on trade came with the duty to defend the occupied lands in the name of the sovereign and to provide appropriate administration of the Natives and settlers, as well as their employees.

Recognizable joint-stock companies first emerged at the end of the sixteenth century. The Russian, or Muscovy, Company, first chartered about 1555, was active through to the end of the nineteenth century. Others, important for their role in opening up trade in newly "discovered" lands but also for acquisition, administration, and settlement of the resultant colonies, were the Eastland Company (c. 1579 to c. 1764), trading in the Baltic countries, and the Levant Company (1581 to 1825), trading in Turkey, Venice, and East India. Many joint-stock companies were ad hoc arrangements, organized for the immediate purpose of financing a single voyage or venture. Each merchant or adventurer subscribed to a capital fund an amount determined by the subscriber and received profit, or suffered loss, in the same proportion to the capital subscription. Even within this scheme, each adventure or voyage was financed separately.[4] This arrangement changed at the end of the sixteenth century with the charter of the East India Company by Elizabeth I. The East India Company functioned much beyond a business in the development of the colonial empire from its incorporation in 1600 until 1858, when the administrative control of India was assumed by Queen Victoria as empress of India.[5]

The HBC is often compared to the East India Company because of the broad role it played in the opening up of that part of North America that was to become western Canada. But differences separate the histories of the two companies. They were both early stock companies, established for the purpose of trade in lands that seemed to have un-ending supplies of commodities sought after by the citizens of Britain and Europe. Both played important roles in the development of the co-lonial empire. In reconfirming the charter of the East India Company in 1660, Charles II gave that company the power to appoint governors in India, to wage war and to conclude peace, to administer justice, to acquire territories, and to seize the ships of interlopers.[6] These quasi-governmental powers proved to be much more all-encompassing than any ever given to the HBC, but one has to wonder if Charles did not have them in mind for North America when he chartered the HBC a few years later.

The search for a Northwest Passage through the Arctic to China, In-dia, and the South Seas was a long-standing prospect that gathered mo-mentum with the navigational interests of Charles II, the exploration pursuits of the Royal Society, and the growing competition for cheaper and faster trade routes. Many had conjectured the possibility, and explor-ers such as Sir Martin Frobisher (1576, 1577, and 1578), John Davis (1585), William Baffin (1615), and, most dramatically, Henry Hudson (1607 and 1608) had attempted to find it without success. The possibility of prosperous trade with a new continent, together with a new route to the treasures of the East, must have been a powerful incentive to a king with expansionist ambitions.[7] Thus in the mid-seventeenth century the HBC was not unique, either in its administration or in the complexity of its interests. There was a long-standing tradition in England of compa-nies with similar mandates and with long-term success. But the fact that the HBC still functions in the twenty-first century and its administrative records are still being deposited in the archives *is* unique.

THE EARLIEST RECORDS

Details of the earliest activities of the governor and Committee of seven who were to direct the voyages and manage the business affairs of the HBC are found in the minute book catalogued in the Hudson's Bay Company Archives as A.1/1. It starts on the 24th of October 1671, al-most eighteen months after the charter was granted and almost four years after the adventurers first met to provide support to a voyage to Hudson Bay by Pierre-Esprit Radisson and Médard Chouart, Sieur des Groseilliers. There may have been books and papers, including a rough minute book, from the first four years, but these were later reported

Minute book, 1671–74 (A.1/1); the earliest document in the archives

"lost and carried away by one of their Servants."[8] The minute recording the order to keep the records of the Company is dated 7 November
1671, but the first minute book is actually backdated to the 24th of
October to include the activities of the previous two weeks. The grand
ledger, which officially starts in November 1671, has entries back to
1667, including lists of the original shareholders and accounts for the
expenditures relating to the voyage of the *Nonsuch* in 1668–69. Other
than the original charter, the first minute book is truly the beginning to
the archival record of the HBC.

The records in the HBCA do not tell the whole story of the Company's origins. The earliest records certainly provide plenty of evidence

and intriguing clues, but we have to look further for more details of
the story that will help us to understand why there was a company in
the first place and why its records were kept, not just for its immediate needs but for over three centuries. Briefly then, we know that
Pierre-Esprit Radisson and his brother-in-law Médard Chouart, Sieur
des Groseilliers, had been very successful in trading for furs but unsuccessful in their attempts to convince Montreal investors that a fur
trade route through Hudson Bay was a reasonable alternative to the
established, and heavily taxed, overland route from Montreal. Their
entrepreneurial spirit led them to search for support in New England,
where, in Boston, they met a commissioner of Charles II, Colonel
George Cartwright, who recognized their expertise in the fur trade and
experience in travel in the northeast of North America and encouraged
them to return to England with him.[9] They arrived in London in the fall
of 1665 and were quickly transported to Oxford, where the court of
Charles II had retreated to escape the plague that was epidemic in London. In Oxford, Cartwright introduced them to Sir George Carteret,[10]
who, on hearing their story, arranged for an audience with the king.
Charles was intrigued by the fur traders' story and provided them with
a small pension and accommodation with his cousin, Prince Rupert, at
nearby Windsor Castle. The next year they moved back to London with
the court when threat of the plague had diminished. Radisson and Des
Groseilliers were put in the care of Sir Peter Colleton while arrangements were made to outfit a voyage to Hudson Bay.[11] All this time they
were in discussions with various members of the court and society. Finally, after a series of delays, they were able to set sail, Radisson in the
Eaglet and Des Groseilliers in the *Nonsuch*, and as the saying goes, the
rest is history.

   The records documenting the story to this point, so important to the
history of Canada, are scattered. The letter of instructions to the captains of the *Nonsuch* and *Eaglet* from Prince Rupert and the backers of
the 1668 voyage to Hudson Bay is found among the state papers of
Charles II in the Public Record Office.[12] The original grants of trade into
Hudson Bay, provided to the backers of the first voyage by Charles II
in 1669 and predating the charter, are also in the Public Record Office.[13] The journal of Captain Zachariah Gillam, written during the
successful 1668 voyage of the *Nonsuch* to Hudson Bay, was published
in 1689 as *The English Pilot, the Fourth Book*.[14] Thomas Gorst, who
accompanied Gillam on the *Rupert* to Hudson Bay on the 1670 voyage, kept a journal, as instructed, a copy of an extract of which is in the

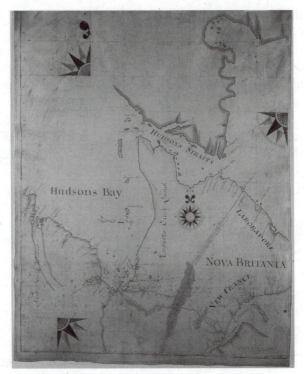

Map of Hudson Bay and Straits by Samuel Thornton (son of
John Thornton), 1709 (G.2/1)

Guildhall Library, London.[15] A map of Hudson Bay by John Thornton
from about 1685, probably based on the maps of Gillam's first voyage,
is in the British Library.[16] Manuscripts attributed to Radisson are
found in the Bodleian Library in Oxford, the British Library, and the
HBCA (E.1/1 and E.1/2).[17]

　　The interests and interconnections of all the players are many. Sir
George Carteret and Sir Peter Colleton were original shareholders in
the HBC. Several of the early shareholders were also members of the
Royal Society, including Prince Rupert when Charles II appointed him
the first governor of the HBC. Rupert was also governor of Windsor
Castle, where he pursued his interests in art and science and the prospect of overseas trade. All of these elements came together to provide
the environment required for the founding of the HBC. Radisson and
Des Groseilliers had specialized knowledge of the virtually unexplored
regions of northeastern North America. The original investors had experience in other chartered companies, such as the East India Company

and the Royal African Company, as well as a scientific curiosity and thirst for knowledge as members of the Royal Society. They all also wanted to make money. The approval of the king, along with members of his court, was the consequence of a growing interest in the idea of trade in furs directly from Canada, together with the hint of copper resources and the enviable possibility of finding a northwest passage to the South Seas.

These courtiers, princes, merchants, and traders, adventurers all, blended their expertise, interests, and finances to provide the backing for a preliminary expedition to Hudson Bay as early as 1666. But the war between England and Holland intervened. Another attempt the following year also failed because of delays in approval that left the expedition too late in the season for safe navigation in Hudson Bay and the northern seas. Finally, in the summer of 1668 a partly successful expedition headed to the bay with Radisson and Des Groseilliers travelling separately in the *Nonsuch* and the *Eaglet*. Unfortunately, the unseaworthy *Eaglet*, with Radisson, had to turn back after two months. His second attempt to reach Hudson Bay on the *Wivenhoe* in May 1669 was also unsuccessful. But the *Nonsuch*, with Des Groseilliers aboard, reached Hudson Bay and returned to England in the fall of 1669, laden with furs and the knowledge that trading directly into the bay was indeed possible. The investors petitioned Charles for a charter, which he granted on 2 May 1670.

Under the Charter, the Company was granted

The sole Trade and Commerce of all those Seas Streightes Bayes Rivers Lakes Creekes and Soundes in whatsoever Latitude they shall bee that lie within the entrance of the Streightes commonly called Hudson Streightes together with all the Landes and Territoryes upon the Countryes Coastes and confynes of the Seas Bayes Lakes Rivers Creekes and Soundes aforesaid that are not already actually possessed by or granted to any of our Subjectes or possessed by the Subjectes of any other Christian Prince or State with the Fishing of all Sortes of Fish Whales Sturgions and all other Royall Fishes in the Seas Bayes Isletes and Rivers within the premisses and the Fish therein taken together with the Royalty of the Sea upon the Coastes within the Lymittes aforesaid and all Mynes Royal aswell discovered as not discovered on Gold Silver Gemms and pretious Stones to bee found or discovered within the Territoryes Lymittes and Places aforesaid.

The first page of the Royal Proclamation Charter of the Hudson's Bay Company, 1670.
Still an active record, the charter, written on five parchment sheets, is on display at
the Company's corporate head office in Toronto. (1987-363-C-25-13)

The HBC was incorporated and immediately sent out two more ships
to the bay. The two adventurers set sail for Hudson Bay on what was
to be a successful trading venture for the Company, Des Groseilliers in
the *Rupert* and Radisson in the *Wivenhoe*. The ships returned in the
fall of 1671, laden with 11,000 pounds of beaver pelts. The cargo also
included otter pelts and moose hides. The next expedition left London
in June 1672. Radisson and Des Groseilliers were kept employed in the
interim as advisers on the purchase of trade items. They made one
more trip together to the bay when the Company sent three ships, the
Rupert, the *Messenger*, and the *Employ*. This time, Des Groseilliers remained with Governor Charles Bayly at Charles Fort in James Bay,

while Radisson returned to London, where he married an English-woman and remained until 1674. Over the next thirty years, Radisson and Des Groseilliers had an on-again, off-again relationship with the Company, alternately aligning their allegiances with the Company in England and the rival Compagnie du Nord in France. In 1684 Radisson returned from France to rejoin the Company, leaving Des Groseilliers to go back to Canada, where he died, probably before the end of the century, without further contact with the Company. Radisson made voyages to the bay in 1686–87 and again in 1688–89. From then until his death in 1710, his connections to the Company were through law suits and petitions he made for arrears in salary or for pension in regard to his service to the Company.

The charter's commitment to colonization and settlement was given little more thought. Within a few years, the details of preparing the annual voyages and marketing the furs required the full attention of the Committee. Not all of the great records of the earliest years of the Company have survived. Many were, unfortunately, destroyed, some were lost at sea, and a few, as mentioned earlier, have strayed into other archives. The conditions of making and keeping records both in London and in Rupert's Land[18] were not easy to control. As a rule, any journals, logbooks, charts, or maps from a post on or a voyage to Hudson Bay were to be handed to the Committee on the return to London. These were later referred to and studied by ships' captains and Company employees in preparing for voyages to or employment at Hudson Bay posts. The earliest known reference to a journal written by an employee while on such a voyage is not in the HBCA but, as mentioned earlier, in the Guildhall Library in London as part of the papers of Robert Hooke, a seventeenth-century philosopher connected with Oxford University. This extract, documented as copied from Thomas Gorst's journal, dates from 31 May to 2 October 1670 and provides the first brief but detailed accounts of day-to-day life at a Company post and of exploration of the coast of James Bay. Gorst was employed as secretary to Charles Bayly when Bayly was sent in 1670 to serve as governor of the Company's small post on James Bay at the mouth of the Rupert River. Bayly remained at Rupert River when Gorst sailed back to London on the return trip. Gorst then returned in 1672 to serve as Bayly's secretary and again in 1674–75 as storekeeper. Journals from the later trips are not extant. John Oldmixon referred to Gorst's journal, which he apparently had in his possession at the time of writing his *The British Empire in America* in 1708, a two-volume "history of the settlement, progress and present state of all the British colonies on the continent and islands of America."[19] How Gorst's journals ended up in the possession of Oldmixon or Hooke is not known, but they have been immortalized in Oldmixon's work, with its first published discussion of the HBC. Gorst's name appears regularly in the Company minutes when he was in London reporting to the Committee his knowledge of the voyages in which he took part to Hudson Bay and assisting Thomas Rastell with the inventory of the returned ships.[20]

THE FIRST KEEPERS

We already know that the very first records of the syndicate that established the Company are no longer extant and the earliest document in the HBCA is the first minute book. The first grand ledger, judging from the dates of its contents, would seem to challenge the minute book as the earliest in the archives, but the ledger is clearly of later origin. It resulted from a resolution dated 7th of November 1671, recorded in the first minute book, which records that the Committee "Ordered That Mr Rastel Doe forthwith give an account to this Comittee not only of the whole charge of Setting out the Shippes & Stocks of the Adventurers this Last voyage to Hudsons Bay, but also of the charge of all former Voyages beginneing from the first joynte Stocke of the Adventurers, & that there bee a true state of the Whole business & every particular man's interest duely Sett Forth & entered in fayre Vellum bookes against tuesday next the 14th day of this instante November, *if it can bee Soe Soone done.*"[21] The earliest information in the ledger must have been copied from the papers of the first years (1667–71), which have now been lost. Obviously, there were gatherings of the chartered adventurers before October 1671, and probably some form of record was kept. What we can be sure of is that once the decision was made to meet regularly and to keep records of those meetings and all dealings of the Company, the record-keeping process was in place. Of course, the job of record-keeping was not to "bee Soe Soone done" since it continues today, and those "fayre Vellum bookes" now stand proudly on the shelves in an air-conditioned and humidity-controlled room in the Archives of Manitoba.

Thomas Rastell, the first clerk hired for the nascent company, had been employed by the adventurers as early as 1669, according to an entry in the first ledger indicating that he was paid £200 on 12th May by the acting treasurer, John Portman.[22] As the clerk, Rastell was initially

Grand ledgers in archives storage (A.14). The second oldest
document in the archives, the first grand ledger (on top shelf)
includes entries recording the expenses for outfitting the voyage
of the *Nonsuch* to Hudson Bay in 1667. It also records the
stock accounts of the first investors, or "adventurers,"
including Prince Rupert and James, Duke of York.

occupied with making and providing records as directed by the Committee. He also took inventory of arriving cargoes and kept track of ships'
provisions for the outgoing voyages, he organized fur auctions,[23] and he
even searched out a supply of appropriate hatchets for trade with the
Natives.[24] Beyond reporting on the "true state of the Whole Business" of
the Company, the minutes of 7 November went on to order

That Mr. Rastell take an account from Mr. Portman of his receiptes
& payments & alsoe of the Sale of the beaver & other goodes &
enter the Same in bookes as aforesayd:

Minute book, 1671–74 (A.1/1, fo. 3d); page showing order on 7 November 1671 for Thomas Rastell to keep the books of the Company

That Mr Rastell take an account also from Sr James Hayes his Secretary of the Copies of all orders & Comissions given to the Comanders & Factors abroad this Last Voyage:
That all Comanders Factors & others imployed by Comission from the Adventurers bee Summoned to give an account each man severally aparte, how they have observed the orders given them:
That an account bee taken of the factors of each Ship Severally of what goods are disposed of abroad:
That an account bee taken also from the factors Severally of the investments of the goods abroad by bills of Ladeing & factoryes ...
That Mr Beane Sende the booke with copies of the Comissions given

to the Comanders & factors abroad, to Mr Rastel, & that all other
papers belongeing to the Adventurers bee comitted also to the charge
of Mr Rastel.

On 14 November the Committee

Ordered, That accordeing to a former order made the 7th of this
instante November Mr Rastel doe take care that bookes of accountes
of all businesses belongeing to the Adventurers bee perfected &
ballanced with all possible expedition.[25]

And on 12 December

That Mr Rastell take an account from all persons of what private
trade can bee discovered accordeing to what papers can bee come
at & give account thereof to the next Comittee & that all orders
bee entred into a booke to bee provided for that purpose.[26]

As can be seen from these few examples, the minute books are full of details of the Company's activities and business arrangements, including
names of the individuals involved and hints at contemporary lifestyle in
high-society London and in the wilderness around Hudson Bay.[27]
    As well as records being kept of the business activities in London,
the Company required them to be kept both at sea and at the posts in
Hudson Bay. The captains of ships making the annual voyage to Hudson Bay were each provided with instructions such as the ones signed
by Charles II for Gillam and William Stannard on the first trip: "You
are to Keepe exact Journalls of all proceedings and observations and to
be curious in your soundings that wee may Know the depth of the wa-
ters in all places w[h]ere you come and according to the best of your
Skill shall provide such mapps as may give us an accompt of the places
where you goe."[28] These orders were based on the "Directions for Seamen" as set down by the Royal Society. The journals were kept and
presented to the Committee on the return to England. In 1696, with
England at war with France, the records show that Captain Henry
Baley was given instructions that went beyond the commercial and exploration interests of the Company. He was required, if necessary, to
act as a warship for the king and to keep notes of any such events.
Copies of the letters from the governor and Committee were written in
bound books and kept in London for reference. Baley's instructions

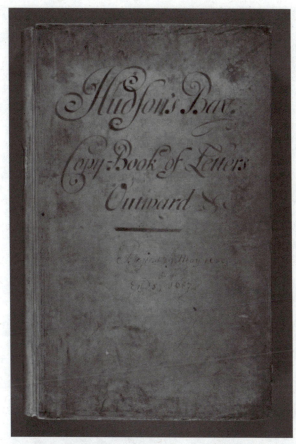

Copybook of letters outward, 1680–87 (A.6/1). Before the invention of carbon paper or photocopiers, all correspondence from the governor and Committee was hand-copied into letterbooks by clerks.

were "to sett forth in warlike manner ye sd ship called the Dering ffrigtt under his own comand ... Provided alwaise that ye sd Henry Baley keepe an exact Journall of his proceedings & therein perticularly take notice of all prizes which shall be taken by him."[29]

From time to time the Committee in London laid down rules for keeping post account books and journals such as when, in 1683, it directed factors of the posts the Company had established around Hudson Bay to keep "Journalls of what hath been done in the respective factories & of all occurrances that have happened to them the yeare past."[30] These daily journals were sent to London each year with the returning fur cargoes.

Albany post journal, 1705/06 (B.3/a/1). Daily diaries of events were kept by clerks at all the posts. The 1705/06 journal from Fort Albany is the earliest post journal preserved in the archives.

Concern for the records is evident throughout the Committee's minutes with references to the "Bookes" and their protection. Clerks hired to keep the books in order took an oath of secrecy, and rules of limited access to the records are evident throughout the history of the Company. Suggestions arose from time to time that the Company was hiding wrongdoings or illicit activities, but the archives do not reveal any such evidence. The records do contain concern for secrecy related to the normal business practice of protecting successful strategies and future plans from competitors. The first clerk to record the events and accounts of the Company, Thomas Rastell, performed that duty at least until 22 July 1674, the last entry in the first minute book. A new clerk, Richard Hobson, was on salary from 5 October 1678 to December 1679, and it is possible that he took over from Rastell. Unfortunately, the minute book recording events from 1674 to 1679 is missing; so this must remain conjecture.[31] By 1679 the shareholders included predominately businessmen, and the attention to more businesslike practices is evident in the records from about that time. Changes were made in the accounting and bookkeeping practices, as the position of treasurer was dispensed with in favour of employing banking houses such as Thomas Cook and Company and Stephen Evans (sometimes Evance) and Company.

A new minute book was started in November 1679 with the entry "Rules and Orders for the better Regulating and Governing of the Company." These early bylaws, which were to be read at the first meeting of the Committee each year, included an oath of loyalty to the Company required of Committee members as well as of all employees:

> I, A.B., doe sweare to be good and true to our Soveraigne Lord & Lady the King & Queenes Matie. that now are his heires and successors, and that I will be faithfull to the Governour and Company of Adventurers of England trading to Hudsons Bay; in the mannagement of their Trade, the secretts of the said Company which shall be given me in charge to conceale, I will not disclose; and dureing the present joynt stock of the said Company, I will not trade to any of the Limitts of the Company's Charter, without leave of the said Company first had and obtained So help me God.[32]

The rules also noted that a copy of the charter "shall be alwaies in the Committee Room to be seen by any of the Company who desire to see same" and that all proceedings of the Committee and its transactions "shall be made publickly at the Board and entred in the Bookes kept for that purpose." The last rule states, "No Bookes or Papers belonging to the Company shall at any time be removed by any person or persons whatsoever from the Committee Roome without Order of the said Committee." This is the first reference to control over the records as a distinct entity. A "New Booke of Orders" was ordered by the Committee and a new clerk hired. John Stone was engaged on a trial basis on 3 December 1679, to examine the "Bookes and Accompts of the Company from the beginning thereof with Ma^r Hobson."[33] Hobson was to give Stone his directions before being paid off.[34] He always described himself as a clerk when witnessing transfers of stock, but Stone, from

the time of his engagement, was always called "secretary." He was, it
seems, the first employee to bear that title officially. He also acted as
accountant. Within a month of Stone's employment, William James
was engaged as a clerk "to Enter all ye Orders of ye Committee in ye
Booke of orders for which he is to have 2s.6d. for such Writing as ye
Deputy Governor shall direct him every Comittee day for wch he is to
attend to receave Instructions."[35]

Starting in December 1679, working-copy books[36] of the minutes
were kept, the contents then copied in the second minute book, or
"Greate Booke" (A.1/2). It is possible that William James is the person
of that name who was associated with the Writing School of Christ's
Hospital from 1658 until he was dismissed in 1675 for being drunk.[37]
He was with the HBC from 1679 until he was discharged from its service at the end of 1681, but no reason is given. The minutes do state
that Onesiphorus Albin, who was to be the new secretary, or Mr Stone
were to take on James's job of writing: "Ordered that M[r] Albin or
M[r] Stone do for the future write all the Orders of the Committee in the
Faire Booke of Orders and That M[r] William James be paid off what is
due to him so farr as he hath written and that he be thereupon discharged our Service."[38]

To reiterate, then, Rastell was working as a clerk, and sometimes per-
forming the role of husband[39] for the Company, from 1671 to some-
time after the middle of 1674. The previous year a Robert Holmes was
hired as husband, leaving Rastell to perform only the duties of office
clerk.[40] We can presume that both Rastell and Holmes left the service
of the Company between 1674 and the fall of 1679 because they are
not mentioned in the minute book that starts in November 1679. Since
Richard Hobson was the clerk from October 1678, perhaps Rastell left
at that time. With the renewed effort to order the affairs of the Company starting in 1679, Stone was hired as secretary and accountant,
with James as clerk until 1681, when Onesiphorus Albin was sworn
into the service of the Company as secretary.[41] Stone remained for one
year, presumably assisting Albin. He left the Company of his own accord but not without some consternation among his employers. The
minutes for 3 November 1682 record that it was considered an inopportune time for Stone to leave.[42]

Albin was a private accountant initially hired by the Company as
secretary and accountant on a part-time basis. He accepted payment of
£80 per year with the understanding that he would be required for no
more than two hours per day. According to Albin, however, he soon

Minute book, 1679–80 (A.1/2, fo. 8d); an example of William James's flamboyant writing style

found the Company's books in "confusion," and the time required of him to spend on Company business was such that it was arranged for him to work full-time and his pay was raised to £180 with periodic gratuities of £50.[43] So he became the first secretary-treasurer, and within a couple of months his duties included those of husband; he was also the first secretary to sign official documents. One of his duties in this regard was to countersign the instructions being sent in 1682 with the ships to Hudson Bay under the words "*By Command of his Highness Prince Rupert Governor and the Committee – Onesiphorus Albin Secretary.*"[44] This authority would come back to haunt him a couple of years later in a court case against the Company.

The minute books at this time also include many details of the secretary's activities. In June paper, books, pens, and ink were purchased from Robert and Plask.[45] Albin was at various times ordered to pay outstanding accounts, to search for insurance documents, and to receive papers and documents relating to the Company's business. He was directed to purchase another iron chest with two padlocks and keys. In that chest he placed the charter, which was kept in a black box, three seals of the Company, and three bundles of papers.[46] One of the seals was removed a week later to be kept in the secretary's office.

The secretary was responsible for keeping all these records in order, and he reported on the Company accounts as kept by the firm of Stephen Evans (Evance) and Company. He packed up and delivered the necessary papers and documents to and from the ships and warehouses, and the letters and journals arriving from Hudson Bay were passed among the Committee members. Because of his authority to sign for the governor and Committee, Albin also took on the responsibility that authority carried. The possibility of his being arrested was dealt with at a Committee meeting in February 1684: "Ordered if the Secretary should at any time be Arrested for Signing Capt. Nehe. Walkers Instructions for his last expedition to Hudsons Bay that Mr. Weymans and Mr. Hayward be Desired to bale him here below and if it be removed above Sr. James Hayes and Sr. Edwd. Dering be Desired to bale him above."[47] Albin was in fact arrested in June, and his bail was paid by Committee members James Hayes and Nicholas Hayward, on behalf of the Company.[48]

Prince Rupert died in November 1682, and two weeks after being elected to succeed him as governor of the Company, the Duke of York (later James II) requested a copy of the charter for his perusal. The secretary retrieved it from the iron chest, a copy was made, and it was delivered to the new governor.[49] For the most part, this principal record stating the Company's purpose and responsibilities remained filed away, safely stowed in the iron chest in the secretary's office.

COURT CHALLENGES

The charter was first challenged in a 1684 court case. In preparing its defence, the Committee once again had the charter removed from the iron chest in order to read it for comparison with the copy in the Book of Orders. The content was verified as "exact according to the Original," and the governor was ready to defend the Company's rights accordingly.[50] The case arose out of the capture of the *Expectation* (alias

Charles) by the Company ship *Diligence*, commanded by Captain Nehemiah Walker, on suspicion of trespassing on the Company's Hudson Bay territory. The case lasted two years, and for the Company it essentially meant that the charter was on trial all that time. Articles from the charter were read and discussed in relation to its authority over a previous charter granted to the Muscovy (Russian) Company by Queen Mary, later confirmed by Queen Elizabeth 1. The degree of frustration the Company experienced is expressed in the final line of the evidence it presented in June 1684: "To the last Article they Answer and believe what they have believed and deny what they have denyed."[51] The Company's defence included details of its record-keeping practices and of Albin's authority in signing orders from the Committee:

> the aforesaid Onesiphorus Alban doth usually signe all orders Instructions and writings that relate to the said Company after the Committee have given directions for the doing thereof which directions are usually taken by the said Alban in a Booke kept for that purpose called the Minutes Booke or booke for Memorandums of what is ordered by the said Committee and that such directions as aforesaid were given to the said Alban about the time aforesaid by Sir James Hayes deputy Governor of the said Hudsons Bay Company Wm. Yong Esq. John Letton and Gerrard Weymans Merchant or by some of them or some other persons as a Committee for the said Company for that aforesaid yeare 1683 ... and that the said Alban did draw up and give such orders and directions as aforesaid to the said Nehemiah Walker or some other of the said Company.[52]

The Company was finally absolved in December 1684 from any claim by the interlopers, but it had been an expensive and time-consuming exercise. The legal action had, however, given a clear vindication of the Company's chartered rights, at least for the time being. It also had taken its toll on the secretary, who, seeking recompense, requested a pay increase from the Company; it was not very encouraging:

> The Secretary now humbley moveing, as he formerly severall times hath done, that the Committee wold be pleased to Augment his Sallery & also to consider him for his past services, he was ordered to withdraw, and the Committee taking his humble request into Consideration, after a long Debate, considereing the present condition of the Compa. Did not thinke it fitt at this present to establish

an Augmentation of Sallery to him, but well weighing how faithfull
& Dilligent the Secretary hath been not only in his owne Station,
but very serviceable also in all the affaires of the Compa. which
was acknowlidged by the whole Committee, It is now ordered that
at present a Gratuety shall be given him of £100 And the Committee
are pleased to promiss for his better Incouragment that when it shall
please God the next shipps shall arrive in safty from Hudsons Bay
he should be taken into farther consideration.[53]

But Albin did receive other benefits from his employers. Soon after he
was hired, he was given an apartment for his family in Scriveners' Hall,
which the Company rented at about the same time: "At this Committee
the lease between the Scriveners Company and Hudson Bay Compa. of
Scriveners Hall was openly read and approved and Ordered the Companys seale to be fixed to it. And allso Ordered that the Secretary take
posession of the aforesaid Scriveners Hall and remove himselfe and
family thither before our Lady day next."[54] Albin had three servants
who assisted with the Committee, subcommittee, and general court
meetings, held there every few days for the next five years. His son,
Joseph, was also hired by the Company for two years, 1682–84. He assisted his father in writing up the minutes[55] and then replaced John
Stone in the warehouse[56] until he was dismissed in November 1684.[57]

Onesiphorus Albin was considered to be faithful and diligent until
28 October 1686, when it was discovered that he had "[a]bsconded
from the Companies Service."[58] His wife appeared before the Committee on that day to demand his wages, and it was "ordered that his Acct.
bee made up, & what Shall bee found due Shall bee justly answered."[59]
Mrs Albin was requested to leave the family quarters in Scriveners'
Hall, but on her refusal to quit until she had been paid, the Committee
ordered two of the servants, George Potter and John Worsell, to
"[c]onstantly lodge in the House every night & one of them at least
Continually remaine heere all the day."[60] On 1 November 1686 the
Committee recorded that Albin was "[e]mbroiled in Severall troubles
& debts" and resolved that as he was unfit for his position, he was "totally discharged from the Companies Service." Albin, claiming that the
Company owed him £700 for wages for himself, for "dyet & wages for
the said servants for 5 years & other Just allowances," petitioned the
king for redress. The petition was referred to the Company, which denied the allegations. Its reply was considered by the king in council on
28 January 1687, and Albin's petition was dismissed.[61] His account,

when finally balanced on 10 August 1697, showed a debit of £412 19s. 2d. which was written off as a bad debt.[62]

The details included here about the first clerks of the Company in London are important to illustrate the early record-keeping practices that established the precedent and standard by which the records have been kept throughout the history of the Company. These are the earliest records. The personal stories and intriguing mysteries that accompany them only add to the wonder of the archives today. Albin was not the only employee to take the Company to court. In 1692 Pierre-Esprit Radisson appealed a decision by the Company to reduce his pension to the £50 the Committee had approved for him in 1684:

Sr. James Hayes and Mr. Yoong made report to this Committe that Mr. Espirett Radison is Lately arrived from france and haveing tendered his Service to the Company that they had caryed him to Windsor and presented him to our Governor His Royall Highness who the Said Mr. Radissons Protestation of fidellity to the Company for the future was pleased to advise he Shold be received againe into faviour the Service of the Company as thereby they had made an agreement with him to receive him accordingly under the wages of £50 p. annum ... This Committee Judging it to be for the Interest and Service of the Company ... Mr. Peter Espritt Radison tooke the oath of fidellity to the Company."[63]

Sir Stephen Evans, who since 1679 had been handling the Company's finances along with Sir Thomas Cook, was the governor of the HBC in 1692; so he was well aware of the Company's financial state and of its obligations.[64] Over the years since 1684 Radisson had been provided with gratuities, a salary when he was "out of the country on the Company's service,"[65] and additional stock in the 1684 three-for-one split. But in 1690, as a result of economic downsizing and a lingering suspicion of his loyalty, the Company had decided to cut Radisson's pension and stock to that of its original 1684 agreement with him.

After lengthy but unsuccessful negotiations with the Company, even with the intervention of the Duke of Marlborough, in whose care he had been put, Radisson made a formal petition to the Lord Keeper of the Great Seal of England in May 1694 for his pension to continue at £50 a year, for the arrears owing for furs he had purchased on behalf of the Company to be paid, and for a court order against the Company to produce its records showing the exact conditions of its agreements with him. The bill of complaint, preserved in the Chancery records in the Public Record Office, instructed the Company to produce its records relating to Radisson's charges. It reads, in part, "that the Company may produce all their bookes wherein any Entrys are made concerning your Orator soe as may appeare to this Court of Justice and reasonableness of your Orators demands."[66]

The Company's reply to the charges was not ready until almost a year later in April 1695, and the case dragged on for another two years after that. It was in its answer to Radisson's complaint that the Company admitted that "all theire books and papers ... for the four first yeares of their said trade and dealings" (1667–71) had been lost or carried away by an unnamed employee. There is no report of the Company producing any of its records in court at this time, but its answer to the bill of complaint refers to specific orders, minutes, memoranda, and letters and concludes "that besides the Minutes orders or memorandums before sett forth there are noe others entered in the said Companys Bookes any wayes relateing to the Complts wages Sallary or gratuity."[67] The response also stated that "these Defendts are ready to aver maintaine and prove as this Courte shall awarde." Three volumes in the Public Record Office attest to that process: A vellum-bound volume (CO 135/2), embossed on the cover with the Company's coat of arms, is the petition from the Hudson's Bay Company of "Transactions Betweene England and France Relateing to Hudsons Bay 1687." A copy of the Company's Charter and other "entries of HB, 1670–1689" was also provided, bound and embossed "Hudsons Bay" (CO 135/1). A volume labelled "Council of Trade, 9 July 1697" (CO 1/68) stated: "The enclosed memorial is a copy of what hath been sent us by the Hudson's Bay Company, upon the same occassion as the other memorials already sent to you in our letters of the 2[d] and 6th Instant."[68]

Finally, in March 1697 an agreement was settled on for a pension of £100 a year, but Radisson did not receive compensation for the furs.[69] However, as Rich points out in his History of the Hudson's Bay Company, it was "the basis for a workable arrangement, and the settlement is probably to be explained in part by the fact that by 1697 the Company again had need of Radisson's services, and particularly of his evidence."[70] The Company charter had been renewed in Parliament in 1690, but only for another seven years. So, beginning in late 1696, the Company began to work on its renewal and to defend adherence to the conditions set forth in the charter.

Political events connected with the death of Charles II in 1685, the short reign of James II, and the arrival of William of Orange in 1689 resulted in an unstable economy in England, intensified by the escalating hostilities with France. In London the Company had a surplus of furs; at sea Company ships were lost to the French; on the bay four of the five Company forts were taken over by French invaders, although trade continued successfully at Albany. Conveniently for the Company, Lord John Churchill (later Earl and then Duke of Marlborough) was its governor during these tumultuous times, and his royal connections were useful, particularly in that he supported the new king, William III. The king cited the French aggression against the HBC's forts and ships in a time of peace as one of his reasons for declaring war against France in 1689.[71]

THE NEED FOR SECURITY

With concern about the French and increasing opposition from other fur companies in England and in North America to the monopoly of the HBC and its charter, Marlborough had the charter confirmed by an act of Parliament in 1690, under the condition that it would be reviewed in seven years.[72] Consequently, the Company's competitors were ready in 1697 to renew their complaints. The Company claimed adherence to the conditions set forth in the original charter and presented, in its defence, five reasons for the continuance of the parliamentary grant that confirmed its privileges and trade. It claimed that it had complied with all articles of its charter; emphasized the great potential for trade in beaver; claimed the cost of the forts it had built, which had subsequently been destroyed by the Natives or the French; claimed the cost of ships and trade lost to the French; and stressed the value of land in Hudson Bay and the subsequent trade that would be lost to the French. But the efforts were unsuccessful, and the parliamentary grant was not renewed. The charter was once again a royal prerogative.

It was an unsettled period for the Company, and suspicious that papers and documents were being supplied to its opponents, the Committee restricted access to any person without proper authority:

The Committee Considering the Inconveniency that may attend the Compas. affaires by delivering out of Bookes & papers belonging to the Comp:a thought fitt to Establish the following order, viz. That for the Future the Secretary deliver out noe Bookes or papers belonging to the Comp:a to any person whomsoever without an order from

the Committee after which he shall take a Receipt from the party he
Delivers them to Expressing the particulars, and if any Booke then to
Mention the first and Last folio thereof.[73]

Shipping was in constant danger from the French until the Treaty of
Utrecht was signed in 1713. Sailing instructions to the captains of Company ships included directions for destruction of records in case of capture at sea. Instructions for Captain Grimington in 1708 read: "In case
you are in Danger of being Taken & se noe meanes of escaping, then
Throw over all your papers in generall, and be shure your signall be one
of them therefore have all your letters & orders & what elce may be of
prejudice to us Ready at hand to destroy tham Except the order for Ran-
someing your Shipp."[74]

Storage of the records that made their way back to London was initially quite casual, but many moves and inconsistent storage conditions
seem to have had little adverse effect on the condition of the records that
are in the archives today. During the first decade of the Company's history, when the Committee met in London at various establishments, the
records moved with the Committee. The first recorded meeting of the
general court of the HBC, on 24 October 1671, was held at the home of
Sir Robert Vyner, one of the first adventurers and also a banker, sheriff
and mayor of London, and the king's goldsmith. His residence on Lombard Street in east-central London was rebuilt after the Great Fire and
has been called a "noble structure."[75] In describing one of Vyner's
homes in Middlesex, Samuel Pepys explains that Vyner "lives, no man in
England in greater plenty."[76] We can only imagine what his home on
Lombard Street provided to the comforts of the Committee members.
The next few meetings alternated between Vyner's and the Tower of
London, a few blocks to the east. The Tower was a convenient meeting
place offered by another original shareholder, Sir John Robinson, who
was lieutenant of the Tower from 1660 to 1678. Robinson was also connected with the Levant and East India companies and served as treasurer
and then deputy governor of the HBC.[77] Prince Rupert's lodgings at
Whitehall, in west-central London near Charing Cross and sometimes
referred to more specifically as Spring Gardens, were periodically used
for general court meetings during Rupert's tenure as governor of the
Company. Exeter House, just west of Whitehall, the home of the Earl
of Shaftesbury, was another early meeting place for the adventurers.
Shaftesbury was lord chancellor of England in 1670 and deputy governor
of the Company from 1673 to 1674. He was also a member of the Royal

Society. Another shareholder was John Foorthe, alderman of the city of London, who offered his quarters at the Excise Office, "where hee is pleased to give accommodation for the Comittee to meete, & for all papers bookes & accounts to be kept there."[78] This was the most regular meeting place until July 1674. A few meetings were also held at the home of Richard Hawkin, who was treasurer of the Company in the years 1673–74, and at least one meeting was held at the Golden Fleece Inn in Cornhill, which would not have been far from Vyner's home on Lombard Street.[79]

The first long-term location for the Company was secured when a committee room was rented at the Golden Anchor in Cornhill from December 1679 to September 1680. Garraway's Coffee House was used for the first sales of furs. For the next two years, 1680–82, Committee meetings were held principally at the home of John Letten, shareholder and Committee member. Company records were also stored at Letten's and he was ordered "to buy an Iron bound chest with 3 Locks and Keys wherein the Pattent & Seale of the Company and such other things as shall be thought fitt by the Comittee may be lodged, of which keyes the Deputy from and for the time being shall allways have the keeping of the principall Key and the others to be disposed of as ye Committee shall think fit."[80]

This "great trunk" was the earliest repository for the Company's records. It cost £9.17s. 6d.[81] An impression of the size of the chest and the kinds of records kept in it can be seen from the varied, but nevertheless interesting, collection of papers listed in the minutes for 25 July 1683:[82]

The Compa. pattent enclosed in a black box lockt up the Key of wch. is in the Same 3 Seales of the Compa. two in Steele and one in Silver upon an Ivory knocker and 3 bundles.

Bundle no. 1:

A Bill of Sale of the barke *imploy* [*Employ*]
A Bill of Sale of the *Craven*
A Bill of Sale of the *George* Ketch to Maximillian Keech by Thomas
  Agres
Maximillians Keeches bill of Sale to the Compa. of the *James* Ketch
Tho. Agres Receipt for £240 of the *James* Ketch
Tho. Agres and others bond to performe covenants
Edw. West and Jno Reynolds bond for Edw. West fidelity to the
  Compa.

Capt. Zach. Gillams Obligation to render an Acco. of Ships Stores
Capt. Neh. Walkers bill of Ladeing Dated 5 May 83
Capt. Jno. Abrahams bill of Ladeing Dated 1 May 83
Wm. Whitegars Obligation to the Governr. and Compa. 79
Capt. Bonds covenant to Render possession ofthe Ship *Craven*
Jno. Nixon Esqr. bond for £5000 Dated 1679
Jno. Abrahams Obligation for £8
Henry Sergeant Esqr. bond to the Governr. & Compa. Dated 27
   Apll. 1683 for £5000
Fran. Rainesfords Charter Party Dated 16th March 1682 for the *Dil-*
   ligence for Hudsons Bay Mr. Ger. Weymans and Jno. Abrahams
   Charter party Dated 21 March 1682 for the *George* Ketch for Porte
   Nellson
The Lease of Scriveners Hall for 7 yeares commencing 25 March
   1682

Bundle no. 2:

John Coles Indenture Dated 1681
Henry Davis Indenture Dated 1676
Joseph Coles Indenture Dated 1678
Henry Coles Indenture Dated 1678
Anto. Beales Indenture Dated 1678
Tho. Ballwoods Indenture Dated 1676
Matthew Snellsons Indenture Dated 1678
Leyton Steels Indenture Dated 1678
Wm. Billings Indenture Dated 1678
Henry Kellseyes Indenture Dated 1676

Bundle no. 3:

4 Deeds of the Mortgage of the Pattent & a Declaration of Trust
   from John Morris etc. a Receipt for £5120 and Memorandums
   concerneing the Same
A bond from Capt. Thompson of £1000 Capt. Sheppard and
   Mr. Brookings bill for £50 James Knowles, Jno. Evins & Rich.
   Smartes Obligation
Jno. Shaws obligation to Governr. and Compa. 1679
Benj. Gorst Obligation to the Compa. 1679
Capt. Greenwayes order for £312.10.–

Capt. Thompsons bond for the payment £132.5.11
Wm. Fraziers obligation to the Compa. 1679
Capt. Shepards bond of £500

Unfortunately, none of these documents have been found in the archives, and the grand iron chest no longer exists. There is no record of its fate. In 1682 a lease was taken on Scriveners' Hall, and the Committee and its records had a home there for fourteen years, including both an office and a warehouse for the furs. It was "ordered that the Screetors trunck and all other things belonging to the Compa. be removed from Mr. Lettens house to Scribners hall of which Mr. Stone & the Secretary is to take care thereof."[83]

When the lease on Scriveners' Hall terminated in 1695/96, the Company moved to the north side of Fenchurch Street into premises situated at the upper end of Culver Court, where it stayed for the next ninety-eight years. The lease was taken originally for thirty-five years at a rate of £75 per year. It was renewed every twenty-one years until 1794. This address became known as Hudson's Bay House and was described by a contemporary author as "a handsome Brick Building whose Front next the Street has been lately repaired and beautified, and carries the appearance of one of the finest pieces of Brick Work with Pilasters, Architraves, etc. in the whole City."[84] The move is recorded in the minutes of the Committee on 18 March 1696 with instructions for safeguarding the belongings in the process: "The Secretary as also the Warehouse Keeper were now ordered to take the first opportunity of Removeing the goods into the new house & to take care that nothing be imbeziled or Lost."[85]

This directive may sound somewhat paranoid, but we should remember all that was going on at this time – Radisson's "complaint," renewal of the charter, and the problems with Onesiphorous Albin. The competitive nature of business in general and competition between the HBC and other fur traders in particular required the Company to take a secretive and protective approach to its business records. Records-creation procedures, secure storage, and restricted access to Company information would take on an even higher priority during the next centuries.

Plan of Fenchurch Street premises 1695/96–1794 (A.37/43).
The buildings at the end of Culver Court, off Fenchurch Street,
were the first permanent location of the Company.

upon no Account to Communicate any of the Company's Affairs

Record-Keeping and Corporate Memory, 1720–1800

Within fifty years of its receiving the charter, the business of the Hudson's Bay Company was conducted as much in remote North America as in the exciting city of London and at the royal court. By 1720 the Company had established itself on firm ground in the area of Hudson Bay with four forts – Albany, York, Eastmain, and Churchill – and had settled into large and secure premises in London. Its charter had been challenged, successfully defended, and confirmed in Parliament. Even when that endorsement was rescinded in 1697, the royal warrant continued as the basis for the Company's presence in North America. But the challenges were far from over, and within a few years its critics would once again launch accusations that would require the British House of Commons to reaffirm the Company's prerogative.

For brief periods of time during the 1700s, the HBC placed a renewed emphasis on exploration to expand its frontiers beyond the small forts at the mouths of rivers. Employees Henry Kelsey, James Knight, Anthony Henday, and Samuel Hearne were sent along the coast, up the rivers, and overland to the west and north in search of more furs and other legendary treasures. The Company was not alone. Exploration from all directions during the eighteenth century would unlock the heart of North America, the movement being predominately westward, including breakthrough expeditions to the interior and the north by Kelsey, Knight, Henday, and Hearne. Enterprising individuals not employed by the Company but whose exploits would have an effect on how it did business were Peter Pond, who explored and mapped the Mackenzie basin in the 1780s, and Alexander Mackenzie, who subsequently followed the Mackenzie River to its mouth and then, in 1793, was the first to reach the Pacific by an overland route. Captain Meriwether Lewis and William Clark accomplished the same task by a southern route to the mouth of the Columbia River in 1805.

For most of the eighteenth century, England experienced financial prosperity and improved economic development. An uneven but general expansion of trade, in which Britain and France drew the major share, reflected and stimulated greater industrial activity. Considerable development took place in the expanding British Empire. Epidemics of smallpox and influenza early in the century and again later reduced populations all over the world, but in England not in the same numbers as the plague in the previous century. Diseases introduced from the Old World had a more devastating effect among the Native population in North America. Stresses imposed by the American Revolution, the French Revolution, and Britain's recurrent wars with France were countered by the energies generated by the industrial revolution and increased employment for the masses. Through the century, although affected by wars, London itself was not a target of hostilities; those took place at sea, in remote areas of England and Scotland, or on other continents. During the eighteenth century, continuous, if not spectacular, prosperity for the HBC is evidence that the war years did little to upset the Company's trade.

Scientific curiosity, economic progress, and a generally enlightened ideology also provided the climate for changes in the arts. Baroque extravagance was replaced towards the end of the century by neoclassicism. The literary world encompassed prodigious writers such as Daniel Defoe (*Robinson Crusoe*) and Jonathan Swift (*Gulliver's Travels*), best known for their political and religious allegories as well as their parodies of British national issues. Their stories of exploration and exotic adventure could easily have been modelled on the lives of HBC servants. By the end of the century a new world order, resulting from the French Revolution, brought immense political and cultural change to Europe and Britain.

Change was also reflected in business and the administration of large enterprises such as the HBC, with its business interests on another continent. Administrative control of diverse business operations with overseas branches resulted in the production of, and requirement for, an increased number of records. Besides the governor and Committee, whose numbers were defined in the charter and hence did not change, the London office of the Company was augmented with extra clerks to assist the secretary and accountant as required. In

North America the Company moved inland and by the end of the century had added posts at Henley House (1743), Cumberland House (1774), Brandon House (1793), and Hudson House (1794) to its established trading posts on the coast of Hudson Bay, which provided the port facilities for the annual voyage and the only communication link with the London office.

Post journals and ships' logs from this time survive in the HBCA in regular series, as does correspondence between the London office and the Hudson Bay posts. These records display a uniformity in style and substance, reinforced by regular reminders in the outward correspondence and confirmed in the minutes of the Committee. The first post journals in the archives date from the early 1700s, adding to the minute books, official correspondence copybooks, grand journals, and ledgers kept since the early years of the Company. Agenda books for meetings of the London committee, subcommittees, and the general court were kept from 1737. Correspondence books of general letters outward from the London office began in 1753 as a separate series from the official correspondence to include copies of letters to correspondents outside the Company and copies of private correspondence to employees in North America. Letters inward from the Hudson Bay posts began, initially sporadically, in 1701 with official correspondence kept in a separate series from more general correspondence after 1712. Records of the Company's fur auctions are found in the HBCA starting in 1786.[1] Ledgers of officers and servants' accounts date from 1719. From 1746 onwards a series of balance books was kept, recording the balance of stock in hand on ships and at posts, including remainders and other assets. These were set out every half-year against debts and dividends due, giving a fair indication of the constant stock-taking and of the increasing investments of the Company. The first complete inventory of the Company's archives would not be taken until 1796.

Generally, lack of funds, space, adequate accommodation, and staff beset public record-keeping in England at the time, but the Company was not alone in its attention to records. A State Paper Office, with its own keeper, was set up in 1703 by the House of Lords during the reign of Queen Anne. Government and Crown papers were kept in various offices, including the State Paper Office, the Tower of London, and various rooms at Westminster and Whitehall. It was not until 1838 that the Public Record Office Act established one record office, putting custodial care of the central government in the hands of the Master of the Rolls.[2] Without any standardization of archival procedures, credit must be given to companies such as the East India Company, active from 1600 to 1858,[3] and the HBC for voluntarily maintaining custody and providing some conservation for the records they kept from the dates of their respective incorporations. Interest in records, libraries, and history was not limited to state and commercial institutions. Like Samuel Pepys in the seventeenth century, individuals collected or lobbied for the collection of significant papers and artifacts. The British Museum and Library was created in 1753 to house the Cottonian Library and the collections of Hans Sloane and Robert Harley. Sloane was a member and past president of the Royal Society.[4] The presence of records relating to the HBC in private collections is an issue that will arise in the discussion of events at the mid-century mark.

Increasingly during the eighteenth century, the activities of the Company took place in North America. All of its forts except Fort Albany were lost to the French from 1697 until 1713, when the Treaty of Utrecht between England and France, one of a series of treaties marking the end of the War of Spanish Succession, restored Britain's (and hence the HBC's) rights to trade and commerce in Hudson Bay. The treaty provided compensation to the Company for its losses during the war years. Throughout the century, the Company continued a competitive rivalry with the French and French Canadians from Montreal while it was reestablishing its positions at Albany, York, Eastmain, and Moose Factory and as well developing a site at the mouth of the Churchill River on the west coast of Hudson Bay. The earliest forts were all established at "the bottom of the bay," at the mouths of rivers flowing into James Bay. New Severn, at the mouth of the Severn River, was the first to be built on the coast of Hudson Bay, followed by York Factory at the mouth of the Nelson River and then Fort Prince of Wales on the Churchill River.

CARTOGRAPHIC RECORDS

The HBCA now contains the largest private collection of maps in Canada, consisting of over 12,000 maps, charts, plans, and sketches, a few dating from as early as 1563. But the full extent of the Company's early mapping activities is not exactly known.[5] It had no mapping department or office in London, and the first maps were purchased or commissioned. The first surveyor on the payroll was Philip Turnor, hired in 1778 for a period of three years to survey inland west of Hudson's Bay. Commercial firms such as those of Aaron and John Arrowsmith and R.W. Searle produced maps based on information received from the Company. Some maps were drawn by or drawn from information provided by Natives, such as those used and copied by Peter Fidler in 1801 from maps made by the Blackfoot chief Ac ko mok ki (also spelled A-ca-oo-mah-ca-ye).[6] Many manuscript maps were made by Company employees. The earliest extant manuscript map prepared by a HBC employee, but now in the British Library, is that of the west side of James Bay by Thomas Moore, dated circa 1678.[7] The earliest map in the HBCA is one drawn in 1709 by Samuel Thornton, who was commissioned to make it by the Company.[8] It is based on James Knight's first-hand observations and illustrates claims against the French for land taken during the War of the Spanish Succession.[9] An annotated version of that map was part of the negotiations for the Treaty of Utrecht in Holland in 1713, which Knight was selected to attend with a member of the Committee.[10] The earliest map by a Company employee in the HBCA map collection is a later one by Knight, probably dating from about the time he was successful in convincing the Company to back a major voyage of discovery to find the Northwest Passage in about 1719. It is a pencil sketch on paper, later over-drawn in ink, of "rivers between Prince of Wales' Fort and the Northern most Copper Mine."[11]

Mapping, another form of record-keeping, was not an exact science in the seventeenth and eighteenth centuries in spite of the fact that exploration of previously unknown parts of the earth's major continents had been taking place since the end of the fifteenth century. With or without accurate maps or charts – or for that matter, accurate instruments of navigation – the captains of Company ships sailed every year into and out of the "bottom of the bay," or James Bay. The charts they relied on were probably based on the results of Henry Hudson's unsuccessful search for the Northwest Passage in 1607/08. And whatever new information was received relating to the mapping of the area occupied by the Company a hundred years later was not shared beyond the Committee room, other than when it was provided as reference material to the captains of the Company ships in preparation for another spring supply trip to Hudson Bay. Confidentiality was reinforced regularly, as evidenced in the 1749 sailing orders to the commanders of the *Mary* and *Success* on their departure for the bay: "you are not upon any acc^t whatsoever to Communicate any of the Company's Affairs or deliver any writing or Journal of your proceedings to any person whatsoever except y^e Govr & Deputy Governor of ye Hudsons Bay Company for the time being."[12] Instructions were clear that maps and charts sent or brought back to England were to be drawn in ink, not in

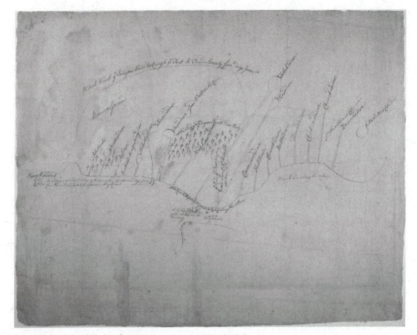

James Knight's sketch of rivers, post-1719 (G.1/19)

pencil, presumably so that no alterations could be made after the fact. But as Richard Ruggles points out, the Company

> did not have at Hudson's Bay House in London a chief surveyor, a cartographer, or geographer responsible for overall exploration programs, for surveying in the field, for drafting maps, for maintaining map files, or for managing public relations with cartographers or scientific societies at home. There was no central drafting room or map room; some incoming maps were maintained in a semblance of order in several map cases and portfolios at different locations in Hudson's Bay House in London. Others, sketched on the pages of journals, or folded and attached to them, were kept in the office files. Still others, drawn on separate sheets, were attached to wooden rails and used as wall maps in the Company's offices. Those drafted on multiple sheets and glued together on a linen or canvas backing might also be used as wall maps before they were stored away.[13]

Some local exploration was carried out by employees of the posts, resulting in sketches and maps of rivers and harbours that added details to the existing information. Few prior to the 1750s have survived in the HBCA. Despite the Treaty of Utrecht, the French presence was still felt to be close by, coming more aggressively from the interior this time, not the sea. All communication between the posts and London was by letter, transported by the yearly supply ship. Instructions from the London office, reports of wars beginning or ending, news of kings or queens dying and their successors' coronations, letters to and from family members, and the annual post report to the governor and Committee were transmitted by this means. The routine of an annual voyage to the bay, which left England in the late spring carrying supplies and new employees and returned in the fall with a load of furs and redundant or worn-out employees, was well established. Except for Knight's enterprises, the first half of the century was not a particularly adventurous period for the Company, but it was prosperous enough to provide dividends periodically to its stockholders and to maintain the British presence in a large part of North America. Between the Treaty of Utrecht and the Treaty of Paris (1713–63) the fundamental conditions of the Company's trade continued unchanged, and Company practices continued stable. The fur trade was its reason for being, and the men who spent years in the remote posts of Hudson Bay made it possible.

RECORD-KEEPING AT ALBANY

The fur trade was based at Albany, Eastmain, Severn, York, Moose Factory, and Charles Fort, with a short period of occupation on Charlton Island. Albany was representative of all the Company posts and had a long and consistent history of success as a fur-trading post on Hudson Bay. Located at the mouth of the river named for His Royal Highness, James, Duke of York and Albany, the Company's second governor, it was established as a place of trade by Charles Bayly in 1674, and the first sturdy buildings were erected in 1679. The post was captured by the French in 1686 but was recovered for the Company and for England five years later. It missed the next round of French aggression when it was the only post on Hudson Bay in the control of the Company between 1697 and 1714. The post was rebuilt in 1721–22 in a new location across the Albany River on the west bank.

A study of Fort Albany in the early 1700s, as recorded in various archival documents, provides a snapshot of the Company's facilities and of the people it employed at that time. The size of the post at Albany can be surmised by the fact that it was home for forty-six men, including the

master or governor (also referred to as the chief factor) and his deputy, a
clerk, a warehouseman-accountant, a carpenter, a gardener, a cooper, two
smiths, a boatswain, two sawyers, a gunner, an apprentice, and a number
of labourers. The staff resided in a three-storey building constructed of
horizontal logs, described by the governor at the time, Anthony Beale, as
the "great house."[14] Another large building was his residence, part of
which served also as a warehouse for stores and furs. The mixture of "domestic bustle" (cows, sheep, goats, kitchen gardens, and hay fields), "business activity" (Natives, furs, and trade), "and warlike preparations"[15]
(palisades and four bastions mounted with cannon) reflects Albany's role
and political position in this period.

   As part of the active routine of the fort, the accountant and the apprentice clerk would spend their days recording the trade transactions
or assisting with the running of the post in one way or another. The
Company required that appropriate and detailed accounting records
and a journal be kept of the daily events and activities. Beale's journal,
like most of the post journals preserved in the HBCA, reveals little of his
personality. As noted by HBC historian Glyndwr Williams, "It reports
the essentials, but eschews speculation; it has no literary pretensions,
and confines itself to the recording of daily events."[16] Beale's journal
and account books were kept by his clerk, Stephen Pitts, who was paid
at a standard clerk's salary of £30 per annum.[17]

   Very little furniture was sent from England;[18] nearly everything in the
post would have been built on site. Tables, chairs, and beds were made
by the carpenters, labourers, or anyone else with the skill, from wood
available locally or from boards left over from construction of the post.
The records show that the staff at Albany had an inkstand and the Company's seal to aid in their record-keeping duties. Paper supplies arrived
annually from England. In 1706 Albany received a fair amount of writing material: three books each containing twenty-four sheets of lined paper (one quire), two reams of loose paper (each ream at this time
contained 480 sheets), a new bottle of ink, and half a pound of sealing
wax.[19] The books and paper supplied by the Company to be used for the
post journal and accounting records provided a standard format for all
the posts' records. Ink was also sent with the other supplies to provide a
uniform medium for writing. Commercial ink used in the eighteenth century would have been an ink-gall or iron-tannin product, made from an
extract of crushed oak galls mixed with water and a mordant such as fer-
rous sulphate. Readers of the original documents in the HBCA notice that
the ink writing is often a rusty colour. It would originally have been

black. The change in colour is not the result of fading, since these books have remained closed for most of their existence, but has been caused by the continuous action of oxidation on the pigment. Keeping the lid on the ink bottle was essential to reducing evaporation and oxidation so that the ink supply at the isolated posts would last until the arrival of the next supply ship. Even more frustrating for the clerks on the shores of Hudson Bay was the problem of frozen ink during at least six months of constant below-freezing temperatures. If they ran out of ink or if the annual supply ship did not arrive as planned, homemade inks could be made from tannic acid, if there were oak trees in the vicinity, or less successfully from carbon.

No mention is made of quills in the list of stores received at Albany. It can be presumed that they were made in situ, as required, from the hundreds of geese that were killed or provided by the Natives on a regular basis. A few quills would not have been missed from the 358 pounds of feathers that were included in the trade inventory for 1705–06.[20] One modern authority on quills claims that the most satisfactory for the purpose of writing are those from Hudson Bay geese.[21] The quill, usually the wing feather of larger birds such as geese or swans, was prepared for writing by drying and removing the exterior membrane; then the end was hardened by heating it in hot ashes before it was cut and shaped to a point. A split was made in the quill from the tip to allow the free flow of ink. The quill pen was a functional and inexpensive writing instrument that remained in use even after other writing tools were introduced in the latter half of the nineteenth century.

In order to find appropriately educated and trained personnel, the Company at times hired its apprentices from London's two large charity schools, Christ's Hospital and the Grey Coat School. The term "hospital" at this time referred to a charitable institution providing housing for the needy or education for the children of needy families. Until the reign of Henry VIII, social services for the poor and homeless had generally been provided by religious institutions. With the dissolution of the monasteries in the sixteenth century, charity hospitals were founded to provide homes and schooling for poor, fatherless, or orphaned boys and girls in the larger cities such as London. The charity schools supplied instruction in the basics of reading, writing, and mathematics. Generally, the boys were apprenticed to commerce and the girls were put out to service as housemaids or governesses.

Christ's Hospital was founded in 1552 and still operates, now outside London, in Horsham where it moved in 1902. Charles II established the

Royal Mathematical School, adjunct to Christ's Hospital, where boys
were prepared for service in the navy by teaching them mathematics and
navigation. These qualifications, as it would turn out, were also ideally
suited to the needs of the HBC. Another option was to hire able-bodied
but not necessarily well- educated youths from the streets of London and
the Orkney Islands. With the firm establishment of the fur trade within
ten years of the Company's receiving its charter, it began the practice of
taking apprentices from Christ's Hospital, known as "Blue Coat Boys"
from their distinctive outfit, to train in the business. The first apprentice
was Charles Coats, who was selected by the Company in 1680. He had
been a student of the Royal Mathematical School, and his first posting
was to the Company ship *Prudent Mary*. Five boys between the ages of
thirteen and sixteen were recruited in 1689, and Samuel Hopkins was
apprenticed in 1715 at the age of fifteen. Two more boys joined the
Company in 1717.

SAMUEL HOPKINS

Between 1715 and 1722 the governor of Albany was Thomas McCliesh
(various other spellings include McCleish, Macklish, and MacLeish).
Samuel Hopkins joined him in the first year to serve his apprenticeship as
bookkeeper. By following a trail of records in the HBCA that identify or
refer to Hopkins, we can put together a story, for a brief period, that illu-
minates the working conditions in its remote posts, reinforces its policies
and procedures, and provides an example of personnel management,
eighteenth-century style.

   Hopkins's unusual story, which furnishes a colourful illustration of
a clerk's life, is documented in the minute, correspondence, and account books as well as in the journals of Albany and York. It begins
on 20 May 1715, when it was recorded that the deputy governor was
"desired to Enquire at Christ Hospital, for a fit Boy, that can write a
Good Hand, In order to serve the Comp[a] in Hudsons Bay as a Apprentice, & to be brought Up to Book-Keeping."[22] Within a few days
Hopkins, the son of a cordwainer (shoemaker)[23] in the parish of
St Giles, Cripplegate, in the city of London, had been taken on for a
seven-year apprenticeship at the annual salary of £5 for the first five
years, £10 for the sixth year, and £15 for the last year.[24] He was sent
to Albany that summer and was immediately set to work. He arrived
with a letter for Governor McCliesh from the London committee,
dated 3 June 1715:

We having taken one Saml Hopkins A Blew Coat Boy as An Apprentice for 7 years, whom we send over on Purpose to keep our accompts at the Bottom of the Bay, We would have you be very kind to him, & give him all the Encouragem^t you Can, And if you are desirous of such another, pray Inform us, & we will take care to send you one, because there are but few but what are Wilde that offer their services to us for that Employment ... We also expect from you that great Care be taken of John Henson & Joseph Adams the Companies Apprentices, as also of Saml. Hopkins who now goes over with you, that they be well used & taught to Read & want for nothing necessary & Convenient for them.[25]

The apprentice writing clerks were hired for their excellent penmanship and knowledge of "ciphering," or accounting. The neatness and readability of their work was crucial to the Committee members' understanding of the Company's business in North America and was critically scrutinized when it was received in the London office. The Albany post journal for the previous two years, 1714–15 and 1715–16, was written by Michael Grimington junior, who at that time was master of the Company's ship *Prosperous*, based at Albany. An example of Grimington's writing from August 1715 illustrates an even, cursive italic script, easily readable and accentuated only by the fashion at the time of extended but controlled ascenders on the letter *d* and descenders on the letter *g*. Hopkins's writing style, taken from an Albany account book for July 1717, illustrates a rounded, upright form. The letters are large with short ascenders, often ending in a curl, and no extended descenders. The writing is legible and efficient-looking.

Hopkins apparently performed his duties appropriately, keeping the journals and account books without comment for four years, until 1719, when the appearance of his work was noticeably different, a detail not missed by the Company. Communication between London and the bay posts was limited to the once-a-year letter and exchange of books with the visit of the annual supply ship. That meant that the books and reports generally left Hudson Bay in late August or early September and arrived in London in October. The committee reviewed them in time for the annual meeting of shareholders in November. Responses and instructions were sent back to the posts on the next ship, leaving London in May or June and arriving in Hudson Bay in July, all going well. So the writing that Hopkins did in the fall of 1719 was sent to London in the summer of 1720, was noted by the Committee, and

Albany post journal, entry for 1715 (B.3/a/9, fo. 1); an example of Michael Grimington's writing style

was commented on in the following year. It was not until the annual letter, dated London, 26 May 1721, arrived at Albany that instructions were received about the sloppy writing: "And now we cannot but take notice how much Sam.l Hopkin's handwriting is alter'd for ye worse since he first, he affecting too much flourishing & makes his letters so small some scarce to be discern'd, w'ch pray acquaint him of, & that he take care to mind his hand for ye future."[26]

Hopkins's apprenticeship was to be completed in 1722, but even with its concerns, the Committee agreed to a further two-year contract, including an increase in wages to £20 per year, with the admonition that his handwriting must improve: "[We] Must again put you in mind that you mend your Hand writing & make your Letters & figures

Albany account journal, 1717 (B.3/d/25, fo.46); an example of Samuel Hopkins's early writing style

Larger & plainer than you have done in Late Years, leaving off so much flourishing for you wrote a much Better Hand when you went over first then now, for we can Hardly Read your letters, & hope you will observe your Governers Directions in all things."[27]

It is possible there was something more wrong with Hopkins than just his handwriting, for in October 1722 he was reported absent without leave. Joseph Myatt had replaced McCliesh as governor of Albany in 1721, and McCliesh had returned to England. On the morning of 3 October, after giving credit for their furs to some Natives, who then left to go hunting, Myatt went to set fishing nets on Albany Creek. He left Hopkins in charge during his absence but on his return was told by the sentry that Hopkins had gone west with the Natives. The reason for

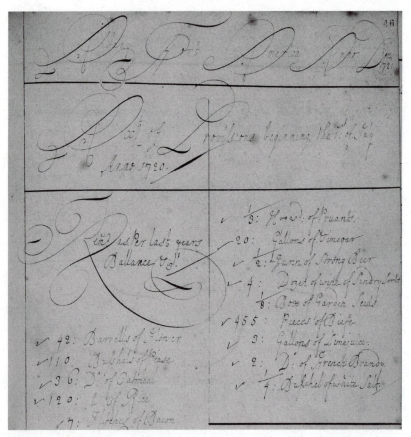

Albany account journal, 1720 (B.3/d/29, fo. 46); an example of Samuel Hopkins's later writing style

his going in such a manner was not known; at least no one interviewed was aware of any provocation. Myatt's own description in the Albany journal for that day provides a colourful narrative of the episode.

3 October 1721 – … The Inds. ytt. Came here yesterday Returned this morning haveing Given them Creditt at 7 this morning took 4 men in the Long Boatt to Sett 3 Netts up Albany Creek In hopes that Last Nights frost had brought fish into the River att my Departure Gave Samuel Hopkins Charge of the ffactory and at my Return found Samuell Hopkins misseing and Makeing A Strickt Enquirie wtt. was become of him the Centrie Gave me An Acctt. he saw him wth his Gunn goe up westward wch is the Last Sight Wee have had of him wch makes me of opinion that he is Gone wth the Inds. that

went from hence the same day Wtt his Reason was for ye same I Cant Devise Not upon any Acctt provokd there to as the whole ffactory can testifie.[28]

The next day Myatt sent a man upriver to track Hopkins, but to no avail. Hopkins, as it turns out, spent the winter in the bush; he reappeared on the 1st of May 1723, just as suddenly as he had left, accompanied by "the Same Indn. he went away" with. Myatt confined him to the post, but two weeks later Hopkins made another bid for freedom, this time unsuccessful. Again, the drama is played out in Myatt's journal:

at 9 this Morning 4 Conowes of Upland Inds. came downe this River to traid traided wth them and at 2 this Even they Departed. this Day Samuell Hopkins Attempted his Escape by Scaileing the workes in the time of traideing wth the Inds. for wch Gave the centuary corporal Punishmt. for his neglect of Duty Imediatly Sent 2 men westward in Search for him at 5 in the Even Returned with him telling me the Inds. would not Carry him I asked his Reason for those Obominable and foolish Proceedings he told me because I laid my Comds. upon him soe farr as this, not to Suffer him out of the Gate without my Liberty.[29]

Hopkins was sent back to England on the August return voyage of the *Hannah*. Whether conditions at Albany had anything to do with his behaviour or his sloppy habits can only be conjecture. But Joseph Myatt had problems of his own at the time, and judging from the wording of the Company's letter to him in May 1723, they were not to be taken lightly:

Wee have Several accounts from too good hands to be disbeliev'd, that many Irregularities & debaucheries are crept into ye Factory where you are, ye certain consequence of which must be disgusting & terrifying ye Natives from coming to Trade with us, & ye ruining & Spoiling our own Servants, & making them uncapable of doing us any Service, besides ye great Scandal this will be to our religion in General & a very great disgrace to us all who have ye power to prevent this Mischiefs & do not make use of it to prevent these disorders we hope these cautions will put you upon yr Guard & remove these grievances, that we may have no further Complaints, who wish you Health & Happiness.[30]

The previous year had seen a drop in trade of 50 per cent as a result of interference from French fur traders with the Natives on their way to

Albany, and Myatt was partially blamed for the unfavourable reports. He was demoted to deputy governor and replaced by Richard Staunton, who arrived on the *Hannah*, the ship that would take Hopkins back to London. Before the ship left, Staunton wrote to the Committee explaining how he would fill Hopkins's position as accountant: "Charles Napper our chirur [surgeon] haveing acted as ye Honrs Accomptt Since Sam^ll Hopkins Elopemt and according to Mr Myats character of him is a very sober & carefull man as by me observed since my arrival your Hon^rs being the best Judges of his abilities. he being willing to Remaine in the Same station, makes noe Dem^s but leaves to your Honrs Pleasure I shall continu him until I heare from you, wch I hope will be sent by the next return."[31]

Hopkins appeared before the Committee in London on 11 December 1723. As he could not give satisfactory answers to questions about his behaviour, his wages were terminated as of the date he had disappeared from Albany, and the Committee resolved not to employ him again.

> This day Sam^ll Hopkins Late accountant at Albany Fort Apearing before ye Comitte & being Asked by the Gou r his Reasons for goeing from ye Factory ye 2d Octb 1722: without Leave of the Governr. Mr Jos Myatt, when he had Left him in Charge of the Factory, & did not Returne till ye 1st of May 1723: being 7/m absent, as Likewise why he attempted A second time, viz ye 17 May 1723: to Escape by Scaleing the workes in Tradeing time, being Taken by Two men at the head of the Isleland & brought back to all which Questions he gave noe satisfactory Answer, upon which ye Sec r was ordered to Cast up his wages to ye 2d Octob 1722 & noe longer, That being The time when he first Absent him selfe from ye Factory, and Resolved That he be neuer Imployed in ye Comp s Service for ye future.[32]

There is no report of Hopkins's defence other than Myatt's journal entry that Hopkins was annoyed because Myatt had forbidden him to leave the fort without permission. No mention is made of any punishment given to Hopkins, unlike the sentry, who received "corporal punishment" for his neglect of duty. The result was a disappointing evaluation by the governor and Committee of a young lad from the heart of London who had shown much promise and who, among his peers, had been given a unique opportunity.

That would seem to have been the end of the story. Hopkins was paid only £6.15.6 for his service in 1722 from 31 May (the beginning of his term) to 2 October (the day he ran away).[33] But the saga continues, for we pick it up again in the minute book for 1724: "The Comitte now Entertained Sam ll Hopkins (who came from Albany Fort Last yeare) notwithstanding his former Miscariages for 2 yeares at L14: pr Ann who is to be sent to Yorke Fort, & A perticular Parragraph is to be Added to Gou r Macklish Gen 'Letter Concerning him.'"[34] Hopkins was sent to York this time to serve once again under Thomas McCliesh, who was chief factor there from 1722 to 1726 and again from 1727 to 1734. He was hired as a labourer and arrived with a letter of explanation for McCliesh from the governor and Committee dated London, 20 May 1724: "Mr Macklish amongst other Servants we've sent you S. Hopkins whome we employ'd at Albany River, you must be acquainted with his deportment there since you came from that place & had it not been out of Charity should not have sent him to you, he go's for 2 years at £14 p.Ann: strickly to Obey yr. orders, & would have you have a particular Eye over him together with an account of all your Peoples behaviour."[35]

McCliesh responded with his own impression of Hopkins and the situation at Albany: "As to the character of our men's behaviour I cannot say but that all men here has been very obedient in the discharge of their duties ... As to Samuel Hopkins's misbehaviour in the Bay after my departure from thence, I think that most of them turned fools and madmen. I must confess that I never knew Samuel Hopkins guilty in defrauding the Company al the six years he served under me, and very obliging, and appears now to be mighty sorry for his former misbehaviour. At the same time shall have a particular eye over him, and according to his behaviour this ensuing year his character shall not be wanting."[36] And a further favourable report followed the next year: "We must confess that Samuel Hopkins has behaved himself very handsomely, and have made him steward [stores man] this year, by reason believe he is naturally honest."[37]

Hopkins continued in service at York Factory, where he appears to have settled down, and there is little mention of him in the records after this. He must have married while in England in 1723–24 because payments are eventually made to his wife. In 1727 he was promoted to the position of bookkeeper, with an increase in wages[38] and no further reports of improper "flourishes." He returned to London in 1731 to terminate his career with the HBC with kind words from McCliesh: "We have according to your honours' orders sent on board the *Hannah* frigate the following persons as passengers vizt. Samuel Hopkins, accountant ... As to their behaviours I cannot say but that they have discharged their duties with honesty to the best of our knowledge, and as for Samuel Hopkins he has been very diligent and honest in the discharge of his duty, and is deserving of your honours' favour."[39]

At the same time McCliesh asked for a second bookkeeper "on account of amount of work to be done in tradeing time." The bookkeeping position vacated at York Factory when Hopkins retired in 1731 was filled the next year by James Isham, who was sent "to be Employed as a writer and to be instructed in keeping Ye accounts, and doubt not he will soon be very usefull to You in that respect by your Instructions & assistance, which Wee require may not be wanting and hope he will be Carefull & diligent in observing the same & desire You will write Us a particular acc.[tt] of his behaviour."[40] Isham had a much more enterprising personality than Hopkins and five years later he was chief factor. Four years after that promotion he was made chief factor at Fort Prince of Wales on the Churchill River when he had to be reminded about his own record-keeping: "Notwithstanding our former directions, your General letter is not wrote in Paragraphs which you must not fail to observe for the future answering distinctly each Paragraph of our Letter."[41] Isham remained there until 1758, making visits to England in 1737, 1745, and 1748. The journal he wrote during the winter of 1743, containing an English-Indian vocabulary and observations of the natural life of the country around the fort, is the first of several observation journals prepared by Company servants in their spare time, perhaps out of boredom with the routine but also to fulfill a personal interest in natural history and the Native languages. Isham's journal was submitted "To The Honourable The Governour Deputy Governour and Committee of the Hudsons Bay Company London," probably in 1743, with the accompanying explanation:

Gentlemen,
Being in a Disconsolate part of the world, where their is Little conversation or Divertisment to be had, I was dubious of that too common Malady the Vapour's, which is frequent the forerunner of other Distempers, therefore to prevent such if possable, I have in cold Days and Long winter Nights, amusd. my self with the following Observations, which I am very Sensible the advantage the Small acct. of the following Language, wou'd be to any person Residing in North America, – the

following Vocabulary of the Language which is cheifly spoke in these parts, with some small Observations on the Country, is most Humbly presented to your honor's perusal by,

> Gentlemen
>> Your Honor's most Obedient
>> and Most Humble Servt.
>>> JAMES ISHAM[42]

These observations may have been Isham's response to the Company's instructions, repeated in 1736, 1737, and 1738, that factors should send home the roots of herbs, plants and shrubs, with seeds, berries, and kernels, while the surgeons should identify them by their Indian names and list their qualities.[43] But the meticulous, yet practical details about the Hudson Bay environment and ecology in Isham's "Observations" seem to have been ignored all together. Many years later, E.E. Rich, editor of the Hudson's Bay Record Society publications, wondered if they were read at all: "The document in the Archives bears no marginal comments such as often denote that a document has been worked through for the benefit of the committee, there is no mention in the minutes of its receipt, and no action can be clearly ascribed to it."[44]

This lack of attention to matters bayside was not new. A few years earlier, James Knight had to remind the Committee that his 1716 journal was "a more particular account of your Country then yett you ever have had from any one heretofore" and suggested that "their Honours should give themselves the trouble to read it."[45] The fact that these journals were somewhat unpolished in presentation and that their appeal and value is in the description of the effect of life in the North on ordinary men may have been the reason for the lack of interest from the London committee, which was looking more for guidance in practical trade issues. Isham's intentions were to provide Indian vocabularies and some solid general knowledge to educate future Company servants sent to the area.[46]

Seventy years after its founding, the HBC had settled into an annual cycle revolving around the fur trade and the weather. In the spring the supply ships left the Thames carrying trade goods, new employees for the posts on the bay, and supplies for another winter at those posts. The ships returned in the fall, laden with furs but also carrying men whose service with the Company was complete or terminated and

James Isham's "Observations on Hudsons Bay," 1743 (E.2/1 fo. 2 and fo. 57). Isham illustrated his detailed descriptions with informative pen-and-ink drawings.

occasionally a Native or two, along with biological and zoological specimens as evidence of the New World. This cycle also included the delivery of blank journals for the writing clerks and accountants and the turnover of journals completed during the previous year or two, signed off by the factors of the posts. Some ships did not make it to the bay before they had to turn back because of the weather, and some did not reach London if an early winter and ice conditions forced them to spend the season at one of the posts. A few ships were wrecked on the way to or from the bay.[47] In those cases, the routine backed up, and, with some obvious deprivations, the servants at the posts carried on until the next shipping season, while in London the Company worried about its possible losses of men and furs. As a precaution against the loss of records, chief factors were instructed for the first time in 1714 to send copies of their books and journals to London, with the intention that the original would be safe at the post if disaster should strike the ship on its Atlantic crossing.[48]

Security of the posts on the bay was interrupted whenever relations between Britain and France were in crisis, and in the eighteenth century the two nations were at war on more than one occasion – in 1702–13 (Spanish Succession), 1740–48 (Austrian Succession), and 1756–63 (Seven Years War). The business strategy of the governor and Committee of the Company was to manage the fur trade in North America, to secure the market for furs in London, and to benefit from opportunities for sales in Europe. They also had to acquire, train, and manage the servants hired to carry out the trade, and under the charter, as frequently pointed out by contestants for trade in North America, there was some responsibility to expand operations on Hudson Bay when and if that was necessary or possible. In the early years an adventurous spirit was exhibited in Company men such as Radisson, Kelsey, and Knight, whose journals or reports stand as testimony in the HBCA. But most of the Company's employees spent all of their time keeping the posts on Hudson Bay open to the trading Natives and themselves fed, clothed, and housed in a harsh climate that eased up for only three or four months a year. Their spirit of adventure was satisfied by the "exotic" location, the limitations of the climate, and the demands put on them by the Company.

CHALLENGES TO THE COMPANY'S MONOPOLY

In the meantime, the Company's monopoly on trade and development in so much of the northern part of North America was not likely to go unchallenged for long. If the HBC did not encourage its men to explore the surrounding country, other enterprising souls were eager to embark on adventures in and around Hudson Bay and to partake of the treasures to be found there. After all, the New World offered fame and fortune, which the Old World could provide for only a select few. Other continents had been colonized and/or exploited, and to some entrepreneurial speculators it seemed unfair that the HBC should have access to a huge territory in North America without sharing it with others looking for new markets in which to invest their lives and wealth. English merchants, New Englanders, the French, and the French Canadians looked for flaws in the Company's chartered claim, and some took action on the assumption that it was invalid. All in the end were unsuccessful, but in the process they made a good case and kept the Company from becoming too complacent.

Among the speculators in the potential of Hudson Bay in the middle of the eighteenth century was Arthur Dobbs, a published economist and historian, engineer-in-chief, and surveyor general of Ireland, as well as a member of Parliament and of the Royal Society. Dobbs's questioning of the rights of the HBC to control such vast territories, as spelled out in the charter, lasted over a twenty-year period that became one of the most critical times in the history of the Company. It was also a key time for the records the Company had kept over the past eighty years. In his enthusiasm for expanding Britain's trading boundaries, Dobbs focused attention on the elusive Northwest Passage. Renewed interest in finding a shorter, northerly route to the lucrative eastern trade in turn drew attention to the monopoly the HBC held over the entire coast of Hudson Bay. The Company had always been protective of its business both in London and in the isolated posts in North America. Any mapping of the Hudson Bay area that had been accomplished was not made public and Company employees were regularly reminded that they were not to discuss or share in any way information related to the Company or its trade. Arthur Dobbs initially approached Sir Bibye Lake, governor of the HBC, in 1734 about a joint venture of discovery. Lake acknowledged such exploration was feasible but Dobbs soon became aware of the Company's reluctance to expend any energy on exploring the northern edges of its territory and was frustrated by the lack of information available. He publicly attacked the Company, claiming it had failed to carry out the terms of its charter. In fact, within a year of their meeting, Lake sent Richard Norton as chief factor at Churchill with specific orders to resume explorations in the northwestern parts of Hudson Bay, using the two company sloops, the *Musquatch* and the *Churchill*. A similar voyage was made in 1736, and the following year Captain William Coats was sent to investigate north of Churchill on the *Mary*.[49]

Dobbs was supported by other commercial interests and powerful mercantile groups, as well as by former Company employees. One of these was Captain Christopher Middleton, who had commanded ships for the Company from 1725 to 1737, accumulating a wealth of experience in Arctic navigation. Middleton's initial interest in Dobbs's speculations was based on theories of discovery, not on any trade rivalry. He provided Dobbs with documents, such as maps and extracts from daily journals, and arranged for personal contact with Company officials, including the governor. By the end of 1740 Dobbs had enough information, and enough friends in the right places, to convince the Admiralty to provide ships for an independent voyage of discovery. Middleton commanded the expedition, leaving London in May 1741. He kept a detailed journal, meticulously recording the weather and tides and describing the coastline, bays, and rivers, but was not successful in finding the passage. His loyalty to the Company returned under the pressure exerted on him by Dobbs to cooperate in an indictment against the Company. In 1744 Dobbs published *An Account of the Countries adjoining to Hudson Bay in the Northwest Part of America*, which exposed the Company to public attack and, as a consequence, resulted in a parliamentary inquiry into its affairs. With Dobbs's publication in print, Middleton found himself having to justify his own actions.

One of the documents transcribed in Dobbs's *Account* was the HBC's charter, the content of which, describing the extent of its powers and privileges, was not generally known at the time. The Company's copy of the charter was kept under lock and key. There were other copies – one in the Plantation Office (later called the Colonial Office and now accessed through the National Archives) and others in the hands of current stockholders or the descendants or heirs of the original adventurers. There were, it seems, also copies translated into French.[50] Dobbs had managed to obtain permission from Colonel Martin Bladen, one of the Lords Commissioner of the Board of Trade and Plantations, to peruse the copy of the charter the Plantation Office held, from which he learned the extent of the Company's privileges in North America.[51]

This episode in the Company's history, which has been covered thoroughly in other publications,[52] is significant for its emphasis on the records, the Company's management of those records, and its ability to provide copies to the parliamentary inquiry. Dobbs and Middleton, both educated and intelligent men, aired their disagreements in a pamphlet war, typical of eighteenth century London. Others joined in the fray, resulting in a spate of publications that make this mid-century period a prolific one for information about the Company, Hudson Bay, and the attitude of the times regarding colonial trade, colonization, and the search for the Northwest Passage.

In 1745 the British Parliament responded to the pressure exerted by Dobbs and others by passing a bill offering a reward of £20,000 for the discovery of the Northwest Passage. This encouraged Dobbs to organize a second expedition in 1747, which was also unsuccessful.[53] Knowledge of Arctic navigation was still so limited that he once again had to recruit former employees of the HBC to command his ships. This time they were William Moor and Francis Smith. Smith was Middleton's cousin and had accompanied him in 1739 on the Company's yearly supply voyage to Moose Factory and Albany and in 1741 on the first Dobbs voyage. He later acted as a witness against the Company.[54]

Had the expedition been successful or even navigated a passage of any distance, it is almost certain the Company would have lost its charter at this time. Early in 1748 Dobbs and a committee made up of the same group of merchants who had supported him previously petitioned the king for a charter of their own to trade in the area of Hudson Bay. The following year a parliamentary committee began hearings into the charges that the HBC had not made sufficient effort to discover a Northwest Passage; had not ever attempted to settle the area provided for in its charter; and had narrowly confined its trade, thus encouraging the French. Twenty witnesses, mostly former employees of the Company, were heard, and the Company itself testified last. Joshua Sharpe, the Company's solicitor, attended the hearings and prepared its case. A draft of his statement was read to the governor and Committee in March 1749, and it was approved at the same meeting that several documents, ordered by the parliamentary committee, were to be examined and prepared for submission to the inquiry. The secretary, Charles Hay, was directed to attend the inquiry with the documents, including Company records that would provide information about its trading business on Hudson Bay not previously accessible other than to the governor and Committee of the Company.[55] The Company's record-keeping paid off in its ability to provide the records for inspection. Among the records required by the proceedings were the journals kept by ships' captains of recent voyages sent out to trade northward from the Company's established posts in response to the accusations that it was not taking full advantage of trade possibilities.

The Company presented its case in a four-page published statement defending its vested property rights as laid out in its charter.[56] Crucial to the Company's case was the testimony of James Isham, chief factor at York. The proceedings were stayed long enough for the Company to recall him from his position on the bay and return him to London on that season's supply ship to act as its key witness. But the parliamentary committee and the Privy Council heard no conclusive evidence against the Company, and what evidence was presented was readily rebutted by the Company. In the end, the status quo remained. The HBC's charter continued unaltered, and Dobbs and his associates did not obtain a charter for a rival company. The final report of the inquiry, presented to Parliament by the chairman, Lord Strange, concluded: "On consideration of all the evidence laid before us, by many affidavits on both sides, we think these charges are either not sufficiently supported in point of fact or in a great measure accounted for from the Nature of Circumstances."[57]

But the opposition was not to be quieted, even by parliamentary proceedings, and reverberations were felt by the Company for a few more years. Dobbs's long and cutting attack on the Company and its monopoly succeeded, in that it raised a general interest in the affairs of Rupert's Land and emphasized the seriousness of the French threat to what were considered British holdings in North America. As a result of his efforts and concerns, a great deal more information, although not always accurate, had been published about Hudson Bay and the fur trade by the middle of the century. The accounts by Middleton, Dobbs, Henry Ellis, Joseph Robson, and T.S. Drage revealed details not known before to commercial interests or to the general public.[58] Robson, who was one of the disgruntled former servants to testify at the 1749 inquiry, also published his version of events in *An Account of Six Years Residence in Hudson's-Bay* in 1752.[59]

The twenty years of attack on its chartered rights inevitably undermined many of the Company's attempts to conceal its operations in secrecy. That feature of its policy was clearly dealt with during the years of attack and inquiry. The publication of many documents from the Company's archives included actual figures for the fur trade over a period of years, but the critics produced more information about the Company than it did, and any records it provided had to be requested. The Company's concern for confidentiality is again evident in the sailing orders presented to the captains of the *Mary* and the *Success* as they were preparing to leave for Hudson Bay in May 1749: "you are not upon any acc^t whatsoever To Communicate any of the Company's Affairs or deliver any writing or Journal of your proceedings to any person whatsoever except ye Govr & Deputy Governor of ye H.B. Co. for the time being."[60]

Several Hudson's Bay Company records disappeared at this time, and it is not surprising to learn that some were found in Arthur Dobbs's private papers. Among the documents belonging to Dobbs in the Castle Dobbs Papers presented to the Public Record Office of Northern Ireland in 1926 were the journals, letters, and memoranda of Henry Kelsey, dating from 1691 to 1722.[61] The Kelsey Papers consist of a volume of 106 pages, including day-by-day accounts of his journeys to the plains and daily life at York Fort and his description of the beliefs and customs of the Plains Natives. Although Dobbs apparently did not use these papers in his attack on the Company in the mid-1700s, they must have been available in 1752 to Joseph Robson when he prepared his publication in support of Dobbs. Since they have come to light, these papers have proved to be a remarkable and complete record of one man's career with the Company. Of course, the detailed descriptions in Kelsey's journals of his travels could only benefit the Company's arguments of its efforts toward exploration and expansion. Kelsey's papers give the earliest detailed first-hand account of life with the HBC at York Factory, at Fort Albany, on trading expeditions, on travel with local Natives, and on board ships as he crossed the Atlantic several times between London and Hudson Bay. Kelsey was with the Company from the age of fourteen in 1684 until 1722. His journals and his own summary of his activities with the Company cover all of those years. Eleven separate records document remarkable details of a period of time in North America that had been only conjecture until they were rediscovered almost 250 years later.

Kelsey is best known for the journey he made in 1690–91 from York Fort to the interior across the plains, the first record of a white man reaching the prairies and observing a Native buffalo hunt. Journals from Albany date from 1705, but those from York do not appear in the HBCA until 1714. Later journals were written by Kelsey at York Factory in 1718, 1721, and 1722.[62] The absence of Kelsey's papers from the archives of the HBC resulted, over time, in inaccurate stories and incomplete geographical information based on Robson's 1752 publication, as well as on snippets of orders and reports in the Company's minute books, correspondence books, and factory journals.[63]

The question of why Kelsey's papers are not in the HBCA has been asked many times. Finding them among Arthur Dobbs's papers did not provide an answer but raised even more conjecture as to their wanderings, to the point that the papers have acquired something of a life of their own. Of the account of Kelsey's famous journey into the plains in 1690–91, Rich surmised that "the Company either did not receive a copy of the account of the journey which Kelsey made or, more probably, the account was allowed to get into the hands of opponents of the Company."[64] When it came into Dobbs's possession is open to even more conjecture. Was it from Middleton? Judging from the version provided by the Company in its defence of that case and the discussion of it in Robson's book, neither would appear to have had the original version. That is the conclusion reached by Arthur Doughty and Chester Martin as editors of the first publication of the Kelsey Papers in 1929.[65] K.D. Davies, writing in the *Dictionary of Canadian Biography*, claims there is no evidence to support either view. He comments:

There is nothing to show that the volume now called *The Kelsey papers* was ever part of the HBC's archives for Middleton to copy or steal. The title page suggests that it was Kelsey's own property, though his action of recording official business in a private book would not have had the company's approval. He may have brought it back to England in 1722 in case Knight's charges against him were revived: the "Memorandum of my abode" (the last document in the book) ends with the arrival of Kelsey's relief and reads like an apologia. Dobbs could have got the volume from Kelsey's family, could even have bought it, before 1749 or after 1749; one's guess at the date must depend on whether one thinks Dobbs a rogue or not.[66]

Dobbs went on to be governor of the American colony of North Carolina and died in 1765. There are 109 pieces in the Dobbs manuscripts, most of them relating to local Irish history or colonization in North Carolina.[67] Five deal with the HBC or the search for the Northwest Passage, including Kelsey's journal, journals of HMS *Furnace* and the *California*, a pamphlet on the Northwest Passage dated 1732, and a fifteen-page manuscript attacking the Company dating from about 1752 (possibly part of Robson's book).[68] It is entirely possible that Kelsey's papers came on the market in the meantime, were brought to the attention of Dobbs because of his interest in the subject, and he acquired by him for his own collection – as a memento, as a trophy, or for reasons only Dobbs would know.

KEEPING THE RECORDS
IN THE LATE EIGHTEENTH CENTURY

The preceding account provides an idea of how the HBC used its records both for private business and against public charges; how its business supplied the subject for all manner of other records – private, public, and legal; how its employees provided records, both private and professional, not all of which the Company took the effort to secure and protect for the long term; and how the stories and lives of the participants continue to be intertwined.

All of this brings us back to the importance of keeping records and a curiosity about how those records were made and under what conditions they were kept. We know that not all of the records of the HBC have made it into the archives. Even when records were kept, surviving the climate in Hudson Bay and the voyage back to London, they are not found in the archives today. Many gaps appear in the records of the bay posts, but even then details can be filled in or surmised from the abundance of London office records. Besides the correspondence transmitted between London and the bay posts, some letters, referred to as "country correspondence," from post to post have survived. Post journals that have survived add the details of day-to-day life not documented in the annual letter from the factor to the London committee. The account books provide item-level descriptions of the goods supplied for Company servants and of both sides of the fur trade.[69] The most noticeable absence of records, apart from the missing minute books, occurs in the early post journals. The first post journal in the HBCA is the already noted 1705–06 journal from Albany (B.3/a/1). The second Albany journal is dated 1706–07 (B.3/a/2). Then several years are missing until the outfit year 1711–12. The first journal from York Factory does not appear in the archives until 1714; the first from Churchill in 1718. Even though posts were established earlier at Eastmain and Rupert House, journals for those posts date only from 1736 and 1777 respectively. The uneven documentation from these other posts has meant that a lot of attention has been focused on the earlier Albany journals and correspondence.

Albany was established as early as 1674, and when Henry Sergeant[70] was sent as "Governour and chiefe Commander of the Hudsons Bay Compa. within the Bay" in 1683, his letter of instruction included a clear directive from the governor and Committee: "We doe expect and accordingly doe hereby expressly require you to send us home every yeare exact Journals of what hath been done both at the place where you shall reside your selfe and at all our other Factories."[71] At the same time John Bridgar, heading out to be governor at Port Nelson, was instructed: "You are likewise by every returne of our ships to send us a perfect Journall and Dayley account of all things that have occurred worthy our knowledge and what hath been done by you & those under your Command."[72]

Managing the post records that did reach London would not initially have been a top priority. It may be that the London committee or head office treated these incoming or branch office records as active but transient, required only for immediate action and with no historical value. We must not forget that the primary purpose of the Company was to make money for its stockholders, not the advancement of geographical knowledge or Canadian history.

There was no specific direction from the Committee to the secretary for the handling of the old records. Several orders over the years concerned

Albany account journal, 1717 (B.3/d/29, fo. 4), showing inventory
of remaining stock on hand at end of the trading season

the keeping and transporting of journals from the bay posts and Company ships, and certain documents were moved around in London for safekeeping or as required by Parliament or lawyers, as with the Dobbs inquiry. Correspondence outgoing from London was always copied and preserved in bound copybooks.

Since the Hudson Bay "mail" reached London only when the ships arrived from their annual trip, incoming correspondence was probably kept in packets according to post or year. A common piece of office furniture even in the 1700s was the pigeonhole desk at which the secretary could sort correspondence by sender, having it readily available for

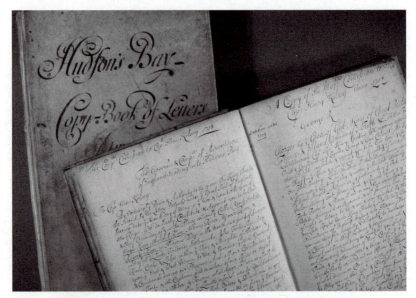

Copybook of letters (A.6/3) and copy of letter from the governor and Committee to Captain Henry Kelsey, 1718 (A. 6/4, fos. 50–1)

reply the next year. Letters were probably stored folded, and when the pigeonholes filled up or the replies had been written, letters could be tied up in bundles and stored with the other records. The earliest letters extant exhibit considerable diversity of ink and paper as well as style. Duplicating letters from the bay improved the rate of survival, but that process, of keeping the originals and sending copies of the yearly letters to London, did not start until 1722.

Although the Company was settled for almost a hundred years in a building on the south side of Fenchurch Street, through almost all of the eighteenth century, references in the minutes suggest that important documents were still kept in boxes and the large iron-bound chest purchased in 1680. On 1 December 1737 the "Committee Examined the Contents of the Iron Chest'"[73] and on 10 April 1746 the "Box Containing the Ballances of the Stock Ledger and the Policy of Assurances on the Company's House which were kept at the late Governor's House as a safety from Fire having since his death been returned to the Committee were this Day Delivered to the present Governor for the like purposes."[74]

The secretary between 1724 and 1737 was Thomas Bird. His work was regularly inspected as noted on 2 July 1729: "the Committee now finished the Examinacon of the Secretary's acc^{tts} and Allowed as same being as followed Vizt ... Ordered that the Sec^r have a Gratuity of One

Escritoire, or writing desk (artifact no. 255), dating from the eighteenth century. Note the folded letters in pigeonholes.

hundred Pounds given him on Account of his having the Care & Management of the Company's Business in the Warehouse and at the Custome House, and likewise in consideration that the Business of the last Year hath been greater than Usual ... £100."[75] A year later it was "Ordered that the Sec[r] have a Gratuity of One hundred Pounds given him for his Encouragem[t] and in consideration of his having thee care and Managem[t] of the Business of the Warehouse and at the Custom House."[76] In 1739 more record-keeping directions were passed from the Committee: "When any Chief Leaves the factory we order as a Stand g Rule that he leaves and delivers all Books, Letters & Papers, relating to our affairs, to his successor who is to give him a Receipt for the same, Mentioning the particulars thereof, And that the General Letters to the Company be always Signed by the Chief and Council as by the first Paragraph."[77]

The recipients of these instructions most often responded immediately by answering the London letter as soon as the ship arrived at the factory so that the reply was ready to depart with the ship once all the supplies had been unloaded and the furs loaded for the return trip. In 1739 Richard Staunton responded with a detailed description of the record-keeping practices at Moose Fort for the year 1738–39 and an explanation of the reality of trying to follow the Committee's orders when there were not enough supplies, living conditions were bleak, and the job of record-keeping was but one of many for the journal writer. His description of the lot of the record-keeper, written on 17 August 1739, can best be appreciated by archivists who today work in climate-controlled environments, wearing white cotton gloves to handle the documents:

Honourable Sirs, Yours from London of May the 17th 1739 came safe to my hands August the 3rd at 10 o'clock at night, whereat I did rejoice that your honours' ships got all safe home the last fall, likewise to hear that you are all well, and according to your honours' command I have sent you my last year's journal which I kept upon cartridge paper,[78] also this year's journal upon the same paper with the other journal book of both years,[79] copied out by William Pitts this year, so that your honours may see my proceeding by my cartridge paper from the first of my arrival ashore to the day of this ship's departure from hence for England, and I do not at all doubt but your honours will pardon the dirtiness of it, for I have many times written with hands as black as a chimney sweeper, and clothes as greasy as a butcher. As for the general letter not being dated it was a fault, for which I ask pardon and hope shall not be guilty of the like again, and as for your general letter being signed by no other persons but Staunton and Howy it was because Captain Middleton did say he would not sign it of his own accord upon which I replied then I would not ask him; and as for any others doing it I thought it not proper for these two reasons, first that your honours' orders being to me that your affairs should not be communicated to any but those whom it may or does concern, and if I know for truth that everything which is spoke or acted upon all affairs should not be communicated to any but those whom it may or does concern, and if I know for truth that everything which is spoke or acted upon all affairs is told in public at the stove's mouth, I think it my duty to keep some things private from such people's knowledge although ordered by you to be one of the Council until I have your honours' further

orders for so doing, being assured that their advice would not
be anyway advantageous for your interests.[80]

There was some thought on the part of the London office about preparing the people being sent to Hudson Bay for the job ahead. John
Newton, sailing to York in 1748 to take over as chief factor, was provided with a collection of inactive records from York Factory for his
study on the voyage:

> As you are a Stranger to the Method in which Our Accounts are kept
> at Hudson Bay We have thought proper to deliver you the following
> Factory Books for your perusal in your Voyage Outward that you
> may make you Self Master thereof by such time as you shall Arrive
> in Hudsons Bay Viz Allowance, Indent, Account Book, Journal and
> Surgeons Indent kept at Y F in the Year We direct that you Send the
> said Books back again in the Packet, at the return of our Ship and
> that in the Journals you shall here after keep you are very full and
> particular which you are to send home Yearly.[81]

Since this was at the height of the controversy with Arthur Dobbs and
the parliamentary inquiry, Newton was also reminded to keep the information confidential. "You are not to Communicate any of the Companys Affairs by Letter or otherwise nor deliver any writings or Journal
of your proceedings to any Person or Persons whatever, save only to
those of Your Council whom you are to Consult on all occasions."[82]

Although the Company had shown considerable enterprise and de-
termination during the post-Dobbs period, it was still slow to expand
its trading alliances from the bottom of the bay. The interior of North
America beckoned, and others (including La Vérendrye and his sons)
were there already, ignoring European charters and treaties. Incentives
were offered to Company employees to venture out on expeditions and
voyages of discovery, with the initial intention of encouraging the Natives to trade downriver at the Company posts instead of with other
traders along the way. With increased interest in exploring beyond the
bounds of the bay, and still smarting from the lack of geographic information it was able to provide to the Dobbs inquiry, the Company began requesting more details from its servants out on the land and
at sea. When it realized that traders from Montreal had reached the
Saskatchewan River and were interfering with the Company's trade
with the Natives there, it sent Anthony Henday west from York in

1754 to search out the Blackfoot and to encourage them to trade with the Company. Henday was expected to keep a journal: "You having a compass, hand Line paper &c. &c. along with you, therefore be Very Exact in Keeping a Journal of your travels and observations Daily, observing the Course, trying the Depth of water in the River or Lakes, when in your Cannoe; ... or travelling by Land all the way, mind to Remark Down Every thing that occurs to your View Daily, mentioning when you come to any River, or Lake, the name, when you meet with any Natives what Nation &c."[83]

Whether the result of vigorous editing or creative interpretation, anomalies sometimes occurred in the fair copies of journals that were sent to London, and Henday's journals are good examples of this problem. They confuse readers as much as they inform. No fewer than four versions exist of the documentation of his inland venture of 1754–55, during which Henday at least reached the area of The Pas, on what is now the border with Manitoba and Saskatchewan, and many have conjectured that he ventured even farther west.[84] Most researchers have interpreted the facts in one or another of the journals as suited their studies or have taken for fact the interpretation of previous researchers. Several scholars, most recently University of Calgary professor Barbara Belyea, have discussed the anomalies and the fact there is no original and no two copies alike.[85] The version that was sent to London in 1755 on Henday's return to York is classified with the York post journals as B.239/a/40, fo. 1–15. The other three versions are included in three different volumes of Andrew Graham's "Observations" (E.1/4, fo. 35–60, E.2/6, fo. 10d–38d, and E.2/11, fo. 1–40d) dating up to 1782. It would seem that Henday left behind a rough notebook from which he had written a fair copy for the London committee but from which he optimistically transcribed his achievements.[86] Graham's versions, written at later dates but probably using the same rough notes, contain substantial differences in factual information. Glyndwr Williams has concluded that historians are "left with an outstanding query to which no obvious explanation offers itself."[87] Belyea's book provides transcriptions of all four versions of Henday's journal in the HBCA, juxtaposing each entry with the other three for ease of comparing. She also supplies context for the text relative to other contemporary documents in the archives and observations and discussions by previous scholars on this period in history, on Henday, and on his journals. Belyea acknowledges the textual ambiguity and concludes the Henday journals "remain deliberately inconclusive."[88]

Anthony Henday's observations copied into Andrew Graham's "Observations," about 1782 (E.2/11, fo. 1), with Graham's comments written in the margins; Henday's observations copied into a York Factory journal, 1755 (B.239/a/40, fo. 1d-2)

Personal journals sent or brought home are not always classified in the archives as business records. If they were written as part of the annual report from a post, they would remain as part of the post journal in Section B, Post Journals. Many personal journals, such as those of Isham, Graham, and Fidler, have been classified as separate documents in Section E, Private Records. Pre-1870 records in this series mainly originated from Canada, but because of their special character, they did not fit into other sections.

Samuel Hearne's journals and those of Philip Turnor, Matthew Cocking, and others who kept diaries of their life at the first inland

Journals kept by Samuel Hearne (B.49/a/1, 1774, and B.49/a/2, 1775) and Philip Turnor (B.3/a/77b, 1779–80, B.135/a/64, 1781, and B.49/a/22, 1790–91). Exploration journals such as these written by Hearne and Turnor provide the first descriptions of northern Manitoba and Saskatchewan.

posts of the Company, such as Cumberland and Hudson House, are the primary authorities for the early written history of Manitoba and Saskatchewan. These exploration journals need to be considered separately from the co-existing factual reports of business required by the administration of the Company. Exploration journals are not always of stylistic merit or grammatical correctness, but they are worthy of note for their expressive spirit and conscious awareness of time and place. The naïveté and inexperience of the writers does not negate or contradict the scientific and historical documentation provided by these explorers, writing down their impressions of a new world. The fact that many of the Company servants who travelled beyond the boundaries of the bay had been hired because of their writing ability means the journals are, for the most part, legible and readable. The tasks assigned to these men went beyond the routine of day-to-day activities at a fur trade post and would have appealed to those with an entrepreneurial and adventurous spirit.

Years later, when Hearne was retired in London and preparing the manuscript of his journals for publication, he applied to the governor and Committee of the Company for permission to study the original journals. He was granted access to the Company's records "with the greatest affability and politeness."[89] The Company's response to this access request brings up the question of how the records were actually kept at the end of the eighteenth century. The first recorded inventory of the HBCA was taken in 1796, shortly after the Company had moved to a second building on Fenchurch Street. When Hearne was doing his research, they were still in the old building where they had been for almost ninety years. But there must have been some order and method of retrieval for the Company's internal use. Some of the records Hearne was interested in may have been stored together as a result of the Dobbs inquiry forty years earlier.

A NEW GOVERNOR

Much of the change in Company policy at the end of the eighteenth century, which included greater emphasis on exploration and mapping can be directly linked to the governorship of Samuel Wegg (1782–99). He led the transformation that moved the Company out of the closed-shop attitude which had plagued the administration for its first century and into the adventurous spirit that epitomized England, and for that matter most of the Western world, by the late 1700s. Servants were hired by the Company specifically for their skills as surveyors. Not only were they tasked with recording accurate and systematic details of the newly explored territories, but they were expected to train others in surveying techniques. Then once their drawings and journals reached London, the information was shared with members of the broader scientific community, particularly through the Royal Society, such as geographers and cartographers involved in the latest scientific ventures. This was the era of naturalist Joseph Banks, Captain James Cook, cartographers Alexander Dalrymple and Aaron Arrowsmith, and inventor extraordinaire Benjamin Franklin and of the establishment of the British Museum and Kew Gardens.

Samuel Wegg, who had been a member of the Hudson's Bay Company committee from 1760 to 1774, deputy governor from then until 1782, and then governor from 1782 to 1799, was a man of these times.

He was a university graduate, a barrister, and a successful businessman. He was also a member of the Royal Society (including membership in the prestigious Club of Royal Philosophers, commonly
referred to as the Thursday Club) and the Society of Antiquaries.
These associations provided contacts with the educated and social
elite of London, which included the leading scientists, naturalists, and
explorers – the cultural leaders of the age. Wegg's broad interests provided him with the attitude necessary to reverse the policies of the
Company, making a clean distinction between commercially important information that was inherently confidential from more broadly
informative scientific facts of limited commercial value but of interest
to those seeking enlightenment.[90]

The Company renewed its practice of hiring apprentices from London's charity schools – Christ's Hospital and the Grey Coat School –
where, as well as a core curriculum, instruction was provided in navigation and cartography. The master of the Mathematical School at
Christ's Hospital from 1775 to 1798 was William Wales, who had observed the Transit of Venus at Fort Prince of Wales in 1768–69 and
then had sailed as astronomer with Captain James Cook in his second
voyage across the Pacific Ocean in the years 1772–75.[91] Eleven more
charity school boys were apprenticed to the Company between 1766
and 1799. These connections with the leading scholars and scientists of
the time helped to dispel some of the historical mystique about the
Company. Cooperative ventures and the sharing of information with
the scientific community meant new undertakings for the Company.
Post employees were encouraged to acquire new skills and to use their
accumulated knowledge in ventures not always directly related to its
business but of use in broader schemes that were presented at this time.

In London the lease on Hudson's Bay House came to an end in 1794,
and a move was made to the southwest end of the same street, near the
Church of St Benedict. The lease for Nos. 3 and 4 Fenchurch Street, which
in turn was called Hudson's Bay House, was entered into in March 1795.
The Company's offices would remain there for seventy years, until 1865.
Soon after this move, the first arrangement of the Company's records was
indicated in the Committee minutes. The secretary was ordered to "pay to
W. John Brome the Sum of Twenty Guineas in consideration of the Labour
& Trouble in classing and arranging the Company's Books from the Com-
mencement of the Company & making an Inventory of & Index to the
same."[92] The resulting "Inventory of Books, &c," is classified as A.64/45.
It includes records dating from 1667 to 1796 with addenda made up

Brome's "Inventory of Books, &c," 1796, showing
listing of York Factory books (A.64/45, fos. 39–40)

to 1819 by later staff members. This inventory lists the records that form the basis of the HBCA and includes a chart laying out their position at the time on shelves, on and under tables, and in bookcases.

For the most part, the Company's records are the conventional records of business of the period. Their format is standardized, and the content is factual and objective, frank in the documentation of details that were not expected to be perused by anyone outside the Committee and the administrative staff. The minute books record decisions made by the governor and Committee. It is sometimes disappointing to find that none of the proceedings or discussion involved is recorded; they are essentially books of orders. But since the Committee initiated most of the business, these minutes are of great importance, providing an almost complete view of the history of the Company's administration. Its methods were basically conservative and cautious with occasional and sometimes brief periods of energy often reflecting the personality or interests of a particular governor or member of the Committee. All other aspects of the business process are reflected in the HBCA. The commissions of ships' captains and of the governors going out to the Hudson Bay posts are there, as are the letters of the governor and Committee to the councils. All were copied into the bound copybooks of letters outward before being delivered to the ships waiting to sail. The same ships returned with replies from the resident governor and council and the private reports of the governor. They also returned with letters from individual servants, mostly private but sometimes official to the Committee, perhaps announcing a decision to return to England or to take another term on the bay. As well, there were the daily journals of the posts and depots and the journals of individuals sent out on specific missions. Correspondence inward and outward was also copied into the post journals, which constitute a large part of the archives.

3

a regular communication

The Record-Keeping of Amalgamation and Colonization, 1800–1830

For most of the years between 1780 and 1820, the story of the Hudson's Bay Company is inextricably interconnected with that of the equally remarkable North West Company. The intense animosity between the two competitors for the North American fur trade continued into the nineteenth century and ended with their amalgamation. The company that emerged from decades of rivalry had the autonomy, control, and name of the HBC with the additional trading territory of the former NWC and a new energy. In the process, the HBC changed its way of doing business, and the fur trade expanded across North America. The Company was made ready for this expansion and eventual colonial settlement by a major reorganization in 1810, and for forty years, from 1820 to 1860, it prospered in what is considered to be its golden age.[1]

In 1800 a total of 506 men worked for the Company in North America: 133 recorded in the area of Fort Albany, 57 at Moose Factory, 41 at Eastmain, 35 at York Factory, 147 at York Inland (Cumberland House, Manchester House, Oxford House, and others), 21 at Severn, and 72 at Churchill.[2] The amalgamation would more than double the size of the Company, increasing its territory to an area in excess of 3,000,000 square miles with fifty-seven posts scattered virtually from coast to coast and a total of almost 2000 employees.[3]

The NWC had been formally organized in 1783 after years of various partnerships, regrouping, and restructuring. More reorganizations occurred in 1787 and 1803. The contest for furs and markets escalated during that time, and the HBC struggled to maintain dominance in its chartered territory. With its headquarters solidly established in Montreal and a mobile force of over 1,000 shuttling between Montreal and its inland posts, the NWC provided a formidable opposition

to the "colourless, methodical and uninspired"[4] Company still cling-
ing to the shoreline of Hudson Bay. With only tentative advances inland, the HBC's finances were at a low ebb by the time the NWC
merged with its other fur trade competitor, the XY Company, in 1804.
The stronger competition for furs, even in an expanding territory,
eventually revealed itself in the Company's bottom line.

Dividends had been paid regularly to HBC shareholders since 1718
(except for three years, 1783–85), but no dividend would be paid from
1809 to 1815.[5] The HBC was still operating under the financing system it had used since 1670 by which money was borrowed every year
from the Bank of England to finance each outfit. That debt was repaid
from the earnings of the fur sales, staff received their wages, and dividends were issued to shareholders from the surplus. No reserves were
kept on hand or for investment, so that the Company accounts almost
always showed a deficit. In times of strife – lost ships, poor trade, or
depressed fur sales – the Company had to go deeper in debt to finance
its next season, which it gambled on being better. Britain was at war
for more than half of the next fifty years, the Napoleonic Wars domi-
nating in Europe and interfering with the normal routes of trade and
commerce. For the Company, this insecurity of low profits and increased costs was only magnified by the clashes with the NWC.

It was time for some tremendous changes. Governor Samuel Wegg
had initiated a revision of policy before he retired in 1799. A new
scheme of trading was introduced with the special appointments of two
inland traders, one each from Churchill and York, and a supervisor
and inspector of posts from Albany. He also introduced a new arrangement by which the chief factors received a share of the profits for the
furs they procured. Wegg retired after sixteen years as governor, to be
succeeded by James Winter Lake, who was following in the footsteps
of three other Lakes who had served as governor of the Company for
fifty-three out of the previous eighty-seven years.[6] Like Wegg, Lake was
actively interested in making the Company's fur trade operations profitable, and he carried on the policies initiated by his predecessor.

More inland posts were established, often within a few miles of existing NWC posts. Some were in operation for only a year or two, but
the strategy only accentuated the NWC's encroachment on the Company's territory. With its new organization, the NWC was also dynamic enough that attempting a takeover of the HBC seemed a
possibility. The fiscal reality of that prospect was probably not feasible, but the threat was substantial enough that the HBC Committee

came up with its own alternative proposals: a coalition of the two companies or a buyout of the competition. One thing was sure: the Committee would not capitulate to the unqualified sharing of the inland fur trade.[7] Early discussions of a merger soon lost momentum, and the Company continued its inland strategy for a few more years. But the idea had been raised.

THE LONDON OFFICE

The administration of the Company remained more or less the same as it had, with the exception of an increase in record-making and record-keeping. In London the Committee and secretary occupied new premises, with an adjacent warehouse, where they would stay until 1865. The building at Nos. 3 and 4 Fenchurch Street was not far from where the Company had spent the previous ninety-eight years. When its holdings were inventoried in 1821, the property, known as Hudson's Bay House, had two buildings. One was a warehouse which included the warehouse keeper's office, his premises, and a bookroom. The other building was the headquarters of the Company and the residence of the secretary. Soon after the purchase, renovations were started to build a new boardroom.

> The Company's two dwelling Houses in Fenchurch Street standing in need of Repairs, particularly that of No. 3, in the back Room of which the Committee usually meet, the same was taken under Consideration: And it occuring to the Committee that a commodious Board Room might be built, at a moderate Expence, agreeably to the original Intention of the Governor & Committee on purchasing the said Premises, Resolved that the same be immediately carried into Execution under the Direction of, & according to a plan submitted to the Board by Mr John Baker, Surveyor of St Pauls Church Yard, who being called in, confidently assured the Committee that the cost & Expence of completely repairing the aforesaid Dwelling Houses together with erecting & completing the said Board Room, on the Site on which at present stand Two Warehouses &c, would not exceed the Sum of £715.[8]

The boardroom was entered through a large entry hall and lobby and there were separate offices for the secretary and accountant. When the Committee met, it was the secretary's responsibility to entertain the members and provide the necessary refreshments on board days. He

Fenchurch Street at far right on a map of Bishops-Gate Ward, London, 1754, engraving by B. Cole (P. 155); and Hudson's Bay House – Fenchurch Street (London), 1854, watercolour by Thomas Coleman Dibdin (P. 22)

was also expected to receive visiting officers from the Company's operations in North America. The governor and Committee met every
Wednesday, precisely at 11:45 AM, with a fine levied on any member
who arrived after that time.[9] The annual general court was held once a
year in November or December. A porter was hired in 1794 "to act as
Doorkeeper & to be assisting about the Company's House and Warehouses And also a Woman Servant to clean & attend the Compy.
House"; £80 per annum was to "Be allowed to the Secretary for both
their wages" and these servants were to "be considered as under the
Sole direction of the Secretary."[10]

The secretary from 1792 to 1817 was Alexander Lean, who in 1813
received a salary of £450 per annum, which included an annual bonus
or gratuity of £50 plus his residence, taxes, coals, and candles.[11] William Smith took over the position after Lean left and remained as secretary until his death in 1843. In 1825 he was earning £500 and shared
the office with the accountant, whose salary at the time was £400, and
three clerks (Mr Siffken and Mr Forster at £200 each and Mr Earnes at
£140).[12] The secretary and accountant each had a clerk or assistant.
Regular office hours were the same as they had been for a number of
years. From Michaelmas (29 September)to Lady Day (25 March), the
secretary's and accountant's offices were staffed from 9 AM to 1 PM and
from 3 PM until the work was done. In the spring and summer the
hours were 8 AM to 1 PM and from 3 PM to the completion of the day's
work. The standard workweek at this time was six days, Monday to
Saturday.[13] The accountant was Arthur Ball, who had been appointed
in 1794 and would remain in the position until his death in 1814. His
salary was £200 (in December 1813, £250). He was assisted by Thomas
Hyde and then, after 1803, by Edward Roberts. Company clerks in
London received £150.[14]

The warehouseman was William Hagell with a salary of £250. The
term "warehouseman" is somewhat misleading. He was, in fact, a fur
broker, managing the comings and goings of furs and trade goods and
arranging sales and auctions. His duties and responsibilities were
considerable enough that his salary was equal to that of the accountant. In 1819 it was agreed that he would receive a commission of
half a per cent on net sales instead of a salary. He was to be "in constant attendance at the Warehouse, assorting lotting and selling the
Goods of the Company, Keeping the Accounts, and superintending
the business of the Warehouse." It was decided that he and his assistants were to

not be concerned in any other business, whatever, on their own
account, and that they shall make themselves generally useful on
all occasions, when required by the Governor & Committee. That,
while the Head Warehouse-Keeper is able to do the whole of the business in a proper and satisfactory manner, without farther assistance,
than [sic] the attendance of a Clerk from the Secretary's Office, at the
time of Landing the Cargoes, & weighing and delivering the Lots after
the Sales, he shall be paid the whole of the said Allowance of ½ P
Cent, but, if farther assistance shall become necessary in assorting
the Goods, for Sale, then the said Allowance of ½ p Cent whsle.
be apportioned at the discretion of the Governor & Committee.[15]

Hagell was the warehouseman until 1837 when he retired and was replaced by his senior assistant, Edward Taylor. Hagell's son was also an assistant in the warehouse, and he eventually took over the top position to
be followed by Hagell's grandson and then great-grandson up to 1912.[16]

Other than the men at the fur trade posts, these were the people
making and responsible for most of the Company's records. The history of business record-keeping in the nineteenth century reflects the
evolution of business practices and the influence of industrialization in
the same period. As the number and size of businesses grew, first royal
and then governmental control eased, to be replaced by liability under
the legal system of the day. In their book *Business Documents*, John
Armstrong and Stephanie Jones explain three main pressures on businesses to create and keep records: "the role of law in requiring the creation and retention of certain documents; the rules of the stock
exchange which required minimum levels of disclosure for publicly
quoted companies; and the creation of records for the internal control
of the firm, what might now be called management information, to
provide data on which to base policy, guide day-to-day operations and
record decisions made."[17] There were no record-keeping standards at
this time, but there were established formats for specific documents
and stylistic regularities that make the archival records of the 1800s as
recognizable as any modern record. And standards were not far off.

As recorded in the Company's inventory carried out in 1796, accounting journals and ledgers, minute books, stock transfer books, and letterbooks had been kept from the 1670s and 1680s. The 1700s show
increased records activity from Rupert's Land, including post journals and
account books, journals of ships' captains and exploration, ships' logs,
and servants' employment records. All of this record-keeping continued in

the 1800s, gradually increasing as legislation required and as the business and its activities grew and diversified.[18] With the owners and shareholders established in London and the primary base of operations situated in Rupert's Land, an isolated area of North American wilderness separated from the Company head office by a vast and unpredictable ocean, careful records presented in a standard form were essential to the success and growth of the daily operations. As labour historian Philip Goldring observes, "central control depended on exhaustive documentation."[19]

Accounting records were always important. As noted earlier, entries in the first grand ledger (A.14/1) date from 1667. The small group of businessmen who formed the Company had the intention of increasing their capital investment; so a careful accounting of cash spent and cash received would ensure any investment income down to the pence. As time passed, the Company's business became more complicated, and as more people were involved in the process, careful records of account provided safeguards for discovering shortages or misuse of funds. Records of previous years supplied recognition of short-term profit-loss anomalies, comparative summaries, evaluative yardsticks, and historical proof of chartered activities. After the introduction of the Joint Stock Companies Registration and Regulation Act in 1844, accounting records were required by governmental regulation for registration and payment of taxes. And independent auditing was first recommended by the Companies Act in 1862 and then required by law as amended in 1900. The detailed books of account for the HBC indicate adherence to common, as well as legislated, process.

Not only do financial records provide details of assets, liabilities, and profit, but daily journal entries furnish historians with information about the men working for the Company and everything from their salary and expenditures to the food they ate and the type of trousers they wore. With a bit of digging, details can be found to satisfy anyone interested in social, economic and labour, women's, Native, and even archival and records history. As Hugh Grant, professor of economics at the University of Winnipeg, has commented, "Company journals and ledgers ... are important historical artifacts in their own right." Early ledgers and journals consist of huge vellum-covered volumes, weighing many pounds. The grand ledger dated 1684–97 (A.14/5) and the grand journal dated 1697–1713 (A.15/5) both measure approximately 50 by 34 by 11.5 centimetres.

The journal – or, in the case of the HBC, the grand journal – was kept as the daily record of transactions, entered in chronological order. The

Grand journals (A.15) on shelves, showing change in format from large bound books to smaller journals kept annually by fur trade outfit

page format inside the bound volumes employed the double entry accounting system and the standardization of procedure that follows through all of the Company's account books, whether from the fur trade posts or the London office.[20] The ledger or grand ledger breaks the daily journal entries down into separate accounts. As Grant explains in his article "Bookkeeping in the Eighteenth Century: The Grand Journal and Grand Ledger of the Hudson's Bay Company,"

> Each individual ledger was continued on the facing sides of a folio. On the verso side of the first leaf is printed the title of the account, and the heading "Dr." above the individual debit entries; on the recto side of the subsequent leaf appears the offsetting title "Per Contra," and credit entries arranged below the heading "Cr." (One can thus appreciate the frustration of the researcher utilizing a microfilm copy of the ledger which places the opposing side of the folio on consecutive frames.) Entries are arranged chronologically, with extra line spacing used to separate fiscal years. When

room on the folio was exhausted, the account was transferred
to the first blank folio found in the ledger book.[21]

Each grand ledger contains numerous separate ledgers for distinctive
aspects of the Company's activities. It can require patience and careful
perusal by a researcher to follow an account through the volume since
an active account may require two, three, or more pages, interspersed
through the ledger.

Through the 1800s until 1891, the business year followed the established cycle based on the fur trade and the weather. That business year,
which ran from June to May of the following year, was referred to as
an "outfit." The year started in June with the outfitting of the ships
with supplies and trade goods and ended the following spring after the
fur auctions, with a financial report of the profit (or loss) over the year.
Then the cycle started all over again. As Goldring explains,

> Trade was organized into outfits, every outfit bearing the date at
> which it was to reach its winter destination for trade. Thus "Outfit"
> 55 consisted of goods "indented for" sufficiently far in advance to
> reach York Factory and to be carried to their destination by the au-
> tumn of 1855. For most districts of the Northern Department, the in-
> dent for Outfit 55 was written up at district headquarters in the spring
> of 1854, discussed by a council of senior officers and scrutinized by
> the officer in charge of York Factory during the same summer, and
> conveyed to London in the autumn. Goods listed in the indent were
> gathered in London over the winter and spring of 1854–55, embarked
> at Greenwich in June, discharged at York Factory in August, and hur-
> ried to the receiving districts along the shallow autumnal rivers to
> reach their destinations before freeze-up. The goods were then ex-
> changed over winter for furs or provisions, and the furs were shipped
> down to York in the spring and summer of 1856. Trade goods such as
> blankets, guns, ammunition and iron goods delivered to the Company
> in London in the spring of 1855 could be converted to cash at the ear-
> liest in the fur auctions of January 1857.[22]

The Company hired clerks, usually on a five-year apprenticeship, to
keep the daily trade journals and to transfer the details of each account
into the ledgers. At the end of May each year, the account books were
closed and tallied; they were then sent to London, along with the post
journal, the year's correspondence, and the other annual records of the

post. The clerks' diligence in a less than perfect environment provided clear and concise accounting records that were amalgamated with those of all the other posts on receipt in the London office. Once the results of the fur sales were in, all this information was summarized in a financial statement for the governor and Committee and for the stockholders. This process provided a check on the business at each of the posts and in London, so that any inconsistencies could be identified and acted on. The bottom line in the London account books more often than not allowed the Company to provide a substantial dividend to its stockholders.

WEDDERBURN'S PLAN

In 1809 William Mainwaring, who followed Lake as governor, and his Committee were acquainting themselves with the Company's affairs when some new characters appeared on the scene. One of these was new committeeman Andrew Wedderburn,[23] who would dominate the Company and have a huge influence on its administration over the next forty-six years. As well, Colin Robertson, a former employee of the NWC but a sympathetic fur trader, arrived in London with a plan to contest the NWC and its shipping route through Montreal. And Thomas Douglas, Earl of Selkirk, a parliamentarian and experienced colonizer, had recently acquired Company shares with the design of obtaining land for his colonizing scheme on the Red River near Lake Winnipeg. These men were energetic, enthusiastic, and entrepreneurial, and all three of them saw the HBC as a means to succeeding in their respective ventures. They were to find equally ambitious and encouraging allies on the London committee.

Immediately on his appointment to the Committee, Wedderburn submitted a plan "for the Improvement of the System of Trade in Hudson's Bay."[24] This innovative plan (referred to in the records as Wedderburn's retrenching system) involved an all-embracing revision of the Company's trade and practices, including a new attitude towards its fur traders, allowing them more autonomy in making decisions and the incentive of a larger share of the profits. With sound economic management and an emphasis on active, efficient, and loyal employees, the plan was to set the Company on a secure footing without provoking the NWC further.

The reorganization had at its heart a meticulous scrutiny of accounts and the elimination of extravagant spending. Each factory would have an accountant, who would also act as storekeeper and be second in

Reference in minute book for 7 March 1810 (A.1/49, fo. 15) to the reorganization plan submitted to the board by Andrew Wedderburn

authority to the factor. He would "make up annually a correct Inventory of the Goods on hand at every trading House within the Limits of the Factory, as also of the outstanding Debts due by Indians, and by the Companys' Servants at the period of closing the Accounts of the

Year."[25] In the past the accounts had been made up by the clerks at each post and checked by the factor. The accounts were to be kept in pounds sterling, rather than in the traditional "Made Beaver."[26] A larger but more accountable administrative structure divided the Hudson Bay territory into departments, factories, and districts. The two departments, the larger Northern Department, which included factories at York, Churchill, Severn, Cumberland House, and Norway House, and their outposts on the Saskatchewan River and west and south of Lake Winnipeg, and the Southern Department, which comprised Albany, Moose, and Eastmain and their outposts, were each under the control of a superintendent. The term "chief factor" came into use at this time as the title for the person in charge of each of the eight factories. The salaries of the superintendents, their clerks, and the accountants were to be charged to the Company, while the salaries of the factors and traders were to be charged to the accounts of the factories. Thus half the net profits of each factory would be distributed in the proportions of one-third to the chief factor, one-third equally distributed to the traders attached to each factory, and one-third to a general fund. Bonuses for the superintendents, the surveyor, and the accountants were to be determined at a later date. Besides these premiums, the Company would pay a base salary according to the following scheme: £150 to the superintendents, £100 to the factors, £60 to the accountants, £50 to the surveyor, £50 to the traders, and £50 to the superintendents' clerks.[27] The Company would never be the same again. Fluctuating profits and markets over the next few years required the plan to be revised periodically.

Many of the resolutions involved revised or increased record-keeping. The same kinds of records continued to be produced, with copies of post journals, correspondence, account ledgers and journals being sent annually to London. But because of the expansion, there are more of these documents in the HBCA for each year than there had been in earlier years.

Wedderburn's retrenchment system was carried out successfully, allowing the Company to be solvent, profitable, and dominant as it moved into new roles and responsibilities. The reorganization continued over the next ten years, interrupted periodically by the incursions of the NWC and by the troubles caused by the Red River Settlement. In 1814 Wedderburn (he changed his name to Colvile later that year) and the Committee reviewed and revised the plan after an analysis of the trade statistics from the previous four years and with the realization that the competition from the NWC had so far been intractable. Colin Robertson was sent to set up an agency for the Company in Montreal, the headquarters of the NWC.

In another major change of the reporting structure, the two forts through which trade was shipped in and out of the bay – York Factory (Northern Department) and Moose Factory (Southern Department) – were designated the regional centres for reporting from the trading districts. In this way the London office placed the responsibility of organizing the information from the smaller posts on the superintendents of these two departments. The intent was to receive more correspondence, particularly from the Southern Department posts, which were in the direct vicinity of the NWC's activity. Arrangements were made for what became known as the winter packet,[28] to be shipped to Montreal through Sault Ste Marie, where an independent intermediary would forward it on the final leg of the trip, so that it would arrive before the middle of February, ready for the first ship to England. The new avenue of communication through Montreal provided the London office with dispatches twice a year – one from the usual late summer sailing by Company ship from Hudson Bay and one from the early spring sailing by commercial shipping from Montreal. The Company expected that the packet would include an account of the transactions of the whole department up to the last possible date before the packet was sent on its way. The letter of instruction to Thomas Vincent, governor of the Southern Department, continued: "You will also find it very useful to keep up a regular communication in this way with all the posts under your command by an interchange of letters, at stated periods in the course of every winter, so that you may have frequent information of the circumstances which occur, particularly at those posts which are most exposed to opposition."[29]

In 1815 the position of governor-in-chief of Rupert's Land was created as a means of better governing the Company's territories during this time of virulent rivalry with the NWC. The content of the general letter sent to all posts that year is an example of the detailed instructions given for preparing reports, annual reports, and journals. Instructions to the Company's servants, often lengthy but precise, were important for the keeping of detailed records in North America and for the transfer of those records to London. The seventy-fourth paragraph explained the instructions that were attached for the preparation of the reports, annual reports, and journals to be sent back by the officers:

Reports: As the information of which we ought to be possessed, with
respect to the present state of our establishments, is in many points
imperfect, and that to which we have access, is too much scattered to
be easily collected together, we have resolved with a view to the rem-
edy of this defect, that every Chief, & Master of a Trading District
be desired as soon as practicable to make a Report addressed to the
Gov[or] of the Department, in which he is situated, as to the present
State of the District under his command.[30]

The reports were to be arranged under the headings of the district, the
posts, the men, the Indians, the Canadians, and the traders, and the following five pages of instructions detailed what should be included in the district reports. This was going to be a very time-consuming project, and it is
not hard to imagine the reaction of the recipients of the letter, even though
the instructions stated that the reports were to be made out "at leisure."

The descriptions of individual posts that were sent on to the manager
of the trading district were to include details about the local situation,
buildings, soil, cultivated fields and gardens, crops and projected yield,
and natural produce, including fish species and supply. The numbers and
occupations of the men were to be listed, including personal information
about each individual and an evaluation of their integrity, ability, intelligence and courage. The Natives were to be described by total number and
number of hunters, the names of individual chiefs and hunters, and the
names of those who traded with the NWC, their general condition and
means of subsistence, and the extent of their hunting grounds. Details
were to be provided about the Canadians or NWC, including numbers of
men and accounts of their establishments within the district, the quantity
and nature of furs, and the trade goods they provided. And a statement
was required of the fur trade in the district balanced with the expenses incurred, the potential for growth, and suggestions for improvements.

The district manager was then to describe the whole district according to geography, topography, vegetation (both natural and cultivated),
and climate. The topographical account was to contain

1. A Plan or Sketch of the various Rivers lakes &c.
2. A description of the Navigation of each River, noticing particularly
   the Falls, rapids & other difficulties.
3. An account of the nature of the country, in the different parts,
   describing the Soil, the Species & Size of the Timber or other
   vegetable growth.

4. The nature and quantity of its productions both such as may be valuable for trade & those which are calculated for the Subsistence of men, specifying the kind of provisions, the seasons at which they can be obtain'd, and the number of men that can be maintained by them.

5. A general account of the Climate, specifying the usual period, when the Thaw commences & the Vegetation begins in Spring, and in like manner that of the setting in of Winter together with any circumstances which may give an idea of the degree of warmth & rapidity of vegetation in Summer as well as of the intensity of cold in Winter.

6. A statement of any advantages or disadvantages to which the district is subject.[31]

The district manager was also to make an annual report of all the posts under his command, including a narrative of the principal occurrences over the past year, explaining in detail any of particular importance; the physical state of each post, again including details about cultivation of crops; the conduct of the officers, specifying each by name and an opinion of their performance; a list of the Natives, evaluating the value of individuals' trade and indebtedness, whether they traded with the Canadians, and commenting on their conduct and condition; a statement of the amount of the trade obtained from the Canadians within the district, including the officers' names and number; and a report on the trade of the district compared with other years, explanations for failure, and also suggestions for improvement.

These reports by the Masters of Subordinate Districts, are to be submitted, in the first place, to the inspection of the Chief, under whose immediate command they have been; who is to examine them, to observe whether any thing material is omitted or misstated, & to report to the Governor, whether they are correct or not. The Chief is also to report on the general conduct of the masters under his command; & to state his opinion, how far it may be advisable to make any alteration on the position, the establishment, or the mode of conduction any of the posts under his command.[32]

The superintendent, then, was to make a general report with reference to the subordinate reports, together with specific comments on his satisfaction with the operations of the districts and an explanation

of his plans for the next year: "with a full detail of his intended arrangements for the ensuing year – the number of men to be stationed
at each post – the change which he proposes to make, in the distribution of the Officers, and in the limits of their commands; as also the
expectations which he entertains, as to the probability of success in
each district."[33]

The requirements for this new reporting procedure did not negate the
obligation of keeping of journals at each post, which were to "contain
nothing but a plain & simple memorandum of facts, without any comment or observations. They must however be distinct & full, containing
all the particulars that may contribute to the better understanding of the
transactions that are mentioned." Climate was of a particular interest.
Thermometers were sent out for distribution to each post and "to such
Officers as are likely to make the observations correctly." A register
was to be kept of the temperatures in all seasons so that the climate of
Hudson Bay could be compared to that of the northern parts of Europe.
"These observations not to be considered as a matter of idle curiosity but
may be of very essential use in enabling us to judge which productions of
European Cultivation may be tried at each of our establishments, with a
prospect of success."[34]

There was no let-up in the requirement for this attention to detail,
and writers at the posts were once more reminded of the importance of
organization and penmanship in the presentation of the journals: "Several of the Journals hitherto sent home are very slovenly and defective.
Besides many most essential omissions, We are frequently told that 'a
man' did this, or that; when it would have been as easy to have given
the man's name. Of all the journals hitherto kept, Mr. [John] Mannalls
at New Brunswick comes the nearest to the proper model."[35]

It is because of precise directions for the keeping of records and the
attention to detail required by the Committee in London that the
HBCA has such a wealth of information, of interest to so many different disciplines.

Each of the trading districts which is under the command of a
master, must have a clerk whose duties will be of the same nature
as that which were formerly to be performed by the accountants
of the Factories, but with those variations which naturally arise
from the reduced scale of the transactions. The clerk will keep
the accounts & all the Books at the post, which when closed for
the year, are to be transmitted to the Accountant of the Factory,

New Brunswick journal (B.145/a/127, fos. 2d and 3); entries written by John Mannall, described by the London office as the "proper model" for keeping post journals

to be examined & checked by him before they are sent home ... These accounts will be signed by the Master of the District & will form materials from which, the accountant will make out the general accounts of the Factory or Department.[36]

With the acceptance of Wedderburn's plan, the Committee arranged to send Edward Roberts, the young clerk in the accountant's office, to Albany, Moose Factory, and Eastmain "for the express purpose of directing [the factors and their clerks] how to keep the Factory Acco[un]ts according to the New System for conducting the Trade in future."[37] The plan included the appointment of an accountant to each factory. Until this time only the larger posts would have had accountants; more generally, it was an apprentice clerk who helped with trade inventories and also kept the books, which were signed off by the factor. With the new plan, each factory would have an accountant-storekeeper, and each trading district would have a clerk for bookkeeping, working under and checked by the factory accountant. Roberts's letter of introduction directed that he be given "every accommodation & assistance that they may think necessary

to facilitate the especial Business of his mission."[38] This was one of the
few times in the history of the Company that a representative was sent
from the London office to the posts on Hudson Bay.

Roberts arrived by ship in Albany on 16 August 1810, and the next
day he began an inventory of the Company's property. It was completed, with some assistance from the doctor, in time for Roberts to sail
for Moose Factory on the Company ship, the *Prince of Wales*, on
28 August. He completed the inventory of the warehouse at Moose
Factory by 3 September, when he sailed for Eastmain for the same purpose. He left Eastmain on 14 September to sail back to Moose, where
he boarded the *Prince of Wales* for England. Roberts had completed a
hectic schedule in a short time frame in order that he could personally
carry home the annual dispatches and first-hand knowledge of the
Company's business methods at the main posts. On his return, he was
introduced to the board,[39] and a few months later he was given a bonus of 100 guineas "for his having executed the Business entrusted to
him to satisfaction of the Company."[40] The minutes of 12 December
1810 record the acceptance of his suggestions for keeping the post
account books:

> The Method of keeping the Accounts of Trading Goods remaining
> at the Factories in the Bay, as suggested by Mr. Edward Roberts, who
> is lately returned from thence, being referred to the Committee of
> Accounts report as follows: That Mr. Roberts' proposed Method
> of keeping the Accounts at the several Factories of Inland Settlements
> in the Bay, for the future, in pursuance of Directions of the Court,
> appear'd to be well arranged and likely to be beneficial to the Com-
> pany, and That Mr. Roberts' assiduity is highly commendable. The
> Committee therefore directs that Books, adapted for the purpose,
> be sent to the Bay the ensuing season.[41]

This was quite a significant accomplishment for a twenty-three-year-
old clerk.

There was so much going on – reorganization, expansion, colonization – and the governor and Committee in London were completely reliant on the written information they received, always months after the
fact, from their bases of operation scattered across the interior of North
America. The staff in the London office on 1 December 1813 included
the secretary, Alexander Lean (£450 per annum, plus house, taxes,
coals, and candles); the clerk, William Smith (£150); the accountant,

Arthur Ball (£250); the clerk, Edward Roberts (£225); the warehouse-man, William Hagell (£250); the assistant warehouseman, Emanual Ster-zel (£150); and the doorkeeper, whose name may have been Keyes (£80).[42] These were the people who carried on the business and incor-porated the changes resulting from Webberburn's plan of 1810 and subsequent reorganizations. Arthur Ball had been the accountant since 1794. He died in 1815, leaving the position open for Edward Roberts to take over.[43] The secretary, Alexander Lean, retired in 1817 after twenty-five years with the Company. "The Board having taken into consideration the letter addressed to them by the Secretary stating his advanced Years and growing Infirmities Resolved that he be permitted to discontinue the Duties of his Office after the 31st Inst."[44] Six months later Lean was provided with a pension of £400 per annum "during the pleasure of the Board."[45] Lean had probably been given six months to move out of the Company's premises, for when William Smith took over as secretary in June 1818, he was provided with the residence un-der the same conditions as Lean, including an allowance for coal and candles. Lean was the only secretary for whom it was recorded that he was to receive an extra allowance of £10 a year for chocolate.[46] No rea-son has been found for this unusual benefit, although it might have been health-related; but it would have been a luxury. Smith had joined the Company as a clerk in 1813 and advanced to assistant secretary four years later and to secretary on Lean's retirement. His starting sal-ary in that position was £300.

After the reorganization and the resulting changes in record-keeping in North America, the London operations remained stable through most of the first half of the nineteenth century. Smith was secretary for twenty-five years, from 1818 to 1843; Roberts was the accountant for sixty-seven years, until 1870; and Sir John Henry Pelly was the governor of the Com-pany for thirty years, between 1822 and 1852. It is possible that Smith had more than one clerk assisting him during this busy time in the Com-pany's history. One or two ships were being sent to the bay each year, and from 1824 on a ship was sent to the Columbia district, which meant they had to be prepared in the spring with trade goods, supplies, new staff, and the head office directives for the coming year. In the fall the ships' return required handling the fur cargoes, preparing them for auction, and deal-ing with signing off or reassigning returning staff and the reports and cor-respondence from the factories and inland posts. Between 1810 and 1820 the staff also had the added duties and record-keeping related to Lord Sel-kirk's attempts to establish a settlement at Red River.

THE RED RIVER SETTLEMENT

The Earl of Selkirk had long been an enthusiastic advocate of planned emigration from Ireland and Scotland, and he envisioned a colony in the fertile valley of the Red River. By buying stock in the HBC, he put himself in a position in 1810 to present a formal proposal to the Company for such a settlement, which also conveniently linked with Andrew Wedderburn's plans for greater self-sufficiency and economy. Wedderburn was Lord Selkirk's brother-in-law, and with his support, Selkirk was granted, for the nominal sum of 10 shillings, a tract of land along the Red River amounting to 116,000 square miles, including a large part of what is now Manitoba, Saskatchewan, North Dakota, and Minnesota. The idea was to establish a colony that would provide relief for the settlers from the poor conditions they faced in Scotland and provide personnel and supplies for the HBC, while avoiding provoking the NWC into open conflict. After Selkirk's death in 1820, the Red River colony was administered with limited success by his executors until in 1836, when it was transferred back to the HBC. The colony then continued, without new immigration, as a place of retirement for Company employees and their families.

Many records relating to Selkirk and the establishment of the colony are not in the HBCA. A large quantity of letters and documents, explaining why the settlement was commenced and detailing its history, were preserved by Selkirk in the ancestral home of the Douglas family at St Mary's Isle, Kirkcudbrightshire, Scotland. Correspondence dated 1771–1820 alone comprised ten volumes. Copies of eight of those volumes were loaned in November 1938 by one of Selkirk's descendants, Sir Charles Hope-Dunbar, for use by E.E. Rich in his work for the Hudson's Bay Record Society. The copies were returned in September 1941 after two copies were made of each by a typing agency. One copy is classified in the HBCA as E.88/1–8 (Thomas Douglas, Earl of Selkirk). Apparently, the second copy was destroyed.[47] While the family copies were on loan, all the originals, including the volumes of maps and plans associated with the correspondence, were destroyed in a fire at St Mary's Isle in November 1940. A large quantity of Selkirk papers previously copied for the Dominion Archives under Arthur Doughty are available on microfilm at Library and Archives Canada. Extracts from the Selkirk papers for the years 1798–1842 in HBCA accession E.88/9 and 10 are copies from the federal archives.[48]

Land registers of the Red River Settlement showing locks (E.6)

Records in the HBCA relating to Selkirk's settlement include census returns, land records, account books, deeds, and agreements. The registers of baptisms, marriages, and burials (E.4) date from 1820 to 1851. The census returns (E.5) include entries for each head of family: the age, country of birth, marital status, number and sex of dependents, number of buildings, livestock, farm equipment, river craft, and acres of land cultivated. The land records (E.6) consist of land register books, memoranda of land sales, land measurements, and sales books, containing maps and plans, for the years 1811–71. E.6/2, a large, leather-covered register sent out from London, its pages printed in the required format to be filled out on site, describes the lots granted by Selkirk and the Company to the individual settlers. A series of account books (E.7) dating from 1811 to 1871 contain detailed reporting of expenditures and payments, together with further information about individuals. Among the miscellaneous papers classified in E.8 is one of the real treasures of the HBCA, a document known as the Selkirk Treaty, which was made between Lord Selkirk, Saulteaux Chief Peguis, and other chiefs, accompanied by a map.

SIR GEORGE SIMPSON

George Simpson dominated the HBC's fur trade concerns in North America through much of the nineteenth century. He joined the Company just before the conclusion of its negotiations to amalgamate with the NWC. His "Journal of Occurrences in the Athabasca Department" is a record of the last campaign of the old Company to gain dominance in the fur trade in the vicinity of the Athabasca River and Lake Athabasca, along what is now the northern Saskatchewan-Alberta border, which lay beyond the territory described in the Company's charter. It was an area said to have a wealth of beaver and one in which the NWC had previously dominated. By 1820 the HBC had ascertained that impeding control by the NWC of that area superseded the risk and expense of securing its trade. Simpson was the person chosen to accomplish that task.

Simpson had been born in Scotland; he was raised by his aunt and grandparents and educated at a parish school, where he mastered the precise copybook handwriting style of the day, as well as basic grammar, arithmetic, and bookkeeping.[49] At the age of about twenty-one he went to London to work as a clerk in the sugar-brokering business owned by his uncle, Geddes Mackenzie Simpson, which later merged with Wedderburn and Company. Andrew Wedderburn, who had precipitated major reorganizations of the HBC in 1806, 1810, and 1814–15, dominated another complete reshuffling in 1820 both in his own company and in the HBC, in response to the trade and settlement crises in North America caused by the NWC. George Simpson, at about the age of thirty-four, emerged from this reorganization with an impressive title in the Company and a substantial salary. Wedderburn, now Colvile, had recommended him as being energetic, intelligent, determined, prompt, and trustworthy in confidential matters. Simpson was dispatched immediately to Rupert's Land, which he had never visited, to direct a campaign to open up the area in the vicinity of Lake Athabasca in competition with the NWC. He delivered, in person, a letter from the colonial minister, Lord Bathurst, which had been written to the heads of both the Hudson's Bay and North West

Selkirk Treaty and map (E.8/1, fos. 10 and 11)

companies, requesting them to instruct their employees to end their rivalry and "to keep the peace."[50]

Simpson emerged from the long winter, having accomplished his task in a swift and efficient manner, to discover that his employer and the NWC had agreed to a "coalition" that would irrevocably change the North American fur trade and his future. His timely presence at the culmination of the negotiations made him an obvious choice for a leadership position with the new corporation. He had left London with not much more than some accounting and business experience and instructions to return on the ship from York Factory the following summer. He ended his first year in Rupert's Land as governor of the HBC's most important region and a future that would see North America as his residence for the rest of his life.

Simpson's management style, as evidenced in the Athabasca campaign, set the standard for administration of the business after the merger. For forty years his shrewdness, high standards, and amazing energy made him a key figure in the Company. Although there are other journals, letters, and reports by George Simpson in the HBCA, the "Journal of Occurrences in the Athabasca Department" has come to represent his personality and strengths. He was capable, businesslike, and unflappable. The vellum-covered volume, known as the Athabasca Journal and classified in the HBCA as B.39/a/18, is a fair copy, written concisely and full of succinct details of the fur trade and information about the participants. The writing is very small, but its neatness makes it easily readable.

Even in his first few months in a job that must have been so completely different from anything he could have experienced previously, and in a less than comfortable environment, Simpson made suggestions for changes in the location of posts, mode and direction of travel, packing of goods and canoes, trade, and interactions with the Natives. His comments on the weather, on the personnel of both the HBC and the NWC, and staffing considerations are interjected with personal opinions about the Natives and mixed bloods, openly sarcastic and often derogatory. His attention to record-keeping, much beyond the administrative procedures required of him, has proved to be a delight to archivists and historians researching this era in the HBCA.

Simpson's journal contains copies of numerous letters to the managers and factors of the Hudson's Bay posts to the north and west along the Peace and North Saskatchewan rivers. The importance he put on the records, including documenting what was being sent out, cannot be questioned. A detailed list of the documents and correspondence is written into his journal and a duplicate packet with exact copies of everything was made up to ensure against loss. Simpson's journal entry for 1 December 1820 explained the preparation that had taken place the previous day:

> I and the rest of the Gentlemen sat up all Night making arrangements for the departure of Mr. Grignon with the Dispatches, they were made up in two sealed duplicate packets addressed to the Governor in Chief; one Copy packed up with the provisions on Mr. Grignon's train and the other sewn up in the hood of Larances Capot: I have given directions that if either are taken by the N.W. the other is if possible to make the best of his way to any of our establishments where he will receive the necessary assistance to prosecute his Journey.[51]

During that winter tensions with the NWC were of course at their peak. Before the coalition was confirmed in March, Simpson was concerned about any information being leaked to the competition. On discovering that the district manager at Fort Wedderburn was keeping a private journal, Simpson admonished his colleague for risking the strategy of the Company and the safety of the residents of the fort. His diligence in dealing with the matter and his manner of handling personnel crises is carefully documented in his journal:

> For several months past Mr. Brown has been industriously occupied in compiling a huge Volume titled "Private Journal." This seems to be a work of great labour not only occupying his attention throughout the day, but his lucubrations are unremittingly devoted thereto. Being labelled "Private Journal" I have hitherto felt a delicacy in asking any questions about it, but within these few days, he seems very solicitous to get possession of a variety of documents (without my privity) which are totally foreign to him in his capacity of District Master of Athabasca Lake; I have therefore to day taken the liberty of enquiring into the object of this ponderous compilation ... I told him that his business was to keep a correct, particular and concise Journal of the Post for the inspection of his superiors ... but that I could allow no Gentleman to interlard his private Journal with the minutiae of the Coys. business and therefore requested it might be discontinued. I took some pains to convince Mr. Brown that my remarks did not arise from any suspicion that *he* would make an improper use of the information he might thus embody, but ... that I did intend suggesting to Govr. Williams the propriety of having every

Gentleman's papers strictly examined previous to leaving the country and that whatever related to public business should be delivered into his possession.[52]

Simpson's ability to perceive the strengths and weaknesses of those he met was supported by his enthusiasm for passing judgment on his associates in his journals, reports, and correspondence. Immediately on becoming governor of the Northern Department in 1821, he maintained a personal reporting system on the clerks in his department, listing them by name and including their nationality, capacity, length of service, salary, and department.[53] The fair copy was written by a clerk, but Simpson signed this list, after adding his own brief remarks on the men, a precursor of the modern personnel evaluation reports used today in most offices. Next to that document in the HBCA is a similar one on NWC clerks of the Northern Department for the same years, 1821–22.[54] These lists formed the basis for a servants' character book for 1822–30,[55] which was copied almost verbatim from the two lists just described by William Smith, secretary to the Company at that time. Additional remarks were added yearly to update the original to 1827 and then again in 1830. When he was asked several years later by the governor and committee to resume this annual personnel reporting, Simpson explained that it had been discontinued for reasons of personal privacy: "In reply to your remarks on the discontinuance of such reports, I have to state that I originated the system myself, and followed it up for several years; but was induced to abandon it, in consequence of the information, which was intended to be strictly confidential, finding its way back to the interior, leading, as may be readily imagined, to personal difficulties and other inconvenient results."[56]

While discontinuing official reports on the Company's clerks, Simpson did keep notes on the chief factors and chief traders in a very private "Character Book,"[57] written at Red River during the winter of 1831–32. As Glyndwr Williams notes in the introduction to the Hudson's Bay Record Society's edition of the Character Book, confidentiality was a major consideration.

It is known that Simpson kept his private papers under lock and key, with not even his confidential secretary (Thomas Simpson at this time) allowed access; and to strengthen the secrecy of the Character Book the commissioned officers were indicated by number only, and the key to those numbers was kept on a separate sheet of paper. How and when the two documents arrived at the Company's London headquarters is not clear. The Character Book presumably remained in Simpson's possession during his lifetime. It may have been sent to the Company with other papers after his death at Lachine in 1860, but is it not listed in the late nineteenth-century "Catalogue of Library &c." It makes its first appearance in the 1923 catalogue under the title "Servants Characters & Histories of Service," and the single sheet identifying the commissioned officers was found and placed with the Character Book in the late 'twenties[58] ... As far as we know, no one except Simpson saw it during his lifetime.[59]

Among the hundreds of letters and reports by Simpson on the shelves of the HBCA, this remarkable little volume, written entirely in his own hand, is one in which he freely expressed his personal assessment of these individuals, revealing to readers as much about himself as about the men being described.

MERGER WITH THE NORTH WEST COMPANY

On 26 March 1821 the governor and Committee of the HBC and William and Simon McGillivray and Edward Ellice, representing the NWC, "agreed to unite their interests."[60] The business of the merged company was to be transacted at Hudson's Bay House in London, the new company was called the Hudson's Bay Company, and the agreement was to be in effect for twenty years. Inventories were taken of each company's assets, including the goods and stores at every one of the depots and posts in North America, the buildings and contents of Hudson's Bay House in London, the NWC office in Montreal, and all company ships. Indentures of all apprentices and engagements of clerks and all other employees were transferred to the new company. The board of the new company was constituted of the governor (or deputy governor) and two members of the Committee of the HBC and two members from the former NWC, the first board consisting of Governor Joseph Berens Jr, Andrew Colvile, Nicholas Garry, Simon McGillivray, and Edward Ellice. Reference was made in the agreement to record-keeping and access to records:

such Board shall have access to and cognizance of all such Information and reports relating to the Trade to be carried on under these presents as shall be received by the said Governor and Company or

Simpson's Character Book (A.34/2) and the index
to the Character Book (A.34/2, fo. 2), which was
found separately

their Successors from their Governors Factors and Agents in North America and all Correspondence Books Documents and papers whatsoever relating to the said Trade and all measures proposed or devised regarding the same and shall from time to time report to the said Governor and Company or their Successors such arrangements and measures as the said Board shall agree to recommend for the management of the said Trade ... [61] [and] ... the said Governor and Company and their Successors shall cause to be kept a proper set of Books of Account for the purposes of the Trade to be carried on under these presents exclusively of their other concerns.[62]

A few months after the coalition agreement was signed, the British Parliament gave full recognition to the Company's rights under its charter by passing "An Act for regulating the Fur Trade, and establishing a Criminal and Civil Jurisdiction within certain Parts of North America."[63] The act removed any doubts as to the powers that existed under the Canada Jurisdiction Act of 1803. The new act extended the jurisdiction of the courts of Lower and Upper Canada to the territories granted to the Company, which in 1821 included the areas known as Athabasca, Mackenzie River, Peace River, and New Caledonia, but did not override the rights of the Company under its original charter.

George Simpson was definitely the dominant force and played the major role in unifying the fur trade across the continent in a way it had never been before. He moved the Montreal office, which had been the headquarters of the NWC, to Lachine in 1826, and it continued to play a role for the HBC for several decades until his death in 1860.

Although not a complete set, the books and documents in the HBCA relating to the NWC provide an important dimension to the story, with information from the position of the HBC's long-time adversary. The account books and servants' contracts are of particularly keen interest to social historians and genealogists. The records surviving from the NWC and its predecessors are classified as Series F, Records of Related and Subsidiary Companies.[64] The earliest NWC records in the HBCA are a post journal (English River) dating from 1786 and two correspondence books dating from 1791 to 1799. The only minute book, for the years 1807–14, has been published by the Champlain Society.[65] Other records include various account books dating as early as 1795, servants' contracts dated 1803 to 1822, and NWC deeds and agreements from 1799. The latest records cover legal opinions and legal cases of the NWC and the North West Company Partners' Trust from 1826 to

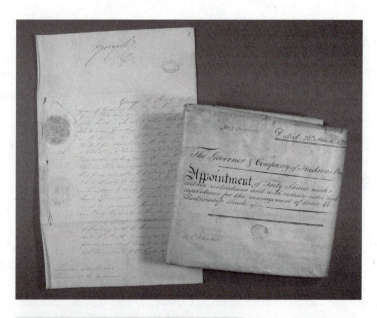

The following notice was objected to by A. Mackenzie as Curator to the Estate of the late Sir Alex.r M.c Kenzie & for himself —

NOTICE is hereby given that, in pursuance and performance of the conditions contained in a certain indenture, whereby it has been agreed that the Indian and Fur Trade, heretofore carried on by the Governor and Company of Adventurers of England, Trading into Hudson's Bay, and the North West Company of Montreal, respectively, should henceforward under certain terms be carried on by and in the name of the said Governor and company and their successors, exclusively the said Indenture having been ratified and confirmed by the said North West Company, the functions of the Agents of the said North West Company, and also of the Agents of Sir Alexander Mackenzie and Company, have ceased and terminated.

McTAVISH McGILLIVRAYS & Co. ⎫ Agents of the
THOMAS THAIN,   ⎬ North West
PIERRE DE ROCHEBLAVE. ⎭ company.
Montreal, 15th Nov. 1821.   tf

NOTICE is hereby given that the undersigned Archibald Norman McLeod, Esquire has retired from and ceased to be a partner of the house or firm of Mc Tavish, McGillivrays & Co.

McTAVISH, McGILLIVRAYS & Co,
A. N. McLOAD.
Montreal, 15th November, 1821,   tf

Licence of exclusive trade with the Indians, signed by George IV (A.37/7); Deed Poll, or "Forty Share Deed," 1821 (A.37/5); and newspaper notice announcing agreement between the Hudson's Bay Company and the North West Company (F.6/2)

Some of the North West Company records in the HBC Archives, catalogued as F.1 to F.7

1831. Like the HBC, the NWC required the keeping of records as part of the business routine: "Regular Books shall be Kept by Each Establishment at Montreal and New York, and General Accounts shall be stated therefrom, and rendered by the one Company to the other up to the 31st of December in each year."[66] Historian Stewart Wallace conjectured about why the book containing the minutes for 1815 to 1821 is missing: "It would seem probable that it too was deposited in Hudson's Bay House after 1821; but if so, it has disappeared. It may have been retained by William McGillivray while he was acting as a member of the advisory board on the fur-trade in 1821–24, or it may have been removed later in connection with one of the litigations which followed the failure of McTavish, McGillivrays and Co. in 1825."[67] It has since come to light that books and papers left in the Montreal offices of McTavish, McGillivrays and Company were sold at auction; they have turned up in various archives, libraries, and private collections, including that of Lord Strathcona.[68]

In Great Britain the 1800s were dominated by the long reigns of George III (1760–1820) and Queen Victoria (1837–1901). Throughout those periods Britain saw immense change in its political, economic, and social history. People of all walks of life were influenced by a revolution in industry that slowly introduced mass employment, unions to lobby for better working conditions, and a prosperous and largely self-made middle class. New cities sprang up to accommodate industry, which was situated for the most part outside the old cities, in what had been the countryside. The government grew during the first half of the century to handle the bureaucracy of policy-making for the increasing population, and by 1855 a permanent civil service was in place, with standard qualifications and standard methods of hiring.[69] Industrial prosperity was offset by overwhelming population growth in England and sporadic but devastating crop failure and famine in Ireland. The people of all classes were looking for better conditions, and many were attracted to the vast and largely unsettled land in North America.

Settlement of the Company's territories, long a controversial but inactive component of its charter, became a reality, particularly through the efforts of Lord Selkirk and his establishment of the Red River Colony in 1812 and James Douglas on Vancouver Island from 1843. Amalgamation with the NWC expanded the Company's territory both in the area covered and in bureaucracy. The majority of the Company's records were generated at the fur trade posts, including the reports sent annually to the London office. Within a few years the Company would find itself in the land business and a principal participant in the settlement of central Canada. Before the end of the century the fur trade, as it had been dominated by the HBC for the previous two hundred years, would come to an end.

4

request the favour of your particular attention

Expanding Horizons Require Detailed Record-Keeping, 1830–1860

With the amalgamation of the Hudson's Bay Company and the North West Company in 1821, the administrative responsibilities of the London office mushroomed. The position of secretary became one of increasing importance in the organization of the Company, and William Smith very capably handled the job for twenty-five years, from 1818 to 1843. Besides the usual correspondence, meeting preparation, and minutes, he also managed the business affairs of and served as executor for many of the servants in North America. The position by this time was becoming more like that of the modern chief executive officer, and the assistant secretary was tasked with the more routine work.

When any of the officers from the Hudson Bay posts were in town, the secretary was expected to receive them. An extra £50 was authorized in January 1820 for "refreshments on the Board Days and other Expenses incidental to his reception of the Company's Officers from the Bay for the last Year."[1] Smith's wife and six children lived with him in the residence provided for him between the Company's offices and the fur warehouse at the rear of 3 and 4 Fenchurch Street. His eldest son, William Gregory, would follow his father into the employment of the Company.

The increased work load on the staff in the London office during the 1820–21 merger period was acknowledged with an overtime bonus in May 1821: "The Secretary and Clerks having been employed during the last nine Months at extra hours equal to nearly three Months time of the usual Office hours. Ordered that they be paid one quarter's Salary respectively in consideration of the said Extra Work."[2] Much

detailed correspondence had to be written, agreements drafted and prepared for signing, and inventories taken of all the Company's holdings
and listed in minute detail. As well, the various officers of the HBC and
the NWC had to be entertained and extra meetings arranged. A year
later another bonus equal to one-quarter of the employees' annual salary was awarded, this time as well to the accountant.[3] One of the
clerks from the secretary's office was also expected to assist at the
warehouse. Under the supervision of the warehouse keeper, the secretary's clerk and a warehouse clerk were to "be present at the opening
of every Package of the Cargoes, and ... take accounts of the same,"
comparing their accounts with the accompanying invoices.[4] The stability of the London governor, the Committee members, and the London
office personnel provided the foundation required for the expansion
and diversification that took place over the next fifty years.

The Company history during the first half of the nineteenth century
is detailed and complicated and has been the subject of many articles,
books, and theses. The interest here will be on where the records and
record-keeping practices intersect with the ideas, plans, movements,
and establishments of the key participants in the Company's activities
and functions. The business diversified dramatically at the same time as
it expanded. Attention was beginning to be diverted from the "old-
fashioned" fur trade to a more diversified trade that responded to the
new frontier, which included farming, gold mining, colonizing, and
other activities. The NWC had reached the Pacific Ocean with the overland expedition of Alexander Mackenzie in 1793 and had built its first
trading post west of the Rockies in 1807. The two most westerly districts of the old NWC covered a vast region previously unknown to the
HBC other than through tales and rumours in the fur trade. The rugged
territory, limited fur profits, and problems with the Aboriginal population had given it a bad reputation.

At the same time as the Company acquired the possessions and
personnel of the NWC in 1821, it was also given, through legislation,
exclusive trading rights to the area for a period of twenty-one years.
An Act for regulating the Fur Trade was passed which gave the British government the power "to issue licences of exclusive trade with
the Indians in all lands beyond the limits of the existing privileges of
the Hudson's Bay Company,"[5] and it used that prerogative to the
benefit of the HBC. The western territories, including most of what
is now British Columbia, Washington, and Oregon, became part of
the Northern Department administered by George Simpson and

eventually the Columbia Department, made up of two trading districts: New Caledonia in the north and Columbia in the south.

Simpson is well known for his far-reaching trips across the continent, visiting, and inspecting the posts, personnel, records, and methods of trade and systems of transport, but when the council of the Northern Department met in August of 1821, Simpson had little direct information about trade on the Columbia River. To ensure a knowledgeable turnover and to oversee the operations, which he based at Fort George near the mouth of the Columbia River, he appointed John Haldane and John Cameron, two long-term NWC men, as chief factors and also sent along two experienced traders – John Lee Lewes, formerly of the Hudson's Bay Company, and James McMillan, formerly of the NWC.[6] Archibald McDonald, a native of Scotland who had been in the service of the HBC since 1812 as a clerk and agent for Selkirk at the Red River, was sent to keep the books. "I have therefore sent Archd. McDonald thither in the capacity of accountant and requested him to give a full and accurate report of it which will be transmitted to the Committee."[7] McDonald was entrusted with the task of taking the inventory of the goods and property in the New Caledonia and Columbia districts,[8] and the results were to be transmitted to Simpson through Chief Factor Haldane, who attended the council meeting in August the following year. Despite the Columbia district's problems and potentially low profitability, Simpson was encouraged to keep a presence in the area as a check on American opposition. This proved to be a good plan, but it was not only the Americans who were active on the West Coast. As at other times in its history, the HBC had to play the role of agent for the British government above and beyond its licence to trade in the area and almost immediately found itself involved in territorial diplomacy with the Russians, who had been showing a keen interest in the West Coast of North America for some time.[9] Records from this period relating to the HBC can also be found in the archives of the Colonial Office and the Foreign Office at the National Archives in Kew, England.

As with any of the Company posts, the standing orders of the governor and Committee in London required the keeping of journals by the chief factors in charge of the posts in the Columbia district. The NWC had required its officers to be similarly responsible; however, the men in charge of the individual posts were not always faithful in their duty, or journals were lost in transit. As a result, there are noticeable gaps in the records from this region in the HBCA.

Fort George, the old NWC post, had been the site of a trading post since about 1811, when it belonged to the Pacific Fur Company and was called Fort Astoria, but it lacked what Simpson required for his vision of a self-sufficient depot. Not long after the HBC took over, a new post, Fort Vancouver (now Vancouver, Washington), was built farther up the river at a site more conducive to farming but still accessible by ocean-going ships for trading purposes. Fort George was abandoned for Fort Vancouver in 1825, but for the four years of HBC occupation there is only one post journal (1824), a report on the district (1824–25), and a few miscellaneous items in the HBCA. There are no incoming or outgoing correspondence books, but there are twelve account books for the years 1821–24, probably resulting from the diligence of Archibald McDonald. Like the other account books in the HBCA, they contain annual inventories and employees' individual accounts. A separate account book (B.76/d/1) contains an inventory of stock on hand in the spring of 1821. Copies of the same inventories and earlier records from the Columbia district and specifically Fort George are also found in the NWC records in the archives. Concern for the records, as well as lack thereof, can be surmised from this letter to Cameron from Simpson in the summer of 1822:

I regret it has not been in the power of Messrs. Lewes and McDonald to compare all Inventories of the Columbia on account of many parcels of goods having been sent from Fort George previous to their arrival but if any error has arisen have the goodness to let it be corrected next season. The accounts of Gentlemen and Servants were intended to have been made up at the Tariff formerly adopted by the N.W. Coy., and Mr. McDonald should be instructed to close them in that way for last year; the Honble. Committee however determine that the Inventories of this Spring be taken at 70 p. Cent advance, at which price the private accounts of Chief Factors and Chief Traders are to be charged, ... Your letter will as a matter of course be with all other public correspondence transmitted to the Committee for their information ... The Columbia Establishment of Clerks & Men is very heavy and Mr. Haldane is of opinion that it might be considerably reduced without injuring the affairs of the Department, to which the Council request the favour of your particular attention.[10]

Company clerks, always integral to the efficiency and accountability of the organization, were especially indispensable during these times of amalgamation and reorganization. Their work and their attentiveness to it have provided the records that document the roles the Company played in the early history of the west. Clerks such as Peter Skene Ogden, who started with the NWC and eventually became chief factor of Fort Vancouver, left behind journals that documented events or expeditions with such detail and "intimate knowledge" that they would become records of reference when precise information was required for territorial definition and mapping.[11] But it was not always so. Several years later, Chief Factor James Douglas wrote with some dismay about the recruits he had been sent at Fort Vancouver to replace those who were leaving the service of the Company for better opportunities: "All our best Clerks are leaving the service, and you have been kind enough to send us Robert Logan and John Fraser to replace them, the first I [positioned] as accountant, as he can count ten without a mistake and the other as shop keeper seeing that he has got the length of the childs 2d Book and can spell words of two syllables ... Pray send no more useless men, our staff lists being already overcrowded with them."[12]

COMMUNICATIONS OVER A VAST TERRITORY

The HBC covered a large territory with a primitive communications network, not the instant electronic information transfer we have in the twenty-first century. News of the amalgamation and the subsequent instructions were sent out in the 1821 season and the resulting inventories and other records requested were sent back across the country in the following trading season. The process of merging the two companies and the impact of the new regime on the staff of both companies at isolated posts all along the way must have been, to some, confusing and unsettling. Allegiances and animosities among them were longstanding, and reluctance to follow the orders of the competitor would be understandable. As in other periods of the Company's history, the fact that there are documents recording the process, detailed and in significant numbers considering the situation, is one of the reasons for the respect the HBCA holds among its researchers and supporters.

By 1825 Fort Vancouver was the centre of the Company's activities in the Columbia Department, and the record-keeping was more consistent under the charge of Dr John McLoughlin, who took over as chief factor in 1825. He and Alexander Kennedy had replaced Cameron and Haldane at Fort George before that post was closed. Besides fur-buying and the trading of commodities, the records that remain from this era

Peter Skene Ogden's Snake Country journals (B.202/a/2, 1824–25, and B.202/a/6, 1826–27)

illustrate the Company's role as governmental agency, collector of details of natural history, geography, meteorology, and anthropology, and
promoter of self-sufficiency by advocating farming and the use of natural resources. Correspondence to Fort Vancouver includes instructions
on animal husbandry and agriculture, indicating that Simpson encouraged these subsidiary activities. Most of the journals that are classified
as B.223/a/1–7, dating from the years 1825–38, are land- or sea-trad-
ing expedition journals made by various employees with Fort Vancouver as their home base. They are not post journals as such, nor do they
contain the particular attention to detail observed in other post journals, such as the early ones from Albany and York Factory. Some of
this lack is made up by McLoughlin's letterbooks for the same time period, which have been published in three volumes of the HBRS series.[13]
References and comments in these letters lead one to seek out reports,
journals, letters, and ships' logs, some of which are not found in the
HBCA. There is ample proof of the difficulties that a frontier region
presented and the variety of issues someone such as McLoughlin had to

contend with. International diplomacy and border disputes involved the Americans and the Russians. Transoceanic and coastal shipping required the acquisition and maintenance of ships, their crews, and cargo. There was also a range of people with whom to interact, including the local Aboriginal people and Company personnel, who might have been British, French Canadian, Métis, or Hawaiian.

There are, in the HBCA, forty-three letterbooks containing correspondence between Fort Vancouver and London dating from the years 1825–60. The letterbooks from the North American posts are often the only source for these records because incoming correspondence from the posts was not consistently preserved in the London office until later in the nineteenth century. Another complete letterbook, found in the possession of a direct descendant of McLoughlin, was edited by Burt Brown Barker and published by the Oregon Historical Society in 1948 as *Letters of Doctor John McLoughlin*. Barker comments, "That it is an original book and was kept in Fort Vancouver is evidenced by the fact that fifty-two of the letters are in the handwriting of Dr. McLoughlin and duplicates of all the letters except ninety have been located in the archives of the HBC in London. So far as is known, these ninety are to be found herein only."[14] McLoughlin's career with the Company ended in 1846 after long-standing animosity with Simpson. He left Fort Vancouver to spend the rest of his life as a private businessman, one of the original founders of Oregon City. Barker writes of McLoughlin:

> one is impressed with the infinite details of the business which Dr. McLoughlin had to supervise. Apparently there was no one to whom these details could be assigned, or, if so, he was unwilling so to assign them. As a result we find him not only passing on matters pertaining to the policy of the company in his district (Columbia), but giving detailed orders as to the location and shifting of men, horses, trappers, freemen, boatmen; also, he supervised the building of saw and grist mills, and the manufacture and sale of their products. He indicated the uses to which the lands were to be put, even as to what to plant in a local vegetable garden. He ordered what a post was to produce and the use to which the produce was to be put, even to the exchange of produce between forts. He had to see that all forts were properly supplied with men, food, horses, trapping materials and goods for exchange. He gave instructions as to the rate of exchange of goods for pelts, whether the goods were blankets, guns, ammunition, food, traps, beads, cloth, clothing, or other articles

of exchange. This rate he would change as competition at any fort made it necessary. The letters are full of such details indicating that his life was one of great activity and that he was in constant touch with every department of his district, which was the largest under the control of the Hudson's Bay Company.[15]

Fort Vancouver and the other posts in the Columbia district were not totally isolated. There were two routes of access to this area. The shipping route by sea from London was across the Atlantic, around Cape Horn, and then up the west coasts of South and North America (the Panama Canal was not opened until 1914). The overland route was by boat and canoe following the rivers, lakes, and portages across the continent from Hudson Bay and then down the Columbia River. Both routes were used, but each took months to complete and had many hazards. Even when the ocean route for shipping the furs was established from the West Coast, mail was still delivered by what was known as the express route – London to York Factory by ship and then by boat and canoe along the well-travelled inland waterways to New Caledonia and the Columbia district. Mail was returned overland in the same way, for it was still faster and more assured than by ship travelling around Cape Horn. This overland route was also the one travelled by Simpson when he made his tours of inspection. Sometimes, duplicate packages of correspondence and reports were sent by both systems to better guarantee the arrival in London of at least one. And copies of the cargo manifests of ships loading at Fort Vancouver were forwarded to London via York Factory using the overland route in case of loss of the ship or its cargo and also so that the Company could prepare its next sales in London, knowing what furs to expect. Even with this attention to making sure the important records arrived in London, there are, as has already been noted, incomplete series in the HBCA.

STAFFING THE POSTS AND KEEPING THE RECORDS

At this time in the history of the Company, the staff at the posts were divided into three groups. Commissioned officers included the chief factors and chief traders, salaried officers comprised clerks and postmasters and their apprentices, and the general workers included interpreters (required to communicate with the Aboriginal traders) and tradesmen (mechanics, carpenters, coopers, etc., needed to keep the post in running order). The fur trade was carried out by guides, voyageurs, labourers, and finally trappers, who either worked for the Company or were independent.[16] The clerks were the record-keepers. They were apprenticed for five years, during which time they kept the account books and wrote all the letters, reports, and journals under the supervision of the chief factor. During the busy season, they also helped out with the fur trade. When their apprenticeship was complete, they left the writing desk to make way for the next apprentice and moved on to serve behind the counter in one of the small fur trade posts. If they were still committed to life with the Company and had shown the necessary competence, energy, and initiative, they would then be eligible for promotion to the profit-sharing rank of chief trader. Apprentice clerks earned a salary of £20 per annum, which increased annually by £5 or £10 to a maximum of £50 in their final apprenticeship year. For clerks, the salary ranged from £40 to £150, which was the salary of clerks in the London office. Promotion to chief trader, under the Deed Poll of 1821, brought an income based on a 1/85th share of 40 per cent of the profits. Each chief factor's share was twice that.[17]

As at all of the other posts, the clerks at Fort Vancouver wrote in journals and letterbooks provided by the Company. The post journal was a chronicle of the day-to-day activities which might also include copies of pages from the account books and copies of both inward and outward correspondence. Post records covered more than business records. Some were meteorological journals, ships' logs, journals of expeditions, astronomical journals, or the surgeon's medical journals. Every item of trade received at or sent out from the post was kept track of, and the account books at the central posts such as York Factory, Moose Factory, and Fort Vancouver record all the items received from London and then distributed to posts in the district. While a ship's cargo was unloaded, the clerk or clerks recorded every item as it was stacked on the dock. They then transferred their notes to the lined account books. The account books also provide the inventories of goods on hand at the end of each season, together with accounts of the individual employees, listed by name.

A handwritten copy was made by the clerk of every letter sent out from the post. By the second half of the nineteenth century, letter presses were available to make copies but the process was somewhat tricky and the resulting copies are not always clear. It involved the transfer of ink from the original letter onto a dampened sheet of lightweight copying paper by applying pressure in a letter press. The print on the "flimsy" copy is often very pale.

Letterbooks contained copies of correspondence written at a post communicating with other posts or with the governor and Committee in London. The standard means of duplication was by copying into bound letterbooks in longhand. Researchers have at times found discrepancies in content between the original and the copy, sometimes leading to conjecture about what the intention was. Likewise, clear intention is unsure if only the copy is extant and the original has been lost. The clerk would write the requested letter, probably dictated by the chief factor or chief trader, in the letterbook and then transcribe this draft onto the appropriate letter paper and in the appropriate format. The letter would be signed by the originator, generally the chief factor. When the letters arrived in London, they were read, scrutinized, and responded to by the secretary and the Committee. Any discrepancies were noted and questions asked in the next annual letter outward to the post. One can only conjecture about what James Douglas at Fort Victoria was chastised for when he responded to Governor Pelly with the following: "I am extremely sorry that you should have had trouble in making out the meaning of some passages of my last letter, and I am no doubt to blame for not expressing myself with more precision and clearness, as it ought to have occurred to me that no person living in a well regulated community can form any idea of the moral and social state of this country."[18] Three years later, Douglas responded to letters from Secretary Archibald Barclay and the Committee: "I have duly noted the contents of these communications, and will give them my best attention."[19] The letterbooks containing letters received at the posts are classified with the post records. There are as well four volumes in the HBCA dating from 1823 to 1875 that consist of copies of private and confidential correspondence between the governor and Committee in London and the officers in North America. These large, leather-bound books were each secured with a sturdy brass lock, and the keys kept by the secretary.

Clerks were also responsible for writing up the annual reports for the post, which were amalgamated with the district reports providing London with information on social and economic conditions relating to each specific area. The reports kept the chief factor and the clerk or clerks, depending on the size of the post, busy at the end of the season, as they included last-minute comments on the productivity of each post, the conduct of the officers and men, the number and health of Natives in the area and changes in their condition, fluctuations in the fur trade, and the means of subsistence of the traders. Some reports also provided topographical descriptions, sketches, and maps. When lists of servants were included, the general format layed out names,

A private letterbook, 1823–46 (A.7/1), with a lock attached.
The key would have been held by the secretary.

parish, position in the Company, wages, winter residence, expiry date
of contract, age, stature, number of years of service, and comments on
character. Some posts kept separate lists for officers, clerks, postmasters, and servants, providing a general statement or abstract of the employee's account that included information as above, together with
wages and other credits, debts, rations, donations to the benefit fund,
bills in London or Montreal, sundry remarks, and a balance.

    Post records, such as those kept at York Factory in the nineteenth
century, are made up of the following, all in separate volumes and classified by letter. Post journals are thus classified as, for example, B.239/
a/1–196, and correspondence books as B.239/b/1–134.

Post records stored on shelves in the HBC Archives, arranged
according to post number

Post journals (a)
Correspondence books (b)
Correspondence inward (c)
Account books (d)
Reports on districts (e)
Lists of servants (f)
Abstracts of servants' accounts (g)
District fur returns (h)
Minutes of council (k)
District statements (l)
Scheme indents (m)
Indent books (n)

Fur invoice books (o)
Expenditure books (p)
Book debts (q)
Scheme distribution and invoice books (r)
Provision shed balance books (s)
Store balance books (t)
Servants' engagement registers (u)
Accounts current (v)
Bills of lading (w)
Servants' ledgers (x)
London fur trade ledgers (y)
Miscellaneous items (z)
Inventories (aa)
Tariff books (bb)
Store transfer books (cc)
Store invoice books (dd)
Invoices of shipments (ee)
Freight check books (ff)
Cash advances to officers/servants (gg)
Fur purchasing agencies (hh)

By 1842 George Simpson, predicting the outcome of discussions that would eventually lead to the Oregon Treaty four years later, made the decision to establish a new headquarters north of the forty-ninth parallel of latitude on Vancouver Island. The best site for the Company's activities on the West Coast was identified on the southern tip of the island, and the building and administration of Fort Victoria was placed under the leadership of James Douglas, who was based at Fort Vancouver. McLoughlin, who had been working under increasingly poor relations with the London committee and Simpson, was relieved of his command in 1846. As chief factor, he was replaced by a board of management consisting of Douglas (chief factor), John Work, and Peter Skene Ogden. The Company's presence at Fort Vancouver was gradually phased out over the next few years.

SHIPPING RECORDS

The move of the HBC out of American territory was part of a major re-organization of the Company that would clearly assert British maritime commerce on the North Pacific. It also put the Company at the centre of British colonization of the West Coast, forming a new regional economy while providing a year-round deep-sea port for trade with Hawaii, California, Alaska, and, of course, London.[20] The Company's business on the West Coast was quite different from the trade centred primarily on furs and carried out by cargo canoes manned by a few men on the network of inland rivers. Although canoes were still used on inland rivers and for short coastal journeys, seagoing vessels were necessary for the Pacific coastal trade.

The Company had always had ships plying the North Atlantic, annually servicing the fur trade posts in Hudson Bay, constantly respecting the weather, and working against the pressure of completing the return trip within the June-to-September shipping season. As well, its canoes and sturdy York boats navigated the inland rivers and lakes, moving trade goods and furs between posts. The Company's growth on the west side of the Rocky Mountains was focused on receiving trade goods from and shipping its furs to London directly by sea. Here there were no seasonal concerns about ice-up. There were, however, storms, and it was a longer voyage from England, the return trip taking as much as two years to complete.

In response to Russian and American competition on the West Coast, Simpson determined to establish a chain of posts from the Columbia River to Alaska. He also anticipated Company vessels acting as an itinerant post to handle the fur trade in the remote inlets where a permanent post was not a viable option. The ss *Beaver*, a steam-driven paddlewheeler that was also rigged for sail, was the first of these vessels to be used for this purpose. She arrived at Fort Vancouver in 1836 and served the Company in various guises until 1874. The ss *Beaver* was followed by the ss *Otter* in 1853 and the ss *Labouchère* in 1859. All were steamboats independent of wind or the weather but, in McLoughlin's view, costly in fuel and upkeep.[21] The countless details involved in acquiring ships, hiring masters and crews, making arrangements for the long voyages, and purchasing fuel and provisions, as well as finding supplies for the fur trade and for the commercial trade, have left many records as evidence of the financial commitment of the Company and the diligence of its staff in carrying out these innovative but complex and detailed arrangements.

Several research tools have been prepared in the HBCA to aid research on the subject of the HBC and its shipping. Ships' histories are available for most of the Company's ships, providing general information on areas and dates of operations, construction details, and major

Book of ships' movements, 1719–1929 (C.4/1), showing records of dates of departures and arrivals of Company ships to Hudson Bay and around Cape Horn to the Pacific Northwest

sources in the HBCA. Some ships' plans are also available, as are paintings and photographs. Comprehensive records, although not always complete, include ships' logs, seamen's wage books, portledge books (recording advances made to seamen), ships' movements books, marine insurance books, freight books, and miscellaneous papers. These records date from as early as 1699, but are most consistent for the nineteenth century. Ships registered in London for service in Hudson Bay, James Bay, the Eastern Arctic, and the Pacific Northwest included barques, brigs, brigantines, schooners, and steamships.

SCIENTIFIC INVESTIGATIONS

The Company's reputation for providing assistance to the Royal Society in the 1700s was renewed again in the nineteenth century when extraordinary contributions were made as interest grew in the field of natural history and science-specific organizations searched for more information about the world. The Royal Horticultural Society, the Zoological Society, the Royal Geographical Society, and the Royal Society all asked for and received assistance from the Company in their endeavours to explore and record the natural world of North America. The resulting correspondence in the London office records and in the journals and letterbooks from HBC posts along the routes taken add another dimension to the chronicles of these travellers and explorers. The British Museum in London and the Ashmolean Museum in Oxford both expressed interest in the natural history collections that the Company was accumulating. In April 1831 the governor and Committee resolved "to present to the British Museum the Birds and Animals in the Company's collection which Mr. Children has selected and which he represents would form a great and valuable addition to the Zoological collection now in that National Establishment."[22] However, there were no specimens available three years later when the Ashmolean Museum requested the same, but the keeper, T.B. Duncan, was asked to provide "a list of what are required."[23] Presumably, it was expected that more animal and bird specimens would be received from the fur trade posts.

In 1824 David Douglas, who has been described as "one of the greatest exploring botanists of all time,"[24] made his way through North America with the assistance of the Company. He had spent the previous year collecting botanical specimens in the eastern United States and Canada for the Royal Horticultural Society. His expedition to the Columbia District was jointly sponsored by the Horticultural Society and the HBC. The details of his trip are explained in a letter to the society in June 1824 when the Company agreed "with great pleasure" to give Douglas free passage for the purpose of making a collection of specimens:

Mr Douglas will be permitted to remain in the Country until the return of the Ship in 1826 or longer should it be considered desirable, and every facility will be afforded him of visiting the Company's different establishments in the Interior, he will however find the fare of the Country rather coarse and be subject to some privations. The Ship that will return in 1825 can bring such specimens as Mr. Douglas may collect during her stay on the Coast and he can take his Passage home with the remainder in the one that will return in 1826. There will also be an opportunity for him to transmit letters in the Month of March by the Overland dispatch for York Factory, which will arrive here putting accidents out of the question in the November following.[25]

Douglas was also given a letter of introduction to the chief factors of the Columbia district: "Mr. Douglas is a Passenger in the William &

Ann, and is sent by the Horticultural Society for the express purpose of collecting Plants and other subjects of natural history, he will remain with you till next Season, and we desire you will afford every assistance in promoting the object of his Mission."[26]

The expedition lasted from the spring of 1825 until the spring of 1827, with specimens of hundreds of newly described species of plants and trees being shipped to the Horticultural Society on Company ships from the West Coast. During those two years Douglas established his headquarters at Fort Vancouver but spent most of his time on excursions into the rainforest, observing the flora and fauna and collecting specimens along the tributaries of the Columbia River. He introduced over three hundred new names to the field of botany, including the Douglas fir (*Pseudotsuga meziesii*). When it was time to return to England, he travelled on the annual express, accompanied as far as Fort Colville by Dr John McLoughlin, overland to York Factory, where he boarded the Company ship from Hudson Bay to London. A subsequent expedition, from 1830 to 1833, to the same area as well as California and Hawaii was marred by disasters. Douglas's daily journals, four hundred collected specimens, and all his provisions were lost when his canoe capsized in turbulent water on the Fraser River in the spring of 1833. He sailed for England the following fall, and it was while exploring the island of Hawaii on a stopover for supplies and cargo that he met an accidental and tragic death. He was thirty-five.[27] The original journals of his first trip are in the archives of the Royal Horticultural Society and have been the subject of several publications.

The Company's cooperation with the Royal Horticultural Society went beyond assistance to collectors. In 1823 the society sent out a variety of seeds for planting at the posts on Hudson Bay, accompanied by orders from Governor Pelly in the annual general letter: "We direct that you will pay full attention to their instructions, as we are desirous of assisting the views of the Society as far as circumstances will permit."[28] A year later the society sent young trees for planting.[29] The Company itself expressed its enthusiasm for natural history collections of its own when a letter was sent to John McLoughlin on receipt of material he had sent to London, separate from that sent by Douglas to the Royal Horticultural Society. "The curiosities collected during the trip of the William and Ann along the Coast were very acceptable, and have made a considerable addition to a small Museum now forming here, and we have to desire that any interesting specimens of Natural history which may be collected should be sent home especially those which do not take up much room."[30]

Assistance provided to other individuals such as naturalist John James Audubon and Joseph Paxton, the designer of the Crystal Palace for the Great Exhibition of 1851, is noted in Company correspondence: "Mr. Audobon [sic] will be accompanied solely by his son and we have to desire that every attention may be shown these Gentlemen at such establishments as they may visit, you will also furnish them with such supplies as they may require, and for which you will take an acknowledgement, and transmit an amount of the same to us."[31] And the "HBC would only charge expedition for passages by ship and inland craft, plus maintenance and necessary supplies and would be willing to afford all possible assistance to the collectors."[32] Through Simpson, the Company also provided a donation of £50 and the promise of specimens to the Natural History Society of Montreal.[33]

As well, Simpson arranged to share cartographic information with John Arrowsmith, one of the founders of the Royal Geographic Society, continuing the relationship the Company had with John's uncle, map-maker Aaron Arrowsmith, and his son Samuel: "Your application to the Deputy Governor for permission to copy the Manuscript Charts &c., &c., of the Company into the Map you are about to publish of British North America has been taken into consideration and I am directed to acquaint you that the Governor and Committee being desirous to afford every information in their Power, have ordered that you have free access at your earliest convenience to the various documents in their possession."[34]

Between May 1846 and October 1848, the artist Paul Kane travelled on foot and by boat, canoe, horse, snowshoe, dogsled, and other means from Toronto to the West Coast through the Northwest with the assistance and companionship of Company personnel, sometimes in the company of the governor of Rupert's Land at the time, George Simpson. As with David Douglas, Kane's visits to Company establishments along the way are noted in the post journals. Any outside visitor would be worthy of note at these isolated outposts. At one point in the trip he helped to deliver mail from Fort Victoria to Fort Vancouver, as he "was very anxious to do anything in my power in return for the hospitality and kindness" he had received. His description of the mail service as it was carried out between posts on the West Coast sheds light on Native entrepreneurship and on a different kind of trade from which the Company did not receive any profit. It also brings to mind the subject of records management and the requirement for standards:

The gentlemen in charge of the various posts have frequent occasion to send letters, sometimes for a considerable distance, when it is either inconvenient or impossible for them to fit out a canoe with their own men to carry it. In such cases the letter is given to an Indian, who carries it as far as suits his convenience and safety. He then sells the letter to another, who carries it until he finds an opportunity of selling it to advantage; it is thus passed on and sold until it arrives at its destination, gradually increasing in value according to the distance, and the last possessor receiving the reward for its safe delivery. In this manner letters are frequently sent with perfect security, and with much greater rapidity than could be done otherwise.[35]

Kane's paintings of the scenes and people along the way have become famous not only as works of art but as anthropological documentation because of their detailed recording of the Native people and their costumes and lifestyle. Simpson had his own collection of specimens of natural history, ethnology, and art, which was augmented with sketches he commissioned from Kane.[36] It is no wonder he was eager to patronize such travel with support by the Company. He had written to Kane: "I should feel greatly obliged if you would take for me some sketches of buffalo hunts, Indian camps, Councils, feasts, Conjuring matches, dances, warlike exhibitions or any other scenes of savage life that you may consider likely to be attractive or interesting, with a view to their being coloured and framed, & of equal size so as to match each other ... I intend the sketches applied for, if you would be good enough to provide them, to be framed and hung up in a room I design as a museum for Indian curiosities."[37] In January 1849 Kane sent ten sketches of now famous scenes to Simpson in Montreal. Four more were to follow when finished. Most of Simpson's collection was dispersed by his descendants, and none of the paintings sent to him are in the HBCA art collection. Kane visited the governor and board of the Company in London in March 1858. Simpson had provided him with a letter of introduction: "I have the pleasure of making Mr. Kane known to the Board, as since his extensive travels in the interior, he has never failed to make public acknowledgement of the courtesy he received at the hands of the Company's Officers, and of the favourable opinion he was led to entertain of their treatment of the Indians and general management."[38] Kane's journal is in the archives of the Stark Museum of Art in Texas. It was published in 1859 in London as *Wanderings of an Artist among the Indians of North America*.[39]

KEEPING RECORDS IN THE COLONIES

The Hudson's Bay Company was unable to influence the outcome of the Oregon Treaty of 1846 between the British and American governments, which established the forty-ninth parallel as the international boundary between the United States and British North America. But the Company's presence, its British presence, in that area for the previous twenty-five years (and that of its predecessor, the North West Company) and the records it had to prove its presence ensured that the Americans did not acquire all of the West Coast to Alaska.[40] In order for the Company to be compensated appropriately for its possessions within the new Oregon Territory, detailed inventories and valuations of its holdings were prepared by James Douglas, John Work, and Peter Skene Ogden, all of which aided, but only marginally advanced, the negotiations. It was difficult to evaluate all the work of the previous twenty-five years:

> The Outlay on shipping, in exploring the Country, in opening roads, the enormous expense of labour, the strong force required as a protection against the Natives, on the other hand the changes effected by means of that outlay in the Country, now covered with luxuriant fields, abounding in all the necessaries of life, and with every element of Comfort; the Indians conciliated, and brought into friendly relations, are sacrificed on the part of the Hudson's Bay Company, and substantial benefits to the Government of the United States, which, judging from the precedent of other Colonies, it would have cost millions to acquire.[41]

At the same time, negotiations were going on between the Company and the British Colonial Office, with the end result that in January 1849 the HBC was ceded Vancouver Island for the purpose of colonization. The grant was based partly on the success of colonization that had already taken place around Fort Victoria and partly on the attempts of the Company at colonization at Selkirk's Red River Settlement. The colonial secretary insisted on a legislative-style government for the new colony to include a governor, elected by royal commission, and an elected assembly,[42] and the continuance of the colony was subject to the renewal of the Company's Licence for Exclusive Trade, which would come up in ten years' time.

James Douglas was appointed the Company's agent on Vancouver Island and moved to Victoria in June 1849. Fort Vancouver was left in the care of Peter Skene Ogden (1849–51), then John Ballenden (1851–53), and finally James Grahame (1853–60) before it was totally abandoned by the Company. The first governor of Vancouver Island was Richard Blanshard, whose term lasted just twenty months (March 1850–November 1851). When he arrived in Victoria, the Company had been well established on Vancouver Island for eight years, and Douglas, as the chief factor, completely dominated the colony. The Company's records inevitably became quite mixed with the governmental records of the new colony. On close inspection, Blanshard detected inaccuracies in the Fort Victoria accounts, and the London office of the Company found a few others. The Company's record-keeping procedures were well established by this time, so there are not many instructions or references in the archival records relating to process except when there was a problem. Before Blanshard left Victoria, he established a council of three members, one being Douglas, to provide a form of representative government for the colony, as required by the British government. Douglas was selected from this council a few months later to be the next governor of Vancouver Island. As such, he was responsible to the secretary of state for the colonies, but he was also still chief factor of Fort Victoria responsible to the governor and committee of the HBC in London. The modern term "conflict of interest" comes to mind with this appointment, but Douglas was determined to function appropriately in both positions.

Both offices required a regular exchange of correspondence with London. The Company, the colony and the colonists were still firmly connected to Britain for support of all kinds. And all were dependent on the expediency of shipping. Communication by this method was surprisingly predictable and timely, but it also required a fair amount of patience when a ship was unexpectedly late. On the 4th of August 1851 Douglas wrote up the latest news in a letter to Barclay but noted: "I have received no letter from you since that of the 15th Feby. replied to in mine of the 25th June and have received no intelligence from Fort Vancouver since the middle of June. We have not heard of the arrival of the *Pekin* nor of the departure of the *Mary Dare* from Fort Vancouver."[43] When the mail did arrive on 7 August 1851, it included Douglas's appointment to the office of governor of Vancouver Island.[44] Since inaccuracies in the record-keeping of the new colony had been exposed by Blanshard, Douglas asked for an experienced clerk directly from Hudson's Bay House in London to assist in putting the books in order.[45] Richard Golledge, who arrived on 15 May 1851, became Douglas's secretary.

But even with help, record-keeping was not one of Douglas's top priorities. Eden Colvile, governor of Rupert's Land, complained in July 1852:

> The Accounts from the Columbia this year [which would have included Fort Victoria] do not appear more explanatory than last, but I do not think this to be attributed to the Accountant at Fort Vancouver, Mr. Hardisty, who, I am informed, has been most assiduous in his duties. Mr. Ballenden complains in his letter of the unusually late arrival of the accounts from Fort Victoria, and the very incomplete state in which they were rendered. Looking at the very numerous Staff of Officers & Clerks, this is somewhat inexplicable. It appears that this establishment consists of 1 Chief Factor, 1 Chief Trader, 2 Clerks, 1 Clerk & Surgeon and three APP. [apprentice] Clerks.[46]

The errors seemed to have been in separating the expenses of the Company from those of the colony. The governor and Committee in London responded with almost immediate aid:

> Owing to the same want of detailed accounts of which Governor Colvile complained, we have been unable to ascertain the causes, but we apprehend that it is in a great measure, if not entirely, attributed to errors in the mode of stating the accounts; we have therefore sent out Mr. John Miles, an experienced Clerk of our establishment here, to investigate the accounts of the last Outfit, and to open the Books of Outfit 1853 on a system which Shall in future exhibit the state of the business in a clear and distinct manner.[47]

As a result of all of this attention to detail, Douglas spent more time checking the books "to remove an impression which appears to have taken possession of the minds of Mr. Ballenden, in Fort Vancouver, and other gentlemen, that the Fur Trade is saddled with the expenses of this colony; an opinion which has no foundation in fact."[48] After 1852, the accounts of Fort Victoria were sent separately to London, rather than from Fort Vancouver.

Douglas was not the only factor to be chastised for sloppy record-keeping. James Anderson, chief factor of Mackenzie district in 1852, and Simpson discussed records management in the district and the policy of access to that information. Simpson commented:

> The careless manner in which official documents are scattered about the Company's establishments, as you describe at Fort Simpson,

had frequently come under my notice in other parts of the country. It is rather surprising that our gentlemen do not take the trouble to collect & fyle them – indeed, the general statements of returns & results of trade should be considered confidential documents furnished to the gentlemen in charge of districts for their information as parties interested in the trade, to be by them handed over or left under cover to their successors when they leave. These office details can hardly be made the subject of a special Minute of Council as you suggest, but must be left to the good judgement of four gentlemen, who now pay more attention to these matters than in former days.[49]

As governor of the colony, Douglas was required to report to the Colonial Office, but as chief factor for the HBC, he continued to send detailed reports to the Company secretary, Archibald Barclay. His despatches, besides reporting on Company business, described events and situations in the community of Victoria that had been built up around the fort. For the London bureaucrats and Company board members, this extra information provided context for decisions made in Fort Victoria on their behalf.[50] Historians must keep an open mind and investigate all options when considering where to look for archival records. For example, a ledger, an account book, and two journals from the colony of Vancouver Island (1848–61) are in the HBCA classified as private records (E.22/1-4), and HBC records relating to the colony can be found in the British Columbia Archives.

AN END TO THE COMPANY'S MONOPOLY

Record-keeping was one aspect of the Company's administration investigated by the new British government of Lord Palmerston in 1857 when the HBC licence to trade was coming up for renewal. The Joint Stock Companies Registration and Regulation Act[51] had been passed in England in 1844. For the HBC, the registration process required lists of stockholders, their addresses, occupations, and number of shares. Operational records such as books of account, board minute books, the register of stockholders, and an annual balance sheet were required for the inspection of shareholders. The act, which provided "a mass of material on every joint stock company registered,"[52] was soon superseded by other acts that stipulated even fuller records creation, particularly of finances and the reporting of accounts at shareholders' meetings. All registered companies were required to keep books recording the "minutes, resolutions and proceedings of general meetings,"[53] and as a model for annual

general meetings held today, shareholders were to receive a copy of the
balance sheet for the previous year for inspection prior to the meeting.
The details of obligatory practices and regulations were developed
through the mid-1800s, requiring more, or sometimes less, detailed information, but this governmental regulatory process is important for its attention to record-keeping, resulting ultimately in the survival of records.

For the renewal process, Palmerston appointed a select committee of seven, chaired by the secretary of state for the colonies, Henry
Labouchere, to investigate problems raised by the Company's administration of and its trading monopoly in British North America, which at
that time was accentuated particularly in the nascent colonies of Red
River and Vancouver Island. Representatives of the Hudson's Bay
Company and those of British, Canadian, and American government
interests were questioned over a period of five months in an effort to
determine "the State of those British Possessions in North America which
are under the Administration of the Hudson's Bay Company or over
which they possess a Licence to Trade."[54] A lawyer for the Company provided copies of its 1821 and 1838 exclusive licences to trade, and as well,
the committee had for reference a copy of the charter, the 1749 report resulting from the Dobbs inquiry, which had reaffirmed the Company's
chartered rights, and a list of shareholders as of 1856. After listening to
twenty-five witnesses, including George Simpson, Richard Blanshard,
Company committee member of long standing Edward Ellice, former employees, and ships'captains testifying in the Company's defence, the select
committee reported to the House of Commons. The report (550 pages in
length) recommended another renewal of the Company's licence to trade,
but it referred a question of the validity of the charter back to the government and the Crown. It recommended the cessation of the Company's
monopoly rule in the Northwest, the transfer of the Red River and
Saskatchewan districts to Canada, and the establishment of a Crown colony west of the Rocky Mountains, thus terminating the HBC's connection
with the colony of Vancouver Island. This plan left the management and
control of what was termed "Indian Territory", the areas considered not
fit for settlement, to the Company. It was a turning point in the Company's history, preparing the ground for the Deed of Surrender to the Dominion of Canada, which would be worked out a few years later.[55]

As a result, James Douglas was made governor of both the main-
land colony of British Columbia and the colony of Vancouver Island
in 1858, with the condition that he resign as chief factor and sever his
interests with the Company. This he did; he would administer both

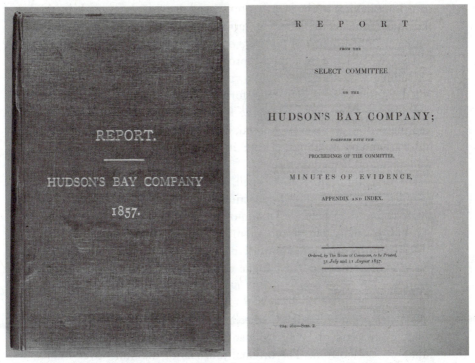

Report from the Select Committee on the Hudson's Bay Company, 1857 (Rare Book J301.K6)

colonies until he retired in 1863. The Company's licence to exclusive trade in North America was terminated in 1859. It gave up or sold its interests in subsidiary enterprises such as mining and agriculture.[56] It had added considerable interest in land sales to its already heightened involvement in general commercial trade. But it was still chiefly a fur-trading company. When the 1821 amalgamation of the two fur trade companies had been completed, the salaried workforce in North America was over 1,900. That number dwindled to less than half and then rose again over the next ten years. By 1837, Simpson reported that the total was over 1,400, but according to labour historian Philip Goldring, this number was actually 1,046.[57] In 1857 the number had risen to about 1,800.[58]

STORIES OF MISPLACED RECORDS

As W. Kaye Lamb noted, "a remarkable proportion of the [Victoria] records and correspondence files have survived, and this is all the more surprising in view of the fact that no special provision was made by the B.C. government for their preservation and care until as late as 1908."[59] In his *Report of the State of the Library and Archives* written in 1934 when Lamb was the BC provincial librarian and archivist, the Legislative Assembly for the Crown colony of Vancouver Island had voted a grant of $1,000 in 1863 for the establishment of a parliamentary library: "For many years the few volumes purchased under this and succeeding grants were housed, unattended, in a single room in the old Parliament Buildings. Those in need of books apparently just walked in and helped themselves."[60]

The first librarian, R.E. Gosnell, appointed in 1893, found an incomplete and disorganized collection. "There were then about 1200 single volumes, principally Dominion and Provincial Sessional Papers, Statutes, Journals, House of Commons and Senate debates, and other official reports, and a few miscellaneous works." By the end of 1897, the task of compiling a catalogue of the library was begun. Gosnell later recalled in an article in the *Daily Colonist* that one of his first jobs was to clean up the litter of accumulated Blue Books and newspapers "with a pitchfork and a wheelbarrow. It had grown hard, almost solid, from years of being trodden on; and what do you suppose I found at the bottom? The original journals of the Vancouver Island Legislature ... and other official documents that had been lost for twenty years." He also recalled that the records room in the provincial secretary's department was a problem: "There was no arrangement of anything. When the shelves had been filled everything was thrown on the floor. The room had never been cleaned or dusted ... since Victoria became the capital of the united colonies, and when every once in a long while a clerk had to go in to attempt to find something, he emerged a mass of dust and dirt, as black as any chimney sweep."[61] Apparently, the chimney of a coal stove used to heat the building ran through the records room.

Stories related years later by Company employees make one marvel that any records survived. The Hudson's Bay Company requested in 1899 and again in 1921 that inventories be made of the records at the various posts. Responses sent to the fur trade commissioner, Clarence Campbell Chipman, indicate that many records were packed up at that time and sent to his office in Winnipeg or, in the case of British Columbia, to Victoria. Later, in 1921, when a concern was expressed by the Company's Canadian office for further information in connection with the incomplete British Columbia district records, a letter from C.H. French,

A selection of Fort Victoria post records (B.226)

district manager at that time, explained that perhaps the Company's officers and staff did not always realize the importance of the records in their care and might have been careless in their management of the records. For example, he himself was party to an unfortunate destruction of records at the time of a visit from Sir Thomas Skinner to the West Coast during his year as governor of the Company, 1914–15:

> [Skinner] instructed that all books and records be sent to the incinerator plant and destroyed, excepting those dealing with the previous ten years business. The execution of this was put in my hands and I have to confess that my instructions were not carried out because I felt that there was nothing contained in these old books that the Company would be ashamed of and in after years they would prove very valuable from an historical point of view. I am now only sorry that more time was not devoted to the task, so that the record retained would have been more complete. As it is, I am afraid that at least half were burned and included in the six drayloads of books which were destroyed at that time.[62]

French went on to suggest other misappropriations: "There are in the archives in Victoria, many records that apparently originally belonged to the Hudson's Bay Company but they had disappeared from the Company's book room long before the cleaning up which we are now talking about, and were not taken by Company's employees but by historians, or would-be historians, who had been given permission to look them over and were unscrupulous enough to carry away those that they particularly wanted."[63] A later letter again explained French's part in salvaging what he could and added more details about the operation: "It seemed to me sacrilegious to burn many of these old journals, log books, etc. and so in a rough way many of them were thrown to one side and practically smuggled to the fur room and there treasured by me until the Hudson's Bay Company's authorities realized their value and were eventually all sent to London."[64]

As a postscript to record-keeping with a distinctive West Coast flavour, F.D. Wilson, who was the clerk in charge of the post at Fort Vermilion from 1897 to about 1908, reminisced years later about the use he made of the old, inactive records:

While I was in charge of Fort Vermilion on the Peace River we operated a Saw Mill and supplied Lumber to Posts up and down the River, on one occasion the cogs on the gear wheels that operated the bull wheel that brought the logs out of the water and hauled them up the jack ladder to a platform level with the saw, got stripped of the cogs and was useless, it would be months before a new one could be brought in, so we had to devise some means to haul the logs up to the saw, we decided to try a friction drive, we had a large flat faced pulley but no friction wheel, one made from wood would slip and be useless, paper if a good quality would do, so we took the paper from four very old ledgers, bolted the paper together with a five inch iron flange on each side, cut the paper down to a six inch pulley with a chisel, having previously made a shaft hole and key seat in the flanges we had only to chisel out the paper and we had a perfect friction pulley that was in use for four seasons. The same device was used at Moose Factory. If you cannot quite catch the idea, ask any Machinist to explain a friction drive, but I trust I have made myself clear.[65]

The Fort Vermilion post records in the HBCA include only eight account books for the years 1822 to 1886.

5

to surrender to Her Majesty

Record-Keeping
in a New Country, 1860–1920

The second half of the nineteenth century was prosperous and provided better conditions of life for the majority of people in Britain. The population was growing, and so was the middle class, with unprecedented numbers in the professions and business. Industry boomed and, with it, advances in transportation and technology. Rail lines traversed the country and steamships plied the oceans. The British Empire expanded to include almost one-fifth of the land on earth.[1] It was a time of efflorescence in the arts and sciences. The first Great Exhibition was held in England in 1851, celebrating British manufacturing and trade. The Hudson's Bay Company exhibited fur specimens, swan and goose quills, and isinglass in the category of manufactures.[2] Of significance to the empire and to the Company was unrest in India and the end of the British East India Company in 1858. Chartered in 1600, that overseas trading company also had a long history of record-keeping which was required of it by its role in governmental administration. The parallels with the HBC are obvious, and the Native unrest that precipitated the demise of the East India Company in 1874 must have been unsettling for HBC officials. Queen Victoria reigned for sixty-four years, ending the century with her grand Diamond Jubilee and then, soon after, died. With her died an era in British history.

Advances in technology were already pointing the way to the fast-paced technological progress we are experiencing more than a hundred years later, at the beginning of the twenty-first century. Communication advanced in several fields. Railways led the way by providing fast, efficient routes connecting distant centres through vast expanses of unsettled territory. The telegraph was invented by Samuel Morse in 1844, and the first telegrams from London were received in Winnipeg in

1871. Alexander Graham Bell invented the telephone in 1876, contributing to expanding instant communication around the world. The invention of the typewriter, though not celebrated quite so universally, took the drudgery out of hand-copying and provided multiple copies of documents without the expense of printing. The HBC purchased its first typewriter for the secretary's office in London, and correspondence sent out from the London office was typed from the beginning of January 1890.[3] More communication and more efficient office equipment, in the end, meant more paper records and the requirement for more office staff. By the end of the century, sophisticated filing systems replaced chronological letterbooks, and vertical filing cabinets replaced flat box files. Women were being trained and hired as stenographers and typists, taking over from the men who had been hand-copiers[4] and radically changing the composition of the office workforce. During the First World, when many male employees left the HBC to join the armed forces, the Company hired women to type and carry out the routine office operations.

It is no longer possible to track the keeping of Company records solely through the minute books, letterbooks, and post journals. The records of the Company during this increasingly complicated period of Canadian history are also those of the Colonial Office, the governments of Upper and Lower Canada and the American territories, other companies promoting a variety of interests, and the individuals involved at all levels of the plans, schemes, and negotiations going on at the time. Original documents or copies of those in the HBCA may be found in Library and Archives Canada, the archives of the provincial governments, the National Archives of the United Kingdom, and various university and private archives in Britain, the United States, and Canada.

In London the governor and Committee of seven, as defined in the Company's original charter and by 1860 representing almost 1,500 stockholders, met at least twice a month. Sir John Henry Pelly had been governor of the Company for thirty years when he died in 1852. After such a long period of stability and continuity, the Company was again on the verge of major changes in its administration and its focus. The next thirty years would see eight governors with terms of only one to six years each.

Edward Roberts, despite being seventy-one in 1860, continued as the accountant for another ten years with the assistance of his son, Edward

Roberts Jr. Roberts claimed, "There is no one in this country that knows more of the accounts of the Company than I do,"[5] and he was probably right. William Gregory Smith was the secretary, and Thomas Fraser the corresponding secretary, having succeeded Eden Colvile in 1858. When Fraser resigned in 1867 in poor health, the duties of secretary were consolidated again, all to be performed by Smith with a salary of £550. Both Roberts and Smith carried on as the Company's accountant and secretary until 1870, in the last years of their careers experiencing immense changes as the Company transmuted from a chartered joint-stock company based solely on an out-of-date fur trade to a public stock business with interests in settlement, land, retail trade, and communications (telegraph and railway), as well as the traditional trade in furs. When Smith retired in 1871 after sixteen years as secretary, William Armit was appointed to the position, which he held until 1893; William Ware then took over to carry the Company into the next century. These are the names researchers find in the minute books and correspondence books of this era.

George Simpson died in 1860, and with him died forty years of authoritative administration in North America. William Mactavish, the governor of Assiniboia, served as acting governor of Rupert's Land for the next two years from his base in Red River, until Alexander Grant Dallas was appointed the new governor-in-chief in 1862.[6] Dallas moved the Company headquarters from Lachine in Quebec, where Simpson had based his operations for thirty years, back to Fort Garry on the Red River. Control of the Montreal Department was left in the charge of Simpson's secretary, Edward Hopkins, and an office in Montreal retained the Company's links with the financial and business community there and in the United States and provided direct access by sea to England.[7] Hopkins was made chief factor and put in charge of the Montreal depot in 1863, a position he held until Donald Smith (later Lord Strathcona) took over in 1869.[8] Dallas was governor for only two years, after which he left the Company and was succeeded by William Mactavish, who became the last governor of Rupert's Land before Confederation.

After the coalition with the North West Company, the HBC's monopoly had trebled, and it continued to monopolize the fur trade as it had for the previous two hundred years. The fur trade remained the raison d'être for most of the Native and the established white and Métis populations, but with a growing emphasis on agriculture and other commercial enterprise. Changes in any of these focal areas were constant, and many more changes would take place before the end of the century.

Demands placed on the Company that it had never had to consider in the past were felt by the officers, whose main focus was still on making money for stockholders in England through the sale of furs.

The large, "modern" trading post and fur depot at Fort Garry served as the Company's inland administrative headquarters after it was built in 1832 near the Red River Settlement. It was also the official residence of the governor-in-chief of Rupert's Land for two years until Simpson moved his residence to Montreal. Fort Garry became the centre for dispatching outfits each spring in brigades of York boats and cargo canoes to the northwest to pick up the furs coming down the North and South Saskatchewan rivers and to deliver them to Hudson Bay for transport to the market in London.[9] Supplies for the fur trade and for the Red River colonists, many of whom worked for the Company, were shipped into Fort Garry from Montreal through the St Lawrence and Ottawa river systems. The officers and clerks of the Company were kept busy year round. They not only had to engage the teams of boatmen, outfit buffalo hunters (primarily Natives and Métis who provided the pemmican, the staple food for the brigades), buy local provisions and import ready-made goods from England, fill the requests from outposts in the district, and outfit and receive the brigades, but they had to keep meticulous account of all these comings, goings, and transactions in the Company's journals and ledgers. The records in the HBCA indicate that the procedures of accounting and documenting the furs trade operations in Rupert's Land continued in the same way as they had in the past, although the Company's trade in furs was definitely in decline as a result of a competitive market. While a more modern business was emerging in London, in Montreal, and even in the increasingly important centre at Red River, the old life continued at the isolated posts throughout the north and the west, still dependent on the lakes and rivers for transportation and the dichotomy of summer/winter activity.

Apprentice clerks learned the proper standards by copying from the old journals. One young recruit from the Orkney Islands, Isaac Cowie, described the process:

I was soon set to work to pen a new set of books. These were a day book, copied in ink from the pencilled blotter which was carried round in the stores, an Indian debt book, a fur receipt book, and one for the receipts and expenditures of provisions. In all these the money and other columns had to be ruled, for the books were all plain horizontally ruled only. At the head of each column in the fur book the names of each kind of skin and whether large or small,

prime or common, were written alphabetically across the double
page, beginning with badgers and ending with wolves; and at the end
of the year the totals of these columns had to tally with the totals of
the "returns of trade" packed for shipment, and if they did not cor-
respond there was a strict investigation.[10]

He went on to describe the "journal of daily occurrences" as

like the log of a ship, supposed to contain a complete record of everything taking place at the post. The weather occupied the first place,
as upon it depended the general business which was all done out in the
open by the hunters and travellers of the establishment ... To a new
man coming to take charge of a post the old journals provided a mine
of most useful information for his guidance in the management of the
routine work as well as the insight it, along with the Indian debt book,
gave him of the character and capabilities of the people.[11]

Each summer the journals and account books of the post's activities
over the previous year were still transported with the furs by canoe,
York boat and ship to London, where they were perused, digested, and
reconciled. Cowie, who went on to serve as a clerk at various posts
from 1867 to 1873, described the process of closing off the books for
the year-end and getting them to London:

The end of each business year – called "Outfit" – was May 31, upon
which date the inventory of everything belonging to the Company at
the fort was taken ... [the clerks] worked from dawn to dark till everything was weighed, measured and counted, both outside and inside the
establishment ... Once the list of merchandise, etc., and articles in use
had been made in pencil it became my task, day and night, to recapitu-
late them in alphabetical order under the various headings, and enter
the result duly priced in the post account book for Outfit 1867. To get
that book complete so as to find out the apparent gain or loss on the
year's trade before the time came for the boatmen to start for the annual voyage to York Factory took up all my time.[12]

THE INTERNATIONAL FINANCIAL SOCIETY

By mid-century the emphasis in North America had shifted to colonization and settlement, with pressures exerted on the Company from several

Isaac Cowie's contract, 1867 (E.86/1, fo. 4), and Fort Ellice post journal written by Cowie (B.63/a/9, fo. 2)

directions. American pressures pushed northward toward the abundant and fertile plains of what are now Manitoba and Saskatchewan. Communication lines, – roads, railways, and telegraph – from the east pushed through the Company's land towards the west. And these pressures did not always come from outside the Company. As in the past, HBC investors held diversified portfolios, favourites at this time being the Grand Trunk Railway and the British North American Association, which were proposing telegraphic communication across the whole width of North America. Conversely, stockholders in these modern companies could see that acquiring control in the HBC could simplify the process of obtaining access to and through the territory long monopolized by the Company.

The colonial secretary in Lord Palmerston's government was Henry Pelham Fiennes Pelham-Clinton, Duke of Newcastle, while from 1858 to 1863 Henry Hulse Berens was the governor of the Company. These two men were brought together by the persuasive Edward Watkin, president of the Grand Trunk Railway, advocate of a transcontinental telegraph, and imperialist supporter, along with another interested party, Sir Edmund Head, who had been lieutenant-governor of New Brunswick from 1848 to 1854 and then governor general of Canada until 1861. Head and Watkin turned out to be the key players in removing the obstacles created by the HBC to allowing the British North American colonies to form the Dominion of Canada in 1867. The Company had always been a factor to consider in any scheme of settlement, trade, or development in or through the Northwest. The requirements of both the railway and telegraph supporters depended on cutting a wide swath through the Company's territory. The freeing up of the fur trade monopoly, the welfare of the Aboriginal and Métis populations, and some form of governmental control over the area were also issues needing attention in any discussions or negotiations for territorial expansion. When pressure from these enterprises took hold the Colonial Office acted as intermediary, but not always as an impartial bystander.[13]

At a series of meetings in July and August 1862 between the Company and representatives of the Colonial Office, Watkin and Newcastle requested Berens to provide an estimate of the monetary value of the Company so that a buyout could be considered. The eventual purchase of the HBC by the International Financial Society in June 1863, with the approval of stockholders, changed the face and direction of the Company. The society was a recently formed syndicate made up of businessmen and financiers, including Watkin, whose purpose was "the undertaking, assisting, and participating in financial, commercial, and industrial operations, both in England and abroad, and both singly and in connection with other persons, firms, companies and corporations,"[14] and it immediately introduced the Company to "the active world of international finance and politics."[15] The Company retained its name and charter, and Head was made the first chairman of the board, still called the governor. The emphasis of the "new" company was the opening up of Rupert's Land to colonization. The prospectus offered share certificates of £20 each to a total of

£1,930,000, stating: "It has become evident that the time has arrived that those operations [of the Company] must be extended, and the immense resources of the Company's Territory, lying as it does between Canada and British Columbia, should be developed in accordance with the industrial spirit of the age, and the rapid advancement which colonization has made in the countries adjacent to the Hudson Bay territories."[16]

Within a month, shares were offered on the open market and the Company was under the control of 1,700 stockholders, up from 1,500 three years earlier. The International Financial Society passed the torch to the stockholders and went on to other ventures. Through all of this wheeling and dealing, the staff in the London office were the same tradition-bound crew, some of whom had been there for fifty years. Watkin wrote about his first meeting with the governor and Committee of the HBC in 1862 in a colourful description of the offices and staff. The meeting took place on the first of December at Hudson's Bay House on Fenchurch Street:

> The room was the "Court" room, dark and dirty. The faded green
> cloth, old chairs almost black, and a fine portrait of Prince Rupert.
> We met the Governor, Berens, Eden Colvile, and Lyell only. On
> our part there were Mr. G.G. Glyn (the present Lord Wolverton),
> Captain Glyn (the late Admiral Henry Glyn), and Messrs. New-
> march, Benson, Blake, and myself. Mr. Berens, an old man and obsti-
> nate, bearing a name to be found in the earliest lists of Hudson's
> Bay shareholders, was somewhat insulting in his manner.[17]

From this description the reader is given the impression that it was indeed time for the Company to change. And in fact, if Watkin and the International Financial Society had not come along, it is perhaps possible that the old fur trade company would have been trampled in the rush of modern business and of colonization and expansion in North America. Watkin was introduced to the accountant, seventy-five year-old Edward Roberts, who showed him the books and told him "many odd things." A year later, after a complete inspection, the auditors reported on Roberts's record-keeping: "We have received every assistance from Mr. Roberts, your valued Accountant, in conduction of the Audit, and although the Books of the Company exhibit a special system, they are very regularly and carefully kept."[18]

International Financial Society, 1863: Memorandum of Agreement for the society, represented by Edward William Watkin and Richard Potter, to purchase the shares of the HBC;
prospectus; and notice to shareholders of opportunity to sell at a considerable profit (F.27/1)

Two years after the purchase, the Fenchurch Street premises were prov-
ing to be inadequate, and the Company entered into an agreement with
the London and St Katherine's Dock Company for the lease of the former
East India Company offices and warehouse, nearby at the corner of Lime
and Leadenhall streets.[19] For the next sixty years, the HBC address was
No. 1 Lime Street, where its offices faced the headquarters of the P & O
Steamship Company. The Lime Street building was elegant and spacious
with three storeys above the ground floor, which was rented out, and a
basement. The boardroom, on the first floor, with its lofty ceiling and antique furniture, was reached by an impressive stone staircase. "Ancient
and rare books of reference and of travel were to be found in the glass-
fronted book-cases and on the walls hung oil paintings and pictures of
peculiar interest to the HBC."[20] Next to it was an anteroom that was
used as a private office by Lord Strathcona when he was governor. The
next floor up housed the secretary's office and the transfer department.
Above that, on the top floor, were the accountant's office and the typists'
room. The fur warehouse was in the same building but separate, with
thick walls and small windows. It had eight "decks," which were accessed by a hydraulic lift for goods or by a stone stairway for personnel.[21]

Even after the move to the Lime Street premises the general courts continued to be held in the boardroom at Fenchurch Street until that building was sold in 1870. With so many stockholders, larger facilities were required, and even the new facilities at Lime Street could not accommodate such a crowd. The meetings were consequently held at two locations, either the City Terminus Hotel on Cannon Street or the London Tavern on Bishopsgate Street. The new Company, with the same structure as the old one (a governor and seven committee members, who were all also active in the world of international finance and politics), was eager to get on with a new approach to the business of settlement and trade in North America. Stockholders were kept informed by annual reports from the directors of the Company, as required by the Joint Stock Companies Act. A workforce of almost seven hundred chief factors, chief traders, clerks, and general workers still manned the posts spread throughout the north and northwest of the country.[22] When the negotiations between the International Financial Society and the old HBC were taking place and changes in operations were being made, these Rupert's Land employees were pretty well left out of the discussion, though they continued receiving directives from London. With so much attention in London being paid to the big picture, it was inevitable that the more mundane operation of the fur trade would be somewhat neglected. Within a few years the neglect in record-keeping procedures was obviously a concern, as is indicated in a letter from the secretary to the chief factor at Moose Factory in June 1867:

> I am directed to state that in former times duplicates of the Reports
> from Gentlemen in charge of Posts and districts to the Governor of
> Rupert's Land were sent home annually for the information of the
> Governor and Committee, but that of late years the practice has fallen
> into disuse – The Board being of opinion that it would be greatly to the
> advantage of the Company's interests if it was revived, I am directed to
> request that you will give the necessary directions of this purpose to all
> the gentlemen in your Department who have charge of Districts.[23]

There are few records of the buyout of the Company for study in the HBCA. In fact, historians have noted that they are "disappointingly meagre."[24] Events and decisions can be pieced together from the always informative minute books, the correspondence books, the private letter-books, and the correspondence with government departments. Newspapers such as the London *Times* also reported on the events. Watkin

Old East India Company building on Lime Street, occupied by
the HBC from 1866 to 1924 (1987-363-H-42-5)

published his memoirs in 1887 as *Canada and the United States; Recollections, 1851–1886* with his side of the story. The colonial secretary's
papers in the National Archives in England contain information from the
Colonial Office, along with all the other events occurring in colonial
North America that occupied the officials and staff at the time.

The Company's minute books indicate a continued pattern of weekly
meetings for the Committee, except during the summer recess from August to October. Decisions are recorded succinctly in the minutes without details of the discussions. The first annual report, for the year
ending 31 May 1866, announced a profit for the stockholders as a result of high prices for the furs sold that year. The report included sections on the Company's ships, the depressed trade on Vancouver
Island, and the ongoing process of arbitration with the United States in
the Oregon Treaty process. The governor's report discussed the "future
policy of the Company":

It has become necessary for us to discuss at some length the question whether colonization on a large scale ought to be undertaken by the Hudson's Bay Company. We have been charged with losing sight of the promises made in this prospectus, which undoubtedly stated that the southern portion of the territory would be thrown open for settlement. How far we are answerable for not having carried out a scheme of this kind will be best understood by a consideration of what we have done, and of what is really required for effectually executing any such project.[25]

The business would never again be what in retrospect was the simple routine of the fur trade – annual export from London of goods and personnel to match the annual bountiful export from Hudson Bay of luxurious and much-sought-after furs. The pressure of settlement on Rupert's Land, of American expansion pushing north, and of unrest among the Aboriginal population (whose members were unable to conceive of the notion of territorial expansion on lands previously open to their roaming) all encroached on the peace generally experienced at the Company's relatively isolated posts. The Province of Canada (resulting from the union of Lower and Upper Canada in 1840) was also growing larger and more prosperous and developing politically, socially, and industrially.

Negotiations between the Company and the Colonial Office continued throughout the late 1860s to establish administrative and governmental control of the settlements in the territories belonging to the Company. At the centre of the concerns were the 10,000 inhabitants of the Red River area, the majority Métis but many of them retired Company families and Scottish immigrants.[26] Removing the responsibility of governance from the Company's officers would allow them to proceed with the more profitable work of trade. At the same time the government of the Province of Canada was negotiating for a general federation to include the Maritimes and what was now referred to as the North-West, an expanded Rupert's Land. The British Parliament was aware that its best defence against the inevitable encroachment of the United States onto British territory in North America would be a federation.[27] In March 1867 the British North America Act was enacted to provide for a Canadian federation that included admitting Rupert's Land.[28] By July, with Confederation and the formation of the Dominion of Canada, the autonomy and powers of the HBC over the vast territory defined in its charter had succumbed to the force of settlement, which would be even further encouraged later in the century by the building of the Canadian Pacific Railway. Emphasis on the fur trade was replaced by an increasing requirement from the settlers for goods for which they paid in cash. When the Company ceded its territories in 1870, it found itself paying more attention to the distribution of land. On 22 June 1869 the Rupert's Land Act provided provisional government to the area,[29] and two years later the Manitoba Act superseded it with special provisions under the British North America Act to establish the province of Manitoba as the fourth province of Canada. On 23 June 1870, at the court at Windsor, Queen Victoria issued an order-in-council admitting Rupert's Land and the North-Western Territory into the Dominion of Canada in accordance with the terms of surrender that had been reluctantly accepted by the HBC in November of the previous year. The Deed of Surrender (schedule C of the above imperial order) was essentially a guarantee of the continuance of the Company's trade without hindrance and with no special taxes or tariffs. Although not as dramatic or artistic a document physically, the Deed is as vivid in its wording and its consequences for the HBC as the original charter, which continued as the Company's right to trade in the new country of Canada.

With the transfer of Rupert's Land to the Dominion of Canada, the Company was paid £300,000. It retained all of its posts and an adjoining block of land as determined by the governor-in-council and the Company, not to exceed 50,000 acres. It could also claim, over the next fifty years, grants of land up to a total of one-twentieth of the fertile belt defined by the United States – Canada border, the Rocky Mountains, the North Saskatchewan River, Lake Winnipeg, and Lake of the Woods. "With all convenient speed," all of this land had to be surveyed into ownership lots, and the Company had the right to retain or sell its deed of title as it saw fit. Its right to continue its trade was confirmed, but the fur trade dominance of the "old" Company was almost immediately overpowered by the advancement of settlement, the sale of land, and the progress of the railway through the new dominion.[30]

LORD STRATHCONA

A dominant character in this next phase of the Company's history was Donald Smith, who had joined the Company as an apprentice clerk and had thirty years' experience as a fur trader, most recently as president of the Northern Department, based at Fort Garry. He had been in London during the 1869 negotiations between the Company and the

Deed of Surrender, 1869 (A.37/19)

Colonial Office for the Deed of Surrender. When he returned to Canada that year, he took charge of the Montreal Department, which, as already noted, had been under the supervision of Edward Hopkins since Simpson's death in 1860.

As a commissioned officer in the fur trade, Smith was affected by the conditions of the Deed of Surrender, which interfered with the partnership agreement with the Company set out in the Deed Poll. That agreement provided remuneration for the commissioned officers based on the fur trade profits, an obvious encouragement to work harder and reap the benefits of a lucrative trade. With the Deed of Surrender, the emphasis on land and general trade took precedence over the trade in furs. The fur trade was to be carried on in the northern areas, which were generally unfit for settlement, while the more accessible land in the south was made available for colonization. The Company's new diversified focus, which had a hint of abandoning the fur trade altogether, combined with a fluctuating world economy, increased emphasis at the posts on carrying out governmental responsibilities, and in some years a decrease in the availability of furs resulted in low profits from the fur trade. The Company was really the only organized entity in the remote Northwest; in fact, it was the chief administrative unit everywhere outside the developing major centres, which were few and far between. No profit meant no pay for the commissioned officers or the shareholders. After two consecutive years of no profit, 1877 and 1878, an amendment was written into the Deed Poll which provided a minimum dividend each year to each partner together with the establishment of a Fur Trade Officers Reserve Fund to be distributed as required at the discretion of the governor and Committee.[31] The last meeting of the "wintering partners" was held in Winnipeg in 1887, and the profit-sharing ended in 1893. No new commissions were offered, and the fur traders became salaried employees.

Sir Stafford Northcote was the Company's new governor (1869–74), and he chose Smith, who was also a friend and confidant of Sir John A. Macdonald, as his chief adviser. Smith represented the Company during the intricate negotiations between the Canadian government and Red River delegates in early 1870 following the Red River Resistance. Northcote travelled from London to Ottawa to support Smith in the negotiation process and to witness for himself the complex situation in order to be able to report accurately to the British government.[32] Of course, Ottawa was a long way from the Red River, but at least he had made his way to North America, the first Company governor to do so. He and Smith spent time together discussing the changing circumstances in the country, the Company's future strategy, and how to reorganize to increase profitability.[33] After his return to London, Northcote appointed Cyril Graham (who had been secretary to the colonial secretary during the parliamentary approval of the British North America Act) to investigate first-hand the situation and business in North America and to provide an independent report. Northcote's instructions were provided in a letter to Graham written in October 1870:

> The Committee of the Hudson's Bay Company have learnt with pleasure that you are willing to proceed to Canada and to visit Rupert's Land this Autumn, and to afford them your assistance in the present position of the Company's affairs ... Amongst the questions which present themselves are these: – Under what supreme executive authority should our staff be placed? It cannot be efficiently directed from London. Should it be placed under a Governor or Superintendent directly appointed by and responsible to, the London Board? and if so, what should be the limits of his authority and his

relations to the other officers, with regard to matters of discipline, promotion of servants, regulation of trade, and so forth? – or should any attempt be made to organize a Committee of Management either at Montreal, Fort Garry or elsewhere in America? Or, should different arrangements be made with regard to different portions of the business; e.g. should the superintendence of the Banking, Land dealing, and general commercial departments be put into different hands from those intrusted with the management of the Fur Trade?[34]

Graham's reports, along with Northcote's observations during the trip to Ottawa, formed the basis for his plan for restructuring the HBC in Canada. The reorganization of the fur trade would have to consider seriously advances in the technologies of rail and steam. The long-range business plan presented to the general court in London in June 1871 introduced one of several successive reorganizations of the "new" Company's revised operations in North America. Northcote's plan concluded:

The points to which I think it desirable that the Board should devote attention are chiefly these:
1. The expediency of reorganising the fur trade, and revising our arrangements with our wintering partners.
2. The expediency of seeking the cooperation of capitalists residing in Canada.
3. The expediency of undertaking Banking business.[35]

The plan included the appointment of Donald Smith as the Company's chief commissioner in Canada in place of the old position of governor-in-chief of Rupert's Land. He was to be located at Upper Fort Garry, near the soon-to-be-booming community of Winnipeg, which was incorporated as a city in 1873.

The frequent reorganizations that the Company went through after 1863 parallel its changing role and the frequent turnover of governors in London at this time. Northcote, the first governor after the Deed of Surrender, held the position for five years. In 1874 he returned to his political career and was succeeded by George J. Goschen, a director of the Bank of England and First Lord of the Admiralty under Prime Minister William Gladstone,[36] whose vision for the Company clearly included expansion of the land side of the business. The administrative organization in Canada was shifted again when Smith was named land commissioner and James Grahame was moved from Victoria[37] to Smith's old but significant position as chief commissioner. An office was established in Montreal from which to manage the Company's land business interests in an effort to separate this new venture from the fur trade, headquarterd at Fort Garry. It also separated the fur traders from any subsidiary profits. As land commissioner, Smith reported directly to the governor and Committee in London, making his position parallel to Grahame's. Montreal was the financial centre of Canada at that time. It was also a port with direct access to London, a rail terminus with access to the west and the United States, and within a few hours' travel of Ottawa, the capital of the new Dominion of Canada.

Smith's record-keeping, especially when it came to accounting, was a point of contention throughout his career. As a young clerk at Mingan, Smith, who had completed his apprenticeship, had his work reviewed by George Simpson:

> Your Countinghouse department appeared to me in a very slovenly condition, so much so, that I could make very little of any document that came under my notice. Your schemes of outfits were really curiously perplexing, & such as I trust I may never see again, while letters, invoices and accounts were to be found tossing about as waste paper in almost every room of the house. I am aware that, during the pressure of summer business, you have not much time to devote to the neat arrangement of papers, but your winters are very long with little or no out-door work to occupy your attention; and if you were but to give a few hours a week to the arrangement of your papers, your bureau would be in a very different state to that in which I found it.[38]

Thirty years later, Smith was reminded by Governor Northcote that the lack of reports from his office had proved embarrassing:

> It seems to us that you must require help in order to keep all the details of the business in proper order. You have an enormous amount of work upon your hands, more than one man can be expected to do without assistance. I was cross-questioned at the [shareholders'] meeting as to the Land Sales and was rather embarrassed by the fact that we had received so little information from you. I did, however, give some particulars, which had for the most part been gleaned from the newspapers. I hope they were substantially right.[39]

And again in 1878, just before he resigned from the Company's service, Smith was chastised by the Committee, in a letter from Armit, for his lack of attention in keeping the London office informed: "Looking at the small amount of work connected with the accounts of the Land Department it was hoped that the details would have been promptly and regularly rendered, but as the Committee are again disappointed in this respect, they direct me to state that a minute was passed directing your special attention to the matter and calling upon you in future to render the accounts in question regularly."[40] Grahame, on the other hand, had taken to heart his five years of apprenticeship, and his aptitude had provided him with rapid promotions and increasing responsibilities.

THE LAND COMMISSIONER

For various reasons, including a depressed economy in North America and in Europe, the land sales business did not take off immediately. Smith's personal interests had broadened into investments, politics, and particularly the railway. He resigned from the Company in 1879. A land office was built in Winnipeg, and Charles John Brydges was appointed land commissioner. He had been general manager of the Grand Trunk Railway under Edward Watkin and was recommended by Sir John Rose, who was Prime Minister Sir John A. Macdonald's finance minister from 1869 to 1870. Rose was a member of the London Committee and soon became deputy governor. Brydges's appointment to such a position of responsibility from outside the ranks of the Company was a step towards separating management from ownership, a new concept in business structure introduced at the end of the nineteenth century.[41] His approach to the management of the Land Department was modern, active, aggressive, and planned. The pace certainly picked up, and his years as land commissioner, from 1879 to 1889, were some of the most exciting in the Company's history.

Brydges outlined his records management strategy in a letter to Armit: "I have asked Mr. Smith to take with us to Winnipeg, all the information in his possession, in regard to lands other than the twentieth portion belonging to the Company, so that we may start a register of all the lands we have to sell, and make the necessary preparations for bringing them on the market. There does not appear to be anything of the kind at present, and it will evidently take some months before we shall be in a position to offer the lands to purchasers."[42] He also recommended the addition of a surveyor to his staff in order "to complete these registers and to get up such plans and information as necessary in order to put proposing purchasers in a position to know what we have to sell."[43]

Within a week of arriving in Winnipeg, Brydges and Grahame sent plans and estimates to Armit for a new building for the Land Department. The Company's fur-trading post, retail store, and officers in Winnipeg were housed in the buildings on the site of Upper Fort Garry. The main post and governor's residence were still a few miles north at the larger Lower Fort Garry. The Land Department office was "a miserable single room, for which $300 a year rent is paid, but is hardly big enough to turn around in."[44] The proposed two-storey building would be situated next to the Dominion Lands Office on Main Street and would include a room to conduct business, a separate but small living space, and "a proper fire proof vault for the safe custody of the books, agreements etc."[45] There was also discussion at this time of a new building, also on Main Street, for the Company's trading establishment. That building, including a retail store and offices for the Fur Trade Department, would open in 1881.

Brydges was assisted in the Winnipeg lands office by an accountant, John Balsillie, who had started his career with the department as an apprentice clerk and was a chief trader with experience in the Red River district when he was appointed to set up the office for Smith in 1872. An accountant was definitely a requirement, as tens of thousands of dollars a month moved through the office during the most active years of the land boom. Brydges soon hired John Dennis Jr, a surveyor whose father had been surveyor general of Dominion Lands and in 1878 was deputy minister of the Interior.[46] During the summer of 1879 Brydges and Dennis began the first of nine annual surveys which would document the land holdings of the Company throughout the Northwest. As Hartwell Bowsfield, editor of Brydges's correspondence for the Hudson's Bay Record Society, explains, "This body of personally gathered information formed an important part of other major survey projects commissioned by Brydges. Together, they provided the foundation for the Company's reputation as a dependable source of information for the immigrant – and for governments and private commercial interests alike."[47]

Brydges's first annual inspection report was submitted to the secretary in September 1879. It is full of details recorded during almost a month "on the road" observing not only the Company's holdings but also the climate, soil conditions, agriculture, mining and business potential, Native conditions, current and prospective settlement patterns, and comments and observations from personal interviews with Company

The Hudson's Bay Company land office on Main Street in
Winnipeg about 1880 (1987-363-w-200-8)

employees, settlers, and other businessmen. Brydges's enthusiasm for the
job was obvious: "I am afraid I shall have wearied everybody by so long
a letter, and I am probably only repeating what the Committee have
heard before, but I have been so greatly impressed with what I have seen
during the last four weeks, that I could not avoid the temptation of making a record of as much as possible."[48]

The survey report followed in a few months.[49] On his own initiative, Brydges immediately published a pamphlet, *Manitoba and the
North-West, The Great Wheat Fields, and Stock-Raising Districts of
Canada: Facts and Information for Settlers with a Map of the Country.* Although he had been given a mandate to manage the Land Department at his discretion, the governor was not impressed by this
unauthorized expenditure for advertising the Company's land for sale.
He felt the Canadian government should be the agent for immigration
and the advertising costs should be its.[50] Brydges's zeal for his job
were not to be curbed, but he required every ounce of energy during
the next two land-boom years in Winnipeg. He built and opened the
new office and hired and managed the clerks, accountant, and full-
and part-time surveyors, all of whom had to work as sales agents
when the office was busy.

Various land records, including *Manitoba and the North-West* (1879), a brochure distributed by the Dominion of Canada to provide "facts and information for settlers, with a map of the country" (PP1879-3); and HBC land sales registers, 1872–79 (RG1/1-21)

Over the next ten years, as fortunes flowed and ebbed, the office staff were augmented or reduced as directed by the London office. And they were not immune to activity going on around them. Commissioner Grahame reported to Armit in 1882 that "the inflated condition of Real Estate" was "producing its effect" on the staff of clerks, "several of whom find themselves in possession of more wealth than they ever anticipated and carried away by the tide," were leaving the Company's service, "expecting to do better for themselves … It is quite impossible to get our employees to refrain from speculating in Real Estate."[51] Brydges himself was under constant observation for land speculation on his own behalf or for assisting others and was investigated and summoned to London to appear before the governor and Committee on more than one occasion. Maintaining the records in order also kept them all busy. In December 1880 Brydges reported that "statements are getting very voluminous, and, excepting in the dead months of winter, are likely to be continually increasing. I need hardly say that it requires a great deal of care to prevent errors arising; and next year it will be necessary to have an accountant employed in Winnipeg, specially to attend to the books – the transactions now becoming so very numerous."[52]

This activity continued over the next two years. "The arrival of emigrants is assuming gigantic proportions, and I begin to be alarmed at what we shall do with the crowds that are coming in. About 3,000 arrived in the City yesterday."[53] Brydges had to rent the "largest room we could get in the city" to hold an auction of land in April 1882, after the land office was inundated with eager buyers the day before. The land office had to be renovated to accommodate the crowds when "it was an every day occurrence to see files of men waiting to, in their turn, reach the limited counter room to make the enquiries they desired."[54] The same scenario was playing out every day at the Dominion Lands Office next door and the nearby Canadian Pacific Railway land office.

These were rapidly changing times for the Company, and many of the administrative procedures developed and set up by Brydges remained the standard beyond his ten years as land commissioner. Unfortunately, long-term control of the Company's records for this period was lost in the rush of expansion and diversification. Many transient records and correspondence of the Land Department were destroyed in later reorganizations. The remaining financial records, ledgers, and registers of farm lands and town lots are classified in two separate series in the HBCA. Western Department land records, classified as "H," contain deeds, ledgers, registers, and other documents regarding land in British Columbia, on Vancouver Island, and in Victoria dating from 1851 to 1889. Land Department records from the office in Winnipeg are classified as Record Group 1 (RG1) and date from 1871 to about 1969. There are virtually no records of the land commissioner's office during Donald Smith's tenure, and any that are written in his hand are almost impossible to read because of his illegible handwriting.

Brydges revised and developed forms to facilitate the registry of land. In January 1880 he sent a sample of the forms of deed, which he requested the London office to have printed up with the amendments as shown:

I enclose you one of the forms of deed, and shall be obliged if you will have printed and sent to me a supply altered in the way which I have marked the enclosed. The present one is simply for the City of Winnipeg; and we shall be wanting to give deeds for town lots in other places, and also for farm lands, the enclosed form if adopted will answer for every thing except Winnipeg. I want the blanks left as shewn, so that in the event of the sale being to more than one person, it can be properly filled in, instead of altering the printed part. I think it would be well if you are having them printed to send me a good supply of these.[55]

Each deed was sent to London for attachment of the Company seal. These would be stamped and then returned to the land office for distribution to the owners.

Brydges's regular overseas correspondence, averaging a letter every week or two, was made possible by modern transportation – trains across the country and steamships across the Atlantic. A letter dated in London on 17 November 1880 was responded to by Brydges in Winnipeg on the 9th of December, just over three weeks later. Railway lines connecting the eastern seaports to the central continent moved the mail quickly to and from Pembina, just across the American border, about 100 kilometres. south of Winnipeg, and by 1885 the CPR had reached Winnipeg with regular service. Telegraph cable had been laid to Winnipeg by 1871; so more urgent requests and replies were transmitted by the Company through that means.

Brydges was regularly criticized for his management of land sales and requested to explain procedures and staffing in the land office. Although his allegiance to the Company was solid enough, there was always the question of land speculation by Company employees and a long-standing animosity between Brydges and Smith.[56] Brydges and Grahame both generated such accusations. As a result, three Company officials – Deputy Governor Sir John Rose, board member Sandford Fleming, and Company secretary William Armit – visited Canada in 1882 to provide first-hand reports to the governor and Committee in London. Although generally favourable, they corroborated mismanagement in the Land Department and recommended administrative changes in Canada. In March 1883 Colvile asked Grahame to resign, with the condition that he stay on until he could be replaced by "a younger and more active man." That younger man was Thomas R. Smith, the assistant secretary to Armit in the London office,[57] who was sent to Winnipeg as temporary manager of the Red River district and manager of the new store on Main Street. He did not report to Commissioner Grahame; instead, he reported to London through the new subcommittee. Colvile had decided to tighten control by establishing a subcommittee in Canada to supervise the local affairs of the Company, with a view to the better regulation and management of its business abroad.

THE TRADE COMMISSIONER

The Canadian subcommittee, consisting of Donald Smith and Sandford Fleming, was to be based in Montreal, and Brydges was instructed to submit copies of all correspondence, reports, and any documents regarding the sale and disposition of lands he sent to London to the Canadian subcommittee. With this corporate shift of power in a reorganized Canadian management, the Company moved another step towards diversification and further away from its roots solely as a fur trader. It was becoming a modern corporation, responding to the expansion and quickened pace brought about by the new technologies of steam and rail. Land sales and the retail trade were growing, but the fur trade continued to provide the profits required to keep all the operations viable and to provide dividends for shareholders. Instead of replacing Grahame with another chief commissioner, the Company appointed Joseph Wrigley as trade commissioner, a position that reflected the growing emphasis on commercial operations. Like Brydges, Wrigley came from outside the Company. He was not a commissioned officer like Smith or Grahame, who had worked their way up through the ranks of the fur trade, and he was not a shareholder. His background was in the textile industry in England.[58]

An organizational chart for the Company in Canada in the 1880s provides a view of the diversification and decentralizing of its management. The key reporting was through the subcommittee to London.

ORGANIZATIONAL CHART FOR THE 1880s
Hudson's Bay Company (London)
    Eden Colvile, governor
    William Armit, secretary
    George Roberts, accountant
Canadian Subcommittee (Montreal)
    Donald Smith
    Sandford Fleming
Trade Commissioner (Winnipeg)
    Joseph Wrigley
Land Commissioner (Winnipeg)
    Charles Brydges
Assistant Trade Commissioner (Victoria)
    Thomas Smith
    Fur Trade Posts

The three main centres of business activity were in Montreal, Winnipeg, and Victoria, with the fur trade posts, even York Factory and Norway House, relegated to a position of lesser importance. This shift was reinforced when, within a few short months of his appointment, Wrigley found himself caught up in the early stirrings of what would become known as the Northwest Rebellion. The Company, the dominion government, and the Canadian Pacific Railway would, within the next two years, attempt to work together to maintain what order they could while the Métis made one last desperate attempt under the leadership of Louis Riel to obtain legal rights to land they had long occupied. The HBC's concerns were based on protecting its fur trade interests as the Natives sympathized with the Métis cause. The Canadian government asked the Company to act as its principal agent for provisioning and transporting the troops being sent to suppress the rebellion. The Company was well set up for the retail trade, with local suppliers as well as wholesale contacts in major centres in the United States, and its system of transport was well established along the North Saskatchewan River, where most of the unrest was centred. All of this ready-made infrastructure was necessary when as many as 4,500 troops were in the field at one time and operations took on a massive scale.[59] In June 1885, towards the end of the campaign, Wrigley's report to Secretary Armit provides some idea of the Company's involvement: "there has been received about a million dollars. Further requirements are likely to reach another half million dollars. It is difficult to ascertain the profit but as well as can be calculated there should be from £15,000 to £20,000. I trust the Board will think that a satisfactory result for the Company. Certainly the Government would have spent considerably more if it had not been for the assistance of the Company."[60]

The Company's final bill to the dominion government for supplies and services amounted to almost $80,000. After some negotiation with the commission that had been set up to handle the war claims and three years of accounting and detailed paper work, the Company received $65,471.05 from the dominion government.[61] But no payment would compensate for the almost two years' interruption to the fur trade. The Company also experienced loss of property because of militia activities and loss of land sales as a result of the disruption of immigration to area. And as a further result affecting shareholders far from the scene of the rebellion, no annual dividend was paid on Company stock that year. If one were to consider the staff time and use of Company facilities, there was little in the way of profit. Wrigley received some recognition for his timely, efficient, and energetic role from Adolphe Caron, minister of Militia and Defence, who reported to Parliament: "I question whether, if it had not been for the help given to the Department by the Hudson's Bay Company and the valuable assistance given us by Mr. Wrigley ... it would not have been impossible to achieve what we have achieved."[62] The trade commissioner's correspondence with government officials and his explanations and requests for authority to the governor in London, together with the account books, provide an interesting context for government and military records of this significant event in Canadian history. Other records include telegrams to and from London and Ottawa and requisitions and vouchers recording all the transport and provisioning contracts. Associated records are also found among the London correspondence, the commissioners' records, and the post records for Winnipeg and Prince Albert.

Wrigley returned to the job of establishing a Trade Department for the Company. In 1885 he had under his management the fur trade posts in the northern, southern, Montreal, and western departments, as well as all of the saleshops. He had begun his management of the Fur Trade Department with a tour of inspection that took him to many of the posts across the prairies and also to the Western Department and Victoria. Throughout his years as trade commissioner, Wrigley continued these visits and he also set up a system by which regular inspections were made of key areas and particular posts.[63] His report to the governor and Committee in 1888 made several recommendations resulting from his observations.[64]

As for the accounting procedures, the simple system that had been in place for many years was sufficient for the fur trade, but it was not appropriate for the mercantile business of the saleshops. The accounting process itself was adequate, but the volume of business from saleshops required more detail for stock control. Wrigley advised that a person with some bookkeeping or accounting experience would be required to introduce the changes to "accounts and financial arrangements." The reporting process from post to department to London could be simplified if more responsibility was taken in the department for the details and only quarterly summaries and a simplified balance sheet sent to London. The inspection reports received between 1880 and 1892, classified as D.25/1–12, provided the information required for the Company to determine its return on capital investments at the fur trade posts over those years. Gone were the days when profit was measured by fur sales once a year.[65]

The records of the commissioner's office, including those of the Canadian subcommittee, are classified in the HBCA in Section D. Grahame developed a distinct group of records for the office. Wrigley continued that administrative style and introduced a more formal system for the submission of accounts, reports, and other documents from the department and district offices. The commissioner's records include correspondence received and sent by that office, as well as the inward and outward correspondence registers, synopses, and indices. Copies of outward correspondence were kept in bound letterbooks, while correspondence inward from both HBC and non-HBC sources was kept as loose pages in file boxes. As a result of the careful record-keeping set up in the early years by the London office, there are nearly complete duplicate series of this correspondence.

Wrigley was dismissed in 1891, as a result partly of failing health and partly from the change in philosophy when Smith took over as governor of the Company in 1889. In response to his dismissal, Wrigley summarized his term as trade commissioner by referring to the records he had created during those seven years in a letter to Armit:

> When I first came out I did not find in the Commissioner's Office anything to help me. There were no statements, no balance-sheets, no information, and no system. A perfect stranger I had to begin to learn probably one of the most intricate businesses in existence. Without troubling the Board with details, I assert that now I have so systematized accounts and statements that cover every Saleshop, and I may add every Post, the Commissioner has control, and by learning the various difficulties in the trade and visiting as many Districts as I could I have such a knowledge of the business as is possessed by few, if any. I think my letters on Inspection Reports, and Memoranda on Accounts, could not be written without an intimate knowledge of the business, nor could the comprehensive Report, which was drawn up in 1888, containing for the first time most important facts and figures necessary for the correct understanding of the business, have been written without a thorough knowledge of the trade.[66]

William Clark served as acting trade commissioner for a few months until Clarence Campbell Chipman arrived in Winnipeg to take over. A native of Nova Scotia, Chipman had served as private secretary to Charles Tupper between 1884 and 1890, when Tupper was high commissioner for Canada in London and finance minister in Ottawa. Chipman was chief clerk in the Department of Marine and Fisheries in Ottawa when he was appointed to the position with the HBC.[67] He had close links with Donald Smith through his political connections, and it was under the governor's mandate that he set about, in the interest of economy, central-izing the Company's divergent interests – land sales, fur trade, and re-tail.[68] He took over the job in May 1891, and by September he was recommending major changes for the various districts. A month later Chipman provided the governor and Committee with a proposal, clearly laid out with objectives, method, advantages, and disadvantages, for re-vamping the accounting procedure from the fur trade–based "outfit" to a more business-oriented yearly account. The year-end would be 31 May, with all districts completing an inventory for that date. Winnipeg would be the head office for the Company in Canada, responsible for receiving reports from all the districts and presenting one "fur trade account" to the London office for presentation to the shareholders at the annual gen-eral meeting, held in November or December.[69]

RECORD-KEEPING IN THE WESTERN DEPARTMENT

With instructions from the secretary to "make the necessary arrangements for taking over the entire control of the Western Department at as early a date as possible ... [with] full authority to make such reduction and alter-ations as you may think necessary and desirable,"[70] Chipman headed to Victoria, where one can only imagine the scene of destruction he left be-hind in the process of restructuring. It does not require much sensitivity to read between the lines of his report to Armit, dated 4 November, to imag-ine the shock and response of Thomas Smith and his staff:

> Accordingly upon my arrival at Victoria I said to Mr Smith that he no doubt was aware from the letter addressed to him by direction of the Board of the object of my visit. I discussed the situation with him in a most friendly yet frank way, which resulted in his asking permission to withdraw from the service of the Company. I told him that I had no desire to inconvenience him in any way but that I felt somewhat lim-ited for time and that I wished to take over the affairs of the Depart-ment without avoidable delay. I added that under the circumstances I would grant him leave of absence from the 1st November instant, and that I had of course every desire that his retirement should appear as emanating from himself ... It was arranged that the several Officers and clerks in charge in the Department should at once be notified by

Mr Smith and by myself of the altered condition of affairs. This was done ... A letter was then addressed to the surplus stock of clerks on hand in the Saleshop and Depot expressing regret that in consequence of a reduction of staff their services would not be required after the 30th November, and in order that they might have an opportunity of looking for employment elsewhere a month's salary was given to them in lieu of a month's notice.[71]

Eight employees received this notice, and those remaining were consolidated in one office. Chipman was satisfied that he made the necessary changes "without friction or disruption of business," and he hoped that his plans for "improved efficiency so far as this part of the reorganization is concerned have been more than realized." Since Smith had been given the same termination date as the rest of the staff, effectively eliminating the office of assistant commissioner, Chipman immediately transferred the Western Department to his own direct supervision and control as commissioner in Winnipeg. Before leaving Victoria, he appointed Robert Hanley Hall officer in charge of the Western Department. He also reviewed and revised the accounting procedures with the accountant, James W. Anderson, having found them to be in what he considered an "unsatisfactory state." A system that required multiple bookkeeping records was updated to reflect the system Chipman was implementing throughout the department. The operating statements were modified to indicate profit and loss, as opposed to credit and debit in the old system, sometimes amalgamating operations from a six-step process to one and moving the Company into more modern bookkeeping methods. "The accounts to be laid before the Shareholders could be much simplified, and would consist merely of a Trading Account, a Land Account, one Profit and Loss Account, and a general Balance Sheet. The present complicated way of calculating the Interest would be avoided."[72]

Needless to say, Chipman's visit to the Victoria store and depot "caused a great deal of extra labor on the part of the Accounting Staff, which I am pleased to say, was most cheerfully afforded."[73] He also visited Vancouver, Kamloops, and Calgary to observe and evaluate the business in those centres for ways to economize. In Winnipeg he was to "establish authority as quickly as possible"[74] by consolidating the Company's operations there in one building and considering the disposal of surplus properties such as the flour mill, the trade commissioner's house, and the Red River bridge. The Saskatchewan steamships were also on the block.

The Canadian subcommittee of Donald Smith and Sandford Fleming
was never officially disbanded, but it became inactive at the end of 1891
with the appointment of Chipman as commissioner, amalgamating the
former positions of trade commissioner, assistant trade commissioner,
and land commissioner and centring the Company's Canadian business
in the Winnipeg offices. Since 1882 the Company had occupied the Land
Department office at 208 Main Street, next to the Dominion Lands Office, and an office building, also on Main Street, south of Broadway on
the old site of Upper Fort Garry, next to the old fort gate. In 1881 a new
retail store was built at 180–184 Main Street with additions over
the next ten years that would extend the building around the corner of
York and Main, providing administrative offices for Chipman in 1892 at
210 York Street. All other offices were vacated at that time, and the land
office moved in with Chipman and his secretary.

Chipman's management style is clearly represented in the archival
records from the commissioner's office during his tenure. The most visual evidence is the use of the typewriter. All of his correspondence and
reports are typed. Since the Company purchased its first typewriter
in 1889 for use by the secretary's office in London, the equipment
Chipman used in Winnipeg may have been his own. Carbon paper was
introduced at this time, but it was initially messy, and the letter press
continued to be the most common means of making copies of correspondence. As for format, the old procedure of numbering paragraphs
in letters to and from London was no longer policy, but Chipman introduced the records management practice of sequentially numbering
correspondence from his office. Some of his letters are filed chronologically; others were withdrawn from the chronological sequence in 1911
and filed according to the new subject classification introduced at that
time. The arrangement of the commissioner's correspondence to London reflects the changeover from the traditional chronological filing
system to the method of subject filing. Chipman began separate series
of correspondence files for the Fur Trade, Stores, and Land departments, all of which are listed in indexed registers. They also include the
annual reports from the land office. Chipman's first report for Outfit
1891 bound together all the reports from the Montreal, southern, and
western departments with his comments and covering letter. After ob-
jecting to the redundancy and unnecessary labour of copying the reports from the various departments, he changed the procedure by
sending a consolidated report each year from 1892 on. Chipman also
introduced separate annual reports for the saleshops (1893–1910) and

stores department (1910–22), which provided profit and loss figures, comparative figures, analysis, and description of market conditions, together with market predictions. Since this was a growing segment of the business, these reports were extensively annotated by the London committee during its study and evaluation.[75]

Profits from the fur trade continued to diminish, but new trends in the Company's operations were emerging. The proceedings of the annual meeting held in London on 3 July 1900 reported that "we can hardly anticipate increase in this branch of the business in future years, indeed, the probability is that as the country opens up by the influx of settlers, miners and prospectors, the receipts from the fur trade will diminish year by year ... and we shall, no doubt, obtain other profit out of it by supplying all those who go into the country engaged in farming, mining, fisheries and other industries."[76] By 1901 Chipman's reorganization had reduced the number of districts in the Fur Trade Department from twenty-eight to eleven. He reported to William Ware, then secretary in London, "Owing to the improvements in transportation, postal and telegraph communication, it is possible for each Officer in Charge of these larger Districts to control them even more effectively than was formerly done by the several Officers of the small Districts."[77] Chipman's centralization scheme did not satisfactorily increase profits and decrease expenses. But he was not the only one at fault. As Douglas MacKay noted in his history of the Company, the emphasis at the turn of the century was on the sale of land, with a corresponding lack of attention to furs and retail sales: "London management could not grasp the reality of cities rising swiftly from tent towns. After ten years of the new century had gone, the old Company found itself surpassed by aggressive, young retail merchant organizations."[78]

HISTORICAL RECORDS

An interest in the Company's historical records was shown by the Canadian government while Chipman was commissioner. In 1898 Joseph Pope, undersecretary of state to Prime Minister Sir Wilfrid Laurier and former secretary to Sir John A. Macdonald, approached Chipman in search of records of Canadian historical significance for the Public Archives in Ottawa. Addressing his letter to "My dear Chipman," Pope explained that the government was proposing to establish a public records office and thus taking "steps to add to their collection any material which may be available outside the Public Offices."

Now it is commonly understood by those who take an interest in such subjects, that there exists scattered throughout the various Posts of the Hudson's Bay Company, a series of MSS, Notes, Memoranda and Diaries, etc., bearing upon the early days of the Company, and containing much information respecting the characteristics of the Indians; the rivalries of Trading Companies; the climatic conditions at the various Posts, etc. It is also very generally believed that, owing to the ravages of time, and other causes, these MSS are gradually disappearing, and it is felt that an effort should be made to rescue documents of this nature while there is time, and safeguard them for posterity."[79]

The first Dominion archivist was Douglas Brymner, whose appointment in 1872 was a Confederation culmination to almost fifty years of earlier historical research and records selection in Lower Canada, Quebec, and the Maritimes. Working out of the Department of Agriculture, Brymner had, or gave himself, a broad mandate to collect history relating to the new country of Canada, not including government records. That task was given to Henry J. Morgan, keeper of the public record for the secretary of state. As the new secretary of state in 1898, Pope was not kind about the over twenty-five years of work in this area:

I do not know if you remember the deplorable system, or rather want of system, which has hitherto existed at Ottawa, with respect to our Public Records; how we have a Clerk in one Department styling himself "Archivist," and another in another Department known as "Keeper of the Records," each looking upon the other as his rival, and neither possessing anything beyond a fraction of the documents worthy of preservation, which are stuffed into inaccessible chambers in attics and basements, their value unrecognised, and their very existence sometimes unknown."[80]

Brymner had, in fact, been in communication with and visited officials regarding the HBC records since 1873. His annual report to the minister of agriculture for that year explained that through Sir Stafford Northcote, the governor, and William Armit, the secretary, he was enabled "to examine the documents in possession of that Company ... [and make] myself as far as possible acquainted with the best means of getting the information desired."[81] At that time he acquired "the Blue Book containing the evidence, with relative documents, taken before the committee of the House of Commons appointed to investigate the

Hudson's Bay Company's claims" (1857). He also learned that the "records of the Council of Assiniboia ... [were] to be found, most probably, at Winnipeg, and steps have been taken to have them obtained and deposited with the other records. It is probable they will throw much light on the history of the North West Territories."[82] Brymner made other trips to London which included visits to the HBC and its archival records. He also set up a program of hand-copying textual and cartographic records in offices in London and Paris.[83] When Pope wrote to Chipman, it was just after the completion of a commission appointed in 1898 to report on the state of public records in Canada. He reinforced his request by pointing out that Prime Minister Laurier, "a man of fine literary instincts," had been informed and that he "warmly approves the suggestion, and I am authorised by him to say to you that the Government will cheerfully defray the cost of collecting and forwarding to Ottawa any documents of Historic interest lying in the various Posts of the Hudson's Bay Company, which you might be disposed to place with the National Deposit. I should be glad if you would give this matter your consideration, and let me know whether you would cooperate with the Government in regard to it."[84]

A copy of Pope's letter was attached to one sent from Chipman to Ware a few days later. He had replied that he did not think there was anything worthwhile at the posts. "This letter is forwarded in case the Governor and Committee may think it advisable to take any action with regard to the Records at present preserved in the London Office, but it is not recommended that the suggestion made by Mr. Pope should be adopted."[85] Although no records were transferred to Ottawa, some of historical importance did make their way to the Company's offices in Winnipeg and London as a result of instructions sent to its officials to carry out an inventory of any books and papers that were to be found in the posts. The records in British Columbia were discussed in this regard in the previous chapter. The post at Lac La Ronge found eight journals and a letterbook dating from 1865: "The old journals have been kept regularly and are fairly legible. The mice have done some damage to them. They have been boxed up. Nothing appears to be recorded of any great interest beyond the daily routine of an inland Posts."[86]

The chief factor at Fort Chimo reported: "I can't find any journals dating back further than 1890. These contain nothing of special importance, simply the state of the weather, the servants' daily employment and the arrival and departure of the natives. There are a number of old Ledgers and Day Books packed in the Office here, but no Journals

among them. The Journals in this list are all in a good state of preservation. Some books were lost by the flood 3 years ago and among them
some journals, but I am unable to give the year."[87]

An employee at the Stuart's Lake post reported: "From information
obtained from Mr. F. McKenzie, Esq., H.B.Co., Pensioner at this Post I
learn that a great many of the old Journals were packed up and forwarded to Victoria, via Quesnelle [sic], and he states that they may be
still lying at the latter Point, if not received at Victoria, from my own
personal knowledge I know there are a great many old books lying in
one of the warehouses at Quesnelle, and possibly some of the missing
Journals are among them."[88]

In 1910 a policy reversal took place, reorganizing the Company's operations by decentralizing the administration and returning to something like the structure of the 1880s. Fur trade operations were divided
into three departments – Fur Trade, Saleshops, and Land – with "the
head of each to be responsible to the Board alone."[89] Chipman would
feel first-hand the effects of this new restructuring phase. The responsibilities of the fur trade were taken from him, but he remained in
charge of the Land Department. Robert H. Hall, whom Chipman had
put in charge of the Western Department, took over as fur trade commissioner, and Herbert Burbidge, son of Sir Richard Burbidge, the
owner of Harrod's department store in London, was hired by the
Company and sent from England to take the position of the commissioner of saleshops. A year later Chipman's "services were no longer
required." He was provided with a pension but was required to va-
cate his residence. Burbidge immediately remodelled the Winnipeg
store, expanding its merchandising policy and, as a result, its profits.
Over the next ten years he took charge of the Company's retail business in Canada, including a building program to erect modern department stores in the larger centres, such as Calgary, Victoria, and
Vancouver, and to enlarge existing saleshops, such as in Edmonton.
Although its head office, fur warehouse, and auction facilities were
there, the HBC never did open a retail store in London. In 1912 the
board decided it wanted more direct connection with the operations
in Canada, and so a Canadian advisory committee was formed:
"With the object of having the best local advice and co-operation for
themselves and the three Commissioners, the Governor and Committee invited Mr. A.M. Nanton, Mr. George Galt and Sir William
Whyte, all resident in Winnipeg, to act as a local Committee in an advisory capacity."[90]

THE FIRST WORLD WAR

The Canadian advisory committee functioned in a consultative capacity only for the next ten years, and the new administrative organization was in place in Canada for about the next twenty years. In 1913 N.H. Bacon took over as fur trade commissioner when Hall retired. He moved the fur trade office to Montreal in 1916 to oversee the Company's assistance to the French government during the war years, discussed later in the chapter. The fur trade annual report for the year ending 31 May 1916 explained this move:

> In view of the fact that so much of my time was engaged in work connected with the Export Department, which necessitated my constant presence in the East, authority was requested from the Governor and Committee to transfer the headquarters of the Fur Trade from Winnipeg to Montreal for the duration of the war. In March 1916 practically the whole staff was transferred and installed in new offices at 17 St. John Street, Montreal. It has been found that the disadvantage of being farther away from the Western Districts has been more than offset by my being able to give more prompt attention to matters of moment and the fact that information as to the fur market is much more accessible in Mont-real than in Winnipeg. The reduction in Administrative Expenses is almost wholly due to the saving in travelling expenses incidental to the transfer of the headquarters of the Fur Trade.[91]

The commissioner went on to praise the people with whom he worked throughout the country:

> I take this opportunity of recording the continued efforts of the members of the Fur Trade Department in the interests of the Trade under adverse and discouraging circumstances since the beginning of the war. The reductions of the staff owing to enlistment, and the marketing of furs in the States and Canada have called for greater exertions by those remaining, and it is with pleasure I have to advise the Governor and Committee that loyal and untiring assistance has throughout been afforded me by all of those in the Active List both in the Country and District Offices, also in the Executive Office.[92]

Bacon quit in 1918, and the office and staff were relocated to Winnipeg.[93] James Thomson, who had followed Hall as manager of the Western

Department and then took over Chipman's position as land commissioner in 1911, took on the responsibilities of the Fur Trade Department until Angus Brabant was appointed in 1920.

The records of the HBC from about 1870 reflect a company responding to industrialization, an expanding frontier, and the pressures of competition resulting from changes to the structure of the country in which it was operating. The impact of the expanding settlement throughout the west was accelerated by the building of major transportation routes by railway companies. The last half of the nineteenth century saw immense growth and expansion of population throughout North America. The isolation and independence of the old HBC was irrevocably altered, and it became more difficult to manage the increasingly complex operations from London. But it had a two-hundred-year history of distant communication with its staff in North America. In the United States, railway companies were pioneers in the advancement of internal communications. With depots and personnel dispersed along miles of track, they required clear channels for exchanging orders, schedules, and reports. The telephone and telegraph hastened dispatches, and technology eventually increased the production of office records as well. The HBC was still a major influence in almost half of what is now Canada, but it was seldom at the leading edge of change and was often slow to realize its inadequacies.

Recurring processes of reorganization, alternating between centralization and decentralization of responsibilities, and the gradual relinquishing of control from London to Canada occurred as the HBC evolved from the fur trade to become a large, diversified, and functionally departmentalized business. Changes in internal communication systems developed to keep control of the records of business as well as the requirements of communicating throughout the divisions and departments in Canada and with the board in London. Joanne Yates has discussed this evolution of business in her book *Control through Communication*: "During this period of change, experience soon showed that the ad hoc managerial methods that had worked satisfactorily for small, owner-managed firms in a less competitive environment were inadequate for larger firms run by managerial hierarchies and competing in expanded markets."[94]

By the end of the 1800s, office procedures were firmly in place that would continue throughout the twentieth century. With more efficient means of writing and copying reports and forms and the increased stratification of a departmentalized company, internal communication flowed through the organization. The historical context of the HBC's methods of communication and record-keeping is important to archival studies and to the study of business. Whereas Yates found in her study of three nineteenth-century American businesses that the records keeping had been what she called a "tip of the iceberg" approach to appraisal – retention of records from only the top levels of the corporate hierarchy – a study of the HBCA produces a treasure trove of records from all levels of the business. Certainly, of the pre-1870 records and excepting the Stores and Land departments, management and functional units are all represented in complete series, lacking only where records have been lost as a result of circumstances beyond the control of normal procedures. From the meticulous minutes of the Company's board of directors to the correspondence from individuals requesting leave from their isolated posts to visit family, the HBCA contains documentation of the organization and as well represents the organic flow of information that provides researchers with evidence of the structure of the business, the style of management, the social history of the directors and the "servants," the history of record-keeping, and the changes in all of those areas over time.

Donald Smith, Lord Strathcona, governor of the Company for twenty-five years, died in 1914, the same year that Britain and Canada went to war. Sir Thomas Skinner, Smith's deputy governor and long-time committee member, took over as governor for the next two years. When he resigned in 1916, Robert Kindersley was elected to the position at the annual general court in August. Kindersley had also been on the Committee for a number of years. He was chairman of Lazard Brothers and Company, merchant bankers, a director of the Bank of England, and chairman of the War Savings Committee. At the same time, Charles V. Sale was elected to the position of deputy governor, and the two businessmen would lead the Company through the next fifteen years. Sale was a partner in an importing firm, Sale and Company, with interests in Japan, where he had spent his early career. With his experience and knowledge of the requirements of transocean shipping, Sale had been invited by Kindersley to sit on the board of the HBC and manage the business with the French government that arose during the First World War in Europe.

During the war and for some years after, the HBC operated what was known as the French government business. An agreement was negotiated with the French ministers of war and finance under which the Company arranged credit for and acted as purchasing and transport

French government business offices and staff in London, 1915–18 (album 33a, 9 and 12)

agent of goods for that war-beleaguered country. A subsidiary, the Bay Steamship Company, was formed to charter and manage a fleet of ships which eventually made 350 voyages, mostly across the Atlantic. Two-fifths of those ships were sunk by enemy action, with the resulting loss of goods and men. Branch agencies were set up by the HBC in Montreal and New York, and agents appointed in ports of shipment all over the world. The operation extended to Russia when similar services were rendered through an agency in Archangel, as well as to Belgium and Romania.[95] Charles Sale was invited by the new governor to manage this business and to sit on the board of the Company. A year later, in 1915, he was made deputy governor. He worked out of an office in Threadneedle House on Bishopsgate Street in London with a large staff in several departments, administering all aspects of this international shipping business. When the war was over, the Company once again had a new personae.

6

custodians of a great inheritance
Developments Evolving from the 250th Anniversary, 1920–1930

From its emphasis on the fur trade, the Hudson's Bay Company had diversified into retail trade and land sales, but its role as "true and absolute Lordes and Proprietor" of almost half the North American continent, as defined in the royal charter, had ended with the Deed of Surrender. In 1920 the Company of Adventurers had been in business for 250 years. The First World War had been over for two years, bringing peace and an end to four years of wartime restrictions and regulation. The world was slowly returning to order, but not without noticeable losses, including an Old World innocence. The HBC had lost employees and ships, but it had continued to make a profit from its expansion into war service, chartering several hundred merchant vessels to transport food stuffs, fuel, lumber, and munitions. The next ten years of rebuilding and growth would come to a resounding halt with the crash of the New York stock market in 1929 and the effect that event had on the economy of the rest of the world. In the meantime, from a records point of view, the changes in the nature of business being carried out in the London offices were pivotal to the Company's old records becoming the world-class archives they are today.

The HBC was a diversified commercial business with successful retail, land, and fur trade departments throughout Canada and one of the largest international fur sale businesses in London. The London office directed the Company's activities which, other than the fur sales, still took place predominantly in Canada. The HBC continued to dominate the north in much the same way it had dominated Rupert's Land, and it was, in most cases, the sole provider of goods, the sole purchaser of furs, and the sole administrative, legal, and quasi-governmental power for numerous isolated communities. Journals were still kept at the northern posts as part of the annual reporting routine, as they had been in the past. These records provide historians with "unofficial" records of the settlement and movement of the Native people and are often used for substantiating land claims and providing evidence in other legal skirmishes.

One senses a renewed dynamic from the records of the London office in the 1920s. The fur trade crisis continued for the next few years; so the new energy must be attributed to the personalities and abilities of key players. Old, established industries, sluggish before the war, either disappeared or received a new lease on life. Those that remained, trading companies such as the HBC, had to be current and innovative to survive. The war had resulted in losses, never to be retrieved, but it had also brought advances in science and technology that were immediately available for civilian access and utilization. The Company established a Development Department to investigate the potential of new products and the utilization of by-products as the result of processing. Information-gathering trips were made to Canada, and a laboratory was set up outside London for further research and development. A variety of new products were marketed, and a few years later a Fish and Fish Products Department was established for this purpose.[1]

New concepts of diversity and efficiency in business affairs brought a revolution in office management. The Company's responsibility as a result of its accumulating and keeping a massive body of records relating to its business as a major British enterprise became evident in the late nineteenth and early twentieth centuries. Its historical business records, its archives, were taking on a life of their own, having stimulated interest beyond the business community and become the subject of scholarly research. A hesitant willingness to grant access to some of these records to certain historical researchers indicates that the HBC had begun to realize that it could benefit from the favourable publicity generated by these authors. It even responded on occasion to this interest in its history by requesting its officers to identify and protect historical records. However, it did not do so consistently. Some researchers were denied access to the existing Company records, and on occasion, instruction was given to destroy old records indiscriminately, at least some HBC officials assuming that this was to be done in order to eliminate information which might have proved embarrassing to the Company.[2] Furthermore, the Company did not have a formal archival service or office responsible for administering custody of and access to its older records. Access was provided by the secretary under the advice of the governor. Because of past experiences with outsiders questioning its rights under the charter and the extensive government investigations involved, the HBC was wary of liberal access to its records. At the same time it would welcome a favourable treatment of its past. But the absence of a consistent records retention and access policy, as well as the lack of a formal archival service to assist researchers, set up a situation that worked against it. The HBC was not indifferent to its obligation to protect and make available its "great inheritance" of archives, but it wanted to do so on its own terms. Of course, economic conditions also had an influence on the Company's priorities. When business was good, money was provided for staff to work on the old records. When finances were limited, commitment to the archives was also restrained and staff were redirected or eliminated.

The secretary of the HBC from 1911 to 1923 was Frank C. Ingrams, who had been assistant secretary from 1893. He and most of the staff in London and in Canada were involved in one way or another during most of that time with war business. In Canada the Montreal office took on a greater role in order to put the HBC closer to a major Canadian seaport, but Winnipeg remained the centre for what fur trade business there was during the war. The Fur Trade Department managed nine district offices and 150 trading posts across Canada and the north. The land and wholesale departments had branches through the west, while the retail department had buying agencies in Montreal and New York and department stores in ten cities in western Canada.[3] But the financial and commercial depression, the interference with shipping, and the uncertainty caused by the war had produced a crisis of unprecedented severity for the fur trade.[4]

The HBC offices in London remained at No. 1 Lime Street, in the heart of the financial district. Considerable alterations were made to the rented building after the death of the governor, Lord Strathcona, in 1914. The secretary's office, the transfer department, and the shipping office were moved to the ground floor, previously rented out.[5] This change provided off-the-street access to all these offices. The accountants took over the second-floor offices vacated by the secretary. The boardroom and governor's office remained on the first floor, still full of antique mahogany tables and chairs, bookcases, oil paintings, and the long-case clock that had faithfully chimed the hours since it was purchased in 1684. The fur warehouse occupied the attached building. Most of the reference books collected and used by the Company officers would have been stored in the boardroom bookcases or in the secretary's office. A total of

270 books were catalogued in 1887,[6] and it was these and the documents and business records kept in the vaults in the secretary's and accountant's offices that were of interest to historians, most of them from North America, who wanted to write about the HBC at this time.

WRITING THE COMPANY HISTORY

The competitive nature of business, particularly the competition between the HBC and other fur traders during the first two hundred years of its activity in North America, had required the Company to take a protective and sometimes secretive approach to its business records. It could not shake off the paranoia that had developed out of these fur trade rivalries. Extreme caution resurfaced every time researchers attempted to avail themselves of the records. The Company had, at various times over the years, placed an emphasis on records creation procedures and secure storage. At the same time, it seemed to be oblivious to the historical value of many of its records. As Douglas MacKay wrote in his unauthorized, popular history of the Company, "if ever an historic organization was indifferent to the glamour of its past, it was this company of adventurers during the first two and a half centuries of its existence. The fluctuations of a business which originated in the subarctic and ended in the luxury trades of Europe were too all-absorbing to permit the cultivation of company annals."[7]

Books had been written about the HBC as early as 1708, but few authors had the benefit of access to the archives. The first book to discuss the Company and the importance of its business was John Oldmixon's *The British Empire in America*, which was written less than forty years after the charter was granted. Oldmixon explained his research methodology in the preface to the second edition of the book, published in 1731:

> The History of Hudson's Bay may be depended upon; for the Author took it from original Papers, he having had in his Possession the Journal of a Secretary of the Factory, the Commissions and Instructions of some of the Governors, and other Memoirs, out of all which he could gather no more, and does not believe, that even by the Company's books much more is to be gathered. Application was made to Persons concerned in the Affairs of the Company, for Matter to continue an Account of them to this time; but it being not come to Hand before the Book was printed, the Events there are not of Importance enough to keep the rest of this History longer from the Publick.[8]

The boardroom in the HBC building on Lime Street, about the 1920s (1987-363-H-42-7)

The journal Oldmixon referred to as being in his possession was that of Thomas Gorst, who served as secretary to Governor Charles Bayly on his exploratory voyage to Hudson Bay in 1670–71. He does not explain the origin of the other documents he had, how he came to have access to them, or whom he contacted at the Company. He was perhaps the first author to encounter "the tight-lipped reserve with which the Company met inquiries, an attitude which was to become second nature to the officers and servants,"[9] as MacKay observed.

By the end of the nineteenth century, interest in writing histories was growing, and the HBC was an intriguing topic for British, Canadian, and American authors and readers. Alexander Begg, born in Quebec and a trader in the Red River Colony in 1867, published several historical works, including the three-volume *History of the North-West*, which he dedicated to Governor Donald Smith: "I wish, then, as an humble token of my great respect for you and the deep gratitude I feel for all your goodness to me and mine, to dedicate to you my work, which I fear is but a poor attempt to chronicle events relating to so great a country."[10] The appendices of Begg's book include copies of the royal charter, the 1821 and 1838 Crown grants to the Company, and the commission issued to Smith.

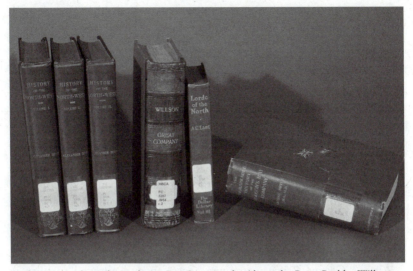

Books written about the Hudson's Bay Company by Alexander Begg, Beckles Willson, Agnes Laut, and George Bryce

British author and natural historian Robert Miller Christy drafted a manuscript for a two-volume history of the HBC that was never published. "The Last Great Monopoly: A History of the Hudson's Bay Company, From its Establishment in the Year 1670 to the Present Time" was written after he consulted a lengthy list of books in the library of the British Museum.[11] Christy was a fellow of the Linnean Society and his interest in the HBC arose out of his travels in Canada and his research as editor for the Hakluyt Society.[12] He was given permission by the secretary, William Armit, to peruse books and documents, but he found the project quite daunting. He explained his frustrations in a letter to a friend: "With the concurrence of the officials of the Hudson's Bay Company, I have undertaken to write a history of the Company & am now actively engaged upon it. I find I have undertaken a most stupendous job – in short, nothing (or very little) less than a history of the whole North-West."[13]

In 1900 Beckles Willson, a Canadian working as a reporter for the *Daily Mail* in London, published *The Great Company (1667–1871), Being a History of the Honourable Company of Merchants-Adventurers Trading into Hudson's Bay*, which he compiled from the Company's archives and other sources. Although it was not an official Company history, Lord Strathcona, the governor from 1889 to 1914, permitted him to have access to the Company's records. In return, Willson recorded his

gratitude "for assistance and courtesies rendered" to him. He acknowledged his indebtedness to "Mr. William Ware, the courteous secretary of
the Hudson's Bay Company,"[14] who, with his staff, would have searched
out and provided the records requested. In his introduction to the book,
Strathcona defines the narrative as "a most interesting contribution
to the history of Canada."[15] Willson went on to write two biographies of
Lord Strathcona. In the 1915 edition, published shortly after Strathcona's
death, he acknowledged access to the Company records: "For the chapters relating to Hudson's Bay Company affairs, I am specially indebted
to Messrs. Roderick MacFarlane, Colin Rankin, W.D.B. Ross, and to
Mr. William Armit, formerly Secretary of the Company. For copies of
the official correspondence in Lime Street, I am beholden to my friend,
Sir Thomas Skinner, the present Governor of the Hudson's Bay Company, who, I hasten to add, is in no sense a party to the misdeeds of the
original body corporate."[16]

Author George Bryce was given access to and allowed to borrow
original material from the Company archives by governors Goschen
(1874–80) and Strathcona (1889–1914) to research his book *The Remarkable History of the Hudson's Bay Company* which was published
in 1900. Bryce's acknowledgments explain the access he was given:

> The writer has had full means of examining documents, letters,
> journals, business records, heirlooms, and archives of the fur trad-
> ers both in Great Britain and in Canada. He returns thanks to the
> custodians of many valuable originals, which he has used, to the
> Governor of the Hudson's Bay Company in 1881, Right Hon. G.J.
> Goschen, who granted him the privilege of consulting all Hudson's
> Bay Company records up to the date of 1821, and he desires to still
> more warmly acknowledge the permission given him by the distin-
> guished patron of literature and education, the present Governor of
> the Hudson's Bay Company, Lord Strathcona and Mount Royal, to
> read any documents of public importance in the Hudson's Bay
> House in London.[17]

Douglas MacKay would later comment that "both Bryce and Willson had
to work from vast quantities of disorderly and unclassified material."[18]

Agnes C. Laut was a popular Canadian-born historian and author of
numerous historical novels. Her two-volume *The Conquest of the
Great Northwest* was published in New York in 1908. She explained
her use of Company records:

I have relied for the thread of my narrative on the documents in Hudson's Bay House, London; the Minute Books of some two hundred years, the Letter Books, the Stock Books, the Memorial Books, the Daily Journals kept by chief factors at every post and sent to London from 1670. These documents are in tons. They are not open to the public. They are unclassified ... The Minute Books consist variously from one to five hundred pages each. Besides the documents of Hudson's Bay House, London, there is a great mass of unpublished, unexploited material bearing on the Company in the Public Records Office, London.[19]

Laut acknowledged her HBC contacts as C.C. Chipman, William Ware, and Governor Strathcona.

The governor of the HBC, through the secretary, provided access to the records based on his perception of the merits of individual applications. It would seem that access was granted to well-known authors who might be expected to write favourable popular histories of the Company which stressed the "romance" of the fur trade in a far-flung wilderness rather than controversial details of Company business practices. At the same time, some historical researchers were denied access. In 1913 W. Stewart Wallace, historian and future president of the Champlain Society, was refused permission to examine the archives of the Company. His recounting of an interview with Lord Strathcona describes the atmosphere:

I can remember the interview as vividly as if it were yesterday. The old man, bending on me his beetling white eyebrows, inquired what it was I wanted to learn from the Company's archives; and since I had no particular line of inquiry I wished to follow, but was anxious merely to go on a sort of general fishing expedition, I fear I was not able to answer his question very satisfactorily. He was most polite in expressing a desire to supply me with any particular items of information of which I might be in search; but he did not appear anxious ... to turn me loose among the Company's archives. There the interview ended.[20]

Wallace, librarian at the University of Toronto for over thirty years, author of more than thirty books, and editor of several Canadian reference books, was eventually given access to the archives of Hudson's Bay House many years later, and he was able to be objective about the earlier disappointment:

I thought at the time that Lord Strathcona's reluctance to grant me access to the records of Hudson's Bay House proceeded from a fear of
what I might discover; but I realize now that my suspicions were wholly
unfounded. The archives of the Company at that time were unorganized,
unclassified, and uncatalogued; and to turn students loose among papers
of such value would have been most improper ... That Lord Strathcona
was right in refusing me admission to the Hudson's Bay House archives
in 1913 is one of the lessons that experience has brought me.[21]

THE 250TH ANNIVERSARY

Plans for the Company's celebration in 1920 of 250 years of business under the royal charter began to take shape in 1919 but the idea had in fact
originated a year earlier from Herbert Burbidge, the stores commissioner
in Winnipeg. "There is such a wealth of educative and interesting history
associated with the operations of the 'old Company' that it should not
be a difficult task to produce something suitable in celebration,"[22] he
wrote. A special meeting of the governor and committee was held in
April to discuss how the event would be commemorated, including
the idea of a history of the Company. Also attending that meeting was
H. Holford Bottomley, a publicity specialist who during the war had
been director of special publicity and propaganda for the National War
Savings Committee and the National War Bonds Campaign. Governor
Kindersley had been the chairman of the National War Savings Committee. The Company had increasingly become aware that its long and colourful history was a valuable asset as a public relations tool, and the
manner in which it planned the anniversary reflected those tendencies.
With a less than one-year time frame and a suggested budget of £50,000,
Bottomley's London advertising company was hired to handle the event.
The anniversary celebrations were to take place in London and in Canada, in each of the cities where the HBC had a store, with the principal
celebration in Winnipeg. There were several components besides the
events to be arranged locally in each town.[23]

Bottomley was sent to Winnipeg to confer with Burbidge, the Canadian
advisory committee, and the commissioners and to discuss the suggestions
of the London board for the best way to celebrate the event. Some of the
ideas were: an illustrated history of the Company, to be distributed to cus-
tomers and schools; a film depicting the history of the Company, as well
as its present activities; opening the new store in Victoria and laying the
foundation stone for a new store in Winnipeg; commemorative medals to
be given to all Company employees; building schools for children at all the

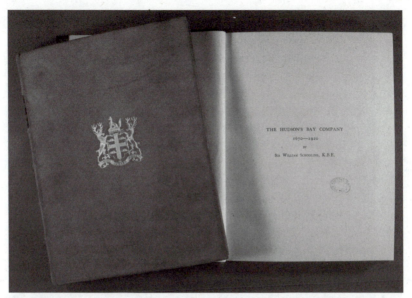

The Governor and Company of Adventurers of England Trading into Hudson's Bay, by
Sir William Schooling, published for the 250th anniversary in 1920

northern posts; making a gift to the city of Winnipeg (or Canada) of the
old stone fort at Lower Fort Garry; a pension fund for Company employees; and a standard scheme of advertising for the Canadian stores.[24] Not
all of the plans were carried out, but the enthusiastic Canadians were in
complete agreement, even adding more suggestions as the project gained
momentum. Clifton M. Thomas, an advertising agent from Chicago, was
hired to set up a publicity office in Winnipeg.

Bottomley contracted S.J. Brown to write a Company history, but by
October it was clear that his work was unacceptable, and William
Schooling, a journalist and personal friend of Kindersley (Schooling had
also been on the National War Savings Committee), was asked to rework
the brochure. He was paid a handsome £525 for the project and by the
first of December he had an outline and had written three chapters. The
final product, known as the "brochure" and titled *The Governor and
Company of Adventurers of England Trading into Hudson's Bay during
Two Hundred and Fifty Years, 1670–1920,* was, in fact, a 129-page,
hardcover book with engraved illustrations. Thirty thousand copies were
printed in time for the anniversary celebrations in May, including a de-
luxe edition bound in leather for special presentations.

The anniversary "brochure" reflected the Company's increasing awareness that it had a responsibility to share the historical material it had
accumulated, and in the introduction, Governor Kindersley expressed a

TABLE OF CONTENTS

vii.

Table of contents for Schooling's book

sense of obligation for the proper custody of records: "The Committee of to-day recognise that they are the *custodians of a great inheritance*, which it is their duty to hand on, enhanced and not impaired, to future generations ... a record which is unique in the history of trading corporations."[25] It is unclear what reference material Schooling used in writing the book, but early in the planning stages Bottomley had asked the secretary to provide a list of books relative to the history of the Company and a copy of the original charter.[26] Presumably Schooling used previously published material, but his book contains neither bibliography nor footnotes. Whether he had access to the records that were stored in Hudson's Bay House at No. 1 Lime Street at that time is not documented.

To celebrate the 250th anniversary, the Company staff in London were invited to a dinner and each was presented with a copy of the anniversary

The 250th anniversary dinner in New York (1981-28-170) and menu for the dinner (E.286)

"brochure." In Canada the plans included local celebrations in each of the cities where the Company had stores, beginning with Winnipeg on the 2nd of May. Governor Kindersley and his wife travelled to Canada to participate in the celebrations in the different cities. Every HBC employee was given a copy of the Schooling's book and copies were provided to Canadian libraries and schools. One hundred copies were also distributed to public libraries in the United States. Banquets were held for staff and pensioners in Montreal, Winnipeg, Edmonton, Calgary, Vancouver, and Victoria. Extravagant pageants were presented in each of these cities in which the whole community took part, and prizes were presented to schoolchildren for writing essays about Canadian history. A dinner was held in New York for staff who were still working there finishing up the business resulting from the wartime assistance to the French government.[27] A Company pension plan was announced; as well, each employee received a bonus equivalent to one month's salary. The anniversary celebrations were a huge success in London and especially in Canada.

A lasting by-product of the anniversary celebrations was the in-house staff magazine, *The Beaver*, published from the Winnipeg publicity office with the intent of improving employees' morale by catering to their needs and interests and creating a family-like company spirit. Readers were encouraged to be contributors. The first issue of *The Beaver*, published in October 1920, was dedicated to Governor Sir Robert M. Kindersley. Clifton M. Thomas served as the first editor.

We propose to make this Journal as newsy and interesting as an H.B.C. Magazine should be, with the wealth of good material at its disposal. But we must depend upon you, our readers, for the gathering and reporting of this material ... Send us the FACTS ... and PICTURES ... Give us notes, narratives, anecdotes, personal news items, history, biography and poems – about the Company, its staff and their activities. Whether you are a trader, clerk, inspector, ship captain, post-manager, stenographer, salesperson, buyer, accountant, department manager – whatever your position in the service, you can help to make "The Beaver" a more interesting and newsy magazine.[28]

In November 1923 Thomas left and Robert Watson, the accountant from the Saskatoon store, took over as editor. With a personal interest in writing and history, he encouraged submissions of articles relating to the history of the Company and its adventurers which proved popular.

Starting with the December 1924 issue, *The Beaver* was distributed quarterly rather than monthly, and over the next ten years it was read increasingly by both amateur and professional fur trade historians. When Watson left in 1933 to pursue his writing ambitions, he was replaced by Douglas MacKay. MacKay was new to the Company but had experience as publicity director of Canada Steamship Lines and then the Saguenay Club in Montreal. He immediately revamped both the editorial content and the format. With a revised subtitle, *Magazine of the North, The Beaver* doubled its distribution to 8,000 and included more advertising of HBC merchandise among the informative and interesting articles and photographs. When MacKay died in a plane crash in 1938, Clifford Wilson was hired as editor of *The Beaver*, Company historian, and curator of the historical exhibit displayed in the Winnipeg store. The magazine by then had paying subscribers and included articles of a scholarly and literary nature, as well as regular reports on staff and Company news from the London office, commissioners' offices, district offices, and stores.[29] With a readership at that time of 11,000, *The Beaver* emerged as a popular Canadian history magazine in 1941.[30]

After writing the anniversary "brochure," William Schooling urged Governor Kindersley to consider having a complete history of the Company written.[31] He presented a detailed proposal suggesting five volumes and requiring considerable examination of the Company's original documents. Kindersley accepted the proposal in April 1920, just before he left for his anniversary tour of Canada.[32] Schooling's fee for writing a history of the HBC was to be £2,000 per year. He would pay for his own secretary, but the Company would be responsible for additional help with copying work and with sundry expenses for paper, books, and some records preparation.[33]

Schooling settled in as the Company historian for the next six years. He hired Kathleen Pincott to help him prepare material for the book, and she became his tireless assistant, whom he later described as "entirely sensible and capable."[34] Pincott and clerks from the secretary's office were given the huge task of arranging the post journals, letterbooks, and minute books, reading them, and then preparing brief extracts from them.[35] Schooling's office was in his home in Kensington, but he regularly visited the HBC office in the city to examine the documents his assistants were working on and to consult books in the library. He also consulted material at the British Museum and the Public Record Office.

Bound volumes of annals prepared by HBC staff for William Schooling, on the shelves
in the HBC Archives (RG20/6a/1–29)

THE MERK AFFAIR

Schooling was the first outsider to have free access to all of the HBC
records, a fact that generated interest and curiosity among his connections in the historical community. During the time that Schooling was
working on the larger history, he was also instructed by Ingrams to
provide assistance in answering research requests regarding the archives. His broad interpretation of those instructions created a controversy that lasted over ten years and for many more years sustained
stories among historians of the inaccessibility of the Company archives.

The researcher involved was Frederick Merk, a professor of history at
Harvard University, whose topic of interest was the history of the early
Oregon Territory on the West Coast of North America. Since the area
was part of the HBC's Columbia Department in the first half of the nineteenth century, his search for original material lead him, at the end of
1920 and early 1921, to London and to the HBC. Merk had been pursu-
ing his research in Europe during the previous year for a paper he was
going to present to the American Historical Society.[36] His contact with
Schooling at this time was fortunate since a fair amount of abstracting
of the Company's archival material had already been accomplished.

Schooling accepted Merk's impressive credentials and provided him with a catalogue listing the manuscript material in the Company's historical record. Merk did not have access to the archives in the London office, but he was provided with a desk at Schooling's Kensington office for the purpose of making transcriptions of the records as they were brought to him. Transcription was a tedious process, and Merk worked at it for several months. He and Schooling came up with an agreement that Merk could take away copies of documents relevant to his research in exchange for copies of the material he had collected from other sources during his research on the topic.

But Schooling must have become nervous about the amount of material Merk had found in the Company's records and asked the board for clarification of records policy. It is not clear from the records available in the archives on this problem whether the governor and board knew that a researcher was working in Schooling's office. The board responded that it had no objection to an exchange of information but requested that copies be provided to the governor or deputy governor for perusal. "The Board are perfectly sure that they can rely on your discretion in the use of their documents and records, but there are certain reasons which might not be so apparent to yourself, which make it necessary to act with caution."[37] Merk completed his search of the Company's records by the end of February, and his notes from nearly sixty items, including the complete text of George Simpson's 1824–25 journal, were examined by Schooling, who then passed them to the deputy governor, Charles Sale, at the beginning of March. Two months later, Sale informed Schooling that it would not be possible to return the transcripts to Merk.

It then seems that Schooling did nothing about the notes until Merk contacted him again prior to returning home in September. Finally, Schooling wrote to Governor Kindersley to tell him about Merk and to present the transcripts with passages marked to which Schooling thought the Company would take exception.

The period referred to is from 80–100 years ago, and I think you will agree that such a corporation as the H.B.C. cannot fitly decline to place its archives dealing with a remote period at the disposal of any serious and responsible historian. There is really nothing in the documents that can do anything but help to improve the opinion that could be formed in America about the relations between the British and the Americans in connection with Oregon. I should therefore be very glad

if you would give me permission … to entrust Dr. Merk with the
copies of these documents on the express undertaking that he makes
no public use of them whatever without previously submitting to
us what he is saying, with the understanding that we can censor his
writings in any way that we think necessary and appropriate.[38]

It was Sale who responded, leaving it to Schooling to provide Merk
with the censored copies and emphasizing his assurance that he would
obtain further permission prior to any publication involving the material.[39] Merk finally received the material in December.[40]

Ten years later and without further contact with the Company, Merk
published his book *Fur Trade and Empire: George Simpson's Journal*
in the United States and Britain, with what he thought were appropriate acknowledgments to the HBC:

I am under obligations to Sir William Schooling, K.B.E., and to
the officers of the Hudson's Bay Company for the greater part of
the documents presented in this volume. I did not have access to the
Company's archives themselves, the documents being selected by
me from a manuscript catalogue and brought for transcription to an
outside office … My transcripts were censored as I have indicated. I
consider it permissible to say that the record of the Hudson's Bay
Company in the Oregon Country, so far as I saw it, contains nothing
that cannot bear the light of day. The standards imposed by the Hon-
orable Committee on its servants were high in themselves … I believe
the Company could but enhance its reputation by throwing open its
archives without restriction to historians.[41]

The Company was not impressed. In 1931 a new publication scheme
was in place and Simpson's journal had been chosen as the first topic.
The Company secretary was now J. Chadwick Brooks, who, on behalf of
the new governor, Patrick Ashley Cooper, wrote to Merk questioning his
lack of attention to the 1921 agreement with Schooling: "we do not
appear to have received from you any copies of what you proposed to
publish, nor do we appear to have given our official sanction to publication."[42] Merk was distressed at the misunderstandings regarding the
publication and suggested that the communication problem was with
Schooling, who by then had been dismissed by the Company. Merk had
presumed that his original agreement was void after receiving the heavily
censored transcriptions. He sent copies of his publications *Fur Trade and*

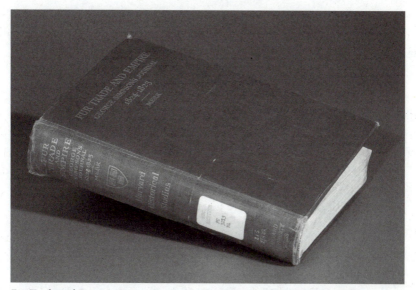

Fur Trade and Empire: George Simpson's Journal, by Frederick Merk, published jointly by Harvard University Press and Oxford University Press in 1931

Empire and *The Oregon Pioneers and the Boundary,* and the Company eventually admitted that the first book was "edited in good spirit and the subject is treated in a satisfactory manner."[43]

CANADIAN HISTORIANS

When the Merk research concerns first came to light in 1921, Deputy Governor Sale had reminded Schooling that no one outside the HBC was to have access to any of the documents or papers he was working on.[44] That policy remained in place over the next five years while he continued work on the history. The Company was making plans to move out of No. 1 Lime Street, and Schooling was given space in the old building for inspecting documents.[45] These arrangements lasted for the next six years, when there were often as many as four full-time assistants employed to work on the records for the book project. A new catalogue of the Company's boardroom library, prepared at that time, listed 330 titles,[46] and an incomplete catalogue of the records stored in the basement at the end of 1922 filled 400 typed pages.[47]

Schooling has not been given much credit in the history of the HBC, but his influence on the archives and the Company's approach to its archival dilemma is unquestionable. When he travelled to Canada

between April and October 1922, Schooling visited Company offices in
Winnipeg, Vancouver, and Victoria as well as former HBC posts, Fort
St James, and Norway House.[48] He carried out research at the Public
Archives in Ottawa, and at the Provincial Archives of British Columbia
in Victoria, he inspected "the entire collection of journals, diaries,
reminiscences ... [and] the H.B. Co. transcripts."[49] While in Winnipeg,
he provided consultation on the selection and disposal of archival material at the Canadian Committee offices and arranged to have eleven
cases of pre-1876 journals and records transferred to the London office. He met and conferred with members of the historical community
in every Canadian city he visited. Schooling was particularly excited
about his visit to Ottawa, where he attended a meeting of the Royal Society of Canada with Arthur Doughty, the dominion archivist, and
where he met Prime Minister Mackenzie King. From that meeting he
reported a "unanimous and very pronounced view that the Hudson's
Bay Company documents had not been made as readily available for
students as is desirable." In Toronto Schooling met with Dr George
Wrong, a professor of history at the University of Toronto, and they attended a meeting of the Champlain Society, which Wrong had helped
found in 1905.

   That society's distinguished record of publication of archival documents relating to the history of Canada underlined the lack of published archival material from the HBC, and as a result, Schooling came
away with a proposal to select, edit, and annotate Company records
for publication by the Champlain Society. He reported on the work of
the society to the Company board of directors: "The fifteen volumes it
has already published are of great value, and I am sure that, even for
the Hudson's Bay Company, there would be a certain distinction in
having some of its documents published by the Champlain Society."[50]
Schooling was also impressed with the level of archival care for historical material in Canada. The Public Archives had been housed in its
own building in Ottawa since 1906 and access to the holdings was
largely unrestricted.

   The criticisms of the Company's access policy that Schooling met in
Canada reinforced his view of the problems which were becoming increasingly obvious in London. He reported that Canadian scholars insisted an important part of the records documenting Canada's history
was inaccessible to them. "The general opinion, in which I concur, is
that, since the Hudson's Bay Company was the effective Government
of a large part of Canada for two Hundred years, its documents for

that period (viz. prior to about 1870) should be freely available, and documents since 1870 should either be withheld, or only open to inspection according to the merits of each applicant and the purpose of the investigation. It would be a great satisfaction in Canada if some such policy as this were adopted."[51] The archives of the HBC were not only unclassified and without permanent housing, but were also completely inaccessible except to all but a few members of the Company's staff. Schooling pleaded with the governor for attention to the archival records: "Another matter in which I am much interested, although not directly concerned, is the permanent keeping and arrangement of the archives. Historically, and even financially, these are of very great value, and unless I wholly misinterpret the opinion of the present Directors, they think that these should be housed, catalogued and cared for in a way befitting their importance."[52] Influenced by what he had seen in Canada, he went on to propose a library and adjacent archives with a librarian and an archivist fully employed by the Company in the management of the records. He added that he would gladly advise the Company on implementing these proposals.

On his return to London, Schooling was filled with enthusiasm for his history book project. "Canada," he said, "has made me appreciate more fully even than before, the privilege of being entrusted with the writing of the History of the Hudson's Bay Company."[53] He was surprised by the amount of material relating to the Company that he had found on his visit to Canada. Indeed he was somewhat intimidated by the wealth of information that was available to him and concerned about whether he could meet the deadline for completing the history with so much documentation to explore. But the board was "beginning to be rather agitated at the expense already incurred"[54] by the three years of work with no tangible results. It asked Schooling for a firm date and financial accounting for completion of the history, but instead he suggested that the history project should be delayed until the archives were in order. And he wanted Kindersley to pursue the proposal for a joint publishing venture with the Champlain Society. But Schooling continued to work on the history project and asked for more accessibility to the records by having them moved temporarily to a house where he could also live. And he felt it was essential to have many of the journals and letterbooks bound in some fashion. He began to refer to the history as an "encyclopaedia," and in order to confirm his facts, he asked for permission to send the proofs "to a number of the best people in Canada for criticism, revision and possible addition." As a result of Schooling's procrastination, the board presented him with a detailed ultimatum on 18 September 1923:

1. No alterations to be made in Sir William Schooling's remuneration.
2. The History of the Company to be completed as quickly as possible and in any case not later than the 31st December, 1925.
3. The Company to rent a suitable house for the period of two years, in which Sir William Schooling will reside, and to provide necessary steel shelving; also a safe for custody of the more important documents whilst in Sir William Schooling's possession.
4. The Company will furnish Sir William Schooling with necessary records, documents, etc., from the Archives at Lime Street. In the case of the more important ones, in period of, any, ten or twenty years at a time, as the work progresses; such documents to be listed, invoiced and checked on the return to the Company, as at present.
5. All records and documents in Sir William Schooling's possession to be kept strictly private, no one being allowed access to them other than Sir William Schooling and his assistant, except by formal consent of the Board; the intention being that no third parties shall gain any knowledge of the Company's affairs until such time as the Board decide to release it.
6. The question of publication to be considered as soon as possible by the sub-Committee appointed by the Board and a decision arrived at as soon as Sir William Schooling is within sight of having the encyclopaedia articles ready for submission to Canadian and *other* historically minded people.
7. Sir William Schooling to exercise every care in the selection of individuals in Canada to whom such records will be sent for criticism and revision and steps should be taken to ensure that such articles do not counteract the provisions of Clause 3.
8. The Board for reasons of policy, will require all proofs to be submitted to them for approval before publication.
9. Only good illustrations, which should be mainly portraits, to be included in the History.[55]

Another house was rented for Schooling at No. 9 Elvaston Place in Kensington. It had plenty of room in which to store the archival material he required for reference but he asked for several renovations and for steel shelving to be installed. He was asking for ten or twenty years' worth of documents at a time, and, in the case of post journals, he wanted them all at one time.[56] Kindersley and the board were concerned with moving so much archival material at a time to Kensington:

> The Board's decision that not more than half of the documents
> shall be at Elvaston Place at one time, is not intended in any way
> to preclude you from having the whole of the documents there
> at one time or another, and you are perfectly free to choose what
> you want and to exchange them as necessary ... You speak of the
> necessity for finishing the history quickly, but in view of the fact
> that you have already been engaged on the work for three years,
> and that by the recent decision of the Board you still have another
> two years in which to complete it, I do not think it can be said
> that we have curtailed you unduly in this respect.[57]

At this time, in late 1923 and early 1924, the premises on Lime Street were being vacated, and the records moved to Beaver House. Much of the material was in packing cases and required time to unpack and to arrange on the shelves. Schooling was also involved in finding appropriate bindings for the archival material and appropriate storage methods for the large and unique map collection.

ARTHUR DOUGHTY AND THE HBC ARCHIVES

In 1922 and 1923 Schooling's attention had again been diverted by an outside researcher. Arthur Doughty was in England on behalf of the Public Archives of Canada, and he would prove to be another major influence on the Company's attention to its archival records. Doughty had been appointed in 1904 to succeed Douglas Brymner as Dominion archivist with the added responsibility of keeper of the Public Archives. Born in England and educated at Oxford, he had spent most of his adult life in Canada as a civil servant in Quebec. As Dominion archivist, he was soon noted for aggressive archival acquisition policies, which included records copying programs in London and Paris.[58] His primary mandate was the encouragement of historical research, which he promoted by preparing a guide to archival material relating to Canada within the country and overseas.[59] Doughty's first trip to England in 1904 to solicit donations of material relating to Canada from members of the British aristocracy had been supported by Lord Strathcona, the HBC's governor. At that time, arrangements were made for records of the Hudson's Bay Company to be part of the Public Archives copying program, which had been active

in London since 1878 and in Paris from 1883.[60] For several months during 1912 and 1913, a Mrs E.J. Ferguson was provided space in the governor's room to copy post journals and Radisson's journals for the Public
Archives. In 1916 Winifred Mayes from the Provincial Archives Department of British Columbia was allowed "to copy certain historical
documents ... relating to the early history of the Pacific North-west."[61]
The list of documents copied by the Canadian archives program included
HBC minutes, minutes of council, exploration journals, some post journals, and several miscellaneous items such as memorial books and official documents.[62]

During his year-long visit to England in 1922–23, for the purpose of
soliciting acquisitions for the Public Archives, Doughty helped to establish the Canadian History Society there under the patronage of His
Majesty the King and with considerable support from Sir Campbell Stuart. Stuart was a Canadian (of United Empire Loyalist descent) from
Montreal who had settled in England after the First World War. He was
the grandson of Charles Brydges, land commissioner for the Company
from 1879 to 1882 and at one time head of the Grand Trunk Railway.
The object of the Canadian History Society was to facilitate the acquisition of records related to Canadian history that were, or were thought
to be, in the custody of members of the British aristocracy. Besides the
king, the membership included Lady Minto (wife of the late Earl of
Minto, who had served as governor general of Canada from 1898 to
1904) and various dukes, marquesses, earls, and lords. Sir Campbell
Stuart, as chairman, Sir Robert Kindersley (governor of the HBC),
Sir William Schooling, and Sir Arthur Doughty served on the executive
committee. An inaugural banquet was held in November 1923, at
which Stuart acknowledged the services of Doughty in organizing the
society and urged the solicitation of new members.[63] A year later a similar society for families connected with French Canada was inaugu-
rated by Stuart in France at a banquet held at the Palace of Versailles.[64]

Doughty re-established the relationship he and Schooling had begun
during Schooling's visit to Ottawa. Together they presented to Governor
Kindersley the idea of publishing the contents of the HBC archives.
Schooling was aware of the magnitude of the archival record of the Company and of the immensity of the project he had undertaken in attempting to write a one-volume history. The new plan included Schooling as
editor-in-chief, Doughty and Dr Adam Shortt, also of the Public Archives
of Canada, as associate editors, and an advisory editorial board of historians from Canada, the United States, England, and Scotland. It was a

grand scheme, proposing Kindersley as chairman and vice-presidents such as "the Prime Minister, past and present Governors of Canada and the like." Schooling even suggested that the king might agree to become a patron. He projected as many as two hundred volumes over a period of ten or twelve years with a cost of £250,000, to be raised through subscription. He also suggested a new building for the archives and a staff of fifteen. Schooling appealed to the business nature of the Company by pointing out the publicity value of such a venture and its duty to make the records public.[65]

Unfortunately, Schooling was by this time trying the patience of the governor and board, and they were not convinced by his enthusiasm. They insisted that he complete the history of the Company as he had been commissioned and in the allotted time. They did, however, appoint a subcommittee to consider the publication of archival records at a later date.[66] Schooling persisted with his recommendations for publishing the records and eventually suggested that, to eliminate any costs involved, the Company could give "permission to some Society of the nature of the Champlain Society, to publish the archives subject to the veto of the Hudson's Bay Company."[67] The Champlain Society had been modelled on the Hakluyt Society in Great Britain.[68]

Schooling admitted that he was overwhelmed by the history project and by the diversions created by the Canadian historians. By the end of October 1924, the board of directors, concerned about his slow progress, acknowledged that some of the problem was caused by interruptions from researchers. An announcement that is extremely significant in the history of the Hudson's Bay Company archives was made by the board at this time: "Recognising the difficulty experienced by Sir William Schooling in resisting the insistent demand of Canadian enquirers for access to the Company's records, the following Resolution was passed: – RESOLVED that, after completion and publication of the History of the Company upon which Sir William Schooling is now engaged, steps be taken to publish such of its archives as may be deemed expedient."[69]

Schooling suggested that instead of a history, the Company should publish the "Annals of the Hudson's Bay Company," which would be a compilation of quotations prepared by his staff over the previous years for his reference from the documents with added explanatory text, notes, and an index.[70] In November the board agreed to the new title for four volumes covering the period 1670 to 1820, but the "Annals" were to be ready for publication by the end of the next year, 1925.[71] Schooling was no more successful at following through on that plan than he had been on any of the others since the history project began, and a year later the project was abandoned.[72] He was asked to return everything he had completed to date, including his notes, to either Oxford University Press or the Company.[73] The Company had spent approximately £17,000 on this failed attempt at making its history known, including more than £13,000 paid to Schooling over the six years.[74]

Schooling may not have succeeded in his attempts to publish the wealth of historical material in the possession of the HBC, but he was the key to discovery of the Company's archives and the opening of that treasure chest to an eager historical community. His overly ambitious attempts to publish a Company history, although unsuccessful, left a good part of the Company's records indexed and extracted in a format that provided future staff of the archives quick and efficient access to volumes of information. Over the six years that he was on the Company's payroll, Schooling's priority changed from writing the history to promotion of a proper archives and an ambitious archival publication program. The history project failed as a medium for providing information from the Company's records. It did, however, make clear to the Company the nature of an archival dilemma it would have to address over the next few years: the extent and importance of its historical records, the inadequate arrangements for their administration in the Company, and growing international academic pressure to obtain better access to them. At this time the Company was not entirely supportive of Schooling's idea of a Company archives that would provide the level of service to researchers he had seen in North American archives such as the Public Archives in Ottawa. But times were changing. The Company moved slowly and hesitantly towards a policy of openness when it acknowledged the importance of its archives beyond the confines of the business and promised to publish at least some of its archival records. And Schooling's repeated pressure for recognition of the archives as a functional unit of the Company eventually elicited a commitment to an Archives Department within the Company. William Schooling had been sixty years old when he wrote the Company's anniversary "brochure" in 1920. He died in 1938 at the age of seventy-eight.

The publication program promised by the Company in late 1924 became an alternative means of attempting to resolve the archival problem after the failure of the official history project. It did not, however, get off the ground until Arthur Doughty was hired by the Company to launch it two years later. At the 1925 annual general court, Kindersley had resigned because of ill health. The new governor was Charles Sale, and, in a major change in the role of the governor in the administrative organization, he was also appointed managing director, the equivalent of the modern chief executive officer, putting him closer to the functional operations of the Company. Sale's years as governor were marked by reorganization and expansion. New facilities were built in London and new stores continued to be built in Canada. But he was also interested in the past, and his involvement with Schooling's project became obvious in the board minutes during his term, which are strewn with references to the Company's history and information from the archives. Sale travelled to Canada every year between 1925 and 1929, visiting offices, shops, and remote posts. On the first of these trips he met with Doughty in Ottawa, and there must have been serious discussion between the two regarding the Company's archives because the London *Times* made a significant announcement on 27 November 1925: "It is believed at Ottawa that Mr. Doughty, the Dominion Archivist, is likely to resign his office and go to England, in order to edit the papers of the Hudson's Bay Company."[75]

A month later the *Ottawa Journal* published a long article on the possibility of the Canadian government losing an exemplary civil servant and "high-class brain." It feared Doughty would be lured away from service to his country by the promise of "first-class remuneration" from private business. The reporter exaggerated the details somewhat in the announcement, stating that "Dr. A.G. Doughty, Dominion Archivist, has received an invitation from the Hudson's Bay Company to take charge of the archives of that company in London; also the information has leaked out that the company offers Dr. Doughty something like double the salary which he received as the deputy minister of a Canadian Government department."[76] The article went on to praise Doughty as having "a dynamic energy, an indomitable courage, and a public spirit which might be characterized as savage" and asked the question "what is to be done about Dr. Doughty's case?" From the time of Confederation the government of Canada, restricted by the level of salaries offered, had had difficulty retaining qualified civil servants, while "private business goes vigorously after what it perceives to be first-class value."[77]

Doughty must have been somewhat embarrassed by this outpouring of praise and conjecture. He immediately wrote to Governor Sale to explain: "I have tried to keep the matter quiet but it has got into the Press and absurd statements have been made as to the great things offered to me ... It cannot however do the Company any harm. On the contrary it [the *Ottawa Journal*] considers it good business on the part of the Company."[78] In fact, no firm arrangements had been made at this time between Doughty and the HBC, and he was reluctant to leave Canada. The government was unstable, politically, during 1926 with the transfer of power from Mackenzie King to Arthur Meighen and then back to King. The Public Archives of Canada was without a minister for most of that time, and no one was prepared to take the Dominion archivist's place.

Doughty did eventually get to London, and in March 1926 he presented Sale with a draft of an agreement outlining a plan by which he agreed to "undertake the direction and supervision of the classification and arrangement of the Records of the Company with the assistance of your staff" while maintaining the confidentiality of any information of which he might become aware regarding the business of the Company. The agreement would not be effective without the consent of the prime minister of Canada. Doughty added that his "direction of the said work shall not imply a claim on the part of the Canadian Government; or of others, to the benefit of my knowledge of the affairs of the Company, or to copy extracts of information of any kind, relating to its records."[79] The remuneration was to be £300 a year.[80]

Prime Minister Mackenzie King approved the arrangement in October and the Company finalized the agreement in December with the first monthly payment to Doughty. He must have worked on the classification of the records at Beaver House, the new fur warehouse, where they had been given separate accommodation after they were moved in 1926 from No. 1 Lime Street. No report of the classification work completed by Doughty has been found in the HBC archives, but in February 1928 he wrote to Sale from the Public Record Office in London to encourage publication of material from the archives: "Now that the records of your numerous posts have been assembled and it is possible to make selections for publication, I shall be pleased to assist you in any way possible."[81] Doughty remained on the Company's payroll at £300 per annum until 1930.

The return of the books and records borrowed by Schooling and the process of reintegrating them and arranging them on the shelves at Beaver House was a convenient time to check the inventory. A monetary value for insurance purposes was determined for the archival material. The total value allocated was £50,000, including the unclassified maps. The highest individual valuation was placed on the two original narratives of Radisson (£500 each) and the "observations on Hudson's Bay" by Graham, Isham, and Hutchins (£250 each). The oldest minute books were valued at the rate of £50 each, as were the earliest and largest of the grand ledgers and grand journals. The book of stock assignments dating from the years 1673–90, noted for the signature of Sir Christopher Wren, was valued at £100.[82]

PUBLISHING THE ARCHIVES

In April 1928 new publication arrangements were made with the Canadian History Society in England and its founder, Sir Campbell Stuart.[83] Sale informed the Canadian Committee of the plans and, in the process, revealed something of the Company's awareness of the public relations value of its archives:

> During the last few months we have assembled our records which make a unique collection despite the numerous fires and clearances effected from time to time at various places and on various occasions throughout the Company's history. We have commenced the task of clearing off the dirt and dust of ages and are engaged in classifying them. It is a task of great magnitude. Doctor Doughty has been with us during recent months and his advice has been very helpful ... [He] returned to Ottawa a few days ago, perfectly satisfied with the fact that the bars of the treasure house are about to be taken down. Whilst Doctor Doughty was here we had several meetings with Sir Campbell Stuart who has been, as you know, the moving spirit in the formation of the Canadian History Society ... We have agreed to combine with this Society in the publication of our records, whilst still retaining control through the fact that we take the monetary risk. In publishing under the auspices of the Society we shall benefit by the prestige of the great names among its members.[84]

The new publication scheme was devised in a manner that would make a wider range of archival information available than could be published in a single official history. Thus the obligation to preserve "the great inheritance" of Company archives could be fulfilled, and it could enjoy whatever "prestige" that may have brought it. At the same time, it would still control access to the information in the records because it retained the final say on which would be published. By December that year the announcement was reported in the *Canadian Historical Review*:

> Students of Canadian history were greatly interested in the announcement as to the historical records of the Hudson's Bay Company, made by Mr. Charles V. Sale, governor, at the meeting of the general court of the Company held in London on June 26 last.
>
> Mr. Sale referred to the immense collection of records in possession of the Company, touching almost every phase of history of the Canadian West from the seventeenth century to the present day. Until recently much of this material was scattered throughout Canada, but, with the provision of space in the new buildings of the Company in London, these documents were taken overseas, and the work of classifying them, together with the documents preserved in England, was begun ... That a company still engaged most actively in business should have in its archives records dealing with such a vast area and of such great historical value provides an almost unique situation. The publication in the near future under competent editorship of important documents from the storehouse of the Company is eagerly awaited, while it is hoped that scholars engaged seriously in research work may have access to other materials which are unlikely to be printed soon, if at all.[85]

Doughty was to be editor with associate or consulting editors appointed from western Canada. The Canadian Committee in Winnipeg reminded the governor of the importance of this selection: "There is an unfortunate tendency in eastern Canada, particularly in Ottawa, to forget the West and it is thought that the Company should not adopt this attitude which has been the cause of considerable feeling at different times that could be avoided."[86] The editorial committee was eventually made up of Chester Martin from Manitoba (later to move to the University of Toronto), A.S. Morton from Saskatchewan, and A.L. Burt from Alberta, all professors of history.[87] Doughty advised the Company "that Mr. William Smith should be sent from the Public Archives to assist in the selection and editing of documents which you decide to publish," and Smith's salary was augmented by the HBC.[88]

The Merk publication had not yet come to light, and Smith spent about three months in London and several more back in Ottawa preparing Simpson's 1824–25 and 1828–29 journals for publication. He encountered the same difficulties as Schooling had with the immense amount of material in the Company archives and a limited amount of time to prepare it.[89] The draft text was finally ready in February, but when Chester Martin read it, he was not satisfied and Doughty was disappointed.[90] Considerable work had been carried out towards a publication, but again with no tangible result. Doughty had to cancel two trips to London that year, and in August 1930 Sale wrote to inform him that the arrangements with him had been terminated.[91] The Company was tightening its belt because of poor profits in 1929 and 1930 and cutting all peripheral spending. Another four years had passed with no publication and with another £4,000 spent.

The requirements of this ambitious publication program again accentuated the necessity of having a well-organized company archives. But with the publishing program discontinued, the Company settled on a more liberal access policy as a means of making its archival information available. The new policy was a response to requests from the academic community for improved access to the archives and an attempt to reconcile the competing concerns of the Company for both confidentiality and favourable publicity. It thus decided to allow outside researchers direct access to the least sensitive records (those created before 1870) but without necessarily permitting publication of information gleaned from them. From 1927 the Company had the beginnings of a formal Archives Department, established to assist Doughty's publication program and to enable researchers to have wider direct access to the Company's historical records, which its new policy allowed.

In 1928 the Archives Department was moved once again, to the sixth floor of the new Hudson's Bay House on Bishopsgate, where there was more space for the staff to arrange and classify the records. Although the work on publication had been discontinued, the Company had a better idea of its documentary heritage, through which it had become more familiar with at least the first two hundred years of its history. It also had an idea of why students of history were so interested.

The secretary of the Company through most of this period was J. Chadwick Brooks, who had been hired in 1922 to assist in the work of reorganization plans. Frank C. Ingrams was officially the secretary until June 1923, but when he asked for a year's leave of absence in April 1922, Brooks, A.H. Doe, and P. Sewell were appointed assistant secretaries to manage the work of that office. Ingrams had been with the Company for thirty-five years, and he may have found the changes and reorganization more stressful than he could handle at that point in his career. When his retirement was announced, the Company acknowledged his well-earned right "to a less strenuous existence."[92] Of the three assistant secretaries, Brooks was the young, educated, and physically active choice for the position. He was a fellow of the Incorporated Secretaries Association and worked well with the business-oriented deputy governor. The changes in the office routine and record-keeping that are obvious in the files from the 1920s can probably be attributed to two men – Charles Sale and J. Chadwick Brooks.

MODERN RECORDS MANAGEMENT

In general, the orderly and effective management of industry and business had been developing intensively since the end of the nineteenth century. Schools of business, professional organizations, and detailed handbooks on all aspects of business management, functions, and methods were readily available resulting in uniform standards for offices and companies.

Administrative routine in the London office was reorganized to include a central records registry system which required that each letter received was recorded, placed in a subject category, and stamped with a number representing the subject. A parallel alphabetical card index was used to cross-reference the numbers assigned. Duplicate copies typed on flimsy blue paper were made of all correspondence, one for the board and one for filing according to subject. Duplicate and even triplicate copies of correspondence were received from the Canadian offices. The official registration stamp, usually found in the upper right-hand corner of the letter, also included a consecutive number for the correspondence of each month, the date of receipt, a box for the initials of the person answering, boxes for the initials of the individuals reading it in each department to which it was circulated (S for secretary, A for accountant, etc.), and a space to indicate whether a duplicate was filed and where.[93] As of June 1927, this scheme was revised so that all original letters received the registration stamp in red ink, with the added note that the letter was to be returned to the central filing department, and all duplicate copies of letters from Canada were stamped in blue ink, indicating that the duplicate was to be filed in the department to which it was forwarded. All original letters from the Canadian office were circulated to the governor and managing director, the secretary, the accountant, and the respective department. Letter registers were kept for all inward correspondence and for outward correspondence to the Canadian Committee.[94] Correspondence from Canada was filed according to a numerical system by department (17 for Canadian Committee, 18 for land commissioner, etc.) until 1928, when all Canadian departments were centrally filed by subject in a Canadian Committee series.

Sale's interest in the history and historical record of the Company, reinforced by Schooling's enthusiasm and his research in the subject and the refreshing energy of Brooks, resulted in a thorough housecleaning of records in all departments and branches of the Company, both in London and in Canada. In April 1922 the governor and Committee received from the Canadian advisory committee a list of old records that had been located at Lower Fort Garry.[95] In all, several tons of records were located in the Canadian offices and fur trade posts and shipped to London. And in the process, a large number of historical artifacts was rounded up which eventually formed the basis for the Company's museum collection. Robert Watson, then editor of *The Beaver*, explained the records situation at the still active Norway House:

> I examined all possible places where old documents relative to Norway House might lie … In the loft of the Mess House (library) I found a box of old correspondence scattered and trodden among rubbish. This I sorted out and examined. They dated as far back as 1832. I took what I considered the more important and typical, bringing them back with me … In the Fur Warehouse I found a great pile of discarded books, amounting to several hundreds. I examined all of these and among them found the following, which I brought back: – Minute Book of Council Meetings, 1870 to 1883, Norway House Diary 1868/1870, Norway House Diary 1911/1915, Tariff 1833, Tariff 1837/38, List of Officers and Servants (Northern Department) 1854. There were numerous other books 1833 to 1865 which I separated from the more recent ones and put to one side in the warehouse along with the Norway House letter books dated 1887/1908. There were no letter books among these prior to that date except one in which copies of letters had been written. This was dated 1858 and I brought it back with me. During the early period of the Post's history, letters would appear to have been copied by hand and filed in bundles with pink tape, as per samples which I have brought back … Mr. Bayer ([a] free trader and previous Post Manager at Norway House) has a remembrance that a Mr. Rackham, who was with the Company at one time, took away a padlocked book of Council or other historical records at Norway House. If

there is any truth in this, it might be possible to find out from
Mr. Rackham what happened to this book. [96]

As a result of Watson's fruitful visit to Norway House, searches were
also carried out at York Factory, Moose Factory, and several other
old posts.[97]

Other changes and innovations occurred in London during the
1920s, leading to the development of order noted within the Company's administrative records. The importance of setting standards and
providing training for staff throughout the Company was an initiative
of Brooks, and policy and procedure manuals were drawn up and circulated.[98] As part of his efforts to standardize records practices in London
and in Winnipeg, Brooks sent Philip Chester, then assistant accountant
in London, to Winnipeg to bring the fur trade accounts in the Canadian
head office into line with the London office system. His suggestions and
recommendations for reorganization and for further cooperation between departments were accepted, and the new system saw the accounting process decentralized. The fur trade accounting records were
transferred from the Canadian head office to a separate fur trade commissioner's office. Chester was then sent back to Winnipeg with an assistant "for the purpose of installing a revised system of accounts."[99]
He remained there permanently, married a Canadian, and was appointed chief accountant. Thus began a long relationship between
Chester, the Canadian Committee, and London. He was appointed general manager of the Company in Canada in 1931 and became a member of the Canadian Committee.

During the decade of the 1920s, the Company's physical image in
London changed considerably with moves into two impressive, custom-
designed buildings. Even with the renovations carried out in 1914–15,
the premises in the old Lime Street warehouses were no longer suitable,
and the lease was terminated in 1923. The building was owned by
Lloyds of London and was to be demolished to make way for its new
corporate headquarters, a structure that would in turn be replaced, on
the same location, by an impressive postmodern glass building in 1986.
A new buying, shipping, and fur warehouse, to be called Beaver House,
was built for the Company on property a few blocks to the west, bor-
dered by Great Trinity Lane, Garlick Hill, Thames Street and Little Trinity Lane. This put the Company at what had been the medieval centre of
London's fur trade district, not far from the old Skinners' Hall. The
modern, custom-designed, 600,000-cubic-foot warehouse could hold

Opening ceremonies at Beaver House, 1926 (1987-363-B-18-41 and 43)

two million pelts at a constant temperature. Improved lighting conditions were incorporated for grading and storing the furs. After the market slump during and immediately after the First World War, Beaver Hall was added on to the warehouse, providing a spacious facility for auctions, with banked seating and microphones. The first auction was held there in 1928. Although Beaver House was not designed for the administrative functions of the Company or for long-term storage of its records, separate but temporary accommodation was provided in the new warehouse for what were then (finally) being called the "archives" while another new administrative building was completed.[100] In the meantime, the rest of the administrative offices and the records department joined Governor Sale and his staff in a nearby office building known as Threadneedle House, also on Bishopsgate, for four years.

A NEW HOME FOR THE HBC

In 1928 a new administrative headquarters building was opened at 52-68 Bishopsgate, next to Threadneedle House. Hudson's Bay House was grand. Designed by Messrs Mewes and Davis, the building was described by one writer as "an ornament to Bishopsgate."[101] The *Financial News* called the building an architectural work of art: "the Renaissance style is extraordinarily safe, its forms are not only pleasant and seemly, but are capable of investing a building with dignity … while striking a note of opulence, it yet impresses by its scholarly style, which has ample room to display itself in a facade of such dimensions. Very tall and broad, the frontage towards Bishopsgate is of a design easily analysable into its constituent parts."[102] The description gives no clues to the activities of the business to be carried out within but an obscure clue, scarcely visible six storeys above street level, was a beaver weathervane topping the lantern feature on the steep roof.[103]

Hudson's Bay House may have been new and "modern" in the context of 1920s London, especially as compared to the outdated Lime Street building, but its interior was still imposing in the classical sense. The style was described as "classic with traces of the Wren influence; singularly appropriate, as Wren was a stockholder and a member of the Committee of the Company."[104] The high ceilings and cornices in the committee or board room on the main floor were carved with beavers, otters, and other North American flora and fauna. Tall glass-fronted bookshelves on either side of the fireplace alcove were flanked by majestic Corinthian columns. A painting of the first governor, Prince Rupert, by Sir Peter Lely hung majestically over the mantelpiece, facing

Architect's presentation sketch for Hudson's Bay House,
68 Bishopsgate, about 1923

the portrait of King Charles II, also by Lely, across the room. On the side wall opposite the windows were portraits of the Duke of York, second governor and afterwards King James II, Sir Robert Kindersley, and Sir John Pelly, governor of the Company from 1822 to 1852.[105] The long walnut table sat on a 16-by-29-foot Persian carpet, purchased especially for the room. The walnut chairs were upholstered in green Moroccan leather, and mounted on the back of the matching governor's armchair at the head of the table was the Company's coat of arms carved in the wood.[106] The Company offices on the main (second) floor and partial mezzanine were accessed by entrances off Bishopsgate at each end of the building. The front of the main floor included the governor's office, offices for his private secretary and the Company secretary, a general office for the clerical staff, and a small accountant's office. Also at the back of the main floor was a large public lobby and hallway, the stenographers' room, the managing director's office, and records storage space. The rest of the building except for the sixth floor and basement, which was used by the Archives Department, was rented out to tenants such as Sale and Company and the Australian Bank of Commerce.

7

rendered available for inspection by students of history
Establishment of the Hudson's Bay Company Archives, 1930–1960

The decade of the 1920s and the governorship of Charles Sale slammed shut in 1930, a year after the collapse of the North American stock market and the worldwide downturn in everything commercial. The Company experienced heavy operating losses in its retail trade that would last well into the 1930s; no dividends were paid to shareholders from 1931 to 1938. The financial situation was reported to the Committee in December 1930:

> The difficult conditions of trading for the current year as foreshadowed by the Governor at the Annual General Meeting on the 27th June, 1930, have proved to be even more severe than was anticipated. Not only has there been a continuous and serious fall in the price of furs, thereby involving the Company in very heavy losses, but the prevailing depression in Canada has adversely affected the Company's other activities, including the Land Department receipts. Unfortunately, there appears to be no immediate prospect of improvement and the present year's working will undoubtedly result in heavy loss.[1]

Discussions raised by these concerns and the response of some members resulted in the selection of a four-member special committee to evaluate the position in which the Company found itself. Its recommendations called for drastic changes that included considerable downsizing of personnel, segregating of the Stores Department from the rest of the operations in Canada, consolidating the London operations at

Beaver House, and temporarily waiving the fees paid to board members. Sale had been a hands-on governor, taking on a more active management role than previous directors of the Company, and some shareholders blamed him for the recent financial losses. In a later speech to shareholders and the other directors, the deputy governor testified to Sale's important role in the Company: "Charles Sale joined the Company at a very critical time in its history. He found it lagging behind instead of taking a prominent part in the growth of that wonderful Dominion. He gripped the situation in the spirit of the earliest Adventurers, and, with his immense energy and great vision and courage, in a comparatively short time revived the old spirit of the Company."[2] But as explained in a letter to shareholders at the end of December before the next meeting, the Company was moving in new directions, and Sale could not accept the recommendations presented by the special committee report:

> The Governor, Mr. Charles V. Sale, does not agree with the recommendations of the special committee so far as they relate to the information of a Canadian Company to acquire and conduct the Company's Stores business in Canada, and, believing as he does that such a fundamental change in the policy of the Company at the present time is not in its best interests, feels that he cannot associate himself with such a change. He has, therefore, tendered his resignation as Governor of the Company, to take effect so soon as his successor is appointed.[3]

For one of the few times in the history of the Company, an extraordinary court was called to receive and consider the report and to pass a resolution on it. Sale attended the meeting but, having tendered his resignation, turned the chair over to the deputy governor, Sir Frederick Richmond. The select committee recommended the segregation of the Stores Department and "the constitution of a separate Company in Canada to own and operate the Stores."[4]

The one common interest of all the shareholders was "the restoration at the earliest possible moment of the prestige and prosperity of the Hudson's Bay Company,"[5] and further, they optimistically believed "that the present difficulties are a passing phase in the history of the Company, and that with good management and good will on the part of everyone interested it will not be long before we may expect better times."[6] Sale's resignation was accepted immediately, and for six months Richmond served as acting governor until a new governor was elected. The drastic changes required to set the Company back on track financially would involve the fur trade, the Land Department, and sale-shops in Canada. All reported to the Canadian Committee, which in 1929 was provided with power of attorney and a year later was entrusted with full power of administration and executive authority for the North American operations. The London board retained its responsibility for broad policy and large capital expenditures. All correspondence and re-porting to and from London was conducted through the Canadian Com-mittee, which was centred in Hudson's Bay House on Main Street in Winnipeg.[7] The Canadian Committee was chaired by George Allan, in a continuation of his role as chair of the Canadian advisory committee. Other members were James Thomson, who had been the land commis-sioner and also the fur trade commissioner from 1918 to 1920, and sev-eral leading Winnipeg businessmen: James A. Richardson (J. Richardson and Sons), R.J. Gourley (Beaver Lumber Company), C.S. Riley (Canadian Fire Insurance Company), and H.B. Lyall (Manitoba Bridge and Iron).

Philip Chester, who had been the chief accountant in Canada since 1925, was appointed general manager in 1930 with control of all the business and affairs of the Company in Canada.[8] His first concern was the reorganization of the Fur Trade Department to reduce expenses, and with that goal in mind, he chose Ralph Parsons to replace Charles French as fur trade commissioner and Frank Martin as manager of the retail stores. Parsons, the last of the fur trade commissioners, reorganized the Fur Trade Department over the next ten years, with consideration of the Company's new emphasis on merchandising. When he retired in 1940, the Canadian Committee decided to discontinue the title of fur trade commissioner and reorganized the Fur Trade Department with a manager reporting to the general manager.[9] Chester named his assistant, Robert H. Chesshire, to the new position. Chesshire, in turn, made sev-eral organizational changes, including consolidating or abolishing dis-tricts, a process that was turned around in 1946 when a major expansion and development plan was introduced for the increasingly important merchandising aspect of the Fur Trade Department. Posts were estab-lished wherever there was a potential for business in furs or merchandis-ing, and older posts were revitalized with new buildings.[10] In some communities the fur trade played a small or non-existent role, with mer-chandising replacing the collection of furs as the chief activity. By 1959, with more than 90 per cent of the business in retail selling, the Fur Trade Department was renamed the Northern Stores Department, and another important era in the Company's history came to an end.

In London the Company's fur sales operations continued to be centred at Beaver House in Trinity Lane and its adjacent auction facility in Beaver Hall. All shipments of new furs were received there, graded, and warehoused in preparation for the auctions held three times a year. The Company's administration offices were in Hudson's Bay House at 68 Bishopsgate. The main-floor offices were used by the governor and his personal secretary, the secretary and his assistant, the accountant, three stenographers, and up to twelve clerical staff.

THE FIRST ARCHIVIST

The archives were located on the sixth floor of the building. The person in charge of the Company's records department, and its only staff member still left by the middle of 1931, was Richard Leveson Gower,[11] who had initially been employed by the Company in the fall of 1923. He had arranged for the archival records to be delivered to and returned from William Schooling, who was working on the history project out of his home in Kensington. He was also one of a team of four staff members who read, arranged, and made extracts of information from the post journals, minutes books, and letterbooks for Schooling's history. The extracts and notes provided a chronological sequence of events of the history of the Company, which was typed and bound, eventually filling twenty-nine "Annals," all indexed by subject.[12] Another set of twelve smaller volumes compiled extracts from post journals as well as listing the names of the writers,[13] and two small volumes gathered information about the Company's ships.[14]

Leveson Gower had also been engaged in the mid-1920s to answer numerous inquiries, primarily regarding the long-standing Labrador boundary dispute, which was finally settled in 1927.[15] Later that year he was sent to Canada for four months to learn about the Company's operations there and to identify and arrange for the transfer of inactive records to London. There is no itinerary in the HBCA's files for his trip, but it is evident from correspondence received from him in London that he at least visited Montreal (Lachine), Ottawa, Winnipeg, and Victoria, coinciding at times with the governor's trip to Canada and the United States that same year.[16] Sale and Leveson Gower both visited the Provincial Archives in Victoria in September, when Sale requested information on HBC forts, especially Fort St James, which he had visited on his travel to the coast.[17] As previously mentioned, important documents concerning the HBC are in the possession of the British Columbia Archives, largely because of the dual role of James Douglas as chief factor for the Company and governor of the colony of Vancouver Island up to 1858, when he ended his employment with the HBC and became governor of the colony of British Columbia. Arrangements were made during the 1930s for copies to be exchanged between Victoria and London to round out each archives' resources. A note in the annual report of the archives department of the B.C. Provincial Library for 1926–27 explains also that Leveson Gower was "left for 4 days to study our mode of indexing and filing ms. [manuscripts] and ms. books, etc. preparatory to putting their [the Company's] own valuable archives in shape."[18]

Despite the fact that quite a bit of ordering and extracting had been accomplished since 1920, the archives still lacked an adequate general catalogue suitable for the use of researchers. When inquiries were received, the practice had been to identify relevant records on a particular subject from which extracts of information were provided to the researcher. Copies of the research material collected were filed so that resource material was accumulated and available for future inquiries, but it was time-consuming for the staff. Leveson Gower was "admirably fitted for the work," Brooks told the governor in the wake of the 1931 downsizing, "possessing as he does a natural aptitude for historical dates and for the work of classification and cataloguing of records, and he obviously derives considerable pleasure from the research which is rendered necessary by the many applications we receive from students of history and others."[19]

Asked by the secretary to report on the records department in early 1931, Leveson Gower identified seven areas to discuss: publications, accessibility to researchers, collection of data and indexing, preservation, sorting and classification, and the library. As a cost-saving measure, the decision had been made to postpone any future publications and his assistants were to be let go. Leveson Gower regretted that decision, especially the loss of Kathleen Pincott, whose knowledge of the material in the archives he respected:

> I therefore beg to point out, with all deference, the great value of Miss Pincott's past services in this connection. Although, it would probably be possible, when the time arrives, for you to obtain another assistant, I cannot stress too strongly the great benefit which would result if Miss Pincott's services were retained, owing to her very extensive knowledge of all periods of the Company's history,

combined with her previous experience in editorial work. Her work in connection with the Company's Archives extends over a period of almost ten years, as she was employed by Sir William Schooling, as Research Assistant for five years from 1921/1926, and since February, 1928 has been employed by the Company here.[20]

It did not help; Pincott left in May and did not return to the employ of the Company.

Further to Leveson Gower's report on the state of the records department, he noted that the preservation of the records had been enhanced since 1928 with the employment of a bookbinder. "All the most important and oldest Books and Documents have now been put into a state of repair which should last for many years to come."[21] Sorting and classifying the records had benefited greatly from locating the records in one place, on the sixth floor of Hudson's Bay House, in 1928, resulting in the identification and sorting of most of the material up to 1870. The library books, located either in the boardroom bookcases or in the records department, had recently been catalogued. The report also broached the subject of accessibility of the archives to outside researchers. "More especially, in view of the fact that it has been decided temporarily to suspend publication ... it has occurred to me that it would be much appreciated in many quarters if, at some future time, the Board would consider the possibility of rendering the Company's Records accessible to Students."[22] The report must have been presented to the interim board, which made a decision that had been long awaited by historians. On 12 May 1931, in view of the decision to postpone the question of publication, "it was decided that the Company's Archives prior to 1870 should be *rendered available for inspection by students of history* and others, at the discretion of Mr. Leveson Gower, the Company's Archivist."[23]

This was a significant turning point in the history of access to the archives of the HBC, and the fact that it was accomplished at what must have been an unnervingly unstable and disruptive time for the Company is even more noteworthy. In attendance at the meeting were Sir Frederick Richmond, deputy governor (in the chair), Vivian Hugh Smith, Sir Hewitt Skinner, A.K. Graham, London manager, Lieutenant Colonel J.B.P. Karslake, and Captain Victor A. Cazalet. But even in his absence, this decision reflects the interest shown in the archives over the previous ten or fifteen years by Charles Sale. For the first time, as a matter of formal policy, researchers were to be allowed direct access to records created before

1870. They would still require the Company's approval to publish information from the records. It had always been the prerogative of the governor to decide who could publish information from the archives. That tight control was ended when implementation of the access policy was delegated to the company archivist, Leveson Gower, who was known as a strong advocate of liberal terms of access for researchers. Correspondence regarding the archives was still received by the board through the secretary, who then informed the archivist. The first application for access to the archives came in September 1931 from J.B. Tyrrell, a well-known Canadian geologist and historian from Toronto, who wished to research Philip Turnor's surveys and the journal of Joseph Howse with the intention of publication. The board replied to the request by deciding "that access to the documents referred should be afforded to Mr. Tyrrell, and that, subject to revision by Mr. Leveson Gower, extracts from them might be published."[24]

The new governor, Patrick Ashley Cooper, was recommended by the Bank of England and took over in June 1931. His personal style would be imprinted on the Company for the next twenty-one years as he studied all aspects of the operations, regularly travelling to Canada. He delegated the functional organization to others, choosing instead to be an objective "critic of management" when required.[25] With F.A. Stacpole as his appointed assistant, Cooper immediately set about disposing of excess property, primarily the barely three-year-old but costly Hudson's Bay House at 68 Bishopsgate. The building would not, in fact, be sold until 1947, but most of it was rented out when the board and administrative offices moved to Beaver House in 1932, leaving only the Archives Department to occupy the sixth floor, basement, and sub-basement. Staff terminations, begun earlier in the year, continued. Between January and September 1931, twelve women and eight men were let go, including stenographers, mail and file clerks, the registrar, and the lawyer, and further reductions were made in October. A gradual turnaround occurred over the next three years as the administrative structure of the Company was gradually rebuilt with appropriately trained and efficient staff. By 1934 the heavy financial losses had turned to profit. Through the years following the restructuring, the well-being of the staff was a constant consideration. Long-service awards were presented annually with some ceremony. There were regular Christmas parties for the staff and their families, and every summer a garden party was given by the governor and Mrs Cooper at their country home. The HBC was a regular stop for Canadians visiting London. The governor entertained Canadian sports teams, Rhodes scholars from Oxford, and Canadian staff on official or personal visits to London. On these occasions, the archives was included on the tour of the Company's operations in London.

Like Sale, Cooper was a modern manager but with an interest in the history of the business. He fully appreciated the importance of its archives both for historical research and favourable publicity, and the Archives Department remained after the downsizing exercise, though not untouched, and still reporting to the secretary. The move to Hudson's Bay House on Bishopsgate in 1928 had provided the archives with adequate space for the records to be stored in an order that made their access more efficient. In 1932 the records were moved to the basement of that building, where they remained, except for six years during the Second World War, when most of the archives were moved out of London to a more secure location.[26] When the dust had finally settled after all the consolidation and re-organization, Brooks pointed out to Cooper that Leveson Gower was the only staff member serving the records and archives and the only person with the knowledge of the records to search out answers to the numerous research questions being received. He recommended the hiring of an assistant to provide an understudy for the archivist. The archives and records must have been important enough to Cooper because the very capable and efficient Alice Johnson, who had worked in the Archives Department until the end of 1930, was rehired in 1934 as assistant to the archivist.

The lack of success of two earlier strategies to write an official Company history and to promote a publication program, combined with academic pressure to loosen restrictions on access and publication, prompted the Company to open up its archives to researchers. If the benefits of the archives were to be obtained, a policy permitting direct access by outside researchers to the records in order to publish information from them was the only alternative. This approach implied that the Company archives should be able to provide the service needed to implement these policies. The archives, which had developed as an ancillary aspect of the two publication efforts in the 1920s, emerged in the early 1930s, in the capable hands of Richard Leveson Gower, as a distinct departmental service with a mandate to encourage access and publication.

GOVERNOR COOPER AND THE ARCHIVES

In 1932, with the intention of making the archives more accessible to outside researchers, the new governor instructed the archivist to contact the Public Record Office in order to obtain someone to "inspect our methods of filing, storing, tabulating, etc., the records, and to advise us whether we are doing all that is necessary in that respect and in the right manner, and if not, to advise us as to the best way in which the work should be done to make the records available for the use of students."[27] As a result, two consultants were invited to inspect the archives and records "with a view to making suggestions regarding the most efficient methods of cataloguing and preserving them and of rendering them available to students in as adequate a manner as possible."[28] Reginald Coupland was professor of colonial history at Oxford University. Hilary Jenkinson was officer of repository and repairs at the Public Record Office and author of *A Manual of Archive Administration*, first published in 1922 and reissued in 1931, which is still recognized as a classic work in the field of archival administration. Sale had sent a copy of the *Manual* to Philip Chester soon after his appointment as general manager in Canada, with a note that he had not read it, "but a hasty glance through leads us to believe you may find it useful, if only in drawing your attention to the experience of others in this direction."[29]

Jenkinson was one of the chief promoters for the formation of the British Records Association in November 1932. The HBC was an institutional member from 1933, the archivist attended the annual meetings and received the association's journal, *Archives*, and from 1935 to 1960 the Company made annual reports of its archival work to the association. The purpose of the BRA was clearly suited to problems and concerns with which the Company had been engaged since 1920 regarding its archives:

> The objects of the British Records Association shall be to promote the preservation and accessibility under the best possible conditions of Public, Semi-Public and Private Archives; to take measure for the rescue and distribution to recognized custodians of documents which would otherwise be dispersed or destroyed; to arouse public interest in, and to create a sound public opinion on, matters affecting the Records; to ensure the co-operation to those ends of all Institutions and Persons interested; to enable such institutions and Persons to interchange views upon matters of technical interest relating to the custody, preservation, accessibility and use of documents; and to receive and discuss Reports on all these matters from its Council, Committees and Sections as provided.[30]

It is no wonder that Jenkinson was interested in the Company's archives, and it is significant that he was requested to inspect them in

1932, a particularly vulnerable period in their history. Among his prolific writings, Jenkinson expressed concern for archival records at such times: "Records, which have survived because no one troubled to destroy them, are particularly liable to perish in times of stress because no one is sufficiently interested to preserve them."[31] A few years later, during the Second World War, the association published pamphlets for the "information of Local Representatives and Local and Private Custodians of Records" to warn of overzealous paper recycling and to prevent the indiscriminate destruction of documents in the national cause of paper salvage. The first pamphlet, *What Should We Try to Save?* was sent to the governor of the Company with a covering letter praising the "laudable efforts being made ... throughout the Country to increase the stock of waste paper" while attempting "to minimise the efforts of misguided enthusiasm without appreciably diminishing the supply of waste paper."[32] The second pamphlet, *What May We Destroy?* included a schedule of the types of records that were important to keep, many of which could be found in the HBC.

Professor Coupland, who inspected the archives in April 1932, "expressed to the Governor his opinion that the housing, tabulating and cataloguing of the records was most satisfactory, especially compared with other records he had seen."[33] It was on his suggestion that Jenkinson was approached. Their separate reports provided recommendations that included conservation measures for the repository and its contents and the installation of steel shelving for archival storage. Jenkinson offered to provide specifications for a shelving system similar to the one used in the Public Record Office. On the subject of public access, both Coupland and Jenkinson recommended that strict supervision would be necessary. Jenkinson's philosophy, as set out in his *Manual*, was that the archivist was "the servant of his Archives first and afterwards of the Student Public."[34] It is not surprising, then, to read in Jenkinson's report to the Hudson's Bay Company that "before any general policy of admission of the public is adopted or (at least) announced,"[35] a summary of the collection inventory should be prepared, a catalogue number attached to every item in the inventory, and then a list prepared by catalogue number. In addition, every document produced for inspection would have to be stamped with the Company's name. Jenkinson had made this point very clear in his *Manual*: "Until some such numbering work as the above has been undertaken, it is not, we must repeat, safe for either the Archivist or the Public to be allowed to deal further with the documents."[36]

Brooks reported these recommendations to the board, which agreed to all the proposals, including the purchase of steel shelving, further expenditures regarding fire protection and lighting fixtures, and steps to complete cataloguing and "marking" the records in order to make "certain of them available to the public."[37]

In February and March 1933 Leveson Gower reported on the work that had been completed since 1922, when Schooling had insisted on some organization of the records to aid his writing of the Company history. One hundred and eighty pages of galley proofs for Schooling's "Annals" were still set up at the printers awaiting the Company's instructions to go ahead with the publication. That never happened, but the printers kept the type standing until 1937, when they were instructed to destroy it, thus ending any further reference to that project. By then, E.E. Rich was editing the first Hudson's Bay Record Society publication and had concluded that, "owing to the numerous corrections, amendments and additions to the draft, the type will not be of use, as the expense of alteration would be greater than the cost of setting up new type."[38] As well, the catalogue compiled when the records were stored at No. 1 Lime Street was no longer useful for locating material. "None of the boxes – with the exception of a few containing correspondence subsequent to 1870 – are still in use as the contents have been extracted and sorted into Files, etc."[39] Post journals were arranged alphabetically by name of post, then chronologically within each category, and indexed; letters inward were arranged in chronological order; and almost two hundred boxes of records, received from Canada since 1922, had been unpacked and sorted. A card index and a subject search file were being compiled from information retrieved while answering research inquiries. Post records other than journals had been divided into three sections: Correspondence Books, District Statements, and Miscellaneous Account Books. Some material relating to areas of individual interest had been arranged accordingly. For instance, records relating to the Puget's Sound Agricultural Society were catalogued together, as were records pertaining to Sir George Simpson. Miscellaneous papers and letters that did not fit into any of the identified categories were arranged chronologically.

With this arrangement in hand, Leveson Gower met again in March with Hilary Jenkinson to discuss the appropriate classification for the HBC records. They developed a plan that reflected both the existing order and Jenkinson's theories of classification based on the administrative provenance of records, as explained in his *Manual*. The first

Four articles about the HBC archives by Leveson Gower,
describing work completed in the archives, published in
The Beaver between December 1933 and September 1935

division of classification was by section (or broad administrative origin) and, within each section, by class (or company record-keeping system) and then by piece (or individual document). It was decided that the Company's archival records would be divided into five sections: Section A, Administration of the HBC in London; Section B, Administration of the HBC in Canada, including the 351 posts; Section C, Logs and other documents pertaining to ships; Section D, Miscellaneous Records, including Sir George Simpson's correspondence, papers, etc. (which had already been separated); and Section E, Private Records. These new arrangements would continue to be fine-tuned but were similar to the previous order, and more work would be required to foliate, stamp, and label the records once they were ordered. One of the mysteries to researchers with access to the original records is the use of labels on the spines of the pre-1870 bound records. These labels are explained in an excerpt from the "Rules Governing Classification of the Records of the Hudson's Bay Company":

(a) The "Pieces" – i.e. Files, boxes, volumes, bundles or parcels – to be arranged in chronological sequence. The particulars recorded on the labels referred to below to be entered in pencil inside the cover of each "Piece" or in an otherwise accessible place.

(b) Each "Piece" to be marked with the distinguishing Section Letter – "A" in the case of London Office Records and "B" in the case of records pertaining to the Company's Fur Trade Posts and Administrations in North America – number of its class and the number indicating its own position within the Class ... Thus, if the "Class" number in Section "B" for all documents and volumes relating to CHURCHILL FORT be 10 and the letter of sub-division for Post Journals is (a) a Journal will be described as follows: – B.10/a/19 – the latter being the "Piece" number of the particular Journal and shewing that it is the 19th Journal, in chronological sequence, of Churchill Fort. For this process two labels are in use, one with the Company's name imprinted thereon and a blue border ..., the other smaller and oval in shape with a red border ... On the first is stamped particulars of the Section, Class Number and Sub-division. The "Piece" Number is stamped on the smaller label, whilst the covering dates are entered thereon in ink. The large label to be affixed to the top of the file, etc., and the smaller label to be attached to the lower portion.

(c) Each "Piece" – i.e. volume, box, file or parcel – to be duly stamped in several places with the Company's metal stamp. In the case of loose papers each must be duly stamped before it may be made available to students. This stamping is carried out in an oil-basis ink.

(d) Each folio within a volume is numbered consecutively with the numerator stamp.[40]

At the same time, the Company embarked on a records management program in Canada and in London with a directive from the London board on 16 May 1933: "It was agreed that the respective managements in London and in Canada be instructed to examine all the Company's records with a view to providing for continuity of collection of all important documents for preservation in the Company's archives at the London head office."[41] The Canadian Committee was asked to investigate the situation regarding current records "so as to provide for continuity of the existing archives and also to ensure that other important records of more recent introduction are collected from time to time and placed in the Company's archives"[42] A list was included of documents considered by the board to be of archival importance. The response was received in September from the office of general manager Philip Chester, with a list of documents considered for permanent retention in the archives. "We have not included in these lists anything of a routine nature, the retention or destruction of which is dealt with in all departments under a regular procedure."[43] A large amount of historical material had been sent to London over the previous ten years and arrangements were made to ship "forthwith any documents which are now due to be sent to London, and thereafter in December each year despatch any which have become due for transfer during the preceding year."[44] A request was also made for a guide on how to manage the photographs that had accumulated in the Winnipeg office. As the Canadian consignments were received in the archives in London, they were appraised and classified. Old pre-1870 documents continued to show up, and those that clearly belonged to an already classified series were allocated to that series after being labelled and stamped.

A NEW ERA OF ACCESS

In 1934 Brooks reported that any Canadian staff members visiting London were being shown the Archives Department and various items of interest contained therein. "We have been gratified at the keen interest taken by the Canadian staff in our Archives and the history of the

Company."[45] The archives were also included as a formal part of the Company's public relations wing and viewed as an important source of historical information that could inspire employee morale and loyalty. Douglas MacKay, who had been in charge of advertising, public relations, and *The Beaver* magazine, was given supervision of the archives and records in the Canadian office.[46] The governor's address to the general court that year testifies to his commitment to the archives:

> Prior to 1924, the Company Archives lay stored in packing cases in the vaults of the Company's warehouse at Lime Street. Since that date the archives have been stored in various parts of the Company's buildings. While we have been busy overhauling our commercial operations, we have not neglected these archives, because we recognize the responsibility to posterity which this stewardship entails ... we hope that in due course we shall have this unique collection in a shape which will make it readily accessible to historical research students. Moreover, in consultation with the Canadian Committee, we have made adequate arrangements to maintain the continuity of our archives.[47]

As more order was achieved in the archives, Leveson Gower published a series of four articles about the history of the archives and the recent process of classification in *The Beaver* between 1933 and 1935. The Company was finally willing to make public information about its archival holdings and the work that had been accomplished in organizing them for research purposes. In so doing, it knew it would invite research inquiries from historians outside the Company. The archives room of the HBC was opened to researchers in October 1933, the first visitor being Arthur S. Morton from the University of Saskatchewan.

In response to his application to carry out research in the Company's archives, Morton had been interviewed by Stacpole during the governor's visit to Canada in 1931. The governor's assistant was forthright in his reasons for making a recommendation for academic research: "I do feel that we cannot leave any stone unturned to gain good impressions in Canada, and although there must be very distinct limits to the lengths to which we can do this, I feel that no harm will be done by having prominent educationists on our side ... University professors, I have found, if properly handled, are in the long run a very cheap and fairly helpful form of unpaid propaganda."[48] Morton was soon sharing space in the reading room with Charles Elton and his assistant.[49] As Douglas MacKay would later observe,

Visitors' book, 1933 (RG20/8/1). The first researcher to sign the visitors' book was Arthur S. Morton on 16 October 1933.

The archives are now freely available to accredited workers in the field of history. As students have probed deeply, no skeletons have yet clattered out of cupboards nor have nations been rocked ... Instead, as orderly scholarship assembles the pattern of the past, the fabric of history appear. Here and there the thread is broken; now and then there is a stain; but it is a whole cloth, woven by the active minds and toiling hands of men, with occasional brilliant strands upon a field of hodden grey. A long and honest piece, and every thread is a story of men and their money, their ships, their guns, their women and children, their furs,

their ambitions, failures, their courage and cowardice, all in
the service of a great Company.[50]

Early visitors to the HBCA have often commented on the afternoon tea
ritual. Morton wrote in September 1937 to "thank the Company for a
profitable summer's work in the Archives" and to express his "appreciation of the renewing cups of afternoon tea."[51] The tea lady in the 1930s
and 1940s was Mrs Sach, who had first been employed in 1893 as Lord
Strathcona's housekeeper. The story of her career and commitment to the
Company was reported in the staff magazine *The Bay*. She was married
to Joe Sach, who had worked as a warehouseman from 1890 until he
sustained a head injury that left him unfit to continue those duties. The
story of their life together and with the Hudson's Bay Company began
after Joe's accident when he was offered the job of caretaker and messenger at the Lime Street building but had to be married;

whereupon Joe, who was engaged to be married hastened things up,
and Mrs. Sach came as a bride to No. 1 Lime Street. She joined the staff
of the Company as Housekeeper while Joe Sach was appointed Messenger. The two were duly installed in the basement of No. 1, where
they remained for ten years. They were then transferred to the top flat
there, which was removed by 83 stairs from the front door ... At Lime
Street her three children were born, and those of us who began our service there can remember little golden-haired Beattie, the youngest child,
running up and down the stairs on her way to and from school.
Mrs. Sach's work with the Company included the serving of lunch
and tea in the Board Room to the members of the Board who met fort-
nightly at Lime Street, and she recalls ... the excitement which attended
the sailing of the Company's ship each year and its coming home. It
was equipped in London, and, near sailing time, the clerks in
Lime Street would work until 1 a.m., Mrs. Sach ministering to their oft-
repeated requests for tea, etc. It was many years before Women
Office Staff were admitted within the portals of Lime Street, but eventually an Addressograph Operator was engaged for a few months each
year, and Mrs. Sach acted as chaperon, giving her meals in her dining
room. About 1915, on account of war conditions, the Company reluctantly gave way to the extent of a handful of Women Staff, who were
very grateful for Mrs. Sach's attentions in the way of kettles of hot water, etc. ... When the Lime Street lease fell in, the Administration and
Accounts moved to 34, Bishopsgate, and the Buying Office and Fur

Mrs Sach and her tea trolley (*The Bay*, winter 1946/47)

Department to Garlick Hill. There was no accommodation for a house-keeper in either of these two buildings, so Mrs. Sach had twelve months' holiday, being paid a retaining fee to come up to the office whenever help was required, chiefly at sale times. She was then asked to attend regularly to serve afternoon tea, and the accompanying photograph shows her at her duties.[52]

THE HUDSON'S BAY RECORD SOCIETY

In March 1934 Brooks reported to the governor and board that the subject of publication had come up again in discussions he had with

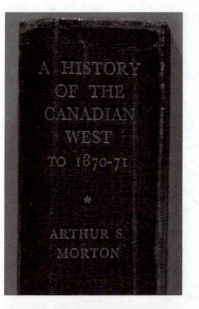

A History of the Canadian West to 1870–71 (1939), by Arthur S. Morton, showing acknowledgments on page ix

the archivist and Professor Morton.[53] "It has occurred to us ... that it might be well worth considering as to whether the Canadian History Society might not undertake the formation of a kind of subsidiary society, somewhat on the lines of the Champlain Society, which might be known by some such name as the 'Churchill Society.'"[54] A few months later Brooks and Leveson Gower argued that, regardless of the approach adopted, Company archival policy ought to strive to achieve the two purposes that it had had trouble reconciling in the past. "The question ... is what steps the Company should take in connection with the publication of its archives, two points being kept in mind, namely – (a) placing the unique archival material within the reach of all students of history and others by publication [and](b) securing to the Company all possible publicity and prestige in connection with such publication."[55] Their report for the board pointed out that the Company would have to make a decision to undertake such publication itself or to arrange for an independent organization to do so.[56] Discussions also had been renewed with Sir Campbell Stuart, chairman of the Canadian History Society of the British Isles, but he thought that the financial climate was inopportune to consider publication and that a separate society would not be the answer to the problem.[57]

Brooks kept pressing the proposal:

There has been a general feeling for some time that the Company should consider the question of publishing the official history because of – (a) the growing interest in the Canadian North as evidenced by the publication each year of books referring to the Company, (b) the increasing numbers of students in Canadian and American Universities who are researching into fur trade and other North American history with a view to publication, (c) the Company's position as owner of the most important volume of material regarding Canadian Western and Northern history involving some obligation towards the history of Canada and of the Fur Trade.[58]

The pressure to publish eventually had an effect and on 22 January 1935 the board recommended

(a) that an H.B.C. Society be formed to undertake publication of the Company's Archives and that a pamphlet inviting membership be issued over the names of influential sponsors representative of the U.K. and North America;

(b) that a small provisional committee be appointed, with Sir Campbell
Stuart as Chairman, to decide the terms of the pamphlet and to arrange
adequate circulation;
(c) that an executive committee be subsequently appointed with a
Director of Publications (part-time) and an Honourary Secretary;
(d) that the volumes published by the Society be available only to
members and not offered on sale to the general public;
(e) that an official history of the Company be published subsequently.[59]

The decision had been made to form a society to facilitate publication,
but it would be another three years before the provisional committee
submitted its recommendations and the society was incorporated. The
record society publication program, however, created a roadblock in
the way of direct access and liberal use of the archives. The restrictions
on publication – the readiness to deny permission to publish material
from the archives in order to protect the Company's own publication
program – were still an unresolved problem.

An incident occurred at this time that exemplifies the Company's un-
willingness to allow publication. Douglas MacKay, former editor of
The Beaver, published a history of the Hudson's Bay Company titled
The Honourable Company. It was advertised as the first history to be
written with full access to the Company archives. MacKay, as has been
noted earlier, was an employee of the Company, first in Montreal and
then at the head office in Winnipeg, where he was in charge of the
Company's general advertising, public relations, internal relations, and
The Beaver magazine.[60] He paid his respects to the Company in the
foreword of the first edition of his book: "To the Governor and Committee of the Company I am indebted for the use of much original material from the archives in London,"[61] but the publication surprised the
London office. The board sent the Canadian Committee "an expres-
sion of the Board's surprise and disappointment that the Committee
should have permitted a history of the Company to be written and published in the United States of America by a member of the Company's
staff without the knowledge of the Board, especially in view of the author's published acknowledgement that he was indebted to the Governor and Committee of the Company for the use of much original
matter from the Company's Archives in London."[62] Four months later
another edition of the book was published by Cassell and Company of
England, and the board was once again caught by surprise. After reading reviews of that publication in the press, the board again recorded

its "disappointment at the failure of the Canadian Committee adequately to control the action of their officers in this matter ... [and] further agreed that, in the circumstances they could not assume any responsibility for this publication."[63]

The episode prompted the Company once again to tighten control of access to its records. The secretary immediately reminded the Company archivist, Leveson Gower: "In connection with the publication of our Archives, I would remind you that, as previously discussed between us, all inquiries for historical information from our Archives must be carefully scrutinised ... All requests for information in regard to which there is any doubt as to its value from the point of view of publication of our Archives must be referred to Sir Campbell Stuart before we make any reply."[64] Brooks also expressed this view to the Canadian Committee, reinforcing the need to protect the Company's own new publication program. He advised that "no archival data which may be regarded as of value in connection with our own scheme should be issued in future,"[65] and in this regard, he enclosed a list of documents to be protected. Pressure to reduce access to outside researchers in order to protect the publication program also came from E.E. Rich, fellow of St Catharine's College, Cambridge, who had been appointed the first editor of what would become the Hudson's Bay Record Society. He was aware of the fact that the number of inquiries being made of the Archives Department was increasing as "the scope and accessibility of the Company's archives became generally known."[66] Rich was concerned that the time required to answer these requests would take the archives staff away from the classification work which was required to make the records available for his publication purposes. As a result, he suggested "that rules be instituted which will discourage casual inquiries and which will provide a system for regulating the procedure in answering serious inquiries."[67] His proposal included a scale of charges, not to include students working in the archives in person, and a list of documents to which access would not be allowed.[68]

The board approved the proposed access rules and charges in December 1937, and "Rules and Regulations Governing Admission to Research" in the Archives Department were appended to the minutes as follows:

i) Except under special circumstances, only the Records of the Hudson's Bay Company up to the year 1870, the date of the Deed of Surrender of Rupert's Land to the Crown, shall be available for inspection. Documents dated after 1870 shall be produced only on such conditions as the Governor and Committee shall determine.

ii) Inspection of the Records is permitted on the express condition that any information obtained therefrom shall be submitted to the Company for approval prior to publication.

iii) Applications to work on the Archives must indicate the definite subject of the proposed research; applications in respect of vague or general subjects cannot be considered.

iv) Any abstracts taken from the Archives, with the Archivist's permission, should be brief and limited to extracts strictly pertinent to the subject in question,

v) No "general collection" of documents or extracts therefrom can be permitted in any circumstances.

vi) No extracts taken from the Archives may be transmitted to third parties without the Company's prior permission.

vii) No extracts taken from the Archives may be deposited in University or other Libraries without the Company's prior permission.

viii) Students are reminded that they work on the Archives by the courtesy of the Hudson's Bay Company and that the Company itself has undertaken the duty of making its records public.

The Company, therefore, discourages the publication of documents or excerpts except by itself and in this matter expects the co-operation of students.[69]

A scale of charges was attached which the Company had come up with after consultation with various institutions such as the Public Record Office and the British Museum.

In respect of enquiries which may be classed as legal, from solicitors and others, there shall be charged a registration fee of 2/6, plus a fee of 7/6 an hour or part thereof for the work involved by the enquiry. Minimum charge – 10/–. In respect of other enquiries there shall be charged a registration fee of 2/6, plus a fee of 2/6 an hour or part thereof for the work involved by the enquiry. Minimum charge – 5/–. The total fee payable, however, may be reduced, if warranted by special circumstances. No fee to be charged to approved students in respect of carrying on research on the Company's Archives.[70]

Numerous inquiries for information from the records were also received in Winnipeg, and although many of those were transferred to the Archives Department in London to be answered by the archivist, others were answered from the records retained in the Canadian Committee offices.

ANNOUNCING—

The Hudson's Bay Record Society

THE Governor and Committee of the Hudson's Bay Company, appreciating the widespread interest of Libraries, Historical Societies, Historians and Collectors in the Archives of the Company, have created the Hudson's Bay Record Society.

The Directors of the Society will be Sir Campbell Stuart (Chairman), Lord Macmillan, Sir Alexander Murray (Deputy Governor of Hudson's Bay Company), Lieutenant-Colonel J. B. P. Karslake and Sir Edward Peacock.

The purpose of the Society is to publish material of outstanding historical interest from the Company's Archives. Mr. E. E. Rich, M.A., F.R. Hist. Soc., Fellow of St. Catharine's College, Cambridge, and Lecturer in History in the University of Cambridge, England, has been appointed General Editor, and the first volume of the series (Sir George Simpson's Athabasca Journal and Report, 1820-21) will be issued about October, 1938. Other volumes will follow annually.

The Hudson's Bay Record Society will work in collaboration with the Champlain Society of Canada, whose members will receive the Hudson's Bay volumes.

Applications for membership in the Hudson's Bay Record Society should be addressed to the Secretary, the Canadian Committee, Hudson's Bay Company, Hudson's Bay House, Winnipeg, or to the Secretary, Hudson's Bay Record Society, 68 Bishopsgate, London, England. Persons who have already applied for membership in the Society in response to the preliminary announcement in The Beaver will receive, in due course, a prospectus setting out in detail the rules and constitution of the Society.

Subscriptions for membership in the Hudson's Bay Record Society are $5.00 per annum in Canada and the United States, or One Guinea in England. Members will receive the publications of the Society as they are issued, post-free and without further charge.

The volumes published by the Hudson's Bay Record Society will not be available for sale to non-members.

Hudson's Bay Company

INCORPORATED 2ND MAY 1670

Announcement of the formation of the Hudson's Bay Record Society, published in *The Beaver*, March 1938

Finally, on 29 April 1938 the Hudson's Bay Record Society was incorporated, with the Company owning all the shares and providing the necessary finances. The recommendations of the provisional committee, which had been presented to the board the year before, were also approved:

i) that a society be formed with the designation "The Hudson's Bay Record Society" with an annual subscription of One Guinea in the United Kingdom and Five Dollars in North America, for which each subscriber would receive one volume per annum;

ii) that copies be available only to the members of the Society, this being in accord also with the policy governing the issue of the volumes of the Champlain Society;

iii) that the first volume, the subject of which would be George Simpson's Athabasca Journal and Report, 1820/21, be published annually on such dates as will accord with the Champlain Society's publication arrangements for their volumes;

iv) that the co-operation of the Canadian Committee be obtained in connection with securing members for the new Society, and their views and suggestions invited in regard to limiting the number of members.[71]

An agreement was arranged with the Champlain Society for a joint publication project that would provide "one volume of the records and archives of the Hudson's Bay Company" a year. Five hundred and fifty copies of each volume would be sent to the Champlain Society "bound in a form and colour similar to other publications made by the Champlain Society." The HBRS would receive fifty copies "bound according to the requirements of the Record Society and containing a statement thereon that they had been published by the Champlain Society for the Record Society." The HBRS could arrange separately with the printers for additional copies which could be bound to its own specifications but had to contain the same statement as above.[72] The much-awaited announcement was made to the historical community:

> The Governor and Committee of the Hudson's Bay Company, appreciating the widespread interest of Libraries, Historical Societies, Historians and Collectors in the Archives of the Company, have created the Hudson's Bay Record Society … The purpose of the Society is to publish material of outstanding historical interest from the Company's Archives … The Hudson's Bay Record Society will work in collaboration with the Champlain Society of Canada, whose members will receive the Hudson's Bay volumes … The volumes published by the Hudson's Bay Record Society will not be available for sale to non-members.[73]

The Champlain Society had been founded by Canadian historians in Toronto in 1905 and modelled after the Hakluyt Society in Great Britain. It was devoted to the "publication of rare and inaccessible materials relating to the history of Canada."[74] It is still an active society. Subscriptions for both societies at this time were $5 in Canada and the

United States or 1 guinea in Britain. Members would receive publications as they were issued and without further charge. The HBRS would, "at its own expense, prepare and edit in every year one volume of the records and archives of the Hudson's Bay Company ..., the form and contents thereof ... subject to agreement between the Record Society and the Champlain Society."[75] In order that the HBRS be accepted for its scholarly contribution and not seen as an organ of the Company, the editors and writers of the introductions would be chosen from the historical community in Britain and North America. They would receive an honorarium from the society for their efforts. Original documents chosen for publication would represent material of significant historical interest from the founding of the Company in 1670 to the time of Canadian Confederation and the Deed of Surrender two hundred years later. The first volume, published in an edition of 500 bound copies, was *Journal of Occurrences in the Athabasca Department by George Simpson, 1820 and 1821, and Report*. It was edited by E.E. Rich and was issued to 469 subscribers in November 1938.

The arrangement with the Champlain Society remained in place until 1950, when the HBC became solely responsible for publication. Rich continued as editor of the HBRS until 1959, after he had written a history of the HBC for the years 1670–1870, published as volumes twenty-one and twenty-two. From 1959 to 1981 members received their publications every second year. Rich's successors as general editors were K.G. Davies (1960–65) and Glyndwr Williams (1969–75).[76] They received considerable editorial assistance from Alice Johnson, who was appointed assistant editor in 1948 and Company archivist in 1950. She researched the documents, wrote many of the extensive notes, and was the sole editor of volume twenty-six (*Saskatchewan Journals and Correspondence: Edmonton House, 1795–1800; Chesterfield House, 1800–1802*), published in 1967, a year before her retirement.

THE SECOND WORLD WAR

The considerable progress made in the work of the archives department was interrupted by the Second World War. Richard Leveson Gower was called up for service in 1939, but before he left, most of the older and more valuable records were packed up and transferred to the governor's estate, Hexton Manor in Hertfordshire, about forty miles northeast of London, where they would remain safe from air raids on London.[77] Before that decision was made, the governor and board had considered but rejected a proposal to microfilm the most valuable records to protect them from war damage.[78] Employees, both men and women, in London and in Canada left the Company to serve in the armed forces, in the Home Guard, or in a variety of other ways. As more and more men were called up for national service, the women members of the staff took over their duties. Cooper was seconded to the Ministry of Supply as director-general of finance for the duration of the war and took his assistant, Stacpole, with him.

Alice Johnson carried on the work of the Archives Department as acting archivist with the help of T.A. Mayhew. Her duties in September 1939 were "[c]arrying out research work and assembling the information on behalf of correspondents' or departmental enquiries; typing and indexing of the various catalogues compiled by Mr. Leveson Gower; filing; keeping up to date Library catalogue; attending to visiting students in the absence of Mayhew. Over the last year a considerable amount of time has been spent on research work and typing for the Hudson's Bay Record Society."[79] Mayhew was charged with "[l]abelling and boxing of classified records; keeping in order both classified and unclassified records; attending to the requirements of visiting students; general duties such as keeping clean and tidy the rooms used by the Archives Department; packing and making preparations for the loading and unloading of boxes during the move to Hexton."[80]

Although requests declined considerably throughout the war period, the archives staff continued to answer inquiries. The limited access required that few students were admitted to the archives facilities in London until the end of the war. Johnson devoted most of her time to helping Harvey Fleming, assistant editor of the HBRS, and when he left in 1940, she took over that job. When Professor Rich was sent overseas in 1943, further responsibility fell to Johnson to ensure continuation of the society's publications. Mayhew, in the meantime, travelled between London and Hexton to consult or retrieve documents and to check on the conditions of storage. There were a few incidents of dampness (the records were stored in the wine cellar), mildew, and insect infestation, all of which were dealt with promptly. Some boxes were returned to Hudson's Bay House for cleaning.[81] Once again, Hilary Jenkinson of the Public Record Office was consulted for his opinion on these conservation problems.[82] Eventually, wartime requirements for fuel led to the prohibition of heating houses and buildings. Special permission was obtained for a ration of coke to heat the basement at Hexton Manor. Jim Cooper, the governor's son, remembers that this heat also benefited those living upstairs.[83] Hexton was used as a retreat where former staff on leave from war service could find relief from the bombing in London. The governor's family also provided shelter to staff and their families who were evacuated from the worst affected areas of London, some of whom remained at Hexton for most of the war.

References to war conditions and concerns about possible air raids are found in the head office records as early as January 1936, and memos to staff explaining procedures under war emergency measures were regular over the next few years. For example, on hearing an air-raid warning, they were instructed to "see that your section attends to the closing of all windows, and that books and documents which are not to be taken to the strong rooms are put in the safes."[84] In the event of damage to Beaver House, staff were to proceed to Hudson's Bay House and to wait there for further instructions. If Hudson's Bay House was inaccessible, "they should return to their homes and take steps daily, by coming up to the City, to ascertain whether the buildings" were accessible.[85] Shortly after the outbreak of war and until 1946, "arrangements were made for Departments to take duplicate copies of current correspondence, transactions, etc., for retention at Hudson's Bay House, so that, in case the originals are destroyed by enemy action at Beaver House, the second set might be available and thus provide for continuity of procedure."[86] By the fall of 1940, air raids were nightly, and consideration was given to the health of the staff. "London and its suburbs are now being subjected to continuous night air raids which interfere with sleep and rest of the staff. It is essential, if the work of the Company is to be carried on efficiently, that the Staff should have adequate rest, and, with a view to ensuring this as far as may be possible, the Company has decided to close the Offices and Warehouse on Saturday morning, until further notice."[87]

The governor remembered these times a few years later when he related that "on more than one occasion, he and the Deputy-Governor had finished a discussion of the Company's affairs, seated underneath the boardroom table, or crouched beneath the window."[88] From almost the beginning of Cooper's term as governor, regular reports from the London office were included in *The Beaver* along with reports from the Canadian offices and districts. During the war this column served as a means of keeping Canadian staff informed of the conditions in the Company and in London and of staff members serving or killed overseas. Copies of each issue of *The Beaver* were sent regularly to Canadian troops overseas, but because of disruption to shipping, these

Hexton Manor in Herefordshire and its wine cellars,
where HBC records were sent for safekeeping during
the Second World War (photos: Deidre Simmons)

did not always reach their destination. Nor did the reports included in each issue from London always reach Canada in a timely fashion. One such report arrived in Winnipeg just before the deadline for the publication schedule, but it was not complete. "Most of the really interesting news (or so we imagine it to have been) had long ago been deposited in the wastebasket of the censor."[89] The "London Office News" for October, which appeared in the December 1940 issue, gives some idea of what the staff in London experienced:

> London has been subjected to intensive and continuous air raids and considerable damage has been done to buildings in the city as well as in practically all the suburbs and outlying districts. Fortunately Hudson's Bay House and Beaver House have escaped so far, the former only having had two incendiary bombs dropped on it, which caused no damage. Beaver House also has only had a few panes of roof glass broken by falling fragments ... The frequent interruptions caused by the raids, when the staff have to seek cover in the shelters, has interfered considerably with work, especially as we have now a depleted staff, which, however, carries on efficiently and unperturbed ... The incessant nightly raids and indiscriminate bombing have also prevented the staff from obtaining much sleep.[90]

Soon after, for reasons of economy and efficient coordination of staff, the Company closed its head office in Hudson's Bay House and moved the operation to Beaver House. The Archives Department and its reduced staff remained in its basement accommodation with the records that had not been transferred to Hexton. In December and again in January 1941 Beaver House was hit but was saved from destruction by efforts of the staff in putting out fires while all adjoining buildings were destroyed. An air-raid shelter had been set up beneath Beaver House where staff could "relax," sleep, or continue their work duties in rather cramped conditions.

Memos in the archives department records indicate that staff were supplied in January 1941 with tins of the Company's brand salmon, HUBAY and LABDOR, to supplement the shortage of rationed meat and a year later were offered a complete hamper of soup, steak and kidney puddings or stewed steak, emergency meals, haricot oxtail, Irish stew, marrowfat peas,[91] potatoes or other vegetables, game pâté, herrings or pilchards, and pickles. In July 1942 a bonus of one month's salary (or wages) was paid to all members of the London staff, and in February 1945 one

Beaver House after bombing in 1941 (album 5, 55) and HBC staff working in the air-raid shelter during the Second World War (*The Beaver*, December 1941)

week's leave with pay was given to every member of the staff, men and women, "in order to establish as far as possible the health of all members of the staff, particularly before the heavy work of accounts, etc., following the end of the Company's financial year."[92] The practice of allowing staff to have Saturday mornings off continued through 1946 "owing to rationing, queueing, ... [and] some difficulty in securing supplies of food." This provision was, of course, "subject to the exigencies of work."[93] In 1943 the governor arranged and the Company paid for medical examinations "with a view to steps being taken to improve the health of the staff under the existing war conditions."[94] Later, halibut oil capsules and vitamin tablets were handed out.[95]

A staff canteen was opened at Beaver Hall in April 1944 to provide hot lunches, as well as morning and afternoon refreshments. The arrangements initially caused consternation among the archives staff and others still located at Hudson's Bay House on Bishopsgate, about a mile away. They pointed out, "it is not possible with the least degree of comfort to go to Beaver House, have a meal and return, in an hour. We feel that any good that will result from better food will be undone by the effort expended in obtaining it."[96] The problem was resolved by providing regular rations for the morning and afternoon breaks, which Hudson's Bay House staff could pick up from the manageress at Beaver House "at convenient periods" to prepare "on the spot." Lunch would not be sent to Bishopsgate, but those who made the effort could receive the mid-day meal at Beaver House.

The archives were at Hexton Manor until 1945, when Brooks notified Johnson and Mayhew that "with the cessation of hostilities the way is now clear for bringing back to Bishopsgate from Hexton all the archives which have been stored in the country for safe custody."[97] In a general reorganization of the London office after the disruptions to staffing and operations during the war, Chadwick Brooks was appointed London manager in 1946, replacing Stacpole, in addition to retaining his long-standing position of secretary. Reporting to the board on all matters of general policy, he would carry out its instructions regarding all London departments and subsidiary and associated companies as well as supervise communications between London and the Canadian Committee.[98]

Leveson Gower returned in February 1947 to carry on as the Company archivist and soon after was in discussion with the secretary's office in connection with the future work of the Archives Department. Brooks wanted to project the completion of classification work on the

Archivist Richard Leveson Gower in the HBC archives reading room with researcher Arthur S. Morton, 1933 (1987-363-A-19-2)

pre-1870 records and establish a plan for classifying the records from 1870 to either 1910 or 1920, with an estimate of the number of permanent staff required to carry out that work.[99] In October he drafted a memo providing staffing requirements for the Archives Department. Leveson Gower suggested a staff of six, to include himself, Johnson as assistant archivist, and two other assistants, one being Mayhew, plus a typist and one other clerical assistant. The classification of the records prior to 1870 had been completed with the exception of miscellaneous papers of subsidiary companies, which he expected to be finished by the end of 1948, when the work on the 1870–1920 period could be started.[100] Gwen Kemp was hired as the new typist and would spend a good part of her time typing transcripts and correspondence for the HBRS, and soon after Janet Briault was hired as a copy typist and microfilm camera operator.

With its full complement of staff, the Archives Department returned to the routine of classifying, answering inquiries, attending to visiting researchers, maintaining the library, providing research and editorial assistance for the record society publications, and handling regular records transfers from Beaver House and Canada. As well, boxes damaged by dampness at Hexton had to be replaced and/or relabelled and cards retyped.[101] J. Chadwick Brooks retired in 1948 after twenty-five years as secretary of the company. During that time, the Archives Department had grown from a centuries-old accumulation of business records to an internationally respected archives regularly visited and cited by respected scholars, historians, scientists, and authors. Brooks was followed by Rudolph Arturo Reynolds.

A NEW ARCHIVIST

Richard Leveson Gower left the service of the Company rather suddenly in January 1949, after the death of his father, to manage the family estate in Surrey. A search was started for his replacement, and the position was posted outside the Company: "Hudson's Bay Company – Applications are invited for the appointment of ARCHIVIST to the Company. Commencing salary between £450 and £550, according to age, qualifications and experience, rising to £750 a year. Candidates preferably between 30 and 35 years of age, must be graduates with sufficient experience of, and taste for historical research to assist in the preparation of material for publication."[102] On 9 March 1949 G. Potter James was appointed company archivist at the salary of £550.[103] This arrangement was short-lived. Potter resigned within a few months, and after some consideration, the appointment of Alice Johnson as archivist was announced in January 1950. Her salary was £525."[104]

The Company had been hesitant to appoint Johnson, partly because she was a woman and also because she did not have a university degree. Reynolds sought outside advice on the matter. He met with Hilary Jenkinson at the Public Record Office to discuss the situation: "I would like to thank you for your kindness in granting me an interview last week and also for the advice which you gave me in regard to the running of our Archives Department and the appointment of an Archivist. I am sure you will be interested to hear that the Board have now appointed Miss Johnson to be the Company's new Archivist."[105]

She ably continued the work of Leveson Gower, recording the details in monthly and annual reports for the next eighteen years. Johnson noted that the advice Jenkinson had offered in 1932 had provided the HBCA with a workable system of classification which she continued to use: "Sir Hilary Jenkinson's recommendations as to the Sections and Classes used in Classification have ... been followed, and the experience

Alice Johnson, HBC archivist from 1950 to 1968 (*The Bay*, summer 1948)

gained has enabled us to fit into the system the different kinds of documents to be found in the Company's archives."[106] Workshop space was set up in one of the strongrooms to carry out some bookbinding as well as picture-framing and minor repairs on documents. Johnson's assistant, Frank Batchelor, took courses at the Public Record Office on bookbinding and repairs and was responsible for most of the conservation work done on the documents during this time.

Researchers who have wondered at the variety of flimsy copies and notes written on the back of recycled letterhead paper, particularly in the search files, will appreciate Johnson's explanation in 1949 that the Archives Department was doing all it could in the way of economy and improvization: "The only new paper used in the Archives Department is for correspondence and economy labels are used on envelopes, where possible. We use a great deal of paper for notes when working on enquiries, but this has always been scrap paper, and until quite recently most of it has been supplied from Beaver House. I need hardly say that in consequence our files do not look as orderly as they would do if standard size and colour of paper were used."[107]

The staff during the 1950s included Johnson, Margaret Nickson as assistant archivist, assistants Frank Batchelor and Robert Harvey, and typists Gwen Kemp and Janet Briault. Visitors were a regular part of the daily routine. The archives attracted a great number of researchers to the small reading room, which also served as office and workroom. During the summer months the work tables were often not available for sorting and classifying because they were taken by researchers. Johnson, though still busy with preparing records for publication by the HBRS, welcomed the growing number of researchers: "We welcome these visitors for we can not only help them, but we ourselves learn quite a lot from our exchange of ideas."[108] Despite the concerns of the late 1930s, there had never been any serious conflict between the Company's publication program and the interests of researchers.

The agreement with the Champlain Society was discontinued in 1950, after more than two years of correspondence and discussion between the two societies. The Champlain Society was required to double its subscription fee after an increase in printing costs made it impossible to provide publications under the original scheme. The board of directors of the HBRS would not agree to any increase in subscription on its part and took "the only course left open to us," which was to "terminate our agreement at one year's notice."[109] The parting was amicable. Campbell Stuart, the chairman of the Hudson's Bay Record Society, expressed his appreciation of the arrangement to W.S. Wallace: "We have particularly appreciated the great benefits we have derived through our association with the Champlain Society, and the Editor tells me how much he has valued the kind assistance and excellent advice he has received from you and many of your colleagues through the years."[110] The Champlain Society, on its part, acknowledged that not all of its members were sufficiently interested in the HBRS volumes, but felt that it had "fully accomplished its objective, namely, to make the archives of the Hudson's Bay Company available to students of Canadian history," and the record society was "well able to carry on without assistance."[111]

MICROFILMING THE ARCHIVES

In 1950 the Company finally decided to microfilm records in its archives dating from before 1870. W. Kaye Lamb, a distinguished archivist, librarian, and historian, had been appointed Canada's Dominion archivist in 1948, and preservation was a priority for him. Well aware of the importance of the HBC to the history of Canada, he drew up a proposal for the Public Archives and the Company to work together to microfilm records in the HBC archives relating to the history of Canada from 1670 to 1870. A copy of the microfilm would be deposited at the Public Archives in Ottawa. Access to the Company's historical records was still an issue for researchers in North America, but the HBC was no longer greatly concerned about the possible conflict with publication of those records. Lamb's proposal would permit easier access, but he acknowledged that the Company's control over the use of records was still important. "While the primary purpose of the microfilm copies would be to provide against possible destruction of the originals, my hope is that we could take advantage of their existence to make the contents of the documents somewhat more accessible to well-known scholars in Canada. Needless to say I recognize fully the Company's absolute proprietorship of the papers, and its right to prevent their use for any purpose that might be detrimental to its interests."[112] This reassurance no doubt helped win the Company's support for the microfilming project, although the mere fact that the records would be more readily available in North America on microfilm indicates that the Company was prepared to entertain and approve more requests for publication of information from the records.

Johnson's description of the project as it started in September 1950 gives the best account of the archives' introduction to this new technology:

A Graflex Photorecord camera has been lent to us by Dr. W. Kaye Lamb, Dominion Archivist, and our own Kodak Library Reader has recently been installed in the Archives Room. We have a Kodak Microfile Camera of the latest design on order and I am assured that it is quite easily operated by the amateur. The camera at present in use is a portable, out-of-date model, and since it cannot be focussed automatically, or the aperture changed with assurance each time the size of the book varies to any extent or the colour of the paper changes, the work is constantly held up whilst tests are being made ...

Dr. Lamb offered and we accepted the services of his operator, but when I found that she knew nothing whatever about cameras and several unsatisfactory reels had been made, I considered it better for the work to be done by a member of the Archives staff. In any case, the clerical work takes up most of the time and as that can only be done by a member of the staff it was a waste of time to call on Dr. Lamb's assistant just to operate the camera for the matter of an hour or two.

Mr. Harvey now understands the camera when filming certain types of records, and so long as we can make the necessary tests and are not expected to work to a rigid schedule we can make satisfactory films with the camera now in use. But the pace is likely to be very slow on account of the deficiencies of the camera. I think Dr. Lamb was much too optimistic about the camera when he lent it to us, and that he did not realise it would take a great deal of experience and skill to use it for microfilming the very many different kinds of archives in our keeping ...

In conjunction with the officials at the Public Record Office and the Recordak Division of Messrs. Kodak Ltd. a scheme has been evolved for carrying out as expeditiously, methodically and economically as possible, the filming of the whole of the archives up to 1870 as a beginning ... We are trying to obtain the best reproductions we possibly can so that they will be of use and not a source of vexation and disappointment in the unfortunate event of the archives being destroyed by fire or other causes ...

The Public Record Office has confirmed my own opinion that it is very necessary indeed to keep exact records of the work carried out. Details have been worked out and the little experience already gained has proved the point. I stress this because, in the early days of the venture, Dr. Kaye Lamb thought such records unnecessary. These records mean that much clerical work is necessary and, if the ordinary work of the department is to be carried on as usual, it will mean that additional help will be required. Since the project is likely to take any time from about two years or more, even with the use of the new camera, I would suggest that instead of employing temporary help, we should engage a permanent assistant to operate the camera and undertake, after a time some of the clerical work. This assistant should also be trained to be useful in other directions, and I hope we should thereby be providing for the future. A permanent assistant is likely to take much more interest and pride in the work than a temporary assistant.

The checking of the microfilms will be carried out by the Assistant Archivist, who is to visit the Public Record Office for advice on the standard to which we must work, and for help in the technique of making corrections ...

It is hoped Dr. Lamb will see reason in our desire to work to our own system, especially as the other work in the Department must continue, and that he will be satisfied to receive anything permitted him as and when we can send it ... We are still in the early stages of the project and are still "buying" our experience, but if we are allowed to carry out our own scheme I am convinced we can do a good job for the Company, and, if Dr. Lamb is patient, supply him in time with anything the Governor and Committee may decide upon.[113]

The microfilm camera was set up originally in the archives room, which doubled as workroom and reading room, but that situation proved inconvenient enough that the microfilming project and its equipment were moved to another Company building on Queen Street, several blocks away. For the next four years, "each item to be microfilmed had to be carried there by a member of the Archives Staff."[114] An announcement of the microfilm project was released to the press in March 1951:

The huge task of microfilming the Hudson's Bay Company's archives – more than 200 years of reports, records, and correspondence, representing in large measure the history of western and north western Canada to 1870 – has been undertaken by the Public Archives of Canada and the Hudson's Bay Company, according to a joint announcement by Dr. W. Kaye Lamb, Ottawa, Dominion Archivist, and Sir Patrick Ashley Cooper, London, Governor of the Company.

The existence of film copies will safeguard against the irreparable loss to scholars and others which would be occasioned by accidental destruction of the original documents, while positive prints filed in the Public Archives in Ottawa will make it possible for research workers in Canada to study the records without making expensive journeys to Britain.

Access to the prints will be governed by the same conditions which govern the use of the original documents in the Company's archives in London. They will be available to responsible scholars for the study of specific subjects, extracts being limited to those pertinent to the subject in question.[115]

The microfilm project was well under way in 1953 when Lamb reported to the Canadian Historical Association, "over 650 reels of film, consisting of facsimiles of over 450,000 pages, have already been received in Ottawa" from the HBC. He expected the microfilming project would be completed in another year when the Public Archives "should have in its possession copies of the entire surviving papers of the Company for the two centuries from 1670 to 1870." The project Lamb proposed was not completed until 1966, but as film was made, it was added to the deposit of microfilm at the Public Archives. Lamb also explained that microfilming had replaced hand-copying in the Public Archives branches in London and Paris; the objective was to microfilm "all the major files in the Record Office that relate to Canada."[116]

Conditions governing the use of the microfilm at the Public Archives of Canada were published in *The Beaver* in 1951, mirroring the rules for access to the archives in London. Application had to be made to the Company, and written acceptance of the conditions was required from all users. A special committee was established in Winnipeg to screen all applications before they were forwarded to London. The committee, in operation from 1951 to 1965, was composed of a Company representative, F.B. Walker, head of public relations, together with Dr Ross Mitchell and Professor W.L. Morton, both authorities in Canadian history from the University of Manitoba.[117] Extracts were still to be submitted to the Company for approval prior to publication, and no extracts from the microfilm could be transferred to third parties or deposited in other libraries or depositories without permission from the Company.[118] Over four thousand reels of microfilm are now available through interlibrary loan from the HBCA and for viewing at the archives in Winnipeg, at Library and Archives Canada in Ottawa, and at the National Archives in England.[119]

Cooper retired in 1952, after thirty years as governor. He was followed by William J. Keswick, who had been deputy governor since 1946. Like Cooper, Keswick was a businessman with government and wartime experience.[120] In November 1955 the Archives Department was transferred from the Bishopsgate building to join the rest of the London office in much more spacious and efficient accommodation at Beaver House. The Company had sold the property in which Hudson's Bay House had been located in 1947. It had never fully occupied the building it had purposely constructed in 1928 and had vacated most of it to tenants when all the Company offices were moved to Beaver House in 1932. At Beaver House the archives took over the main-floor space of the buying office, which moved to a site in another part of London. One of the considerations of the move had been that the underground accommodation of the archives was not a "good advertisement for the Company" to the many visiting students of history from all over the world.[121] "The contents of 1042 shelves, weighing thirty-two and a half tons, were moved and at the same time the steel shelving in use at Bishopsgate was dismantled and re-erected in five rooms at Beaver House."[122]

Classification, microfilming, and HBRS publication continued in the new location, as did research inquiries and research visitors. The public relations function of the archives was an important part of the work of the staff. Inquiries were regularly, and increasingly, received from the Canadian government and from universities and individuals, primarily in Canada and the United States, for information about former Company posts or former employees. Requests about various aspects of the Company's history regularly came from journalists and feature writers from the London press and from overseas. In 1958, charges for searches carried out by staff increased from 2s.6d an hour to 10s.0d an hour.[123]

The London administration of the Company employed approximately 160 that year. The two main departments were the secretary's and the accountant's. The secretary from 1948 to 1970 was R.A. Reynolds, who, besides his duties to the governor and Committee, was responsible for legal affairs, staffing and staff policy, subsidiary companies, head office correspondence and correspondence with the Canadian Committee, London buildings, share transfers and shareholder relations, public relations, the archives and the HBRS. The Company became an overseas trading corporation in 1957 for taxation reasons. The general courts of the HBC were held in London, and the accountant and his staff of five prepared the published annual financial reports, including the accounts from London and Canada. The accountant's office also provided services to subsidiary companies the Company operated in England, made additional financial arrangements as required for the London fur business, and dealt with insurance and other financial-related aspects of managing the London properties.[124]

Despite the regular rounding up and transfer of inactive records to the archives from the administration offices in London and Canada, old records continued to surface from obscure corners, having been overlooked for many years. In 1951, much to the surprise and dismay of the archivist, Alice Johnson, known for her careful attention to detail and efficient preservation of the records, a quantity of old accounting records,

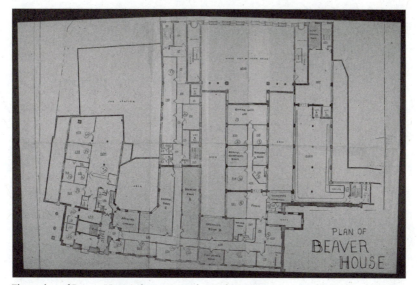

Floor plan of Beaver House about 1955; the Archives Department is located in the lower centre of this plan, in rooms A, B, and C (RG20/5/2)

some dating from the 1890s, was found in one of the strongrooms. The fur trade annual reports, commissioners' reports, saleshops and stores accounts and reports, Land Department accounts and reports, and some Winnipeg head office and Canadian Committee office accounting records were important additions to the series being classified in the archives. But as a result of years of improper storage conditions, many were badly mildewed and had to be passed through a cleaning process before the archivist could amalgamate them with the other archival records. The archivist reported, "at present they are in 'The Dump' being cleaned, aired and thymolized, page by page," a time-consuming and smelly process.[125]

The HBCA also received a number of old post journals from Canada in the 1950s. These journals, which recorded the daily events and activities at the Company posts, had been discontinued in the 1940s when they became redundant because of the more convenient two-way radio communication between the posts and the Winnipeg office;[126] so the additions filled in blanks or completed series already on the shelves in London. By 1958 the detailed records retention schedule of the Canadian Committee office clearly identified which records were to be destroyed, which were to be kept permanently in that office, and which transferred to London for deposit in the archives. Details from the disposition schedule for the accounts records provide an example from a much longer list:

(a) Annual – all departments	Permanently in C.C.O.
(b) Subsidiary company accounts	Permanently in C.C.O.
(c) Monthly	20 years, then destroyed
(d) General ledgers	25 years, then to London
(e) Pensions payroll	10 years, then destroyed
(f) Income tax returns	
(i) Company	Permanently in C.C.O.
(ii) Employees	5 years, then destroyed
(g) Vouchers – originals	20 years, then destroyed
(h) Bank statements	2 years, then destroyed
(i) Cancelled cheques	6 years, then destroyed
(j) Daily cash statements	2 years, then destroyed
(k) Buying office vouchers	1 year, then destroyed[127]

Up to 1941, issues of *The Beaver* included a section for news and announcements regarding staff and their families living at Company posts in Canada's North. When that feature was discontinued, a new staff magazine, the *Moccasin Telegraph,* was introduced directed specifically at the northern Canadian audience; its first issue appeared in August 1941. In June 1942 Cooper announced that "in order to keep members of the London staff serving with the Forces in various parts of the World and others who have been released for National Service in touch with the Company, a News Letter should be prepared and a copy despatched to each member regularly."[128] The newsletter, a simple typed sheet of two or three pages, was prepared by Brooks and his staff. The first issue was distributed in July and a total of nine issues followed, twice a year until 1946. That newsletter would evolve after the war into a quarterly staff magazine. The first issue of *The Bay*, based somewhat on the Canadian staff magazine *The Beaver*, was issued in August 1946. It was edited by Frank Batchelor, assisted by Lorna Headley, an executive committee of five, and a general committee of eight. The magazine published photographs and articles on interests and activities of the staff, an editorial, a crossword puzzle, short stories, a "children's corner," and in each issue a "Bay Personality" profiling a member of the London staff or one of the directors. The magazine was discontinued in 1970 on the retirement of Frank Batchelor from the service of the Company. When the eastern Bay stores were transferred to the Northern Stores Department in 1964, a French edition of the *Moccasin Telegraph* was also published. With some changes in appearance and format, both editions were produced until 1990, three years after the northern stores were sold off to become a separate company, named The North West Company.

The records of the Canadian operations were managed from Winnipeg, and each administrative change is reflected in them. When the Fur Trade Department was renamed the Northern Stores Department, its active records became the records of the new department. In the archives the Northern Stores Department is classified as Record Group 7 (RG7), separate from but overlapping with the Fur Trade Department (RG3). Even though the name change occurred in 1959, RG7 includes Fur Trade Department records dating from 1931, with a few even earlier anomalies. For this period, the records of the Canadian Committee office, dating from 1911 to 1970, are a parallel source for valuable information about the Company's activities in the north. Prior to 1930, these records should be used with London office records in Section A as well as the commissioners' and Canadian subcommittee records in Section D.

8

to deposit its Archives in Winnipeg

Transfer of the Hudson's Bay Company Archives to Canada, 1960–1974

The Company continued to enjoy the public relations value of its history at the same time as it permitted access to and publication from its archives. The positive experience of its archival program during the mid-twentieth century laid the groundwork for resolution of the remaining problems of access to the archives: the limitations of their geographical location in London (which the microfilm program had not fully resolved) and the matter of access to the post-1870 records.

There had been interest in transferring the archives of the HBC to Canada as early as 1932. The Company had briefly considered handing the archives over to either Oxford University or the Canadian government as a response to fiscal restraints resulting from the Depression.[1] Nothing was done at the time but that passing reference to a Canadian home for the archives was a premonition of what would actually occur forty-two years later. There was considerable Canadian and American interest over the years in the contents of the archives and access to them. The records became more accessible with their opening to students in the 1930s and even more so after the records began to be microfilmed in 1950. General access to the pre-1870 material was no longer an issue and documents dated after 1870 would be provided to researchers under conditions as determined by the governor and Committee. Access to the records was also conditional on any information obtained from them being "submitted to the Company for approval prior to publication."[2] These access regulations remained the same as long as the archives were in London.

Historians were satisfied enough with these arrangements but there were major changes ahead for the Company and the archives which would eventually provide more convenient access in North America.

William J. Keswick was governor until 1965, when he resigned. The deputy governor, the Right Honourable Viscount Derek H. Amory, then took over. Lord Amory was a former chancellor of the Exchequer in the Macmillan government and had just returned from Canada, where he had served as Britain's high commissioner. As in the past, the changes of governor signalled changes in the organization, in the function of record-keeping, and, as a result, in the records as each man brought his own special knowledge, aspirations and interests to the Company's top job. The Company had continued to diversify its operations throughout the 1950s and 1960s. As part of this planned expansion, the Fur Trade Department was reorganized in 1959 as the Northern Stores Department. The Company held major investments in natural-resource companies: Hudson's Bay Oil & Gas, Siebens Oil and Gas, and Roxy Petroleum. It moved into eastern Canada through acquisitions of competitive companies such as Morgan's (1960) in Quebec.[3] A new marketing strategy introduced the Company's modern retail identity as "The Bay" (La Bai in Quebec), followed by an ambitious program of building its new department stores in suburban shopping malls. The Company was expanding, and with that expansion came a broader organizational chart and more levels of middle management. The appointment in 1969 of a newly created position, manager of general merchandise and sales, recognized a commitment to sales development and the idea of central merchandising.[4]

THE COMPANY'S THIRD ARCHIVIST

With the approach of its three-hundredth anniversary in 1970, even more changes were in store for the Canadian and London offices. In London the Company archivist changed for only the third time since the department was set up in 1931. Alice Johnson retired in 1968 after thirty-four years working in the archives, eighteen of those as archivist. She had completed her work as editor of volume twenty-six for the HBRS the previous year.[5] Her successor was Joan Craig, who brought a youthful energy to the job of archivist along with a university degree. The sixteen-page annual report prepared by Craig for the London secretary in January 1969 is evidence of her attention to detail, a characteristic that had been demonstrated by all the staff working with the archives since the 1920s. In addition to routine correspondence, department memos, and telephone inquiries, fifty-six written inquiries on a variety of subjects had been received and answered by the Archives Department

Joan Craig, HBC archivist from 1968 to 1973

over the previous twelve months. No fewer than seven authors' manuscripts based on the Company's archives were read for permission to
publish. Considerable staff time was also spent on answering twenty-
three requests for photographs of documents, maps, or pictures, resulting in 124 photographs, copies of which were simultaneously put on file.
During that same year, the Archives Department received 267 readers
and visitors, including Glyndwr Williams, who was working on the next
volume for the HBRS, and Alice Johnson, who was preparing material
for the *Dictionary of Canadian Biography*. Among other researchers
were J. Russell Harper, who was preparing his two-volume study of the
work of Paul Kane, and Professor L.G. Thomas, who was editing the
second edition of A.S. Morton's *A History of the Canadian West to
1870–71*. Permission was granted that year to twenty-seven Canadian
researchers for access to the microfilm at the Public Archives in Ottawa.

The staff of the Canadian Committee offices in Winnipeg were also
busy answering inquiries regarding the history of the Company, referring seven of those requests to the archives in London for further research. The HBCA received new accessions, some purchased and some
donated, from outside the Company, and archival material continued

to be received from the administration departments in London and in Canada, either newly available or previously overlooked. As agreed with the Public Archives of Canada, the microfilming program (up to 1870) had been completed in 1966, but microfilming continued for specific projects by the Company or outside institutions. In 1969 the Smithsonian Institution requested copies of mid-nineteenth-century correspondence between the Company and Joseph Henry, first secretary of the institution, for a publication on Henry.

As a feature of its three-hundredth anniversary year in 1970, the Company announced that all documents in the archives dating to 1900 would be made available to researchers. Considerable work had been completed during the 1960s and early 1970s by the London staff – Joan Craig, Miss Gales, and Miss Collier – on the classification of records dating between 1871 and 1900. That work followed on the completion of the microfilming of series 1, pre-1870 records, with research copies deposited in the Public Archives of Canada. The classification work concentrated on series A.11, London official correspondence inward (1701–1870), and series A.12, London correspondence inward from the Company's representatives in Canada (1823–70). Twenty-seven linear feet of commissioners' correspondence was classified and catalogued, ready for foliating and labelling before being opened for inspection by researchers.

As well as classification and microfilming, the archives staff completed a catalogue of the artworks known as the HBCA Picture Collection, assembled since the early eighteenth century. The original catalogue identified paintings, drawings, and prints of Company posts, portraits, ships, Aboriginals, and natural history.[6] Much of the art was hung on the walls of Beaver House, and the rest was stored in the archives. The boardroom and its adjacent foyer displayed the handsome portraits of King Charles II, who granted the first charter; Prince Rupert, the first governor; James, Duke of York and later James II; John Churchill, the Duke of Marlborough; George Simpson; and other governors of the Company. A nineteenth-century Arrowsmith map of North America also hung in the boardroom, along with paintings of ships and shipping and an 1870 drawing of Fort Garry. Other paintings were located in the secretary's office, the deputy governor's office, the board dining room, the main entrance, and the auction facility, Beaver Hall. In 1973 the paintings, selected antique furniture, and silverware were valued for the purpose of export at £39,900.[7]

The photograph collection was also identified at this time. A small number of historic photographs had accumulated, dating from as early as the 1860s and made up of glass plate negatives, slides, prints, and albums by professional and amateur photographers, including staff. In the collection were an increasing number of photographs taken in-house, starting in the 1920s, of archival records, such as textual documents and maps, used for illustration in books, magazines, and journals. The Company's library, managed by the Archives Department, continued to grow with new additions of books, journals, and pamphlets. Authors using the archives for reference had always been requested to deposit one copy of their publications in the library, and as access expanded, the number of publications increased. Archives staff continued to take classes in binding and repairs for in-house application.

Since 1955 the Company archives had occupied several rooms on the first floor of Beaver House on the same level as the administrative offices and the boardroom. The archivist's office looked over Little Trinity Lane and across to the offices of the Company of Painters and Stainers. Visitors to the archives entered from the stairwell lobby, past the library and two large archives storage rooms, to the archives office, which also served as the reading room. Records and catalogues were stored on shelves in all of these rooms, as well as in the nearby auditor's room, deputy governor's room, and even in the governor's cloakroom. Other rooms on the second floor and on the ground floor of Beaver House were used to store unclassified archival material, including wartime records of the French government business and Bay Steamship Company records.

Glyndwr Williams, editor of the HBRS from 1969 to 1975, reminisced with this author that Beaver House was a "total mystery" to him. His first experience with the archives had been as a young PhD student. After walking down the long, narrow hallway with rooms on either side, the researcher arrived at the archives room on the left, across the hall from the archivist's office. Inside, he was greeted by the assistant archivist, Marjorie Gambles (later Mrs Wright), who was there until 1963. Joan Murray (later Mrs Craig) took her place in the archives room until 1968, and Gwen Kemp was there until 1974. Records were retrieved as requested, and researchers' notes were left at the end of the day to be examined by the staff before being returned the next morning. The notes were examined to make sure that documents were not being copied *in toto* and also to verify they pertained to the subject of research as stated by the researcher. For researchers, it was always a puzzle how the staff had time to peruse the notes, sometimes from several researchers on a busy day, within the normal working

The HBC archives office, London, 1974; *left to right*, Christine Dobeck, Gwen Kemp, and Stephanie Lund (1974-2-11)

hours. In fact, the archivists have admitted they often had to stay late to complete the work. For Williams, "one of the wonderful things" about working in the archives at Beaver House was the smell of the furs which, after forty or fifty years, permeated the whole building. He said he had the "feeling of being in the middle of fur trade history."[8] The reading room was not very big, and since it also served as an archives workroom, researchers shared the space with staff. If more than two or three researchers were working at one time, the staff had to forgo their working space and/or visitors had to double up at the tables, which were already crowded in among the bookshelves, catalogue drawers, and filing cabinets.

Archives staff provided editorial assistance on the HBRS publications, answered queries from head office in London and from the Canadian Committee office in Winnipeg, and provided limited research for outside inquiries at a charge of £1 per hour. The results of any research completed by staff were kept in subject files for future reference. These search files have become an excellent source of information on all types of subjects and can prove a good starting point for any kind of research in the archives. A cross-referenced card catalogue leads the way into these treasures.

A NEW HOME FOR THE ARCHIVES?

Interest in transferring the archives to Canada was raised again in 1964, this time from outside the Company by a well-known Winnipeg physician, Dr William Ewart. He had become aware of the immensity and significance of the archives when he worked in England a few years earlier and had the opportunity to visit Beaver House. Ewart was deeply impressed with the extent of Canadian historical information in the archives. When he returned to Winnipeg, he took up the cause. In February he wrote to J.E. Woods, chairman of the Canadian Committee of the HBC, to Maitland B. Steinkopf, the secretary of the Manitoba Centennial Corporation, and to Dr H.H. Saunderson, president of the University of Manitoba, to propose that "perhaps the Hudson's Bay Company could be persuaded to turn over some of these private documents for us [Manitobans] to preserve for the future."[9] Ewart conceived of the transfer as a project to celebrate the centennials of the Dominion of Canada (1967) and the Province of Manitoba (1970), as well as the tercentenary of the Hudson's Bay Company (1970). The response from the Company came from the secretary of the Canadian Committee, Rolph Huband, thanking Ewart for his letter: "We will certainly look into the possibility ... we shall be pleased to examine your suggestion with our Archives experts in London and with officials of the Provincial Centennial Corporation."

The response from the Manitoba Centennial Corporation was not encouraging. It expressed "little hope for a change in the status quo" because the microfilm of the HBC records for the years down to 1870 was available, albeit through restricted access, in the Public Archives of Canada. The same restrictions would most certainly pertain to any deposits of Company archives in Winnipeg. The executive secretary of the Centennial Corporation wrote to Ewart: "It should also be kept in mind that an approach to the Bay asking for copies locally, would mean challenging a known Company policy of not multiplying copies of their material."[10] This comment referred to the long-standing rule governing the copying of any records *in toto* and limiting publication of even extracts taken from the archives to the discretion of the Company.

Ewart tried again a year later, asking Huband to reconsider the proposal. He emphasized the historical importance of the archives to Manitoba, the West, and Canada and the contribution of the Company to the preservation of Canadian history. At the same time, Ewart asked the premier of Manitoba, Duff Roblin, for his support in persuading "the adventurous traders to part with the precious documents that they have preserved and protected over the centuries in the shadows of London Town"[11] and to provide them on a permanent loan to the people of Canada, who, he said, were "now willing and able to accept the responsibility of such an undertaking."[12] Ewart persuaded Roblin that the prestige of the premier's office and his "reputation of interest in Canadian history would lend weight to this appeal to a private company."[13]

Roblin responded with full support for "the suitability of bringing this historic collection of unequalled importance for western Canadian history to become a centre of scholarship in Manitoba."[14] He had also made inquiries among his cabinet colleagues and found "that this possibility has in fact been raised in a very informal way with the Canadian authorities of the Hudson's Bay Company as a very suitable means of marking the third centenary of the Company in 1970."[15] By this time, letters of support for the idea had also been received from the Manitoba Historical Society, the library committee of the University of Manitoba, Manitoba historian W.L. Morton, the chairman of Great-West Life Assurance Company, and the vice-president of the University of Manitoba. At this point in the plan the University of Manitoba library was the most obvious repository for the Hudson's Bay Company archives.

Hugh Saunderson, the president of the University of Manitoba, also approached senior officials of the HBC in Winnipeg with the idea but found that the timing was inopportune. There was no need on the part of the Company to move the archives to Canada as long as the head office was in London.[16] However, it must have been feeling some pressure from all this lobbying. Governor Keswick had been briefed about the archives issue on his trip to Canada in 1964. J.R. Murray, the Company's managing director, wrote to David Kilgour, the chair of the Canadian Committee and president of Great-West Life Assurance, about the campaign, suggesting that it be discussed at the next meeting of the committee. His candid evaluation explains the situation from the Company's point of view:

The matter is, I think, both political and serious enough for us to consider it at a C.C. meeting and, if you agree, we will put in on our agenda for next Friday. At this stage, it should perhaps be discussed informally, and later this month, when I am in London, I will follow it up with the Governor, with whom the suggestion was very gingerly raised when he was here a few months ago. He did not say much then, but from the look on his face, this proposal will probably get a very chilly reception ... Our problem is going to be how to turn down the request and still leave everyone reasonably satisfied. Politically, I feel we should do the turning down here, rather than leave it to our friends in London to say no to an enthusiastic group of Manitobans.[17]

After the meeting, Kilgour sent a letter informing the chair of the University of Manitoba library committee, B.L. Funt, that the Company was aware of the interest in a transfer, and if it ever thought of "turning over some parts of their accumulated records to any public body, the University of Manitoba might be thought of as a very logical candidate," but he did not think that it would be worthwhile to make a formal request for the archives at this time.[18] Informally, Kilgour told Ewart that the Canadian Committee had an interest in acquiring the archives for Manitoba but that "present business deals regarding the actual transfer of the Company operations to Canada might be jeopardized by directing too much attention to the Archives at this same moment."[19] The idea was put on hold for the next few years, but inquiries regarding the location of the HBC archives arrived regularly in both the London and Winnipeg offices.

THE HBC MOVES TO CANADA

The Company had indeed begun negotiations with the British government to move its head office to Canada. It was becoming more and more obvious that the Company could no longer be run efficiently from a head office outside the country where most of its business was carried out. There were also new tax regulations introduced by Britain in 1965, for overseas trading companies, resulting in increased taxes on dividends, which affected shareholders in both countries. The process of moving the Company to Canada would take five years to complete. In April and May 1967 the board met in London to discuss the practical aspects of transferring the business to Canada:

The Board having considered all the information available to date and having concluded that the balance of arguments indicated that it would be in the long term interest of the Proprietors that the domicile of the Company should be transferred to Canada RESOLVED that (i) an outline draft of the arguments supporting an application for permission to transfer the domicile of the Company should be prepared;

(ii) the Governor should be asked to seek an interview with the Chancellor of the Exchequer with the object of ascertaining the likely reaction of the United Kingdom Government to an application for permission to transfer and to send him the outline draft of arguments in advance;

(iii) thereafter and dependent on the result of such interview with the Chancellor of the Exchequer, the Chairman of the Canadian· Committee should seek an interview with the Minister of Finance in order to obtain his reactions to the situation.[20]

Soon the word was out, and in March 1968 Prime Minister Lester Pearson wrote to Murray in London regarding the Company's plans to transfer the head office to Canada:

> In connection with these changing plans of the Hudson's Bay Company, I wonder if you have given thought to the archives. While I know that they are the private property of the Company, they must also be recognized as the single most important source of English documentation for much of Canada's early history. I know that there might be some reluctance to move them out of London but bringing them here would be a gesture much appreciated by the people of Canada; and especially by historians ... While a copy of all the major documents in the collection is now in the Public Archives, possession of the originals would be a great enrichment of our national historic heritage. If the Hudson's Bay Company were able to entertain such a gesture, in whole or in part, a microfilm copy would, of course be available for deposit in Great Britain so that scholars there might have access.[21]

In 1969 Amory was reported to have stated that "regardless of whether or not the firm's over-all headquarters move to Canada ... he had 'some sympathy' with the idea of moving the company's archives to Canada ... This history has much more direct interest to the people of Canada."[22]

On 2 May 1970, the three-hundredth anniversary of the HBC, it announced its intentions to move, contingent on approval from the shareholders. The Company had "carried on trade in the territories now comprising Canada from the time of its incorporation until the present day without interruption; and ... in view of the expansion in size and complexity of the Company's operations it has become important to the continuing growth and prosperity of the Company that it should become resident in and directed from Canada where 95 per cent of its assets and

98 per cent of its employees are located."[23] An extraordinary general court was held in London on 28 May, and the stockholders gave approval to the move. The next day Queen Elizabeth granted new charters (one in Britain and one in Canada)[24] transferring the head office of the Company from London to Winnipeg, the Canadian headquarters of the Company since 1860. The 1970 charter "annulled all provisions of previous charters except the incorporation section of the original 1670 Charter."[25] A new, additional Canadian charter, granted simultaneously in Ottawa, continued the Company as a corporate body, subject to the laws of Canada.

The first Canadian governor, George T. Richardson, was elected on 28 May 1970 at the last board meeting to be held in Britain. Once the head office move had been made, there was much speculation as to the future of the Hudson's Bay Company archives. The University of Toronto and the Public Archives of Canada both expressed interest in being the future location for the archives. The Public Archives had a long-standing relationship with the Company dating from the early contacts with Douglas Brymner and the publication program undertaken in the 1920s by Arthur Doughty to the microfilm project that began in 1950 with the encouragement of W. Kaye Lamb. To the historical community, the Public Archives of Canada seemed an obvious location for the HBC archives. The Public Archives had moved into a new building in 1967, and as Wilfred Smith, Dominion archivist, pointed out in a letter to the HBC, it had in 1970 a staff of three hundred and a building with "many miles of air-conditioned and temperature-controlled shelves and ... the finest research facilities in Canada."[26] Furthermore, the archives staff was "accustomed to the enforcement of any restrictions on access which may be imposed by donors."[27]

While most of the staff in the London and Winnipeg offices were involved for most of 1969 and 1970 in various projects relative to the Company's tercentennial celebrations, the move of the Company's headquarters to Winnipeg occupied the governor, Lord Amory, and the secretary, R.A. Reynolds, in London and J.R. Murray, managing director, and Rolph Huband, secretary of the Canadian Committee, in Winnipeg. The Company felt no pressure to consider the fate of its archives until the office transfer was complete. Beaver House, in London where the archives were still housed, would remain open, and in a letter to the president of the University of Toronto, Huband explained it would be a year or two at least before any decision regarding the archives was made.[28] A month later Amory wrote to Smith at the Public Archives saying: "We have taken, as yet, no decision about the future of our archives as to whether they remain here or be removed to Canada." Three months later, on his way to Winnipeg, he made a quick visit to the new archives building on Wellington Street in Ottawa.

Amory was in Winnipeg to host the Company's three-hundredth anniversary celebrations. While there, he met with the new president of the University of Manitoba, Ernest Sirluck, who urged him to consider his university as a possible custodian of the archives. Sirluck was "greatly encouraged by [the Governor's] sympathetic reception to our proposal."[29] Amory assured him that "the future of the archives would be considered within the next few months and that representations from the University would be given very serious consideration."[30] Dr Sirluck followed up this interview with a four-page letter to the governor setting out "the main points of the argument for the University of Manitoba as the depository of the Hudson's Bay Company Archives."[31] He emphasized "massive accessibility, massive support, elaborate servicing (including an active publications program), optimal preservation and security arrangements." Accessibility of the archives to researchers would be available through the extended hours of operation of a university library, which included weekends and evenings. Sirluck also noted the expertise available at the university in the areas of teaching and research in a variety of related disciplines and promised to develop the research potential of the archives by orienting "its program of library acquisitions in such a way as to develop the largest potential for the Archives."[32] He quoted an impressive increase in the library's budget that could enable the university to fulfill such a commitment. As to the appropriate servicing of such a collection, he proposed to assign the time-consuming processing work of arranging and describing the collection to research teams made up of faculty members and graduate and undergraduate students. Publication would continue as a result of academic research projects oriented to the archives.

In December 1970, with advice from Provincial Archivist John Bovey, the new premier of Manitoba, Ed Schreyer, wrote to Richardson to encourage relocation of the archives to Winnipeg, specifically to the renovated Civic Auditorium, which was being prepared as the new Provincial Archives Building. The provincial government's proposal totally ignored the lobbying from the University of Manitoba.[33] Richardson also wrote to Amory asking him to confirm the Company's decision to move the archives to Canada and to support the proposal of the University of Manitoba over the Public Archives of Canada. He told Amory that the "Canadian directors

have agreed informally that if the Archives are to be moved,
Manitoba is the preferred location because:
a) It played a key role in Company history.
b) The Head Office is now in Winnipeg.
c) The President of the University of Manitoba has expressed
enthusiastic interest in taking on the Archives.
d) The principal alternative – the Public Archives in Ottawa
already has microfilm of the Archives for 1670 to 1870.

Richardson also attached a list of specific questions related to preparing
for relocation of the archives, including export permission required from
the British government, deposit of microfilm in Britain and other North
American institutions, movement of staff to Canada, access policy, continuation of HBRS publications, and timing of the move.[34]

Control of the export of archives from Britain had been the subject
of a private member's bill, introduced by David Marquand, in the
House of Commons only the year before. The bill had not passed, but
it did generate a subcommittee report and active discussion. The loss of
literary papers and business archives to North American bidders had
increased dramatically in recent years, and prices had increased greatly
since the value of the pound sterling was low compared to the American and Canadian dollars. Archivists in Britain responded to the failure
of the bill by calling for a fresh inquiry and "recommendations which,
without insisting that every archive should be subject to control and retained in this country, encourage owners and dealers to offer accumulations first to institutions in the United Kingdom, ensure that record
offices and libraries are better able than at present to afford to take advantage of this priority of treatment, normally guarantee that where
documents are exported a photocopy of some sort will remain, and act
as a deterrent to the fragmentation of archive accumulations."[35] The
annual conference of the British Records Association in 1970 devoted
its discussion program to the topic of exportation of historical records.

Both the honorary secretary of the Business Archives Council, E.C.
Ingrams, and the secretary of the Royal Commission of Historical
Manuscripts, Roger H. Ellis (also president of the Society of Archivists), had called Joan Craig after the announcement of the transfer of
the Company's headquarters to Canada. Craig expressed her concerns
to the Company secretary, R.A. Reynolds: "Without a doubt there
would be an outcry if the Company wished to take its records out of

this country. Until 1870, the date of surrender of Rupert's Land to the Crown, the archives are the record of the administration of the Crown's 'Plantacions or Colonyes in America" (H.B.C. Charter of 2 May 1670) and as such a part of the country's heritage ... Western Canadians of course will argue, and rightly so, that the Company's records document the early days of their country."[36]

In January 1971 the Company was clearly willing to place the archives in Manitoba, but wanted Manitobans to sort out the question of the repository. Significantly, the main concern in this regard was optimum accessibility to the archives for research and publication. According to Rolph Huband, "The Company suggests that, before it commences discussions on relocation, a decision as between the University of Manitoba and the Provincial Archives should be made by the Provincial Government in consultation with the University on the basis of physical facilities and maximum use of the material for research and publication. The Company expresses no preference except to say that the approach of Dr. Sirluck was instrumental in activating serious consideration of a move."[37] J.R. Murray later admitted that the letter from Schreyer had come as a surprise[38] and until then he had thought the only competition would be between Ottawa and the University of Manitoba. Meetings were set up with Richardson and Schreyer and at this point the ball really started to roll.

Having already expressed her resistance to removing the archives from Britain but accepting the inevitable, Craig briefed the new London secretary, Graham Logan-Brown, in October 1971, emphasizing that "the opinions expressed are dictated solely by what I consider as of prime importance namely the welfare of the archives."[39] She stressed that one of the major responsibilities of the Company should be to maintain "their physical safety and their impartiality and authenticity as archives." For this purpose, she suggested continued Hudson's Bay Company custody in either London or Winnipeg or transfer of custody to a national repository in London or in Canada. In a point-by-point critique of Dr Sirluck's letter, Craig questioned his comprehension of the contents or extent of the archives and considered his proposals unsubstantive and "at variance with proper archival principles." She also expressed concern that his motives were too parochial, not recognizing the broader context of the archives' importance to the contemporary Company and to the history of the rest of Canada, and concluded: "I hold the view most strongly that the University of Manitoba is not a suitable place for the deposit of the Company's archives." Her recommendations were as follows:

Should it be decided to transfer the archives to Canada, I am one
hundred percent in favour of their being in the custody of the
Company in Winnipeg. My reasons are:

  a. Archives are not merely old documents of interest to historians,
  but form a continuing process to the present day. The essential
  qualities of archives are that they are documents forming part of
  an official transaction, preserved for official reference in official
  and continued custody.

  b. For the sake of unity with the series of Administration,
  Northern Stores, Land Department records, etc., now forming
  a separate archive at Hudson's Bay House [in Winnipeg].

  c. First and foremost the Company's archives are Company
  documents. The Company, not a province, not a nation, is the
  unifying factor.[40]

If the Company decided to transfer the archives to Canada to be maintained by an institution other than the Company, Craig said, "the requirements of satisfactory custody, together with their national
importance, lead me unhesitatingly to the conclusion that the only fit-
ting repository is that of the Public Archives of Canada, Ottawa,"[41] although she admitted that no one from that institution had ever
approached her on the subject.

Meetings continued with the provincial government, particularly between the provincial archivist and Mary Liz Bayer, assistant deputy
minister for cultural affairs, who kept the premier advised. The province was quite prepared to house the HBC archives in its newly renovated archives building and suggested at that time that "it would be a
very welcome gesture if the Company would consider contributing an
annual amount to cover all or part of the salary of an archivist who
would work exclusively on the Hudson's Bay material."[42] There were
inherent cost and space requirements for such a large amount of treasured material, questions of accessibility to the archives, including
staffing, and the commitment to the HBRS publications. Discussions,
meetings, and correspondence continued through the year, but with no
seeming rush. The Company was busy with the move of its head office
and with reorganizing the offices left in London, including the archives.
Early in 1972 Huband asked three Company employees with vested interests in the archives for their comments on the now inevitable transfer, either to Ottawa or Manitoba. Shirlee Anne Smith, public relations
officer (and future Keeper of the HBCA), Malvina Bolus, editor of *The*

Beaver, and her assistant Helen Burgess, all wrote back that they preferred the Public Archives of Canada, especially if the Company was indeed to relinquish financial responsibility for the maintenance. But, they thought, long-term control over the use and publication of the archives should be retained by the Company, and microfilm would have to be provided to the Company's head office. Also, publication should continue through the HBRS under the control of the Company.[43] These were basically the same recommendations as Craig in London had made. But within a few months, Huband and Murray had recommended Winnipeg as the location for the HBC archives.[44]

In June, Huband set out the current scenario for the executive committee and the board of directors of the Company. He acknowledged that the general consensus of all of "our historical people," including the Company archivist and the editor of *The Beaver*, favoured Ottawa because of its national scope. The University of Manitoba was hinting at providing a new building for the archives, but the Manitoba government was very keen and had modern facilities available in the Provincial Archives. There was some concern about their financial commitment. Huband's own recommendation, despite pressure from the Public Archives, was "to negotiate with the Manitoba Government for a permanent deposit of Hudson's Bay Company Archives material with the Manitoba Archives"[45] under specific conditions. He estimated the cost of moving the Company archives at about $25,000 and annual operating costs, based on the current costs, at about $50,000. The executive committee met in Montreal on 15 June and "unanimously agreed that the Archives should be relocated in Canada,"[46] but as to location, the question was referred to the board. On 20 June a telegram arrived at Hudson's Bay House in Winnipeg: "English Directors opinion is that archives should go to Canada. Location being matter for Canadian Directors to decide."[47] When the Canadian board of directors met two days later, it deferred the matter, after agreeing "that an independent expert on Archives be engaged to advise the Company on the terms and conditions under which the Archives material might be relocated to Canada."[48]

Thus a meeting of archival experts and Company officials was held in Winnipeg in July 1972. In attendance at the meeting were J.A. Hammond, executive vice-president of the Glenbow-Alberta Institute; Hartwell Bowsfield, archivist at York University and former provincial archivist of Manitoba; Joan Craig, HBC archivist, who had arrived from London for the meeting; Shirlee Anne Smith, HBC public relations officer; Rolph Huband, secretary of the Canadian Committee; and J.R. Murray, managing director of the Company. Provincial Archivist John Bovey attended the meeting briefly to outline plans for the modernized and expanded facilities and to conduct a tour of the Provincial Archives building under renovation. After considerable discussion of "the purposes and objectives of the Company with respect to its Archives material," the meeting participants agreed that the principal objective was availability to scholars, and the secondary objectives were publication and the reputation of the Company. With that focus in mind, the consensus, as reported to the Executive Committee in August, was that the original material in the HBC archives should be deposited with the Public Archives of Canada, which "has the best facilities in Canada for storage, preservation, and repair." It was also agreed that the HBRS should continue, at least on an interim basis, and copies of the microfilm would be "made available to other Archives institutions."[49]

At the end of November, Huband was still recommending that the Company explore all aspects of the subject with the Manitoba government before arriving at any decision on the matter. The Company had definitely made the decision to relocate the archives to Canada, but it was, despite the recommendations of its advisory committee, still considering both Ottawa and Winnipeg. An important insight into the Company's view of the transfer is evident in a position paper Huband prepared for the Manitoba government at that time. He explained that the purpose of the archives after relocation to Canada ought to be twofold: to provide the "widest possible accessibility to scholars" and to provide "maximum encouragement of publication."[50] This approach, when combined with the proposal to allow access to the records older than thirty years (excepting personnel records), was quite a departure from the long-standing formal policy of restricting access to records created before 1870 and of reserving the right to deny permission to publish information from the archives. In December, Huband wrote to London to inform Craig that some of the directors had a strong preference for Winnipeg and were preparing to discuss it further with the Manitoba government.[51] Craig was concerned that the Company seemed to be ignoring the recommendations of the advisory committee which had met in July. As she recalled, "the Manitoba facilities left a very great deal to be desired."[52] Huband explained that the results of the July meeting had been communicated to the board, which had then "decided there were other factors besides pure facilities which should be taken into consideration – Canadian regionalism and the Company's historic identification with the West, and the Company's relations with the federal and provincial governments."[53]

In the meantime, Schreyer had written to Richardson to say he saw no major problems in accommodating the HBC archives:

> Space allocation for present requirement and reasonable future requirement can certainly be made in the Provincial Library and Archives building; we can accommodate the requirements of the Hudson's Bay Record Society; we would certainly agree that we want all the material to be made readily available to scholars and researchers. The Provincial Archives would welcome the sharing of information, microfilm copies etc., of archive material ... The only point which seems to us to require clarification is the extent of the expectation of the Hudson's Bay Company for long-range acceptance of all Company records ... When this point has been resolved, we can proceed with our planning.[54]

Negotiations continued and a draft agreement had been prepared by March 1973. In May, Huband informed the Public Archives of the decision to place the Company archives in the Provincial Archives of Manitoba: "The Board of the Company has agreed with the Manitoba Government to deposit our archives in the Provincial Archives of Manitoba."[55] He explained that the decision was based on a number of factors: "Winnipeg has been the Company's Canadian headquarters since 1860 and the corporate head office since 1970. The Archives and Library Building of the Provincial Government is presently being renovated and will meet the recognized specifications for the management and storage of archives. The present trend towards regional, cultural development encouraged by the Federal Government has also influenced our decision."[56]

Dominion archivist Wilfred Smith responded almost immediately to the decision to locate the records elsewhere. He offered a five-year budget of almost half a million dollars to be allocated for staff and conservation if the decision was reconsidered in favour of the Public Archives.[57] With regard to this significant financial commitment, Richardson immediately contacted Schreyer with two questions:

> (a) To what extent if any is the standard of care and service contemplated in the Manitoba/HBC agreement inferior to that outlined in Dr. Smith's letter? [and]

(b) If there is a significant gap between the levels of service contemplated at Manitoba and at Ottawa, what can be done to close it?[58]

Those questions were then put to Bovey, who responded in detail, if not with money.[59] In the end, the decision, as explained later to Smith, was based more on "the Company's historic connection with Winnipeg"[60] and the expanded facilities planned for the Provincial Archives of Manitoba, which now included amended plans for document restoration equipment and the government's commitment to supply the necessary staff. Another consideration had been the fact that microfilm would continue to be made available at the Public Archives in Ottawa.

THE ARCHIVES IN WINNIPEG

The official public announcement of the agreement was made in Winnipeg on 31 July 1973 by the HBC and the Manitoba government. Premier Schreyer and Governor Richardson jointly signed the agreement to transfer "approximately 4290 linear feet of minute books, correspondence, journals of exploration, account books, maps and ships' logs" from Beaver House in London to the Provincial Archives building in Winnipeg. Schreyer noted the significance of the transfer: "Fortunately for Canadians, the Hudson's Bay Company has always had an awareness of its history."[61] Richardson explained the Company's position: "Following the transfer of our head office to Canada in 1970 it was a natural decision to relocate our Archives in Canada. Because of the Company's long and involved association with the Northwest, and the excellent facilities offered by the Manitoba Government, it was a natural decision for the Company to deposit its Archives in Winnipeg where the Company also has its head office."[62]

The agreement, between the Governor and Company of Adventurers of England Trading into Hudson's Bay and Her Majesty the Queen in Right of the Province of Manitoba, allowed the Company to retain ownership of the archives, which would continue to be known as the Hudson's Bay Company Archives. Responsibility for custody of the records and the cost of administration of the archives was transferred to the government of Manitoba with provision for "the necessary staff and office space to enable the H.B. Archivist to give the same level of service to the public and the same priority to the classification of records as are presently being provided by the Company."[63] The selection of the archivist was to be made in consultation with the Company but that person would report directly to the provincial archivist. Public

BETWEEN

THE GOVERNOR AND COMPANY
OF ADVENTURERS OF ENGLAND
TRADING INTO HUDSON'S BAY,
also known as HUDSON'S BAY COMPANY
(hereinafter called 'The Company')
OF THE FIRST PART.

AND

HER MAJESTY THE QUEEN IN RIGHT
OF THE PROVINCE OF MANITOBA
(hereinafter called 'The Government')
OF THE SECOND PART.

WHEREAS the Company has carried on business in the territories now
comprising Canada from the time of its incorporation on the 2nd of May,
1670 until the present day without interruption,

AND WHEREAS the Company has preserved its corporate records covering that
period and since 1920 has made these records available to the public in the
Hudson's Bay Archives (hereinafter called 'H B Archives') located in London, England,

AND WHEREAS the Head Office of the Company was moved from London, England to
Winnipeg, Manitoba, Canada in 1970,

AND WHEREAS the Company desires to find a new and appropriate location for the HB
Archives, which constitutes an important source for Canadian historical research,

AND WHEREAS the Government is planning to re-locate the Manitoba Archives in
new facilities and a new location on Memorial Boulevard in Winnipeg,

AND WHEREAS it is desirable and in the best interests of both parties and of
the people of Canada to have the H B Archives located in Canada,

AND WHEREAS the Company has decided to deposit the H B Archives in the
custody of the Government and the Government has decided to accept such custody,
the parties therefore agree as follows:

The agreement to deposit the HBC archives with the Provincial
Archives of Manitoba being signed in Winnipeg, 31 July 1973
(1987-363-A-19, 1-10); *left to right*, John Bovey, W.C.
Lalonde (in costume), Edward Schreyer, Shirlee Anne Smith,
and George Richardson

access was significantly widened since the rules of admission to the Provincial Archives would be applied. There would be no restrictions on publication except for subjects designated by the Hudson's Bay Record Society for its exclusive publication rights, and that restriction was eliminated with the demise of the society in 1983. Permission was still required from the Company to publish lengthy excerpts from the records. Under the agreement, the Hudson's Bay Company would continue to deposit records of historical importance in the archives.

THE FIRST CANADIAN KEEPER

Joan Craig announced her intention to resign as Company archivist in the fall of 1973, leaving her position open to an archivist from Canada. In September, Shirlee Anne Smith was appointed to the position with the responsibility of not only succeeding Craig but also spending the next year in London supervising operations of the archives and moving the records from Britain to Canada. Smith had been the librarian in the Winnipeg office since 1957 and had spent much of her time on work related to projects connected with the Company's history and its archives. She was also a public relations officer and, as we have seen, a key player in the relocation decision. On completion of the move, Smith would be employed by the Manitoba government as Hudson's Bay Company archivist.[64] She reported to work in London a week after her appointment was announced and five days before Craig's departure. A considerable amount of work had been completed by Craig over the previous two years in identifying the concerns and problems of moving the three-hundred-year accumulation of treasured documents and records, some in fragile condition. But decisions had to be made as to how the archives would be packed (boxes or crates) and what method of shipment would be used (sea or air). Inventories for shipping purposes had to be much more detailed than day-to-day working lists of records and their locations. Every item, down to the last unclassified letter and the last piece of red tape, had to be accounted for and packed. With a proposed estimated time of arrival in Winnipeg in the late summer or early fall of 1974, time had to be allowed for the packing and the shipping process. There was also the prospective problem of the staff in London leaving as they found other jobs. Gwen Kemp, the assistant archivist, stayed on until the last day. She saw the last of the packing cases off on 30 September and started her new job at the University of London two days later.[65]

Shirlee Anne Smith, keeper of the HBC Archives from 1974 to 1990 (1974-2-1)

The usual number of researchers continued to arrive every week to access the records, written research inquiries had to be answered by the archives staff, and the HBRS publication schedule had to be met. Smith in London and Huband, assisted by Robert Oleson, in Winnipeg kept the move on track with regular correspondence and telephone calls. Huband, as the Canadian secretary, was responsible for making the decisions on the move. An export licence had to be applied for with enough time allowed for administrative processing. As a condition of obtaining an export permit, the British government required the Company to deposit a copy of its archival records from 1670 to 1904 (up to seventy years before the move to Canada) in the Public Record Office, London. Microfilms of the records from 1670 to 1870 were already available, and the Company was given ten years to microfilm those from 1870 to 1904. Microfilming of the later records, in fact, did not begin until 1980 and was completed in 1998.

The decision was made to send the archives by ship from London to Montreal and then by rail to Winnipeg. The shipping costs were £13,302.[66] Six twenty-ton containers were transported on two ships so that, in the case of disaster, not all would be lost.[67] The Company's

Mr Clark packing boxes at Beaver House for the move to
Winnipeg (1974-2-28)

charter and some of the famous portraits were sent separately by air to
Toronto, where the offices of the Company's senior directors were by
then located. The headquarters location had been a prime consideration in the negotiations for relocating the archives, but the corporate
office of the Company was quietly moved from Winnipeg to Toronto in
1978, although the registered office, the officially designated headquarters of the Company, remained in Winnipeg until 1987.[68]

The first containers arrived at the Provincial Archives building in
Winnipeg on 30 September 1974. Smith, with the assistance of staff in
the Provincial Archives, immediately began unpacking and shelving
the records as they came out of the crates. The packing had been done
in a way that kept the classified documents in series order for efficient

Packed boxes awaiting shipment to Canada (1974-2-37)

handling. The last container arrived on 1 November, and less than three weeks later the entire archives, nearly 4,200 linear feet of manuscript material, books, microfilm, and paintings, had been unpacked and placed in retrievable position on the stack shelving. "The success of the entire operation exceeded every reasonable expectation, not one item being lost and only one ledger cover slightly dented."[69] With the assistance of one clerk-typist, Shirlee Smith, the first "keeper" of the HBCA, immediately re-established the archives office and began answering research correspondence. The official reopening took place on 17 April 1975 with an enthusiastic response from historical researchers. Statistics for 1975 – 17 April to 31 December – indicate that of 3,788 research visits recorded at the Provincial Archives, 1,347 were to examine the archives of the Hudson's Bay Company. D.E. Vernon, the deputy minister of Tourism, Recreation and Cultural Affairs, paid tribute to Shirlee Smith in the governmental report to the Company up to the end of 1975:

Nobody is more responsible for the success of the transfer of the Company's archives from London to Winnipeg than she is, and she

The move into the Provincial Archives of Manitoba building was completed in November 1974. Keeper Shirlee Anne Smith showing some of the records to Maurice Tarr and Tom Heggie of Parks Canada (photo: Parks Canada)

is equally responsible for the successful re-establishment of archival operations, and in fact the expansion of services to researchers, in 1975. Without her unflagging energies and complete devotion to her work, I do not see how the great archival events schemed out in the 1973 Agreement could have become realities with so much speed and so few difficulties.[70]

In the spring of 1991, Smith was succeeded as keeper by Judith Hudson Beattie, who had been working in the archives since 1981.

Postscript

When the Hudson's Bay Company archives moved to Canada in 1974, Hartwell Bowsfield of York University in Toronto took over the editorship of the Hudson's Bay Record Society from Glyndwr Williams. Publication of records from the HBCA continued with volumes thirty-one to thirty-three. Then in 1983, after forty-five years, the society was dissolved. The Company, suffering from the economic realities of the early 1980s, high interest rates and reduced consumer spending, had determined it could no longer support the society. Subscriptions were providing only one-quarter of the cost of the publications, and that did not include the substantial administrative and staff support from the head office and the archives. Historians and history buffs from North America and beyond expressed their dismay at the decision of the Company to cease publication. Its response to the historical community explained that it was downsizing in a number of areas of responsibility, but the Hudson's Bay Record Society was the only victim among its history-related activities.[1]

Publication of *The Beaver* magazine, microfilming of the archives, and the position of archivist were not affected by the reductions. Its commitment, since the beginning of the society in 1938, was testimony to the Company's recognition of its role in the history of Canada. The HBRS publications had contributed to scholarly research in Canada and made available the archival record in a readily accessible format. In order to continue this commitment, historians at the University of Winnipeg established the Hudson's Bay Company Archives Research Centre to facilitate scholarly research and publishing on aspects of the HBC territory, known from 1670 to 1870 as Rupert's Land.[2]

In London the corporate offices and the Archives Department were gone from Beaver House, but the subsidiary company, Hudson's Bay and Annings, remained in residence for several more years to carry on the London fur auction, which included furs from all over the world, not just from the trapping was head of around Hudson Bay. In 1979 Ken Thomson, a Canadian who was head of a worldwide publishing empire, bought 75 per cent of the Company to become the major shareholder, effectively completing the move to making the Hudson's Bay Company a solely Canadian company. Profits continued to follow the ups and downs relating to general economic conditions through the 1980s. The Company responded by restructuring its retail business and selling off subsidiary interests.

In 1988 the London fur auction house was sold.[3] Garlick Hill, the historic fur trade district of London in which Beaver House was located, had been designated a Conservation Area in 1980.[4] No buildings could be demolished without permission of the local planning authority of the City of London. Markborough Properties, the real estate branch of the Hudson's Bay Group, however, received permission to demolish Beaver House in 1982 in order to develop the property into a complex containing offices and fur trade facilities.[5] The Royal Bank of Canada Centre, a two-building, five- and seven-storey, postmodern complex, was built on the site and opened in March 1988 by Her Majesty, Queen Elizabeth.

There are few remaining visual reminders of the Hudson's Bay Company's presence in London. One is the classical portico of the 1920s Beaver House, which was carefully dismantled and re-erected inside a spacious glass atrium between the two Royal Bank towers. Visitors now enter the building off Queen Victoria Street, and special permission is required from security to gain entrance to the atrium area to view the portico, displayed like an ancient archaeological treasure. Other symbols of the fur trade are equally hidden. A weathervane in the shape of a beaver is just visible on top of the lantern feature on the roof of Hasilwood House, formerly Hudson's Bay House, in Bishopsgate. As well, architectural elements in the frieze above the first stage of the building include a North American Native feathered headdress carved in the stone.

Many changes have occurred in the Hudson's Bay Company Archives through the years. Once settled into its new home in Winnipeg, the Archives became even more of a meeting place for Canadian and American researchers interested in the multitude of subjects contained therein. Use of the material in the archives increased dramatically to the point that wear and tear on the documents was soon noticeable. A report prepared by the Canadian Conservation Institute for the Provincial Archives of Manitoba in 1977 recommended the withdrawal of the earliest material from use by researchers.[6] These early records would remain accessible to researchers on the microfilm copies only. Agreements with the Company in 1973 and 1976 had stipulated that the provincial government would, at its own expense, keep the archives in good repair and in the same condition as when the records were delivered to Winnipeg.[7] As a result of the CCI report, a professional conservator was hired, and a modern conservation facility was set up in the Provincial Archives by the Manitoba government in 1982.

When the records were moved to Canada, some of 1870–1900 material and most of the post-1900 material was still unclassified, and new accessions continued to arrive from the Company in administrative units that did not conform to the classification system in place for the pre-1870 archives. That system, developed in the 1930s by the Company archivist and Hilary Jenkinson and based on record type and chronology, was no longer adequate for describing the records of a modern corporation. A decision was made to adopt record group classifications for the ordering of unclassified and new material which would recognize the function of the record and the activities of the record-keepers within the administrative unit.

The record group concept had been developed in the United States and Australia in the mid-twentieth century. It was formalized by T.R. Schellenberg as a methodology to control the voluminous government records in the National Archives of the United States.[8] He established the term "record group" to describe major archival units created to facilitate manageability of the larger "archive group" of the government bureaucracy. Essentially, the record group concept, based on organization and function, provided control of the records of the more fluid administrative organization of the modern government records and more logical access to archival researchers. Jenkinson had stressed continued adherence in the archives of the original order of the originating office, a concept that worked best with historical records but broke down with modern records that arrived in the archives when the administrative unit was still active and evolving. Schellenberg's stress was on usability of the record in the archival context; Jenkinson's was on the preservation of the record, with reference access of secondary importance. The record group approach provided a logical relationship to the structure of the creating administration which could be followed organizationally to succeeding records creators.[9]

Alex Ross, an archivist and records manager hired in 1981, recommended the concept to the Keeper, Shirlee Anne Smith, by explaining that it was more flexible than the system used to organize the archival records in the past. "By adopting the record group approach, an archivist is able to arrange and describe a body of records much more conveniently and effectively than would be possible if the relatively inflexible archives group concept was adhered to ... the principle of provenance is not compromised and basic archival units, which are readily manageable are established."[10] Ross worked out that this approach would be particularly useful in dealing with the more recent records in Section D, which included land, fur trade, and stores department records.

His plan was approved. The original classification system remained in place for the pre-1870 material, but some reclassification was necessary in the records created between 1870 and 1920 in order to bring together records dealing with one administrative unit. It was during that period that the administration of the Company evolved from its emphasis on the fur trade to land sales, the retail store trade, and various subsidiary businesses. Each record group (RG) is described in a finding aid, readily accessible to users of the HBCA.[11]

The Company began formulating a plan to transfer ownership of its archival records and museum artifacts to the people of Canada in the early 1990s. The HBCA records were already well looked after in the Provincial Archives of Manitoba (now the Archives of Manitoba). The HBC museum collection was on display at Lower Fort Garry and played a role in the Parks Canada interpretation of the Company and the history of the fort. It had been gathered together in the 1920s, as an outcome of the Company's 250th anniversary, and was first displayed in 1922 in the Winnipeg store on Main Street. A historical exhibit featuring much of the collection had been given designated space on the third floor of the new Portage Avenue store when it opened in 1925. Clifford Wilson was director of the museum from 1939 to 1957, while he was also editor of *The Beaver*. He catalogued, documented, and augmented the collection during that time. Within three years of his leaving for another job, the historical exhibit was closed in 1960. The material was packed for storage while the Company negotiated an agreement with the province of Manitoba to take it on permanent loan. A further agreement with the federal government, through Parks Canada, provided for the collection to be transferred to a purpose-built museum at the National Historic Site of Lower Fort Garry.[12]

When Parks Canada informed the Company in 1992 that Lower Fort Garry was "no longer the best location for the HBC Museum Collection,"[13] the HBC again set about considering its options. Interest in acquiring the museum collection was received from the Manitoba Museum of Man and Nature in Winnipeg, as well as from the Canadian Museum of Civilization in Ottawa/Hull.[14] The Company, in considering the financial aspects of a transfer of ownership, requested a ruling from Revenue Canada on the income tax benefits of donating both the HBCA and the museum collection to the province of Manitoba.

> The Hudson's Bay Company proposes to donate the Hudson's Bay Company Archives to Manitoba in order to: (i) ensure that the Hudson's Bay Company Archives are preserved and maintained in an appropriate setting which is conducive to promoting public knowledge and understanding of our culture and heritage; (ii) ensure continued public access to the Hudson's Bay Company Archives; (iii) preserve and maintain an important historical and cultural resource; and (iv) obtain a charitable deduction, the tax savings from which will, in part, be used for charitable purposes including the ongoing maintenance and preservation of the Hudson's Bay Company Archives. This is a technical requirement to enable the Company to proceed with making an offer of financial support to the Museum and to relocate the collection to the Museum from Lower Fort Garry. The financial support would derive from a foundation established through net tax savings from a Gift to the Crown.[15]

The response from Revenue Canada provided the scope for a transfer plan, and in 1993 the Hudson's Bay Company donated its corporate archives to the Provincial Archives of Manitoba and its museum collection to the Manitoba Museum. The resultant tax savings to the Company from the donation (the archives alone were valued, for tax purposes, at $60 million) was used to set up the Hudson's Bay Company History Foundation to provide capital and operating funding for the future care, management, and interpretation of the two donations. This private charitable foundation, governed by a board of directors that includes current and former officers of the Company, Canadian historians, and one director nominated by the government of Manitoba, was established to advance knowledge of and interest in Canadian history through financial assistance to qualified recipients.[16] It also supports Canada's National History Society, which publishes *The Beaver: Canada's History Magazine*.[17]

Deed of Gift, or donation agreement, January 1994

A requirement of the donation agreement, which included negotiations with the Canadian Cultural Property Export Review Agency, was that the HBC would hire a records manager to guarantee the continued transfer of inactive corporate records of historical value to the HBCA. A records management program was implemented by the head office in 1998 and three years later was expanded to include electronic records management.

With capital funding provided by the foundation, the HBCA constructed new vaults for the safekeeping and presentation of its rare and unique records. The permanent structure, built into the old concert hall space of the Manitoba Archives building, was opened in 1994. Its environmental controls ensure the preservation of paper-based material while also considering the prime conditions for leather, vellum, and parchment. A separate cold storage vault was fitted out to preserve microfilm, motion picture film, photographs, and photographic negatives. A visual storage area in the new vault was added to provide supervised viewing of selected archival treasures on display.[18]

Of the more than 2,000 metres of archival material stored in the HBCA vault, the largest accumulation is of textual records. Because of the Company's meticulous record-keeping and wide-ranging interests, it also has extraordinary collections of books, maps, architectural drawings, photographs, and documentary art. The HBCA maintains a library of published works related to the history of the HBC and/or based on research in the archives, as well as a rare book collection. Many of the books were in the London office library created by the governor and Committee, primarily from the nineteenth century. Other books came from the fur trade libraries.[19] The HBCA has the largest holding of fur trade maps in North America – nearly 12,000 maps, charts, and plans dating from as early as 1563. There are thirty-seven atlases, some from as early as 1733. Architectural drawings date from the late 1700s and include drawings of Hudson Bay forts, Company ships, department stores, and Company buildings in London and in Winnipeg. The photograph collection consists of approximately 130,000 images, documenting the Company, its employees, establishments, and activities. Over 55,000 images were transferred to the HBCA in 1987 from the offices of *The Beaver* magazine. The documentary art collection consists of approximately 1,350 prints, drawings, paintings, posters, calendars, and advertising art. The earliest works are an engraving, *A View of London in 1560,* dated 1738 and the pen-and-ink and watercolour drawings James Isham made at Fort Prince of Wales (Churchill) in 1743.[20] The HBCA also preserves special media, including a hundred motion picture film and video tape recordings featuring commissioned and amateur footage of HBC posts and ships, as well as images of the people, geography, and wildlife of the North. A total of 485 sound recordings cover radio broadcasts of HBC events and oral history taped interviews with retired personnel.

Over eighty libraries and other institutions have a microfilm copy of the HBCA Finding Aid, and through interlibrary loan, any library with a microfilm reader has access to microfilm copies of most of the material in the archives. The current policy at the HBCA provides free and open access to the records of the Company, while safeguarding rights to privacy (individual and corporate), legal rights, and preservation considerations. All categories of Company records except Land Department and

Judith Hudson Beattie, keeper of the HBC Archives from 1990
to 2001 (photo: Mary Ford)

personnel records and minutes are open to researchers after thirty years.
Land Department records are fully accessible, regardless of date of creation, and minutes of the Company and its subsidiaries are accessible after fifteen years. Personnel records are available fifty years after the last
date on the file. Present policy encourages publication of the Company's
records, while attempting to ensure that accurate, fully referenced versions are provided. Many eminent scholars have taken advantage of this
policy, and even recent requests for publication on websites have met a
favourable reception. Requests for access to restricted records must be
made to the manager of the HBCA, and special permission can be granted
to consult the originals if the microfilm copy is illegible.[21]

Judith Beattie retired as keeper in 2001, and Maureen Dolyniuk assumed the redefined position as manager of the HBCA. The history of

The author in the HBC storage vaults and display area opened in 1999

the archives continues as new material is added by donation and as purposeful researchers delve into the hoarded wealth of documents and find new gems of information previously overlooked by meticulous historians, anthropologists, biologists, climatologists, genealogists, archivists, and researchers from a myriad of other disciplines.

The Hudson's Bay Company, based in England and in Canada, is also an excellent case study within which to study record-keeping practices over a period of three centuries. This author found untapped treasures about the administration of the HBCA in previously uncatalogued material, now arranged and described as RG20, the Records of the Hudson's Bay Company Archives.

In January 2006 the board of directors of the Hudson's Bay Company announced its acceptance of a takeover bid from Maple Leaf Heritage Investments Acquisition Corp. Two months later, chief shareholder Jerry Zucker assumed the role of governor and chief executive officer. The Hudson's Bay Company Archives, Archives of Manitoba, continues to be the HBC's corporate archives. The first major accrual of the already significant archives of the Hudson's Bay Company, approximately 1,500 linear feet of inactive records, were transferred in 2007.

Secretaries of the Hudson's Bay Company

LONDON

1681–86	Onesiphorus Albin
1686–89	Richard Banner
1689–1724	William Potter
1724–37	Thomas Bird
1737–45	Thomas Burrows
1745–63	Charles Hay
1763–80	William Redknap
1780–92	John Deseret
	Thomas Hutchins, corresponding secretary, 1783–90
	Alexander Lean, corresponding secretary, 1791–92
1792–1817	Alexander Lean
1818–43	William Smith
1843–55	Archibald Barclay
1855–71	William Gregory Smith
	Eden Colvile, corresponding secretary, 1855–58
	Thomas Fraser, corresponding secretary, 1858–67
1871–93	William Armit
1893–1911	William Ware
1911–23	Frank C. Ingrams
1923–48	J. Chadwick Brooks
1948–71	Rudolph Arturo Reynolds
1971–72	Graham R. Logan Brown, London secretary
1972–[84]	John Richard Dawes, London secretary

CANADA

1960–93   A. Rolph Huband
                 Secretary, Canadian Committee, 1960–70
                 Secretary, head office, 1970–93

Archivists of the Hudson's Bay Company

RICHARD HENRY GRESHAM LEVESON GOWER, ARCHIVIST, 1931–1954

Richard Leveson Gower was initially employed with the Hudson's Bay Company in the fall of 1923, when he was twenty-nine years old. His first job was to deliver material to William Schooling, who was writing the history of the Company. He then became one of the assistants abstracting this material for the Annals. From 1926 to 1928 he was engaged in answering the numerous inquiries about the records, received primarily from North America. He was sent to Canada for four months at the end of 1927 to visit Company offices and to arrange for the transfer of inactive records to London. Leveson Gower was appointed the first Company archivist in May 1931, in charge of a small Archives Department and over 250 years' worth of historical records at Hudson's Bay House in London.

With the threat of war in 1939, he arranged for the packing and relocation of the Company archives to Governor Cooper's estate, Hexton Manor in Hertfordshire, about forty miles northeast of London, where the records remained safe from air raids on London. The bulk of the move had been completed when Leveson Gower was called up for service as a captain with the Grenadier Guards, the regiment he had served with in the First World War. He was assigned to the Rail Ordnance, in charge of all troop movements in Britain. Apparently, he had, from an early age, a fascination with railways and had memorized the railway timetables. He was promoted to the rank of major before he returned to civilian life in 1947. Leveson Gower continued as archivist of the HBC until 1949, when he resigned to assume management of the family estate in Surrey on the death of his father, Granville Charles Leveson Gower.

That estate was the 8,000-acre Titsey Place, which had been in the family since it was purchased in 1534 by Sir John Gresham, lord mayor of London and uncle of Sir Thomas Gresham, founder of the Royal Exchange. The house went through several renovations and expansions and, ironically, was requisitioned and occupied during the Second World War by Canadian troops. The Leveson Gowers were active in the historical community of Surrey as early as 1864, when Richard's grandfather served as vice-president of the Surrey Archaeological Society and wrote articles about the estate and its Roman archaeological site. Other notable members of that society in the early 1900s were "neighbours" Sir Hilary Jenkinson, the archival authority, and Gertrude Jekyll, of gardening fame. Richard joined the society in 1927 and during the 1950s was vice-president to Jenkinson's presidency. The Titsey Estate was often the destination of society outings, with tea served in the garden.

Richard Henry Gresham Leveson Gower had travelled by train each day from Titsey to London to his job as clerk and then archivist for the Hudson's Bay Company, making the unimpressive salary of £360 in 1937 and £600 when he returned from service in 1947. He died in 1982. Richard and his last surviving brother left no heirs, and so to preserve the estate on their deaths, they set up the Titsey Foundation. David Innes assumed the position of governor of the foundation. The manor house and grounds are open to the public in the summer months.

ALICE JOHNSON MCGRATH, ARCHIVIST, 1954–1968

Alice Johnson was born in 1907 and lived in London all of her life. She joined the Hudson's Bay Company in 1926 as a junior secretary in the secretary's office. She was soon transferred to the Development Department and two years later to the Archives Department as the records assistant. She left the Company in 1930 to work for an advertising agency but returned in 1934 to the Archives Department. When the archivist, Richard Leveson Gower, was called up for active war service in 1939, Johnson took charge of the HBC archives. Although the records were stored outside London for five years, she was still able to provide considerable research and editorial assistance to the editors of the Hudson's Bay Record Society. Johnson did her part to support the war effort. Researchers who have noticed the variety of flimsy copies and notes on partial pages of recycled paper, particularly in the search files, will recognize that the Archives Department was doing all it could in the way of economy and recycling. She also served on night-time fireguard duties at Beaver House.

Alice Johnson was married in 1946, becoming Mrs Edward McGrath, but for the most part she continued to use her maiden name in connection with her work. After Leveson Gower returned in 1947 to the job of archivist, Johnson devoted most of her time to work on the HBRS publications. She was appointed assistant editor in 1948 and was the sole editor and wrote the introduction to *Saskatchewan Journals and Correspondence: Edmonton House, 1795–1800; Chesterfield House, 1800–1802*, published in 1967. Johnson was appointed archivist of the Hudson's Bay Company in 1950. Readers of the record society publications who appreciate the informative footnotes and biographies can thank her for the attention to minute detail and for finding those details in the volumes and boxes of archival material. She also wrote numerous articles for *The Beaver* and contributed eighteen biographies to volume 1 of the *Dictionary of Canadian Biography*. In 1968 Alice Johnson was presented with an Award of Merit from the Association for State and Local History at the annual meeting held in Nashville Tennessee. She accepted the award in person, on her only trip to North America. She retired in 1968 at the age of sixty-one and died in 1987.

JOAN MURRAY CRAIG,
ARCHIVIST, 1968–1972

Joan Murray joined the Hudson's Bay Company archives in 1963 to replace the previous assistant archivist, Marjorie Gambles. She married Rodney Craig in 1964. When Alice Johnson retired in 1968, Joan Craig was appointed archivist. Like that of her predecessors, her effective management style is evident in the detailed reports she made regularly on the work in the archives. She travelled to Canada in 1971, meeting staff at the Company offices in Winnipeg and then visiting Montreal and Lachine, Quebec. There were already rumblings about the Company moving to Canada, and on her return to London, Craig became very much involved in the discussions and preparations for the eventual transfer of the HBC archives to Winnipeg. She resigned in the fall of 1973, just five days after Shirlee Anne Smith arrived in London to supervise the move. She has since raised two daughters and now enjoys retirement with her husband in Buckinghamshire, England.

SHIRLEE ANNE SMITH,
KEEPER, 1973–1990

Shirlee Anne Smith spent her entire professional career working either directly or indirectly for the Hudson's Bay Company. After receiving a BA degree in history, she was first employed by the Company in 1957 as librarian at Hudson's Bay House in Winnipeg. She was also responsible for various historical programs promoted by the Company and through the early 1970s she was a key player in the decision to relocate the HBC archives to Canada. In 1973 she was posted to London with the responsibility of not only succeeding Joan Craig but also spending the next year supervising day-to-day operations of the archives and the moving of tons of archival material and artifacts to Winnipeg. She was the first Canadian keeper of the HBCA, and in addition to opening the archives to researchers in North America, she spent a considerable amount of her time advising, encouraging, and persuading students to complete research in the archives for post-graduate degrees. Smith has conducted workshops, written articles and book reviews, and edited numerous manuscripts for publication. In addition to being a past president of the Manitoba Historical Society, she has also served on a number of boards and committees, among them Canada's National History Society, the National Archival Appraisal Board, and the City of Winnipeg Advisory Board on the Arts.

Since leaving the HBCA in 1990, Shirlee Smith has continued to be involved in the archival community as a consulting archivist, researcher, and writer. She was one of the consulting appraisers on the National Archival Appraisal Board evaluating the HBC archives for the Company's donation of that national treasure to the Province of Manitoba in 1994. She is a member of the Order of Canada and has received the Distinguished Service Award from the University of Manitoba and the Prix Award from the Province of Manitoba.

JUDITH HUDSON BEATTIE,
KEEPER, 1990–2002

Judith Hudson Beattie joined the Hudson's Bay Company Archives in March 1981 as head of research and reference. Her education included history degrees from Carleton University and the University of Toronto, the National Archives of Canada archives course, and records management training at the Archives of Ontario. When Shirlee Anne Smith left the HBCA in the fall of 1990, Beattie served as acting keeper until March 1991, when she was appointed keeper. During her tenure, a highlight was the donation of the records by the HBC to the Province of Manitoba in 1994, preceded by several years of negotiation, planning, and dedicated work by the entire staff. The appraisal process and the creation of the Hudson's Bay Company History Foundation provided funds to support the future maintenance of the archives. The resulting dramatic increase in funding and staffing levels also allowed the development of new programming initiatives. The most visible results were the state-of-the-art vault built within the Archives of Manitoba building and the refit of the former vaults to accommodate the maps, paintings, and framed art.

Prior to her retirement in 2001, Beattie focused on outreach and promotional activities. Her retirement coincided with the publication of *Undelivered Letters to Hudson's Bay Company Men on the Northwest Coast of America, 1830–57* (UBC Press), a book she co-authored with Helen M. Buss. Through writing, speaking engagements, and a weekly broadcast on CBC Radio North, Judith Beattie continues to bring stories from the Hudson's Bay Company Archives to the attention of others.

Notes

AM   Archives of Manitoba

BCA   British Columbia Archives

BL   British Library

GH   Guildhall Library

HBC   Hudson's Bay Company

HBCA   Hudson's Bay Company Archives

PRO   Public Record Office (now National Archives)

INTRODUCTION

1 Armstrong and Jones, *Business Documents*, 1.

2 Jenkinson, *Selected Writings*, 197.

3 Ibid., 274.

4 Historians who were lobbying at this time for access to the records of the Hudson's Bay Company included Arthur Doughty, George Wrong, W.S. Wallace, A.S. Morton, Chester Martin, and Frederick Merk.

5 A.1/169, fo. 254, Committee to Leveson Gower, 12 May 1931.

6 The other consultant was Reginald Coupland, professor of Colonial History at Oxford University.

7 RG9/615.3.1, Lamb to Reynolds, 28 July 1950.

8 The archives of still active Canadian companies that also acknowledge their heritage, such as the railways (Canadian National, 1836, and Canadian Pacific, 1881), banks (Scotiabank, 1832; TD/Canada Trust, 1855, CIBC, 1867), insurance companies (Sun Life, 1865; Manulife, 1887; Great-West Life, 1891), and oil companies (Imperial Oil, 1880), cover a considerably

shorter period of history. The records of Molson's Brewery, founded in 1786, are deposited in Library and Archives Canada as the Molson fonds.

CHAPTER ONE

1 Hartley, ed. *The Royal Society*, 1.

2 PRO, Guide to the Public Record Office, 1.

3 Quoted in Mullett, "The 'Better Reception, Preservation, and Convenient Use.'" 197.

4 Robert, *Chartered Companies*, 13.

5 The archives of the East India Company are in the India Office Library and Records, which is administered by the British Library.

6 Robert, *Chartered Companies*, 65–93.

7 "And so in Elizabeth's time the English Muscovy Company were the first Westerners to organize trade with the interior of Russia, though early in the following century they lost it for a while to the Dutch. The corresponding attempts of Frobisher and of Davis to reach India by the North-West Passage led to the Hudson Bay fur trade of Stuart times, one of the main streams of British Canadian history" (Macaulay, *England in the Eighteenth Century*, 252).

8 "butt these defendants know nott who settled the same all their bookes and papers which they kept att that time and for about the first four yeares of their Trade haveing been lost and carryed away by one of their Servants so that these Defendants cannott give any account of any transaction or Trade for the four first yeares of their said trade and dealings nor of any remarkable passage or accident that happened within that time" (quoted in Nute, "Two Documents," 45). See also PRO C33/286, fo. 335–6, The Joynt and severall Answer of the Governour and Company.

9 "Between them they probably possessed more experience and knowledge of the French-Canadian system of fur-trading then any other two men could claim, and their experiences had left them with a deep conviction that the best approach to the furs of the far north was not by the normal Canadian route of the St. Lawrence and the Great Lakes, but by a sea voyage to Hudson Bay and so to the northern outlets of the fur areas instead of to their southern approaches" (Rich, *History*, 1: 24).

10 Carteret and his son, Philip, are among the first recorded investors of the HBC. George Carteret had a long-standing connection with the king and was a member of the Royal Society. For more information, see his biography in Rich, ed., *Minutes*, 1671–1674, Appendix G.

11 Colleton had colonial interests in the Caribbean and was a member of the Royal Society. He was also one of the first investors in HBC stock (1667).

12 PRO, SP29/251B/180, fo. 71–71d, Instructions to Cap.^{ne} William
    Stannard.

13 The text of some of these papers has been transcribed by Nute in "Radisson
    and Groseilliers," 418–25.

14 Fisher and Thornton, *The English Pilot*.

15 GH, MS 1757, fo. 134, Collection of papers dating from 1641–95 made by
    Robert Hooke.

16 BL, Map 5414, art. 20 (originally MS Sloane 3244, roll 23), Chart of
    Hudson's Bay and Straits, and Port Nelson, 1685.

17 For more information about archival material relating to Radisson,
    see Warkentin, "Pierre-Esprit Radisson," "Discovering Radisson,"
    "Radisson's Voyages," and "Who Was the Scribe?" and Warkentin
    and Podruchny, *Decentring the Renaissance*.

18 As stated in the charter: "And that the said Land bee from henceforth reck-
    oned and reputed as one of our Plantacions or Colonyes in America called
    Ruperts Land."

19 Oldmixon, *The British Empire in America*. For a transcription of Gorst's
    Journal, see Nute, *Caesars*, 286–92.

20 A.1/1, fos. 11–14, Committee minutes, 4 March, 2 April, and
    12 April 1672.

21 Ibid., fo. 3d, Committee minutes, 7 November 1671; emphasis added.

22 A.14/1, fo. 110d, "Thomas Rastall, £200," 12 May 1669.

23 A.1/1, fo. 8, Committee minutes, 19 December 1671.

24 Ibid., fo. 23, 4 December 1672.

25 Ibid., fo. 5d, 14 November 1671.

26 Ibid., fo. 7, 12 December 1671.

27 The first three volumes of the minutes books have been published by the
    Hudson's Bay Record Society: volume 5 (1671–74), volume 8 (1679–82),
    and volume 9 (1682–84).

28 PRO, SP29/251B/180, fo. 71–71d, Instructions to Cap.^{ne} William Stannard.

29 A.6/2, fo. 105, William III to Capt Henry Bayley, 26 May 1696.

30 A.6/1, fo. 28, Instructions for Henry Sergeant, Esqr, 27 April 1683.

31 The second minute book appears to have gone missing between 1815 and
    1894. It is included in an inventory of the records taken probably in 1815
    (A.64/52). That inventory is annotated up to 1894. A draft inventory taken
    between 1890 and 1908 (A.64/56) notes on folio 28, "Strong Room Con-
    tents, 1894, Minutes Books 1671–1893 (missing 1675–79)." For the gap
    between the first minute book (1671–74) and the second minute book
    (1679–84), the grand ledger and grand journal provide some continuity.

32 A.1/2, fo. 2, Committee minutes, 28 November 1679.

33 Ibid., fo. 3, 3 December 1679.

34 A.1/3 fo. 1, rough minute book, 3 December 1679.

35 A.1/2, fo. 5, Committee minutes, 23 December 1679. James's hand, with its large, ornamental flourishes, is evident from beginning of A.1/2 to 24 October 1681, when the writing becomes much plainer.

36 Working-copy books include A.1/3 to 7 and A.1/81 to 147.

37 "William James (fl. 1658–75)," in Heal, *The English Writing-Masters*, 201–2.

38 A.1/2, fo. 54d, Committee minutes, 25 November 1681.

39 The *Oxford English Dictionary* defines "ship's husband" as an agent appointed by a ship's owners to see that a ship in port is well provided in all respects.

40 A.1/1, fo. 23, Committee minutes, 8 December 1673.

41 A.1/2, fo. 52, Committee minutes, 14 November 1681.

42 Ibid., fo. 91, 3 November 1682.

43 Ibid., fo. 146, 28 May 1684, and A.1/8, fo. 8.

44 Ibid., fo. 84, 26 July 1682. The instructions read: "If it shall happen that you meet wth. any ship or other vessell sayling or trading within the said Bay without our Lycence you are to seize them, together wth. all Goods which shall be on board, the one halfe to the use of his Majesty, the other halfe for the use of the Compa. & to bring them home wth. you for England & them safely to Deliver at your Arrivall here to the order of the Dept. Governour & Committee of the said Company."

45 Ibid., fo. 82, 28 June 1682.

46 Ibid., fo. 116d, 25 July 1683. The black box is no longer in the archives.

47 Ibid., fo. 133, 1 February 1684.

48 Ibid., fo. 148, 18 June 1684.

49 Ibid., fo. 100d, 15 January 1683.

50 Ibid., fo. 146d, 23 May 1684.

51 "The Company's Evidence, 3 June 1684," quoted in Rich, ed., *Minutes, 1679–1684*, 283–5. See also PRO, Admiralty, 24/121, no. 114, Charles Boone, John Davall & Company v. Hudson's Bay Company.

52 Rich, ed., *Minutes, 1679–1684*, "The Charter Challenged, 30 April 1684," Appendix A, 278–80.

53 A.1/7, fo. 30d, rough minute book, 28 May 1684.

54 A.1/2, fo. 67, Committee minutes, 8 March 1682.

55 Ibid., fo. 96d, 29 November 1682: "Jos. Albin the secretaries sonn into the Compa. service on the 3 Day of this Month in Mr Stones room took the Oath of Fidelity to the Compa. and his wages to commence from that Day att £25. p. Ann.".

56 A.1/2, fo. 91, Committee minutes, 3 November 1682.

57 A.1/7, fo. 45, rough minute book, 19 November 1684.

58 A.1/84 fo. 42, Committee minutes, 28 October 1686.

59 Ibid.

60 Ibid.

61 "Albin, Onesiphorus," in Rich, ed., *Minutes 1679–1684*, 317–18.

62 A.14/5, fo. 27, "Onesiphorus Albin," 10 August 1697.

63 A.1/7, fo. 28, 12 May 1684.

64 Rich, *History,* 1: 170 and 284–5.

65 Ibid., 179.

66 "Radisson's Bill of Complaint and the Company's Reply," quoted in Nute, "Two Documents," 45. See also PRO, C6/303/9, Bill of Complaint, 1694.

67 Nute, "Two Documents," 48.

68 PRO, C33/286, fo. 335–6, "The Joynt and severall Answer of the Governour and Company," 1695.

69 Nute, *Caesars,* 268, and Rich, *History,* 1: 308.

70 Rich, *History,* 1: 309.

71 HBCA Search File "Charter": "Chronological Summary of Occasions when Hudson's Bay Company's Charter has been Formally Recognised, Together with Comments by Law Officers in Respect of its Validity," 1689.

72 Ibid., 1690.

73 A.1/20/fo. 27, Committee minutes, 31 August 1698.

74 A.6/3, fo. 92d, Governor and Committee to Grimington, 26 May 1708.

75 *An Historical Narrative of the Great and Terrible Fire of London, Sept. 22, 1666* (London, 1764), quoted in Rich, ed., *Minutes, 1671–1674,* n1.

76 Latham and Matthews, eds., *Diary of Samuel Pepys,* 6: 215.

77 "Robinson, Sir John," in Rich, ed., *Minutes, 1671–1674*, Appendix G, 250–1.

78 A.1/1, fo.7d, Committee minutes, 12 December 1671.

79 "List of Meetings," in Rich, ed., *Minutes, 1679–1684*, xi-xvi.

80 A.1/2, fo. 21d, Committee minutes, 4 May 1680.

81 Ibid., fo. 116, 25 July 1683.

82 Ibid.

83 Ibid., fo. 69d, 22 March 1682.

84 Maitland et al., *The History and Survey of London,* 2: 997.

85 A.1/18, fo. 10d, Committee minutes, 18 March 1696.

CHAPTER TWO

1 See Harry Duckworth, "The Hudson's Bay Company's Fur Sale Books" (unpublished paper available through the Centre for Rupert's Land Studies, Winnipeg, 1988).

2 Hallam, "Problems with Record Keeping," 219; and PRO, *Guide to the Public Record Office.*

3 The archives of the East India Company are administered by the British Library as part of the India Office Records.

4 Miller, *That Noble Cabinet,* 36–41 and 63–71.

5 Ruggles, *A Country So Interesting,* 3.

6 G.1/25, Ac ko mok ki's map is illustrated in Ruggles, *A Country So Interesting,* plate 19, and discussed on 199–200. See also Beattie, "Indian Maps," 166–75.

7 BL, Add. MSS 5027, fo. 64, "West Side of James Bay," by Thomas Moore [1678].

8 Samuel Thornton was the son of a professional chart maker, John Thornton (active c. 1680–1762), who drafted several maps and charts for the Company that have not survived in the HBCA. One dating from 1685 is catalogued as Add. MSS 5414, fo. 20, "Map of Hudsons Bay," in the British Library.

9 There are two copies of this map in the HBCA: G.1/1 and G.1/2, annotated with the English suggestion of a north-south line dividing French and English territory, part of which ran along the forty-ninth parallel. These maps are discussed in Ruggles, *A Country So Interesting,* 28

10 "as in the Map now delivered": A.9/3, fo. 143, and A.9/7, fo. 142, copies of letter from the governor and Committee, 4 August 1714.

11 G.1/19, [Sketch of rivers between Prince of Wales' Fort and the "Northern most Copper Mine" – giving Indian names]. See Ruggles, *A Country So Interesting,* 31 and 193.

12 A.6/8, fo. 41, "Orders Rules and Instructions to Capt Wm. Coates Commander of the Ship Mary," also A.6/8, fo. 46, "Committee to Thomas Mitchell Master of the Success sloop," 16 May 1749.

13 Ruggles, *A Country So Interesting,* 3.

14 B.3/a/1, fo. 12d, 27 October 1705.

15 Williams, ed., *Hudson Bay Miscellany,* 4.

16 Ibid., 6

17 A.15/5, fo. 137, "Account of wages Debit to Sundry Persons now in the Comp^s Service in Hudsons Bay," 1706.

18 See A.1/7, fo. 27d, Committee minutes, 12 May 1684: "Ordered the Secretary buy for the factory of Port Nelson pewter, a shute of curtain vallances & 4 Russian Leather Chaires & Delivered the same to Mr. Geo. Geyer."

19 B.3/d/15, fo. 59–61.

20 B.3/d/15, fo. 18, Albany account book, 1705–06: "Trade for Outfit 25."

21 Fairbank and Wolpe, *Renaissance Handwriting,* 42.

22 A.1/33, fo. 148, Committee minutes, 20 May 1715

23 The *Oxford English Dictionary* defines "cordwainer" as "a worker in cordwain, a shoemaker; *cordwain* is a kind of pliable fine grained leather used esp. for shoes, made originally in Córdova (Spain) from goatskin and now horsehide."

24 A.1/33, fo. 151d, Committee minutes, 31 May 1715.

25 A.6/3, fo. 135, Instructions to Thomas Macklish, 3 June 1715.

26 A.6/4, fo. 52d, Governor and Committee to Macklish, 26 May 1721.

27 Ibid., fo. 64d; see also, A.1/120, fo. 16, Committee minutes, 2 May 1722.

28 B.3/a/11, fo. 7, 3 October 1722.

29 Ibid., fo. 25d, 17 May 1723.

30 A.6/4, fo. 144, Governor and Committee to Myatt, 17 May 1723.

31 A.11/2, fo. 47d, Richard Staunton to Governor and Committee, 21 August 1723

32 A.1/120, fo. 51d, Committee minutes, 11 December 1723.

33 A.16/1, fo. 5, Officers' and Servants' Ledger, 1721–23.

34 A.1/120, fo. 62, 20 May 1724.

35 A.6/4, fo. 86d, Governor and Committee to Thomas Macklish, 20 May 1724.

36 A.11/114, fo. 28–29d, McCleish to Governor and Committee, 16 August 1724.

37 Ibid., fo. 35, McCleish to Governor and Committee, 26 August 1725.

38 Ibid., fo. 41d, Thomas McCleish to Governor and Committee, 16 August 1727.

39 Ibid., fo. 61, McCleish to Governor and Committee, 7 August 1731.

40 A.6/5, fo. 58, Governor and Committee to Macklish, 11 May 1732.

41 A.6/7, fo. 14, Governor and Committee to Isham, 5 May 1742. Isham had been chastised six years earlier for his letter-writing style by the governor and Committee: "Finding an Intricacy in Your Answers to our letters wee order that you do answer them methodically Paragraph by Paragraph as they are numbered" (A.6/6, fo. 3, 18 May 1738).

42 E.2/1, fo. 4, Isham to the Governor and Committee, Observations and Notes.

43 A.6/5, fo. 97d, Governor and Committee to Isham, 18 May 1738, and A.6/6, fo. 19d, Governor and Committee to Thomas White, 2 May 1735.

44 Rich, ed., *James Isham's Observations*, lxv–lxvi.

45 A.11/114, fo. 4, Isham to Governor and Committee, 17 September 1716.

46 If Isham's personal observations were not put to any constructive use, his journal of transactions, written during the winter of 1746–47 when the *Dobbs Galley* and *California* took shelter at York, was. It included copies of letters between Isham and the captains of the two ships, William Moor

and Francis Smith. The "Journal of the most material Transactions, and Copys of Letters between Mr. James Isham & Council at York Fort, and Capt. William Moor, Capt. Francis Smith and their Council during their Wintering in Hayes River Commencing 26 August 1746 [and] Ending 24 June 1747" was sent home to London with the regular business records for the year, providing a timely and relatively objective record of events that were later questioned in the parliamentary inquiry into the Company's activities on Hudson Bay.

47 Relatively few shipwrecks occurred on these annual voyages. According to William Barr, between 1670 and 1913 only twenty-one supply ships were wrecked. See Barr, "Shipwrecked on Mansel Island," 177.

48 A.6/3, fo. 126d, Instructions to Captain James Knight, 25 May 1714: "You are also to send us coppy's of the Councill Bookes signed by your self, Deputy & Councill, to the time the ship comes away together with a copy of Journalls to all places wether you shall tend to make Discovereys and what may be expected from each place."

49 Coats's journal edited by John Barrow, was published by the Hakluyt Society in 1852.

50 "and in 1680 two further copies, translated into French, also were in circulation in Paris"; see Rich, *History*, 1:128.

51 Ibid., 557, and Williams, *The British Search*, 39.

52 For example, Williams, "Arthur Dobbs and Joseph Robson" and "The Hudson's Bay Company and Its Critics"; Moodie, "Science and Reality."

53 Clarke, *Arthur Dobbs*, 64–5.

54 Moor's journal of the voyage is in Dobbs's papers in the PRO, Northern Ireland. A copy, the log of the *California*, is in the HBCA, E.18/2.

55 A.1/38, fo. 48, Committee minutes, 13 March 1749.

56 E.18/1, fo. 152–65, The Case of the Hudson's Bay Company, 1749.

57 Ibid., fo. 213–34, *Report from the Committee Appointed to Enquire into the State and Conditions of the Countries Adjoining to the Hudson's Bay and of the Trade Carried on There* (London, 1749).

58 Documents in the HBCA that illustrate the events leading to the inquiry are classified in E.18/1–2, Parliamentary Select Committee, 1749. Formerly known as the "Arthur Dobbs folder," it also includes papers of the inquiry itself.

59 Glyndwr Williams discusses the thesis that Robson's book was strongly influenced by, if not written by, Dobbs in "Arthur Dobbs and Joseph Robson."

60 A.6/8, fo. 46, Orders Rules and Instructions to Thomas Mitchell 16 May 1749.

61 PRO, Northern Ireland, D.O.D. 162/7, 23, 37, 44, 62. Information provided in copy of letter from Brian Trainor, deputy keeper, Public Record Office

of Northern Ireland, to Glyndwr Williams, 11 March 1957, found in HBCA
Search File "Dobbs, Arthur."

62 Classified as B.239/a/5–7.

63 "Kelsey" in Davies and Johnson, eds., *Letters from Hudson Bay*, 376–93.

64 Rich, *History*, 1:299.

65 Kelsey, *The Kelsey Papers*.

66 Davies, "Kelsey, Henry," in *Dictionary of Canadian Biography*, 2:314.

67 Clarke, *Arthur Dobbs*, 108.

68 HBCA Search File "Dobbs, Arthur," Trainor to Williams, 11 March 1957.

69 All of these records have been perused by historians and scholars in other
fields for publications on all variety of subjects. Key early records have been
published by the Hudson's Bay Record Society and the Champlain Society.

70 Henry Sergeant succeeded John Nixon as governor in Hudson Bay in 1683.
He was accompanied by his son, his wife, and her companion. Mrs Sergeant
and Mrs Maurice were the first women to live at a bay post. The practice
was definitely not encouraged by the Company. See Rich and Johnson, eds.,
Copy-Book of Letters Outward, 388–91.

71 A.6/1, fo. 58, Instructions for Henry Sergeant, 27 April 1683.

72 A.6/1, fo. 66, Governor and Committee to John Bridgar, 27 April 1683.

73 A.1/34, fo. 66, Committee minutes, 1 December 1737.

74 A.1/37, fo. 57, Committee minutes, 10 April 1746.

75 A.1/121, fos. 135–6, rough minute book, 2 July 1729.

76 Ibid., fo. 385, rough minute book, 24 June 1730.

77 A.6/6, fo. 67, Governor and Committee to Thomas Bird, 17 May 1739.

78 The *Oxford English Dictionary* defines "cartridge paper" as "a thick, rough
paper used for cartridges, drawing, and for making strong envelopes" and
cartridge as "a paper, metal, etc. case containing a charge of propellent explo-
sive for firearms or blasting with a bullet or shot if intended for small arms."

79 Staunton's journals for 1737–38 and 1738–39, which were returned to him
in 1740, as well as the copy made of them by William Pitts, which had been
retained in London, are missing from the Company's archives. There are
other examples in the HBCA of records kept on cartridge paper.

80 A.11/43, fos. 19–24, Staunton to Governor and Committee, 17 August 1739.

81 A.6/7, fo. 139d, Instructions to Capt. John Newton, 5 May 1748.

82 Ibid.

83 A.11/114, fo. 173d, A Copie of Orders and Instructions to Anth[y] Hendey
upon a journey in Land, 26 June 1754.

84 Belyea, *A Year Inland*, 338.

85 Ibid., 15–36. Other published transcriptions have used only the 1782
version of Henday's journal. The editions include Burpee, "York Factory to

312 Notes to pages 76-89

the Blackfeet Country," and Williams, *Andrew Graham's Observations*. The journal has also been discussed in Morton, *A History of the Canadian West*; Rich, *History*; and Ray, *Indians in the Fur Trade*.

86 Williams, "The Puzzle of Anthony Henday's Journal," 56
87 Ibid.
88 Belyea, *A Year Inland*, 31.
89 Hearne, *A Journey from Prince of Wales's Fort*, li.
90 Ruggles, "Governor Samuel Wegg."
91 Ball and Dyck, "Observation of the Transit of Venus," 53.
92 A.1/47, fo. 80, Committee minutes, 2 November 1796.

CHAPTER THREE

1 Rich, ed., *Journal of Occurrences*, xiv.
2 A.30/10, fo. 3-13, Names etc. of the Company's Servants at Hudson's Bay, 1800.
3 Galbraith, *The Hudson's Bay Company as an Imperial Factor*, 21.
4 Rich, *History*, 2:122.
5 MacKay, *The Honourable Company*, 339-44. The years 1783-85 were when York was taken by the French, and during the period 1809-15 Britain was involved in the Napoleonic Wars.
6 Sir Bibye Lake (1712-43), Sir Atwell Lake (1750-60), and Bibye Lake (1770-82).
7 Rich, *History*, 1:261-4.
8 A.1/48, fo. 86d, Committee minutes, 29 June 1803.
9 A.1/49, fo. 6, Committee minutes, 29 January 1806, and fo. 108, Committee minutes, 20 December 1809.
10 A.1/47, fo. 44d, Committee minutes, 26 November 1794.
11 A.1/50, fo. 96-96d, Committee minutes, 1 December 1813.
12 A.1/55, fos. 15-16, Committee minutes, 6 July 1825.
13 A.1/46, fo. 5, Committee minutes, 17 December 1783.
14 A.1/50, fo. 96-96d, Committee minutes, 1 December 1813.
15 A.1/52, fo. 11, Committee minutes 27 January 1819.
16 HBCA Search File "Fur Brokers."
17 Armstrong and Jones, *Business Documents*, 2-3.
18 The Abstracts of Servants' Accounts in the HBCA resulted from an act of Parliament (1 and 2 Geo. IV, c. 66) passed in 1821, "which demanded that registers of persons employed be sent home and that duplicate registers be sent to the Government." The abstracts are organized by category of person – officers, clerks, servants, etc.

19 Goldring, "Labour Records," 85.

20 For a thorough discussion of the subject, see Ray, "The Early Hudson's Bay Company Account Books," 3–38, and Spraakman, "The HBC's of Management Accounting," 26–30.

21 Grant, "Bookkeeping in the Eighteenth Century," 148.

22 Goldring, *Papers on the Labour System*, 1: 7.

23 Andrew Wedderburn changed his name to Colvile in 1814 and is often referred to in records and publications as Andrew Colvile, without reference to his original family name.

24 A.1/49, fo. 115, 7 March 1810.

25 Ibid., fo. 116.

26 "Made Beaver" referred to the standard unit of trade in barter between the HBC and the Natives: one prime beaver skin in good condition. The unit of value was changed to a monetary one for the sake of contemporary bookkeeping methods.

27 A.1/49, fo. 122–4, 2 May 1810.

28 The *Oxford English Dictionary* defines "packet" as "a parcel of letters or despatches, esp. the State parcel or mail to and from foreign countries."

29 A.6/18, fo. 265, Governor and Committee to Thomas Vincent, 29 March 1815.

30 Ibid., fo. 200, General letter to Hudson Bay, 9 April 1814.

31 Ibid., fos. 200–1.

32 Ibid., fos. 208–9.

33 Ibid., fo. 209.

34 Ibid., fo. 213.

35 Ibid., fo. 211.

36 Ibid., fo. 153.

37 A.6/15, fo. 17, Letter to George Gladman, Eastmain Factory, 31 May 1810.

38 Ibid.

39 A.1/49, fo. 134, 21 November 1810.

40 Ibid., fo. 32, 13 March 1811. A guinea was worth a little more than £1, or 21 shillings, a substantial sum considering that Roberts's salary as a clerk was £150 per year.

41 A.1/49, fo. 10, Committee minutes, 12 December 1810

42 A.1/50, fo. 96–96d, Committee minutes, 1 December 1813.

43 A.1/51, fo. 131, Committee minutes, 11 January 1815.

44 Ibid., fo. 86, Committee minutes, 10 December 1817.

45 Ibid., fo. 118, 17 June 1818.

46 A.1/47, fo. 45, 26 November 1794: "And that the usual Allowance of Ten pounds p. Annum for chocolate be also allow'd the Secretary." Chocolate

was introduced to Europe by Columbus, and its medicinal use originated from its Mexican heritage. See Dillinger et al., "Food of the Gods."

47 HBCA Finding Aid, E.88.

48 A.102/1886, correspondence with E.E. Rich, 15 June to 14 September 1941; A.102, Secretary's Dossiers; and HBCA Finding Aid E.88.

49 Rich, *History*, 2:371–2, and Rich, ed., *Journal of Occurrences*, 466.

50 E.88/6, fos. 985–6, Bathurst to Berens, 19 February 1820. See also Morton, *Sir George Simpson*, 35.

51 B.39/a/18, fo. 67. See also Rich, ed., *Journal of Occurrences*, 177.

52 B. 39/a/18, fo. 83. See also Rich, ed., *Journal of Occurrences*, 227: "A 'Journal of transactions and occurrences at Fort Wedderburn', 6 June 1820 to 10 February 1821, kept by Brown, is classified as B.39/a/16. This, however, is obviously not Brown's private journal. The entries in this journal for 17 January 1821 contain no reference to his conversation with Simpson about his private journal." Brown continued with the Company until just before his death in 1827.

53 B.239/f/12, HBC Clerks, Northern Department, 1821/22.

54 B.239/f/13, NWC Clerks, Northern Department, 1821/22.

55 A.34/1, Servants' Character Book.

56 A.12/10, fo. 64, Simpson to Fraser, 12 March 1859.

57 A.34/2, Governor Simpson's Character Book.

58 Williams, ed., *Hudson's Bay Miscellany*, 156.

59 Ibid., 162.

60 Wallace, ed., *Documents Relating*, 322.

61 A.37/7, fo. 1–6, Licence of Exclusive Trade with the Indians, 5 December 1821.

62 Ibid.

63 1 and 2 Geo. IV, cap. 66, 2 July 1821.

64 F.1 to F.7, North West Company.

65 Wallace, ed., *Documents Relating*, 246–92.

66 Ibid., 243.

67 Ibid., 246.

68 Wallace, *The Pedlars from Quebec*, v–viii. A series of NWC correspondence, dating from 1791 to 1799, was deposited in the HBCA by the trustees of Strathcona's estate in 1938 and classified as F3/1–2.

69 Pellew, *The Home Office*, 14.

CHAPTER FOUR

1 A.1/52, fo. 52, Committee minutes, 19 January 1820.

2 Ibid., fo. 117, Committee minutes, 24 May 1821.

3 A.1/53, fo. 37, Committee minutes, 22 May 1822.

4 A.1/52, fo. 128, Committee minutes, 14 November 1821.

5 1 and 2 Geo. IV, c.66, 2 July 1821, and subsequent royal licence, 5 December 1821.

6 Innis in Fleming and Rich, eds., *Minutes of Council*, xxx.

7 Simpson to Colvile, 8 September 1821, quoted in Fleming and Rich, eds., *Minutes of Council*, 399.

8 D.4/11, fo.3, Simpson to Lewes and Simpson to McDonald, 9 August 1821.

9 Lamb in Rich, ed., *Letters of John McLoughlin* (first series, 1825–38), xvii.

10 D.4/1, fos. 60d–62d, Simpson to Cameron, 18 July 1822.

11 Rich, ed., *Peter Skene Ogdens Snake Country Journals*, vii.

12 BCA, Add. MSS 635 Donald Ross, Douglas to Ross, 27 November 1849.

13 Rich, ed., *Letters of John McLoughlin* (HBRS volumes 4, 6, and 7).

14 Barker, ed., *Letters of Doctor John McLoughlin*, i.

15 Ibid., iii.

16 MacDonald, *Good Solid Comfortable Establishment*, 36. See also Burley, *Servants of the Honourable Company*.

17 Barker, ed., *Letters of Doctor John McLoughlin*, 344–5.

18 A.11/72, fos. 59–62, Douglas to Pelly, 5 December 1848.

19 A.11/73, fos. 161–64d, Douglas to Barclay, 26 August 1851.

20 Mackie, *Trading beyond the Mountains*, 257.

21 Lamb, "S.S. Beaver," and Williams, "Simpson and McLoughlin," 49–55.

22 A.1/57, fo. 64, Committee minutes, 13 April 1831.

23 A.1/58, fo. 104d, Committee minutes, 7 May 1834: "Read a letter for T.B. Duncan Keeper of the Ashmolean Museum, Oxford. Ordered him to be informed that the Company have not any specimens at present and that he be requested to furnish a list of what are required."

24 Davies, *Douglas of the Forests*, 11.

25 A.5/7, fos. 159–59d, Smith to James Sabine, secretary, Horticultural Society, 26 June 1824.

26 A.6/21, fo. 12d, Governor and Committee to Chief Factors, Columbia District, 22 July 1824.

27 Gray, "David Douglas."

28 A.6/20, fo. 222, Governor and Committee to Williams and Simpson, 28 May 1823.

29 A.6/57, 17 November 1824.

30 A.6/21, fo. 189, Committee to McLoughlin, 20 September 1826.

31 A.6/24, fo. 58d, Governor and Committee to Simpson, 3 June 1836.

32 A.6/62, Governor and Committee to Paxton, 10 January 1838.

33 A.6/21, fo. 167d, Governor and Committee to Simpson, 7 June 1828, and
   D.5/3, fo. 451, A.F. Holmes, Corresponding Secretary, Natural History
   Society of Montreal to Simpson, 28 April 1830.

34 A.5/9, fo. 147d, Smith to Arrowsmith, 15 September 1831.

35 Kane, *Wanderings of an Artist*, 247–8.

36 Stewart, "Sir George Simpson: Collector."

37 Simpson to Paul Kane, undated [1847], in Kane Family Papers; cited in
   Harper, *Paul Kane's Frontier*, 330.

38 D.4/54, fo. 73d, Simpson to Smith, 25 February 1858.

39 Discussions of Kane and his journal can be found in Harper, *Paul Kane's
   Frontier*, and MacLaren, "'I came to rite thare portraits.'"

40 Williams, "The Simpson Era," 55.

41 B.223/b/38, fos. 2d–3, Board of Management (Douglas, Work, and Ogden)
   to Simpson, 19 March 1847, and D.5/19, fos. 396–418, Board of Management to Simpson, 14 March 1847.

42 Rich, *History*, 2: 754.

43 A.11/73 fo. 152, Barclay to Douglas, 4 August 1851.

44 A.6/29, fos. 65d–68d, Barclay to Douglas, 16 April 1851.

45 A.11/72, fos. 201–206d, Douglas to Barclay, 3 April 1850.

46 A.12/13, para. 54, Colvile to Governor and Committee, 21 July 1852.

47 A.6/30 fo. 81d, Governor and Committee to Sir George Simpson and the
   Council of the Northern Department, 6 April 1853.

48 A.11/73, fo. 557d, Douglas to Simpson, 5 September 1852.

49 D.4/73, fo. 134, Simpson to Anderson, 20 August 1852.

50 Lamb, "British Columbia Official Records," 18.

51 7 and 8 Vict., c. 110, 1844.

52 Armstrong and Jones, *Business Documents*, 4.

53 Ibid., 5.

54 Great Britain, Select Committee on the Hudson's Bay Company, Report.

55 Rich, *History*, 2:774.

56 Careless, "The Business Community," 113.

57 Goldring, *Papers on the Labour System*, 33.

58 PRO, CO6/23, Colonial Office, 1857 Hudson's Bay Company and Individuals, item 3: "I have the honor to enclose copies of the Registers received from
   Hudson's Bay of all persons employed by the Hudson's Bay Company within
   their Territories for the year 1856 and preceding years," John Shepherd to
   the Right Honourable Henry Labouchere, Colonial Office, 9 February 1857.

59 Lamb, "British Columbia Official Records," 25.

60 BCA, C/D/30.8/L16, "Report on the State of the Library and Archives,"
   1934, 1.

61 "Sorted Library Books with Aid of Pitchfork," *Victoria Daily Colonist,* 5 February 1925, 9.

62 RG20/5/3, French to Chipman, 23 January 1922.

63 Ibid.

64 Ibid., French to Leveson Gower, 19 November 1930.

65 Ibid., Wilson to FitzGerald, Deputy Chairman, Canadian Advisory Committee, 27 June 1922.

CHAPTER FIVE

1 McElwee, *History of England,* and Robbins, *The Eclipse of a Great Power.*

2 "Section III, Manufactures, Class 16, Leather, Saddlery and Harness, Skins, Fur, and Hair," in Great Exibition, *Official Descriptive and Illustrated Catalogue.*

3 A.6/59, fo. 41. The first typed letter from the London Office was to the commissioned officers in Canada, dated 21 January 1890.

4 "Women were called typewriters and the machines they used were called type writers" (Delgado, *The Enormous File,* 72).

5 "Testimony of Edward Roberts," in Hudson's Bay Compagny, *Evidence for the United States in the matter of the claims of the Hudson's Bay Company,* 13.

6 Dallas had been on the board of management for the Company at Victoria and was married to a daughter of James Douglas. See Rich, *History,* 2:812.

7 McDonald, *Lord Strathcona,* 118.

8 "Hopkins, Edward Martin," HBCA biography sheet.

9 For more information on Fort Garry, see MacDonald, *A Good Solid Comfortable Establishment.*

10 Cowie, *The Company of Adventurers,* 225.

11 Ibid., 227.

12 Ibid., 280–1.

13 Rich, *History,* 2: 816–49. The story of the International Financial Society and the Hudson's Bay Company is also covered by Galbraith in *The Hudson's Bay Compagny as an Imperial Factor* and Mitchell in « Edward Watkin and the Buying-out. »

14 Quoted in Rich, *History,* 2: 836, and in Galbraith, *The Hudson's Bay Compagny as an Imperial Factor,* 386.

15 Rich, *History,* 2: 838.

16 F.27/1, fo. 94–5, *The International Financial Society Limited Prospectus: Issue of Stock in the Hudson's Bay Company,* 1863.

17 Watkin, *Canada and the States,* 124–5.

18 HBC, Reports and Proceedings, Report of the Auditors, 16 June 1866.

19 A.2/3, fo. 99, Minutes of General Court, 5 July 1866.

20 London Correspondent, "Passing of No. 1 Lime Street," *The Beaver,* March 1925, 67.

21 The floors of buildings in Britain and Europe are numbered from above the ground level. The first floor is equivalent to the second floor in North America. The term "deck" dates to the early days of the Company when the ships' crews continued their service on land as warehouse porters, sorting and storing the furs they had brought back with them from Hudson Bay. See "Show Week in the H.B.C. London Fur Warehouse," *The Beaver,* April 1921, 6.

22 Goldring, *Papers on the Labour System,* 1: 60–1.

23 A.6/41, fos. 244–5, Smith to James Anderson, Moose Factory, 24 June 1867.

24 Mitchell, "Edward Watkin and the Buying-out," 219.

25 A.2/3/102, Report of the Governor and Committee of the Hudson's Bay Company to the Shareholders, 5 July 1866.

26 Rich, *History,* 2: 855. The Company had repurchased the Red River Colony from Selkirk in 1836 for £80,000.

27 Galbraith, "The Hudson's Bay Land Controversy," 472, 475. The Red River Settlement could not be defended against attack from the United States, hence the urgency of linking British Columbia with the Canadian Confederation through Rupert's Land by means of the existing communication facilities.

28 De Brou and Waiser, "The British North America Act," in *Documenting Canada,* 1.

29 De Brou and Waiser, "The Rupert's Land Act," ibid., 24–5.

30 When the Deed of Surrender was finally transferred into Canadian law in 1872, it became the basis for the Dominion Lands Act.

31 Tway, "The Wintering Partners."

32 McDonald, *Lord Strathcona,* 165.

33 Ibid., 166.

34 A.7/4, pp. 148–55, Northcote to Graham, 30 October 1870.

35 A.10/80, fo. 853d, conclusion of Northcote's plan.

36 HBCA Search File "Governors."

37 A.33/3, fo. 161, Agreement between Company and Grahame, 27 January 1874.

38 D.4/67, pp. 254–5, Simpson to Smith, 4 September 1845.

39 A.7/4, p. 175, Northcote to Smith, 3 December 1872.

40 A.6/51, fo. 225, Armit to Smith, 19 June 1878. According to his biographer, Donna McDonald, Strathcona was a keeper of records that are now

scattered among libraries, archives, and private collections in the United Kingdom and North America. She reports: "Following Lord Strathcona's death, papers were shipped from Montreal to London, including copies of all letters written up to 1892, a series of daily journals covering most years from 1869 to 1891 and ten boxes of personal and business letters and other papers" (McDonald, *Lord Strathcona*, 8).

41 Bowsfield, ed., *The Letters of Charles John Brydges*, xli n3. See also Stardom, "Twilight of the Fur Trade."

42 A.12/18, fos. 10–11, Brydges to Armit, 21 April 1879.

43 Ibid.

44 Ibid., fo. 19, Brydges to Armit, 24 May 1879.

45 Ibid.

46 Ibid., fo. 12.

47 Bowsfield, ed., *The Letters of Charles John Brydges, 1879–1882*, xlix.

48 A.12/18, fos. 146–7, Brydges to Armit, 17 September 1879.

49 Ibid., fos. 202–9, Brydges to Armit, 24 October 1879.

50 A.6/52, fos. 242–3, 11 February 1880, Armit to Brydges. This report was also published in London in 1882 by Sir Joseph Causton and Sons.

51 A.12/50, fos. 39d–40, Grahame to Armit, 20 January 1882.

52 A.12/19, fos. 528, Brydges to Armit, 30 December 1880.

53 A.12/21, fo. 123, Brydges to Armit, 17 April 1882.

54 Ibid., fos. 358–72, report from Brydges, 23 November 1882.

55 A.12/19, fos. 68, Brydges to Armit, 29 January 1880.

56 Smith, "'A Desire to Worry Me Out.'"

57 Smith had been promoted to the position of assistant secretary in May 1882 with a salary of £500. Had he stayed in London, he would have been in position to replace Armit, who retired ten years later.

58 Stardom, *A Stranger to the Fur Trade*, 21.

59 Rea, "The Hudson's Bay Company and the North-West Rebellion."

60 D.13/7, fo. 200, report from Wrigley to Armit, 8 June 1885.

61 Rea, "The Hudson's Bay Company and the North-West Rebellion," 56. See also records in E.9/27–30, Red River and North West Rebellion.

62 Stardom, *A Stranger to the Fur Trade*, 21.

63 Ibid., 105–6, and Ray, *The Canadian Fur Trade*, 71.

64 HBC, Reports and Proceedings, Report of the Commissioner on the Trade of the Company, 25 August 1888.

65 Ray, *The Canadian Fur Trade*, 71.

66 D.13/10, fo 258, Wrigley to Armit, 18 February 1891.

67 Nigol, "Efficiency and Economy," 1–2.

68 D.13/11, fos. 159–60.

69 D.21/1a, fos. 195–99, Report from Chipman, 9 September 1891.

70 A.6/60, fos. 106–7, Armit to Chipman, 7 October 1891.

71 D.21/1a, fo. 236b–236c, Chipman to Armit, 4 November 1891.

72 Ibid., fos. 195–9.

73 D.21/3, fos. 74–83, Chipman to Armit, 27 January 1892.

74 A.6/59, fos. 657–60, Instructions to Chipman, 26 May 1891.

75 HBCA finding aid for Section A, "General Introduction to Classes A.74–A.81," "Introduction A.74/FT Annual Reports," and "Introduction A.75/s Annual Reports."

76 HBC, Reports and Proceedings, 3 July 1900.

77 A.12/FT229.3, fo. 224, Chipman to Ware, 4 December 1900.

78 MacKay, *The Honourable Company,* 306.

79 A.12/FT276.2, fos. 1–3, copy of letter from Pope, 11 March 1898.

80 Ibid.

81 "Report of Douglas Brymner on Archives," in Canada, Parliament, *Sessional Papers,* 1873, no. 9. (Ottawa, 1873), 151.

82 Ibid.

83 Heney, "London and Paris Offices" 14–15.

84 A.12/FT/276.2, Chipman to Ware, 11 March 1898.

85 Ibid., copy of letter from Pope to Chipman, 3 March 1898.

86 Ibid., Chipman to Ware, 19 January 1900.

87 Ibid.

88 Ibid.

89 A.1/159, p. 221, minutes of a Special Committee, 15 September 1910.

90 A.2/8, Lord Strathcona's Report to the Shareholders, London, 8 July 1912.

91 RG3/1A/2, p. 7, Fur Trade Annual Report, 1915–16.

92 Ibid., p. 11.

93 A.12/229.3, fos. 259–60, Thomson to the Governor and Committee, 17 October 1918.

94 Yates, *Control through Communication,* 1.

95 HBCA Search File "French Government Business" and introduction to finding aid, RG22, AFG.

CHAPTER SIX

1 The Development Department was in operation from 1925 to 1931 and the Fish and Fish Products Department from 1934 to 1940. See Morton, "'We Are Still Adventurers.'"

2 See French's account, discussed in Chapter 4: RG20/5/3, French to Chipman, 23 January 1922.

3 "Establishments of the Hudson's Bay Company in Canada, 1921," *The Beaver*, May 1921, 4–5.

4 HBC, Reports and Proceedings, 5 August 1921. For more information on the fur trade crisis at the end of the nineteenth and beginning of the twentieth centuries, see Ray, *The Canadian Fur Trade.*

5 London Correspondent, "Passing of No. 1 Lime Street," *The Beaver*, March 1925, 66–8.

6 A.64/55, Catalogue of HBC Library, 1887.

7 MacKay, *The Honourable Company,* 34.

8 Quoted in Tyrrell, ed., *Documents Relating to the Early History*, xi. Oldmixon published his two-volume *British Empire in America* in 1708, with a second edition in 1731 and German editions in 1721, 1727, and 1776.

9 MacKay, *The Honourable Company,* 43–4.

10 Begg, *History of the North-West*, v–vii.

11 AM, MG9 A75–1, Bibliography of the Hudson's Bay Company, 1887. The draft manuscript of "The Last Great Monopoly," in Christy's handwriting, was donated to the Archives of Manitoba by the family of Dr Charles N. Bell, Christy's correspondent. Various other correspondence, research notes, and writings of Christy are classified in the Hudson's Bay Company Archives as E.49, Robert Miller Christy.

12 Christy was the author of *Manitoba Described* (London: Wyman & Sons, 1885) and the editor of *The Voyages of Captain Luke Foxe of Hull and Captain Thomas James of Bristol, in Search of a North-West Passage, in 1631–32* (London: Hakluyt Society, 1894).

13 AM, MG14 C23, pp. 118–19, Christy to Charles N. Bell, 30 May 1885.

14 Willson, *The Great Company (1667–1871)*, x.

15 Ibid., xxix.

16 Willson, *The Life of Lord Strathcona*, x.

17 Bryce, *The Remarkable History*, vi–vii. A notebook kept by the secretary in the London office (A.64/36) lists a number of items borrowed by Dr Bryce, including minute books, stock ledgers, a letterbook, Radisson's journals, reports of Dobbs's voyage, and various correspondence.

18 MacKay, "Books Relating."

19 Laut, *The Conquest of the Great Northwest*, xviii–xix.

20 Wallace, "The Champlain Society," 43.

21 Ibid. The records were not classified until the 1930s. As a librarian, Wallace would have appreciated the security implications of opening them up to researchers without an appropriate filing system in place.

22 A.12/S/misc./1402, Burbidge to Governor and Committee, 26 July 1918.

23 A.10/520, Hudson's Bay Celebration Suggested Scheme, n.d.

24 RG2/2/127, Ingrams to Nanton, 30 April 1919.

25 Schooling, *The Governor and Company of Adventurers*, xii; emphasis added.

26 A.10/519, Bottomley to Ingrams, 15 April 1919.

27 See previous chapter for more information about the French government business.

28 "To Our Readers," *The Beaver*, October 1920, 5.

29 Geller, "Constructing Corporate Images," and Dafoe, "Annals of *The Beaver*." Malvina Bolus was the editor from 1958 to 1972, she was followed by Helen Burgess from 1972 to 1985, Christopher Dafoe from 1985 to 1997 and then Annalee Greenberg, who is the current editor. Since 1994 *The Beaver* has been published by Canada's National History Society from offices in Winnipeg.

30 "Twenty-first Birthday," *The Beaver*, September 1941, 48.

31 A.102/2406, Schooling to Kindersley, 10 March 1920.

32 A.5/132, fo. 451, Ingrams to Schooling, 22 April 1920.

33 A.102/2406, Schooling to Kindersley, 29 March 1920.

34 A.92/167/5, Schooling to Governor Sale, 20 February 1928. Kathleen Pincott worked in the London head office from 1928 to 1931.

35 Extracts taken from minute books and letterbooks for the years 1670–1861 were indexed and bound in twenty-nine volumes called Annals (RG20/6a/1–29). Post journals were arranged alphabetically and indexed in another series, RG20/6b/1–12. Many of these extracts were also filed by subject in the vertical files, where they are easily available to researchers in the HBCA.

36 RG20/2/163, Leveson Gower to Brooks (including copy of letter from Schooling to Kindersley, 31 October 1921), 25 February 1932. Correspondence regarding the Merk controversy is catalogued in A.5, London Correspondence Outward; A.10, London Correspondence Inward; and RG20, series 2, Archives Department Administration Subject Files (London). Record group 20, the records of the Hudson's Bay Company Archives, was arranged and described in 1992 by the author and includes records accumulated in London (c. 1920–74) and those accumulated in Winnipeg (1974–90).

37 A.5/135/35, Sale to Schooling, 1 March 1921.

38 A.10/458, Schooling to Kindersley, 31 October 1921.

39 A.5/138/230, Sale to Schooling, 4 November 1921.

40 E.181/1, Merk to Hartwell Bowsfield, 27 March 1968.

41 Merk, *Fur Trade and Empire*, xxxv.

42 RG20/2/163, Brooks to Merk, 26 February 1932.

43 Ibid., 15 April 1932.

44 A.1/165, fos. 38–9, Committee minutes, 22 March 1921.

45 A.10/458, Schooling to Ingrams, 31 January 1922.

46 RG20/11/4, Index Catalogue of the HBC's Records.

47 RG20/1/2, Schooling to Kindersley, 5 April 1923.

48 A.10/458, Sale to Schooling, 5 March 1921.

49 BCA, GR975, Archives Department Annual and Monthly Reports.

50 A.102/1165, Report of Schooling to the Governor, 27 November 1922.

51 Ibid.

52 Ibid.

53 Ibid.

54 Ibid.

55 A.92/167/6, Kindersley to Schooling, 18 September 1923.

56 A.92/167/2, Schooling to Kindersley, 14 November 1923.

57 A.92/167/6, Kindersley to Schooling, 22 November 1923.

58 Heney, "London and Paris Offices." The program of hand-transcribing manuscripts and maps that was established in London and Paris continues today in the form of microfilming.

59 Wilson, "'A Noble Dream.'"

60 Ibid., 19–20.

61 A.10/454, Scholefield, Provincial Librarian and Archivist, to Ingrams, 6 June 1916.

62 RG20/2/46, Lists of HBC papers in Canadian archives, various dates.

63 Doughty, *The Canadian Archives*, 17–48. See also "Canadian History" in Stuart, *Opportunity Knocks Once*, 128–63.

64 Doughty, *The Canadian Archives*, 19–20, 45.

65 A.93/14, Schooling to Kindersley, 5 April 1923.

66 A.1/166, fo. 208, Committee minutes, 8 May 1923.

67 A.92/167/2, Schooling to Kindersley, 19 July 1923. Doughty was a member of the Champlain Society.

68 The Hakluyt Society, founded in 1846, has published over 350 volumes related to exploration, geography, ethnology, and natural history through subscriptions. These have included publications of rare and inaccessible materials relating to the history of Canada.

69 A.1/214, fo. 134, Committee minutes, 28 October 1924.

70 A.92/167/2, Stirling to Schooling, 19 November 1924.

71 A.92/167/7, Stirling to Schooling, 27 November 1924.

72 A.92/167/8, Stirling to Schooling, 29 May 1926.

73 Ibid., 30 June 1926. No notes or galley proofs relating to Schooling's work have been found in the HBCA.

74 A.102/1761, Report on the Publication History of the HBC, 12 April 1932.

75 A.92/misc./190, copy of newspaper clipping, n.d.

76 A.92/misc./185, copy of newspaper clipping, n.d.

77 Ibid.

78 Ibid., Doughty to Sale, 17 December 1925.

79 A.102/2404, Doughty to Sale, 17 March 1926.

80 Ibid., 2 April 1926.

81 A.92/misc./194, [Doughty] to Sale, 14 February 1928. Copies of a number
    of letters from Doughty to the Company were found in various files.
    Doughty is not identified on the typed copy of this letter, but I have deter-
    mined from the dates and content that they are in fact from him. Doughty's
    handwriting is quite illegible, and copies were probably made to make the
    letters more readable to Company staff.

82 RG20/5/3, Records to Insurance Department, 22 October 1926.

83 A.1/169, fo. 71, 13 March 1928.

84 A.102/1758, Sale to the Canadian Committee, 27 April 1928.

85 "Notes and Comments," *Canadian Historical Review* 9 (December 1928):
    281–2.

86 A.102/1758, Lecky, Secretary, Canadian Committee, to Governor and
    Committee, 14 May 1928.

87 A.102/1761, Publication History of the HBC, 12 April 1932.

88 A.92/misc./194, [Doughty] to Sale, 14 February 1928.

89 A.92/misc./199, Doughty to Sale, 16 January 1929.

90 Ibid.

91 A.102/598, [Sale] to Doughty, 7 August 1930.

92 HBC, Reports and Proceedings, 26 June 1923.

93 Introduction to HBCA finding aid A.92, London Office Correspondence,
    1919–54.

94 RG20/2/55, Notes Concerning Filing System, 1973.

95 A.1/165, fo. 225, Committee minutes, 25 April 1922.

96 RG20/1/9, Watson to the Canadian Committee, 18 June 1927.

97 Ibid.

98 RG2/54/9, Report on Staff Organisation & Training, 20 February 1925.

99 A.102/2404, Sale to Chester, 17 May 1924.

100 London Correspondent, "Our 255th Anniversary: Opening of New
    London Premises," *The Beaver,* June 1925, 115–16, and *From One Flag-
    ship to Another,* brochure distributed for the opening in 1988 of the Royal
    Bank of Canada Centre (on the site of the former Beaver House).

101 Edwards, "Hudson Bay House."

102 Ibid.

103 The building is now called Hasilwood House, and the weathervane can still be seen, looking somewhat incongruous among the more modern buildings in the Bishopsgate neighbourhood.

104 "The Company in London," *The Beaver*, September 1935, 31.

105 These portraits now hang in the HBC head office on Bay Street in Toronto.

106 HBCA Search File, "London," Hudson's Bay House, Inventory of Antique and Valuable Furniture, c. 1928.

CHAPTER SEVEN

1 A.1/170, p. 174, Board minutes, 9 December 1930.

2 A.2/103, p. 12, General Court minutes, 16 January 1931.

3 HBC, Reports and Proceedings, 30 December 1930. A copy of the letter from Brooks to shareholders is attached to the minutes.

4 A.2/103, p. 12, General Court minutes, 16 January 1931.

5 Ibid

6 Ibid.

7 Section A, Unclassified, Department Records – Head Office, Canada, ca. 1931.

8 RG2/7/34, address made by G.W. Allan, chairman of the Canadian Committee, in Calgary, 28 December 1931.

9 RG2/1/25, Canadian Committee minutes, 25 April 1940.

10 RG2/10/37, Canadian Committee annual report, 12 September 1946.

11 Pronounced "Lewson Gore."

12 The "Annals" are classified as RG20/6, Research Tools.

13 RG20/6b/1–12.

14 RG20/6c/6 and 7.

15 RG20/1/14, Leveson Gower to Graham, 25 February 1931.

16 RG20/1/9, Archives Department Correspondence (London), 1927.

17 BCA, GR975, Guest Book Archives Department, 1923–34.

18 BCA, GR299, British Columbia Provincial Library, 1919–1943, Monthly and Annual Report of the Archives Department.

19 Section A, Unclassified, Department Records – Head Office, personal and confidential memorandum from Brooks to Cooper, 15 July 1931.

20 RG20/1/14, Leveson Gower to Graham, 25 February 1931; emphasis added.

21 Ibid.

22 Ibid.

23 A.1/170, p. 254, Board minutes, 12 May 1931; emphasis added.

24 A.1/171, p. 31, Board minutes, 22 September 1931.

25 A.2/105a, General Court minutes, 29 July 1931.

26 The archives were moved from Hudson's Bay House to Beaver House in 1955.

27 RG20/2/18, Brooks to Leveson Gower, 11 May 1932.

28 Ibid, Leveson Gower to Brooks, 20 May 1932.

29 A.92/106/3, fo. 12, Sale to Chester, 19 March 1925.

30 RG20/2/41, *The British Records Association Rules*, 1932.

31 Jenkinson, "The Choice of Records for Preservation," 543.

32 RG20/2/36, British Records Association to the Governor and Committee, 5 June 1942.

33 RG20/2/18, Brooks to Leveson Gower, 11 May 1932.

34 Jenkinson, *A Manual of Archive Administration*, 106.

35 RG20/2/18, Archives of the Hudson's Bay Company, by Hilary Jenkinson, 2 June 1932.

36 Jenkinson, *A Manual of Archive Administration*, 73.

37 A.1/171, p. 121, Board minutes, 27 September 1932.

38 RG20/2/164, Brooks to James MacLehose, 8 July 1937.

39 RG20/5/12, Work Completed by the Records Department since 1922, 4 February 1933.

40 RG20/2/40, Records Pertaining to the Various Administrations of the Hudson's Bay Company in North America, 1 February 1935.

41 A.1/171/196, Board minutes, 16 May 1933.

42 RG20/5/3, Brooks to Canadian Committee, 23 May 1932.

43 RG2/10/18, Chester to Governor and Committee, 30 September 1933.

44 Ibid.

45 A.102/194, Secretary to Canadian Committee, 9 February 1934.

46 A.1/171/160, Board minutes, 10 January 1933.

47 "Governor's address, 1934 General Court," *The Beaver*, June 1934, 57.

48 RG20/2/132, Stacpole to Brooks, 29 October 1931.

49 RG20/8/1, Visitor's Book, 1933–50.

50 MacKay, *The Honourable Company*, 310.

51 RG20/2/176, Morton to Brooks, 10 September 1937.

52 "Bay Personality – Mrs. Sach," *The Bay*, winter 1946–47, 12–15. Mrs Sach retired with a pension from the Company in June 1948. She died thirteen years later in 1961.

53 A.S. Morton, professor of history at the University of Saskatchewan, spent fourteen months at the Hudson's Bay Company Archives, from June 1933 to August 1934, researching material for his subsequent publication, *A History of the Canadian West to 1870–71*.

54 RG20/2/164, Brooks to the Governor, 7 March 1934. The original suggestion for the name of the proposed society was made in a note written by

Leveson Gower dated 1/3/34 in this same file. Some of the enthusiasm probably developed from daily contact in the reading room with A.S. Morton.
A handwritten note labelled "Professor Morton's Views on Hudson's Bay
Company Publications'" dated 14 July 1934, is also found in the file. An
earlier proposal, from Douglas MacKay in the Canadian office, had suggested a series of books to be published under the name "The Rupert's
Library" (RG20/2/164, MacKay to Chester, 16 October 1933).

55 RG20/2/164, HBC Archives and History – Publication, 14 November 1934.
56 Ibid.
57 Ibid., Brooks to Governor, 16 March 1934.
58 Ibid., 14 November 1934.
59 A.1/209, p. 64, Board minutes, 22 January 1935.
60 A.1/171, Board minutes, 10 January 1935: "Reporting the engagement of
Mr. Douglas MacKay, of Montreal, to take charge of the Company's general
advertising, public relations, internal relations and the 'Beaver' Magazine."
61 MacKay, *The Honourable Company*, xi.
62 A.1/209, p. 197, 6 October 1936.
63 A.1/209, p. 223, Board minutes, 9 February 1937.
64 RG20/2/164, Brooks to Leveson Gower, 13 February 1937.
65 Ibid., Brooks to Canadian Committee, 5 March 1937.
66 RG20/5/14, Rich to Brooks, 1 June 1937.
67 Ibid.
68 Ibid.
69 A.1/210, p. 41, Board minutes, 14 December 1937, Appendix.
70 Ibid. The charges are in sterling.
71 A.1/210, p. 19, Board minutes, 27 July 1937.
72 A.102/2736, Agreement between Hudson's Bay Record Society Limited
and The Champlain Society, 20 June 1938.
73 "Announcing the Hudson's Bay Record Society," *The Beaver*, March
1938, 2.
74 Wallace, "The Champlain Society," 43.
75 A.102/2736, Agreement, 20 June 1938.
76 K. G. Davies was fellow of New College, Oxford, and, later, professor of
history at the University of Bristol. Glyndwr Williams was reader and then
professor of history at Queen Mary College, London.
77 RG20/1/21, Leveson Gower to Mr Lubbock, 18 July 1939.
78 A.1/210, p. 127, Board minutes, 14 February 1939.
79 RG20/1/21, Johnson to Brooks, 7 September 1939.
80 Ibid.
81 RG20/10/1, Mayhew to Brooks, 20 May 1942.

82 RG20/2/1, Secretary to Johnson, 11 March 1942.

83 James Cooper, personal communication with the author, 9 May 1998.

84 RG20/2/1, Secretary to Archives Department, Air Raid Precautions, October 1938.

85 Ibid., Air Raid Emergency, 12 May 1941.

86 Ibid., War Emergency Measures, 27 May 1941.

87 RG20/1/21, Secretary to Miss Johnson, 26 September 1940.

88 "Winter Packet," *The Beaver*, December 1944, 49.

89 "London News," *The Beaver*, September 1944, 50.

90 "News of the Fur Trade," *The Beaver*, December 1940, 51.

91 Marrowfat is a term used for a variety of large pea often used for canning.

92 RG20/1/21, Secretary to Archives Department, Staff Welfare, 28 February 1945.

93 RG20/1/22, Staff memorandum, 14 October 1946.

94 "London Letter," *The Beaver*, December 1943, 43.

95 RG20/1/22, Staff memoranda, 14 and 23 August 1946.

96 RG20/1/21, HBC staff to the Secretary, 17 April 1944.

97 RG20/2/1, Brooks to Johnson and Mayhew, 16 May 1945.

98 A.102/2454, Brooks to Hollis, 12 March 1946.

99 RG20/5/14, Brooks to Assistant Secretary, 8 August 1947.

100 A.102/194, Archivist to Brooks, 21 August 1947. See also RG20/1/22, Staff memorandum, 6 October 1947.

101 RG20/2/48, Johnson to Brooks, 26 January 1949.

102 RG20/5/14, undated note signed by R.A. Reynolds, Secretary [January 1949].

103 A.1/221, p. 272, Board minutes, 9 March 1949. Leveson Gower was making £380 immediately before the war (A.102/228e).

104 A.1/221, p. 339, Board minutes, 11 January 1950.

105 RG20/5/14, Reynolds to Johnson, 13 January 1950.

106 RG20/2/119, Archivist to Secretary, 4 January 1950.

107 RG20/1/22, Johnson to Reynolds, 19 January 1949.

108 RG20/2/119, Archivist to Secretary, 22 September 1950.

109 A.102/2736, Stuart to Wallace, 29 June 1948.

110 Ibid.

111 Ibid., Walker to Stuart, 26 February 1949.

112 RG9/615.3.1, Lamb to Reynolds, 28 July 1950.

113 RG20/2/106, Johnson to Reynolds, 22 September 1950.

114 RG20/2/40, Work in Hudson's Bay Company Archives, 1948–54. The microfilming project was moved back to a more suitable room in the Bishopsgate building in 1954, a few months before the whole department moved to Beaver House.

115 RG20/1/112, press release, 10 March 1951.

116 Lamb, "The Federal Archival Scene," 66–7. In 1970 there were 1,858 reels available to researchers in Canada.

117 RG2/8/1025, Canadian Committee to the Governor and Committee, 18 May 1951.

118 "Archives Available," *The Beaver*, June 1951, 50.

119 An online finding aid is available on the HBCA website.

120 William Johnston Keswick started his career in China with the family business, Jardine, Matheson and Company. He returned to England, where he served in the War Cabinet Office with the rank of brigadier, before being seconded by the governor of the Bank of England "to undertake special work connected with the British economy." See "Our Directors," *The Bay*, summer 1947, 4–5.

121 A.102/4033, Secretary to Deputy Governor, Buying Office Rental, 7 October 1953.

122 RG20/2/40, Work in Hudson's Bay Company Archives, 1956–60.

123 Ibid.

124 A.102/4033, HBC London Administration, 20 June 1958.

125 Thymol is an organic fungicide used in paper fumigation. See A.102/917, Johnson to Assistant Accountant, 2 May 1951.

126 RG20/2/40, Work in Hudson's Bay Company Archives, 1948–54.

127 RG2/10/18, Canadian Committee Office, Disposal of Records, 20 June 1958.

128 RG20/1/21, Secretary to Archives Department, 12 June 1942.

CHAPTER EIGHT

1 RG20/2/18, HBC Archives, Reports and Recommendations, 22 September 1932. J.C. Brooks suggested "handing the Archives over to Rhodes House ... to the Dominion Government, Ottawa, or the Public Record Office in London" as alternatives to continuing to provide adequate accommodation for the records in Company buildings.

2 A.1/210, p. 41, Board minute, 14 December 1937.

3 Takeovers and diversification continued through the 1970s and beyond, when the Company acquired control of the real estate development company Markborough Properties (1973), and with the acquisitions of Freiman's (1972) and then Zellers, Simpsons, and Fields (1978). Other takeovers followed of Robinson's (1979), Towers/Bonimart (1990), Woodwards (1993), and K-Mart Canada (1998).

4 "Organizational changes announced by Company," *The Bay*, October 1969, 1.

5 Johnson, ed., *Saskatchewan Journals and Correspondence.*

6 Phillips, "Art in the Archives," *The Beaver,* March 1937, 10–15.

7 RG20/2/152, Valuation for Insurance by Pawsey & Payne, Fine Art Dealers, London, 1 June 1973.

8 Glyndwr Williams, personal communication with the author, 30 April 1998.

9 RG9/615.7.1, Ewart to Steinkopf, 13 February 1964.

10 E.157/1, Joseph Martin, Executive Secretary of the Manitoba Centennial Corporation, to Ewart, 6 August 1964.

11 E.157/2, Ewart to Roblin, 8 February 1965.

12 Ibid.

13 Ibid.

14 E.157/1, Roblin to Ewart, 16 February 1965.

15 Ibid.

16 Ibid., Saunderson to Ewart, 22 February 1965.

17 RG9/615.7.1, Murray to Kilgour, 11 February 1965.

18 RG20/2/181a, Kilgour to Funt, 12 February 1965.

19 E.157/2, Ewart to Roblin, 25 March 1965.

20 A.1/226, p. 285, Board minutes, 18 May 1967.

21 RG9/615.7.1, Pearson to Murray, 8 March 1968.

22 E.157/2, copy of newspaper clipping in file: "Jottings from the Business World" by Sheldon Bowles, *Winnipeg Free Press,* 10 March 1969.

23 "Our First Canadian Charter," *The Beaver,* autumn 1970, 64.

24 Ibid.: "The Charter of 1970 granted at Westminster annulled all provisions of previous charters except the incorporation section of the original 1670 Charter. On the same day, the Canadian Charter granted at Ottawa continued the Company as a body corporate and subject to the laws of Canada."

25 Ibid.

26 RG20/2/181b, Smith to Amory, 7 May 1970.

27 Ibid.

28 RG9/615.7.1, Huband to Bissell, 12 May 1970.

29 Ibid., Sirluck to Amory, 9 October 1970.

30 Ibid., note to file by Huband, 12 January 1971.

31 Ibid., Sirluck to Amory, 9 October 1970.

32 Ibid.

33 Ibid, Schreyer to Richardson, 29 December 1970.

34 Ibid, Richardson to Amory, 29 December 1970.

35 Ibid.

36 RG20/2/181b, Craig to Reynolds, 16 November 1970.

37 RG9/615.7.1, note to file by Huband, 12 January 1971.

38 Ibid., Murray to Amory, 16 February 1971.

39 Ibid., report from Craig to Logan-Brown, 18 October 1971.

40 Ibid.

41 Ibid.

42 RG20/2/181C, note for directors from Huband, 16 June 1972.

43 RG9/615.7.1, notes from Smith, Bolus and Burgess to Huband, 29 February and 2 March 1972.

44 Ibid., telegram from Murray to Huband, 30 May 1972.

45 RG20/2/181C, note for directors from Huband, 16 June 1972.

46 RG9/615.7.1, extract of minutes of meeting of the Executive Committee, 15 June 1972.

47 Ibid., telegram from Collins to Richardson, 20 June 1972.

48 Ibid., extract of Executive Committee minutes, 22 June 1972.

49 Ibid., notes to members of the Executive Committee, 11 August 1972.

50 Ibid., position paper prepared by Huband, 29 November 1972.

51 RG20/2/181C, Huband to Craig, 22 December 1972. George Richardson was most certainly one of the directors with a preference for Winnipeg, and he was, of course, also the governor of the Company.

52 RG9/615.7.1, Craig to Huband, 16 January 1973.

53 Ibid., Huband to Craig, 26 January 1973.

54 RG20/2/181C, Schreyer to Richardson, 11 January 1973.

55 RG9/615.3.1, Huband to Smith, 23 May 1973.

56 Ibid.

57 AM, GR1664–702, EC0016, Smith to Richardson, 1 June 1973.

58 Ibid., Richardson to Schreyer, 8 June 1973.

59 Ibid., Bovey to Bayer, 25 June 1973.

60 Ibid., Richardson to Smith, 11 July 1973.

61 "HBC Archives Transferred," *Moccasin Telegraph*, winter 1973, 7.

62 Ibid.

63 RG9/615.3.1, copy of agreement, 31 July 1973.

64 Ibid.

65 Gwen Kemp, personal communication with the author, 6 May 1998.

66 RG20/2/183, invoice from Pitt & Scott Ltd., 21 October 1974.

67 "We chose September to ship the Archives because according to our insurance specialists there were fewer marine incidents in the North Atlantic in September than any other month" (notes received by the author from Shirlee Anne Smith, 10 January 2005).

68 There was no announcement of the move. The 1977 annual report listed the head office at 77 Main Street, Winnipeg. The 1978 annual report listed the registered office at 77 Main Street and the corporate office at 2 Bloor Street East, Toronto.

69 RG9/615.8.1, Vernon to Huband, 14 July 1976.
70 Ibid.

POSTSCRIPT

1 RG14, "Hudson's Bay Record Society – cessation of, 1981–85," Thomson to Pannekoek, 16 October 1981.
2 Ibid., Easton to McGrath, 18 June 1985. The centre was later renamed the Rupert's Land Research Centre and is now known as the Centre for Rupert's Land Studies. It hosts biennial colloquiums, publishes the *Rupert's Land Newsletter*, promotes awareness of the Hudson's Bay Company Archives in Winnipeg, and co-publishes, with McGill-Queen's University Press, a series of documentary volumes on aspects of the history of Rupert's Land.
3 Newman, *Merchant Princes*, 548–9, and "Hudson's Bay Company," in *International Directory of Company Histories*.
4 "Garlick Hill Nominated."
5 *Daily Telegraph*, 22 June 1982.
6 RG20/3/3, Report prepared by the Canadian Conservation Institute fo the Provincial Archives of Manitoba on the "Hudson's Bay Company Collection," 31 March 1977.
7 RG9/615.7.1, copy of Agreement, 31 July 1973, and RG9/615.3.1, copy of Agreement, 29 November 1976.
8 Schellenberg, *Modern Archives*.
9 Bureau of Canadian Archivists, *Rules of Description*.
10 RG 20/3/9, memo from Ross to Smith, 28 April 1981.
11 The record group system also conveniently fit into the fonds/series system of description developed by the Bureau of Canadian Archivists in the 1990s and used as the basis for the Keystone Archives Description Database, which provides an online guide to the holdings at the Archives of Manitoba, as the provincial repository is now known.
12 Coutts and Pettipas, "'Mere Curiostities.'"
13 AM GR5622 TB1 Q1473/171, letter from Huband to Carson, 26 July 1993.
14 Ibid., Management Plan – HBC Collection.
15 Ibid., Blake, Cassels & Graydon to Revenue Canada, 20 May 1993.
16 This author was one of the first recipients of a grant from the foundation, which made it possible to undertake research travel in England in 1998.
17 Canada's National History Society also funds the Pierre Berton Award, presented annually for distinguished achievement in the popular writing of Canadian history, and the Governor General's Awards for Excellence in Teaching Canadian History.

18 The museum collection is on permanent display in an exhibit hall built to the custom requirements of the more than six thousand artifacts relating primarily to three hundred years of Aboriginal and fur trade culture.

19 Beattie, "'My Best Friend.'"

20 Information about the HBCA can be found on its website, http://www.gov.mb.ca/chc/archives/HBCA.

21 Access Policy, HBCA, 2007.

Bibliography

ARCHIVAL SOURCES

ARCHIVES OF MANITOBA
GR1664–702, EC0016, Schreyer Administration
GR5622 TB1 Q1473/171, Provincial Archivist

BRITISH COLUMBIA ARCHIVES
Add. MSS. 635, Donald Ross
C/D/30.8/L16, "Report on the State of the Library and Archives," 1934
GR299, British Columbia Provincial Library
GR975, Archives Department

BRITISH LIBRARY
Add. MSS 5027, fo. 64, "West Side of James Bay," by Thomas Moore [1678]
Add. MSS 5414, fo. 20, "Map of Hudsons Bay," by John Thornton, 1685
Map 5414, art. 20 (originally MS Sloane 3244, Roll 23), Chart of Hudson's Bay and Straits, and Port Nelson, 1685

GUILDHALL LIBRARY
MS 1757, fo. 134, Collection of papers dating from 1641–95 made by Robert Hooke

HUDSON'S BAY COMPANY ARCHIVES
Note: Archival records cited in the notes are from this repository unless otherwise noted.
Section A: Governor and Committee (London Office) Records

Section B: Post Records
Section C: Ships' Records
Section D: Governor's Papers and Commissioner's Office
Section E: Private Records
Section F: Records of Related and Subsidiary Companies
Section G: Cartographic Records
Section H: Western Department Land Records
RG2: Records of the Canadian Committee
RG3: Records of the Fur Trade Department
RG7: Records of the Northern Stores Department
RG9: Head Office/Corporate Head Office, 1908–
RG14: Hudson's Bay Record Society, 1938–79
RG20: Records of the Hudson's Bay Company Archives
RG22: French Government, 1914–28

PUBLIC RECORD OFFICE (NOW NATIONAL ARCHIVES OF THE
UNITED KINGDOM)

Admiralty 24/121, no. 114, Charles Boone, John Davall & Company v. Hudson's Bay Company

Admiralty 51/379, pt. I–III, Log and journal of the *Furnace*, 1741–42

c6,303/9, Bill of Complaint, 1694

c33/286, ff. 335–6. *The Joynt and severall Answer of the Governour and Company of Adventurers of England tradeing into Hudsons Bay Defendants to the bill of Complaint of Pier Espritt Raddison Complainant (1694–97)*

c06/23, Colonial Office, 1857 Hudson's Bay Company and Individuals, item 3

SP29/251B/180, fo. 70–71d, State Papers, Domestic, Charles II, 1668, Instructions to Cap.ne William Stannard Comander of the Eaglett Ketch and Captaine Zachariah Guillam Comander of the NonSuch Ketch in relacon to the Voyage now undertaken for Hudsons Bay

OTHER SOURCES

Armstrong, John, and Stephanie Jones. *Business Documents: Their Origins, Sources and Uses in Historical Research*. London and New York: Mansel Publishing, 1987.

Ball, Tim, and David Dyck. "Observation of the Transit of Venus at Prince of Wales's Fort in 1769." *The Beaver*, autumn 1984, 51–6.

Barker, Burt Brown, ed. *Letters of Doctor John McLoughlin*. Portland: Oregon Historical Society, 1948.

Barr, William. "Shipwrecked on Mansel Island, Hudson Bay: Dr. Henry Briet-zcke's Arctic Health Cruise, 1864." *Polar Record* 28, no. 166 (1992): 177–90.

Beattie, Judith Hudson. "Indian Maps in the Hudson's Bay Company Archives: A Comparison of Five Area Maps Recorded by Peter Fidler, 1801–1802." *Archivaria* 21 (winter 1985–86): 166–75.

– "'My Best Friend': Evidence of the Fur Trade Libraries Located in the Hudson's Bay Company Archives." *Épilogue* 8, no. 1 and 2 (1993): 1–32.

Begg, Alexander. *History of the North-West.* Toronto: Hunter, Rose & Co., 1894.

Belyea, Barbara. *A Year Inland: The Journal of a Hudson's Bay Company Winterer.* Waterloo: Wilfrid Laurier University Press, 2000.

Bowsfield, Hartwell, ed. *The Letters of Charles John Brydges, 1879–1882.* Hudson's Bay Record Society Publications, 31. Winnipeg, 1977.

Brown, Jennifer S.H., and Elizabeth Vibert, eds. *Reading beyond Words: Contexts for Native History.* Peterborough: Broadview Press, 1996.

Bryce, George. *The Remarkable History of the Hudson's Bay Company.* London: Sampson Low, Marston and Company, 1900.

Bureau of Canadian Archivists. *Rules of Archival Description.* Rev. ed. Ottawa: Bureau of Canadian Archivists, 2003.

Burley, Edith I. *Servants of the Honourable Company: Work, Discipline, and Conflict in the Hudson's Bay Company, 1770–1870.* Toronto/New York/Oxford: Oxford University Press, 1997.

Burpee, Lawrence J. "York Factory to the Blackfoot Country – the Journal of Anthony Henday, 1754–55." *Proceedings and Transactions of the Royal Society of Canada,* 3rd series, 1 (1907): 2, 307–64.

Careless, J.M.S. "The Business Community in the Early Development of Victoria, British Columbia." In *Canadian Business History: Selected Studies 1497–1971,* ed. David S. Macmillan. Toronto: McClelland and Stewart, 1972.

Clarke, Desmond. *Arthur Dobbs Esquire 1689–1765: Surveyor-General of Ireland, Prospector and Governor of North Carolina.* London: The Bodley Head, 1957.

Coutts, Robert, and Katherine Pettipas. "'Mere Curiosities Are Not Required ... '" *The Beaver,* June/July 1994, 13–19.

Cowie, Isaac. *The Company of Adventurers: A Narrative of Seven Years in the Service of the Hudson's Bay Company during 1867–1874.* Toronto: William Briggs, 1913.

Craig, Joan. "Three Hundred Years of Records." *The Beaver,* autumn 1970, 65–70.

Dafoe, Christopher. "Annals of *The Beaver.*" *The Beaver,* February/March 1994–October/November 1995.

– "Early Days at *The Beaver.*" *The Beaver,* December 1994/January 1995, 2–3.

Davies, John. *Douglas of the Forests: The North American Journals of David Douglas.* Edinburgh: Paul Harris, 1979.

Davies, K.D. "Kelsey, Henry." In *Dictionary of Canadian Biography,* 2: 314. Toronto: University of Toronto Press, 1969.

Davies, K.G., ed. *Letters from Hudson Bay 1703–40.* Assistant ed., A.M. Johnson. Introd. by Richard Glover. Hudson's Bay Record Society Publications, 25. London, 1965.

De Brou, Dave, and Bill Waiser. *Documenting Canada: A History of Modern Canada in Documents.* Saskatoon: Fifth House Publishers, 1992.

Delgado, Alan. *The Enormous File: A Social History of the Office.* London: J. Murray, 1979.

Dillinger, Teresa L., et al. "Food of the Gods: Cure for Humanity? A Cultural History of the Medicinal and Ritual Use of Chocolate." *Journal of Nutrition* 130, no. 8 (2000): 2057S–2072S.

Doughty, Arthur G. *The Canadian Archives and Its Activities.* Ottawa: King's Printer, 1924.

Doughty, Arthur G., and Chester Martin, eds. *The Kelsey Papers.* Ottawa: King's Printer, 1929.

Edwards, A. Trystan. "Hudson Bay House." *The Beaver,* June 1930, 13–14.

Fairbank, Alfred, and Berthold Wolpe. *Renaissance Handwriting: An Anthology of Italic Scripts.* London: Faber and Faber, 1960.

Fisher, William, and John Thornton, eds. *The English Pilot, the Fourth Book.* London, 1689; repr. Amsterdam: Theatrum Orbis Terrarum, 1967.

Fleming, R. Harvey, and E.E. Rich, eds. *Minutes of Council Northern Department of Rupert Land, 1821–31.* Introd. by H.A. Innis. Hudson's Bay Record Society Publications, 3. London: 1940.

Galbraith, John. "The Hudson's Bay Land Controversy, 1863–1869." *Mississippi Valley Historical Review* 36, no. 3 (1949): 457–78.

Galbraith, John S. *The Hudson's Bay Company as an Imperial Factor, 1821–1869.* Toronto: University of Toronto Press, 1957.

"Garlick Hill Nominated a Conservation Area." *The Fur Review,* February 1981, 16, 18.

Geller, Peter G. "Constructing Corporate Images of the Fur Trade: The Hudson's Bay Company, Public Relations and *The Beaver* Magazine, 1920–1945." MA thesis, University of Manitoba/ University of Winnipeg, 1990.

Goldring, Philip. "Labour Records of the Hudson's Bay Company, 1821–1870." *Archivaria* 11 (1980/81): 53–86.

– *Papers on the Labour System of the Hudson's Bay Company, 1821–1900.* Manuscript Report Number 412. 2 vols. Ottawa: Parks Canada, 1980.

Grant, Hugh. "Bookkeeping in the Eighteenth Century: The Grand Journal and Grand Ledger of the Hudson's Bay Company." *Archivaria* 43 (1997): 143–57.

Gray, A. Grace. "David Douglas." *The Beaver*, March 1938, 27–9.

Great Britain. Parliament. House of Commons. *Report from the Committee, Appointed to Enquire into the State and Condition of the Countries adjoining to Hudson's Bay, and of the Trade Carried on There*. [London], 1749.

Great Britain. Select Committee on the Hudson's Bay Company. *Report from the Select Committee on the Hudson's Bay Company; together with the Proceedings of the Committee, Minutes of Evidence, Appendix and Index. Ordered, by the House of Commons, to be printed, 31 July and 11 August 1857*. [London, 1857].

Great Exhibition, London, 1851. *Official Descriptive and Illustrated Catalogue of the Great Exhibition of the Works of Industry of All Nations*. London, 1851.

Hallam, Elizabeth. "Problems with Record Keeping in Early Eighteenth Century London: Some Pictorial Representations of the State Paper Office, 1705–1706." *Journal of the Society of Archivists* 6 (October 1979): 219–26.

Harper, J. Russell. *Paul Kane's Frontier*. Toronto: University of Toronto Press, 1971.

Hartley, Sir Harold, ed. *The Royal Society: Its Origins and Founders*. London: Royal Society, 1960.

Heal, Ambrose, *The English Writing-Masters and Their Copy-Books, 1570–1800: A Biographical Dictionary & a Bibliography*. Hildesheim: Georg Olms Verlagsbuchhandlung, 1962.

Hearne, Samuel. *A Journey from Prince of Wales's Fort in Hudson's Bay to the Northern Ocean, 1769, 1770, 1771, 1772*. Ed. Richard Glover. Toronto: Macmillan Company of Canada, 1958.

Heney, Jane. "London and Paris Offices." *Archivist* 19, no. 2 (1992): 14–15.

Hudson's Bay Company. *Evidence for the United States in the matter of the claim of the Hudson's Bay Company pending before the British and American Joint Commission for the Settlement of the Claims of the Hudson's Bay and Puget's Sound Agricultural Companies*. Washington, 1867.

International Directory of Company Histories. Vol. 25. Farmington Hills, Mich.: St. James Press, 1999.

Jenkinson, Hilary. "The Choice of Records for Preservation: Some Practical Hints." *Library Association Record*, November 1939, 543–4.

– *A Manual of Archive Administration*. Oxford: Clarendon Press, 1922, 1931.

– *Selected Writings of Sir Hilary Jenkinson*. Ed. Roger H. Ellis and Peter Walne. With a new introd. by Terrence M. Eastwood. Chicago: Society of American Archivists, [2003].

Johnson, Alice M., ed. *Saskatchewan Journals and Correspondence: Edmonton House, 1795–1800; Chesterfield House, 1800–1802.* Hudson's Bay Record Society Publications, 26. London, 1967.

Kane, Paul. *Wanderings of an Artist among the Indians of North America.* London: Longman, Brown, Green, Longmans & Roberts, 1859.

Kelsey, Henry. *The Kelsey Papers.* Introd. by John Warkentin and including the introd. to the 1929 edition by Arthur G. Doughty and Chester Martin. Regina: Canadian Plains Research Center, University of Regina, 1994.

Lamb, W. Kaye. "British Columbia Official Records: The Crown Colony Period." *Pacific Northwest Quarterly* 29, no. 1 (1938): 17–25.

– "The Federal Archival Scene." *Canadian Historical Association Reports,* 1953, 61–8.

– "S.S. Beaver." *The Beaver,* winter 1958, 10–17.

Lancaster, Joan. "The India Office Records." *Archives* 9 (1970): 130–1.

Latham, Robert, and William Matthews, eds. *The Diary of Samuel Pepys.* Vol. 6, *1665.* London: G. Bell and Sons, 1972.

Laut, Agnes C. *The Conquest of the Great Northwest (Being the Story of the Adventurers of England known as the Hudson's Bay Company).* New York: The Outing Publishing Company, 1907–08.

Leveson Gower, Richard. "The Archives of the Hudson's Bay Company: An Outline of the Work Accomplished in London since 1924 of Assembling These Priceless Records Which Are the Source Material of Western Canadian History." *The Beaver,* December 1933, 40–2, 64.

– "The Archives of the Hudson's Bay Company: A Second Article on Assembling of the Old Records in London Describing the Section Allotted to the Minute Books." *The Beaver,* June 1934, 19–21, 66.

– "The Archives of the Hudson's Bay Company: The Third Article on the Records in London Describing Early Letter Books." *The Beaver,* December 1934, 37–9.

– "The Archives of the Hudson's Bay Company: In This Fourth Article on the Valuable Archives of the Company the Archivist Describes the Arrangement of the Original Letters Received in London and Gives Some Interesting Extracts." *The Beaver,* September 1935, 22–4.

Macaulay, George. *England in the Eighteenth Century.* 3rd ed. London: Adam & Charles Black, 1962.

MacDonald, Graham. *A Good Solid Comfortable Establishment: An Illustrated History of Lower Fort Garry.* Winnipeg: Watson & Dwyer Publishing, 1992.

MacKay, Douglas. "Books Relating to the Hudson's Bay Company." *The Beaver,* December 1934, 55–60.

– *The Honourable Company: A History of the Hudson's Bay Company*. Indianapolis and New York: Bobbs-Merrill Company, 1936.

Mackie, Richard Somerset. *Trading beyond the Mountains: The British Fur Trade on the Pacific 1793–1843*. Vancouver: UBC Press, 1997.

MacLaren, I.S. "'I came to rite thare portraits': Paul Kane's Journal of his Western Travels, 1846–1848. *American Art Journal* 31, no. 2 (1989): 7–21.

Maitland, William, et al. *The History and Survey of London from Its Foundation to the Present Time*. Vol. 2. London, 1756.

McDonald, Donna. *Lord Strathcona: A Biography of Donald Alexander Smith*. Toronto: Oxford, 1996.

McElwee, William. *History of England*. 3rd ed. London: English Universities Press, 1973.

Merk, Frederick. *Fur Trade and Empire: George Simpson's Journal*. Cambridge: Harvard University Press; London: Oxford University Press, 1931.

Miller, Edward. *That Noble Cabinet: A History of the British Museum*. London: Andre Deutsch, 1973.

Mitchell, Elaine. "Edward Watkin and the Buying-out of the Hudson's Bay Company." *Canadian Historical Review* 34, no. 3 (September 1953): 219–44.

Moodie, D.W. "Science and Reality: Arthur Dobbs and the Eighteenth-Century Geography of Rupert's Land." *Journal of Historical Geography* 2 (October 1976): 293–309.

Morton, A.S. *A History of the Canadian West to 1870–71; Being a History of Rupert's Land (the Hudson's Bay Company Territory) and the North-West Territory (Including the Pacific Slope)*. London and New York: T. Nelson & Sons, 1939.

– *Sir George Simpson, Overseas Governor of the Hudson's Bay Company: A Pen Picture of a Man of Action*. Toronto: J.M. Dent, 1944.

Morton, Anne. ""We Are Still Adventurers": The Records of the Hudson's Bay Company's Development Department and Fish and Fish Products Department, 1925–1940." *Archivaria* 21 (winter 1985–86): 158–65.

Mullett, Charles F. "The 'Better Reception, Preservation, and Convenient Use' of Public Records in Eighteenth-Century England." *American Archivist* 27, no. 2 (April 1964): 195–217.

Newman, Peter C. *Caesars of the Wilderness*. Markham, Ont.: Penguin Books, 1988.

– *Company of Adventurers: The Story of the Hudson's Bay Company*. Markham, Ont.: Penguin Books, 1987.

– *Merchant Princes*. Toronto: Penguin Books, 1992.

Nigol, Paul G. "Efficiency and Economy: Commissioner C.C. Chipman and the Hudson's Bay Company, 1891–1911." MA thesis, University of Manitoba, 1994.

Nute, Grace Lee. *Caesars of the Wilderness: Médard Chouart, Sieur des Groseilliers and Pierre Esprit Radisson, 1618–1710*. New York: Appleton-Century and the American Historical Association, 1943; repr. St Paul: Minnesota Historical Society Press, 1978.

– "Radisson and Groseilliers' Contribution to Geography." *Minnesota History* 16, no. 4 (December 1935): 414–26.

– "Two Documents from Radisson's Suit against the Company." *The Beaver*, December 1935, 41–9.

Oldmixon, John. *The British Empire in America*. London, 1708, 1741.

Pellew, Jill. *The Home Office 1848–1914*. London: Heinemann Educational Books, 1982.

Phillips, W.J. "Art in the Archives." *The Beaver*, March 1937, 10–15.

Public Record Office. *Guide to the Public Record Office*, 1. London: Her Majesty's Stationery Office, 1963.

Ranger, Felicity. "Export Control of Archives." *Journal of the Society of Archivists* 3 (October 1969): 570–2.

Ray, Arthur J. "Adventurers at the Crossroads." *The Beaver*, April-May 1986, 4–12.

– *The Canadian Fur Trade in the Industrial Age*. Toronto: University of Toronto Press, 1990.

– "The Early Hudson's Bay Company Account Books as Sources for Historical Research: An Analysis and Assessment." *Archivaria* 1 (winter 1975/76): 3–38.

– *Indians in the Fur Trade: Their Role as Trappers, Hunters, and Middlemen in the Lands Southwest of Hudson Bay, 1660–1870*. With a new introd. Toronto: University of Toronto Press, 1998.

Rea, J.E. "The Hudson's Bay Company and the North-West Rebellion." *The Beaver*, summer 1982, 43–57.

Rich, E.E. *The History of the Hudson's Bay Company 1670–1870*. Vol. 1, *1670–1763*; vol. 2, *1763–1870*. Hudson's Bay Record Society Publications, 21–22. London, 1958–59.

– "The Perpetual Governor." *The Beaver*, autumn 1974, 18–22.

– ed. *James Isham's Observations on Hudsons Bay, 1743 and Notes and Observations on a Book Entitled A Voyage to Hudsons Bay in the Dobbs Galley, 1749*. Hudson's Bay Record Society Publications, 12. London, 1949.

– ed. *Journal of Occurrences in the Athabasca Department by George Simpson, 1820 and 1821, and Report*. Introd. by Chester Martin. Hudson's Bay Record Society Publications, 1. London, 1938.

– ed. *The Letters of John McLoughlin from Fort Vancouver to the Governor and Committee*. First series, 1825–38; second series, 1839–44; third series, 1844–46. Hudson's Bay Record Society Publications, 4, 6, 7. London, 1941–44.

– ed. *Minutes of the Hudson's Bay Company, 1671–1674.* Hudson's Bay Record Society Publications, 5. London, 1942.

– ed. *Minutes of the Hudson's Bay Company, 1679–1684. Second part, 1682–84.* Hudson's Bay Record Society Publications, 9. London, 1946.

– ed. *Peter Skene Ogden's Snake Country Journals 1824–25 and 1825–26.* Assistant ed. A.M. Johnson. Introd. by Dr Burt Brown Barker. Hudson's Bay Record Society Publications, 13. London, 1950.

Rich, E.E., and A.M. Johnson, eds. *Copy-Book of Letters Outward &c Begins 29th May, 1680, Ends 5 July, 1687.* Hudson's Bay Record Society Publications, 11, London, 1948.

Robbins, Keith. *The Eclipse of a Great Power: Modern Britain, 1870–1975.* London and New York: Longman Group, 1993.

Robert, Rudolph. *Chartered Companies and Their Role in the Development of Overseas Trade.* London: G. Bell and Sons, 1969.

Ross, Alex, and Anne Morton. "The Hudson's Bay Company and Its Archives." *Business Archives* 51 (1985): 17–39.

Rudolph, Robert. *Chartered Companies and Their Role in the Development of Overseas Trade.* London: G. Bell and Sons, 1969.

Ruggles, Richard I. *A Country So Interesting: The Hudson's Bay Company and Two Centuries of Mapping, 1670–1870.* Montreal and Kingston: McGill-Queen's University Press, 1991.

– "Governor Samuel Wegg: 'The Winds of Change.'" *The Beaver,* autumn 1976, 10–20.

Schellenberg, T.R. *Modern Archives: Principles and Techniques.* Chicago and London: University of Chicago Press, 1956.

Schooling, Sir William. *The Governor and Company of Adventurers of England Trading into Hudson's Bay: during Two Hundred and Fifty Years, 1670–1920.* London: The Hudson's Bay Company, 1920.

Simmons, Deidre. "Annals of the Fur Trade: The Making of the Hudson's Bay Company Archives." *The Beaver,* June/July 1994, 4–12.

– "The Archives of the Hudson's Bay Company." *Archivaria* 42 (fall 1996): 68–78.

– "'Custodians of a Great Inheritance': An Account of the Making of the Hudson's Bay Company Archives." MA thesis, University of Manitoba, 1994.

"A History of the Hudson's Bay Company Archives." In *Papers of the 1994 Rupert's Land Colloquium,* 333–43. Winnipeg: Centre for Rupert's Land Studies, University of Winnipeg, 1997.

"The Hudson's Bay Company Archives: The Role of the Hudson's Bay Record Society." *Épilogue* 2, no. 1 (1996): 1–13.

"Samuel Pepys, the Bodleian Library, and Hudson's Bay Company Connections with Oxford." In *Papers of the 2002 Rupert's Land Colloquium.* Winnipeg: Centre for Rupert's Land Studies, University of Winnipeg, 2002.

Smith, Shirlee A. "'A Desire to Worry Me Out': Donald Smith's Harassment of Charles Brydges, 1879–1889." *The Beaver,* winter 1987/88, 4–11.

Spraakman, Gary. "The HBCs of Management Accounting." *CGA Magazine,* February 1998, 26–30.

Stardom, Eleanor J. *A Stranger to the Fur Trade: Joseph Wrigley and the Transformation of the HBC, 1884–1891.* Winnipeg: Centre for Rupert's Land Studies, 1995.

– "Twilight of the Fur Trade." *The Beaver,* August-September 1991, 6–18.

Stewart, Susan. "Sir George Simpson: Collector." *The Beaver,* summer 1982, 4–9.

Stuart, Sir Campbell. *Opportunity Knocks Once.* London: Collins, 1952.

Tway, Duane. "The Wintering Partners and the Hudson's Bay Company, 1867–1879." *Canadian Historical Review* 41, no. 3 (1960): 221–3.

Tyrrell, J.B., ed. *Documents Relating to the Early History of Hudson Bay.* Champlain Society, 18. Toronto, 1931.

Wallace, W. Stewart. "The Champlain Society." *The Beaver,* September 1934, 42–4.

– *The Pedlars from Quebec and Other Papers on the Nor'Westers.* Toronto: Ryerson Press, 1954.

– ed. *Documents Relating to the North West Company.* Champlain Society, 22. Toronto, 1934.

Warkentin, Germaine. "Discovering Radisson: A Renaissance Adventurer between Two Worlds." In *Reading beyond Words: Contexts for Native History,* ed. Jennifer S.H. Brown and Elizabeth Vibert, 43–70. Peterborough: Broadview Press, 1996.

– "Pierre-Esprit Radisson c. 1640–1710." In *Canadian Exploration Literature: An Anthology,* 2–26. Toronto: Oxford University Press, 1993.

– "Radisson's Voyages and Their Manuscript." *Archivaria* 48 (fall 1999): 199–222.

– "Who Was the Scribe of the Radisson Manuscript?" *Archivaria* 53 (spring 2002): 47–63.

– ed., *Canadian Exploration Literature: An Anthology.* Toronto: Oxford University Press, 1993.

Warkentin, Germaine, and Carolyn Podruchny, eds. *Decentring the Renaissance: Canada and Europe in Multidisciplinary Perspective, 1500–1700.* Toronto: University of Toronto Press, 2001.

Watkin, Sir E.W. *Canada and the States: Recollections 1851 to 1886.* London: Warwick House, 1887.

Williams, Glyndwr. "Arthur Dobbs and Joseph Robson: New Light on the Relationship between Two Early Critics of the Hudson's Bay Company." *Canadian Historical Review* 40 (1959): 132–6.

– *The British Search for the Northwest Passage in the Eighteenth Century.* Imperial Studies Series, no. 24. London: Longmans, Green, 1962.

– "The End of Company Monopoly and Rule." *The Beaver,* autumn 1970, 56–9.

– "The Hudson's Bay Company and Its Critics in the Eighteenth Century." *Transactions of the Royal Historical Society,* 5th series, 20 (1970): 149–71.

– "The Puzzle of Anthony Henday's Journal, 1754–55." *The Beaver,* winter 1978, 41–56.

– "The Red River Affair." *The Beaver,* autumn 1970, 38–43.

– "Simpson and McLoughlin." *The Beaver,* autumn 1970, 49–55.

– "The Simpson Era." *The Beaver,* autumn 1970, 51–61.

– ed. *Andrew Graham's Observations on Hudson's Bay 1767–91.* Hudson's Bay Record Society Publications, 27. London, 1969.

– ed. *Hudson Bay Miscellany 1670–1870.* Hudson's Bay Record Society Publications, 30, London, 1975.

Willson, Beckles. *The Great Company (1667–1871), Being a History of the Honourable Company of Merchants-Adventurers Trading into Hudson's Bay.* London: Smith, Elder, & Co., 1900.

– *The Life of Lord Strathcona & Mount Royal.* London, New York, etc.: Cassell and Company, 1915.

Wilson, Ian E. "The National Archives 1872–1997: 125 Years of Service." *Archivist,* no. 113 (1997): 28–39.

– "'A Noble Dream': The Origins of the Public Archives of Canada." *Archivaria* 15 (winter 1982–83): 16–35.

Yates, JoAnne. *Control through Communication: The Rise of System in American Management.* Baltimore and London: Johns Hopkins University Press, 1989.

Index

British Museum, 46, 130; fees, 240. *See also* British Library

British North America Act (1867), 155

British Records Association (BRA): and exportation of historical records, 274; HBC member of, 226; pamphlets, 227

Brome, W. John: inventory of books, 80

Brooks, Chadwick, 212, 296; appointed London manager, 249; and publication plans, 237; retires, 251; secretary of HBC, 198, 211

Bryce, George: *The Remarkable History of the Hudson's Bay Company*, 188

Brydges, Charles John, 160–5: and correspondence with London, 165; first annual inspection report, 161; as land commissioner, 160; *Manitoba and the North-West*, 162; records management strategy, 160; reporting to Canadian subcommittee, 166

Brymner, Douglas, 175, 203, 272; and access to HBC records, 174; first Dominion archivist, 174

Burbidge, Herbert: commissioner of saleshops, 176; plans for 250th anniversary, 190

Burgess, Helen (assistant editor, *The Beaver*), 277

Burt, A.L.: on editorial committee, 210

Business Archives Council, 274

business records: types in HBCA, 82

buyout of HBC: by International Financial Society, 152

Canada, Province of, 154

Canada's National History Society, 291

Canadian advisory committee, 177, 176, 220; old records sent to London, 213

Canadian Committee, 209, 210, 240, 297; and changes to reporting structure, 220; and deposit of Canadian records in HBCA, 231; interest in transfer of archives to Manitoba, 270; letter registers, 212; records, 200, 258–9, 261; reminded of publication regulations, 239; and research requests, 264

Canadian Conservation Institute: report on HBC archival records, 288–9

Canadian Cultural Property Export Review Agency, 292

Canadian historians: and access to HBC records, 199–200

Canadian Historical Review: announcement in, 210

Canadian History Society, 204, 237; publication scheme with HBC, 209

Canadian Pacific Railway, 167; land office in Winnipeg, 164; and settlement of HBC territory, 155

Canadian subcommittee, 166, 169; disbanded, 172; records, 261

Carteret, Sir George, 19

cartographic records, 46–8

cartridge paper, 74

catalogue: of boardroom library, 199; of library, 109

census returns, 103

central records registry system: in London office, 212

Champlain Society, 237; agreement with HBRS, 243, 253; joint publishing venture with HBC, 201; meeting attended by Schooling, 200; and publication of HBC records, 200

"Character Book" (Simpson), 108–9, 110

charity schools: apprentices from, 80; Christ's Hospital, 51, 52; Grey Coat School, 51

Charles II: audience with Radisson and Groseilliers, 18; confirms charter of East India Company, 16; grants charter to HBC, 20; instructions for captains of ships, 27; in Oxford, 18; portrait, 217, 265, restoration, 13, and Royal Mathematical School, 52; state papers in PRO, 18

Charles Fort, 21, 49

charter (of HBC), 111, 182; challenged, 32; compared to Deed of Surrender, 155; confirmed by act of Parliament, 37; copy in committee room, 29; copy in Dobbs's publication, 65; granted by Charles II, 20; in iron chest, 32; new charter, 272; renewed, 36; retained, 149; sent separately to Canada, 284; validity of, 138